THE SWAMP FOX

ALSO BY JOHN OLLER

Jean Arthur: The Actress Nobody Knew

An All-American Murder

American Queen:
The Rise and Fall of Kate Chase Sprague—Civil War
"Belle of the North" and Gilded Age Woman of Scandal

THE SWAMP FOX

How Francis Marion
Saved the American Revolution

JOHN OLLER

DA CAPO PRESS

Designed by Trish Wilkinson
Set in 10.75 point Goudy Oldstyle Std

Library of Congress Cataloging-in-Publication Data

Names: Oller, John, author.
Title: The Swamp Fox : how Francis Marion saved the American Revolution / John Oller.
Description: Boston, MA : Da Capo Press, 2016. | Includes bibliographical references and index.
Identifiers: LCCN 2016018548 (print) | LCCN 2016019425 (ebook) | ISBN 9780306824579 (hardcover) | ISBN 9780306824586 (e-book)
Subjects: LCSH: Marion, Francis, 1732-1795. | Generals—United States—Biography. | South Carolina—Militia—Biography. | United States—History—Revolution, 1775-1783—Biography. | South Carolina—History—Revolution, 1775-1783—Campaigns. | Georgia—History—Revolution, 1775-1783—Campaigns. | United States—History—Revolution, 1775-1783—Campaigns.
Classification: LCC E207.M3 O45 2016 (print) | LCC E207.M3 (ebook) | DDC 973.3/3092 [B] —dc23
LC record available at https://lccn.loc.gov/2016018548

Published by Da Capo Press, an imprint of Perseus Books, a division of PBG Publishing, LLC, a subsidiary of Hachette Book Group, Inc.
www.dacapopress.com

Da Capo Press books are available at special discounts for bulk purchases in the U.S. by corporations, institutions, and other organizations. For more information, please contact the Special Markets Department at 2300 Chestnut Street, Suite 200, Philadelphia, PA 19103, or call (800) 810-4145, ext. 5000, or e-mail special .markets@perseusbooks.com.

10 9 8 7 6 5 4 3 2 1

Title page art: Francis Marion as a Continental officer (*New York Public Library*)

NOV 2 8 2016

For my family

Contents

Photographs following page 160

Maps

Author's Note

ANYONE WRITING ABOUT Francis Marion immediately confronts the task of sifting fact from folklore. The mythmaking began with the first and highly embellished biography of him, written in 1809 by Mason L. "Parson" Weems, the same man who fabricated the famous story of George Washington chopping down the cherry tree. The romantic tradition continued with the Walt Disney television series that ran from 1959 to 1961, starring Leslie Nielsen as the Swamp Fox, and took another turn in 2000 with the popular film *The Patriot*, in which Mel Gibson portrayed a Rambo-like action figure loosely, if inaccurately, based on Marion. As stated on an interpretive marker at Marion's gravesite in Pineville, South Carolina, much about the Swamp Fox remains obscured by legend, even though his achievements are "significant and real."

Beyond the more blatant fictionalizations of Marion's life, the original documentary sources are often fragmentary and conflicting (e.g., Was there an ambush at Blue Savannah? Was Marion actually present at Lower Bridge?). I have tried to synthesize the various sources to arrive at sound conclusions as to what most likely happened, making use of much new information that has come to light since the last major Marion biography in 1973, including scholarly research, archaeological findings, pension records, military rosters, and genealogies, not to mention the Internet. In most cases I have reserved the more detailed discussions of conflicting accounts and theories for the endnotes, which I encourage readers to consult.

Some terminology, for readers not steeped in American Revolutionary War history, and geography, for those unfamiliar with South Carolina—as I once was—may be helpful at the outset.

TERMINOLOGY

In describing those Americans who fought for or otherwise sided with the cause of colonial independence from Great Britain during the Revolutionary War, I use the terms *patriots*, *Whigs*, and *rebels* more or less interchangeably. Those who remained loyal to the British Crown are referred to as *Tories*, *loyalists*, or sometimes *king's men* or *friends*. Where the context is clear, I also use *Americans* to refer to the patriot side, even though the Tories were Americans too.

Trained, uniformed, full-time soldiers who fought in the American Continental Army are described as *Continentals* or *regulars*; their British army counterparts are *redcoats* or *British regulars*.

The American militia, also known as *partisans*, were amateur, unpaid soldiers who furnished their own horses, hunting rifles, and ammunition. Some historians take pains to distinguish between the state-regulated "militia" and the purely volunteer "partisans," but for much of the period in question here (1780–1782) there was little or no distinction between the two. Another group of South Carolina soldiers were the so-called state troops who were raised in 1781 for more definite terms of service.

On the loyalist side there were two groups of soldiers: the *loyalists* or *Royal Militia* (or just *militia*), and the *provincials*. In the southern theater of war the Tory militia operated essentially like the American militia/partisans and were generally southern born and bred. The provincial soldiers were trained and paid by the British and often were commanded by British regular army officers. Most of the provincials were recruited from among American Tories living in the North, particularly the pro-British areas of New York, New Jersey, and parts of Pennsylvania.

GEOGRAPHY

The South Carolina Lowcountry is usually defined as the area within fifty miles of the Atlantic Coast, parallel to the two largest port towns, Charleston and Georgetown. Everything else is the backcountry or upcountry, although the latter term is sometimes reserved for the mountainous region in the northwestern tip of the state, near the original land of the Cherokees. Of the three great partisan leaders in South Carolina, Francis Marion operated mostly in the eastern third of the state, encompassing the Lowcountry and portions of the backcountry; Thomas Sumter, a backcountry man, had the middle third of the state; and Andrew Pickens led the partisans in the northwest third of the state, closest to Indian Territory.

Frequent reference is made in these pages to South Carolina's major rivers and ferries. The two most important rivers for our purposes are the Santee and the Pee Dee (spelled *Peedee* or *Pedee* at the time). Most of Marion's most famous engagements took place in between or near these two rivers and their various branches and tributaries.

The Santee, the largest river in the state, held great strategic importance during the Revolution. It has its origins in the mountains of western North Carolina as the Catawba River, which becomes the Wateree in South Carolina and merges with the Congaree in the middle of the state to become the Santee, flowing southeast and emptying out on the coast below Georgetown. (See maps, pp. xiv–xv.)

The Pee Dee (sometimes called the Great Pee Dee, to distinguish it from its tributary, the Little Pee Dee) begins farther east in the Appalachian Mountains of North Carolina and flows south-southeast through the northeastern part of South Carolina until it reaches Georgetown.

Bridges across the major waters of inland South Carolina were relatively uncommon during the Revolution. Most wide river and creek crossings were made in flatboats at state-franchised, privately operated ferries that consisted of two sides, with a landing on each bank. The most important of these was Nelson's Ferry, the principal crossing point on the Santee for travelers or troops between Charleston to the south and British army headquarters to the north. Other ferries frequently used by Marion, because they were near his base of operations, were Witherspoon's, Britton's, and Port's Ferries. Marion's men often camped at these and other ferry landings to provide quick access to water crossings.

In the years before and during the Revolution the South Carolina Lowcountry was divided into numerous local parishes as part of the dominant Anglican Church system.

In referring to cities and towns I generally use the modern spelling, such as Charleston, not Charles Town, and Winnsboro, not Winnsborough.

A Note on the Text

As an aid to readability I have modernized capitalizations and punctuation in the original texts of letters and military orders. I have generally maintained the originals of spelling, grammar, and English usage, even if they would be considered incorrect by today's standards. As a result, Marion in particular may come across to modern readers as semiliterate, and he has sometimes been described as such. But despite a lack of formal schooling, he was about as educated as most American-born men of his time and class.

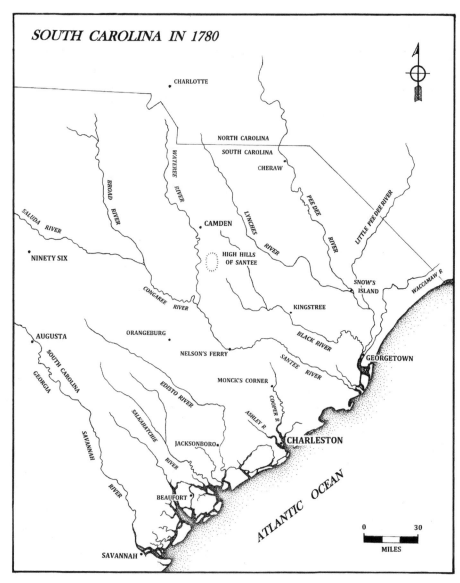

South Carolina in 1780

The Principal Theater of the Campaigns of Francis Marion

THE SWAMP FOX

An eerie, shrill whistle pierced the humid night air above Gaillard's Island in the Santee River Swamp. A second call followed, then another. Like the cry of the whip-poor-will, the sound penetrated through the pines, the moss-draped cypress trees, and the tall canebrakes surrounding the patriot militia camp. There, among their palmetto-thatched huts, the men sat and talked around small campfires they had lit to ward off the mosquitoes and deer flies that swarmed the surrounding marshes and creeks. These oozing, misty morasses were made all the more impenetrable by the alligators and water moccasins that inhabited them.

The bird calls on this night were not, however, those of the whip-poor-will but a series of signals by sentries concealed in the nearby tree-tops. At times a guide to friends searching for the secret lair, at other times a warning of the approach of foes, the whistles on this August evening were a summons for men to gather for an expedition south to reinforce a fellow patriot force being harassed by Tories. A nearly hundred-mile march, commencing at night over unfrequented roads, lay ahead of the men encamped at Peyre's Plantation.

It was time again for the Swamp Fox to move out.

The Darkest Hour

JULY 25, 1780—GENERAL GATES'S CAMP AT
HOLLINGSWORTH'S FARM ON DEEP RIVER NEAR
BUFFALO FORD, NORTH CAROLINA

They were a motley-looking bunch, the twenty or so militia volunteers
who rode on horseback that day into the camp of General Horatio Gates,
the newly appointed commander of the American Continental Army in
the South. Some were white, some were black, and among them was a
Catawba Indian or two, enemies of the British and Cherokees. A few of
the soldiers were barely in their teens. One of Gates's officers, noting the
"wretchedness of their attire," described the newcomers' appearance as
"so burlesque" that the Continentals had to restrain themselves from
laughing at them.

At their head rode a diminutive, forty-eight-year-old man who, at
around five-foot-two and 110 pounds, possessed the physique of a
thirteen-year-old boy. His knock knees, deformed since birth, nearly
touched one another, his hook nose and narrow face gave him a homely
appearance, and he walked with a pronounced limp. Yet his flashing
black eyes and steely demeanor, along with his blue Continental uniform, rumpled though it was, cautioned the mocking soldiers not to
laugh at the ragged group in his presence.

It was a precarious moment for the patriot cause. Two months earlier,
in May 1780, the port of Charleston had fallen to the British after a six-
week siege—the greatest disaster the Americans would suffer during the

entire war. The British quickly established a chain of forts and outposts from the Atlantic Coast to the western mountains to control South Carolina's interior. They planned to roll up through the Carolinas and Virginia one by one and eventually trap George Washington between New York and the redcoat advance from the south, finally ending the rebellion.

Francis Marion, a Continental officer at the time of Charleston's fall, had been absent from the city, having gone to the countryside to nurse an injured ankle. According to legend, he fractured it when he leapt from a second-story window to escape an officers' dinner party in downtown Charleston shortly before the siege began. By eighteenth-century custom the host had locked all the doors to prevent the guests from leaving before the merriment was over. Marion, a light drinker at best, looked for a way out and jumped. A reckless act at the time, if true, it proved to be one of those lucky quirks of history.

After the British captured the city, and realizing he was a marked man in British eyes, Marion hid out among friends' and relatives' plantations along the Santee River in South Carolina's Lowcountry. He was accompanied by his faithful African American body servant (valet), a slave named Oscar who went by the nickname Buddy. Marion's mentor, General William Moultrie, wrote that Marion "was so lame he was obliged to skulk about from house to house among his friends," sometimes hiding in the bushes; as his ankle improved "he then crept out by degree and began to collect a few friends, and when he got ten or twelve together he ventured out."

In early July, Marion rode with his dozen followers to Cox's Mill, North Carolina (near present-day Ramseur), to offer his services to the southern Continental army. The army's interim commander, the German-born, nearly sixty-year-old Johann Kalb, had recently arrived there with fourteen hundred men. Kalb, self-christened "Baron de Kalb," was not a nobleman but rather a soldier of fortune, serving in the French army as a protégé of Lafayette. In April, Washington had sent him south from New Jersey to offer relief to Charleston, but on the way de Kalb learned that the city had already fallen. Exhausted by the five-hundred-mile march, plagued by insect bites, and lacking regular food, he and his men were awaiting the arrival of Gates, the hero of Saratoga, who had been chosen by Congress to succeed Benjamin Lincoln, the surrendering general at Charleston.

Around July 10, after Marion and his ragtag bunch reached Cox's Mill, de Kalb sent them out to scour the area for intelligence and provisions. Two weeks later, on July 25, Marion and his little band, now numbering around twenty, were back at Hollingsworth's Farm, a few miles from Cox's, to witness Gates's arrival. As Marion learned, Gates was preparing to march the army immediately on the British garrison at Camden in north central South Carolina, then under the command of Lieutenant General Charles, Earl Cornwallis.

Gates may have respected Francis Marion's experience as a military man, but he had no place for Marion and his band of "irregular" fighters. English-born and a former major in the British army, Gates was of the school trained to fight set-piece battles in an open field. He was disinclined toward the kind of ambush tactics practiced by Native American warriors, a style of warfare Francis Marion had learned while fighting the Cherokees on the Carolina frontier during the French and Indian War. Primarily an infantry commander, Gates also had no appreciation for the important role cavalry would play in the southern theater, where the open terrain and the great distances between settlements placed a premium on mounted patrols. To Gates, that Marion's men rode into camp on horseback was nothing to applaud.

On July 27, the first day they set out, Gates allowed Marion and his little band to ride up front with him, a gracious gesture to make up for the slight they had received from the Continentals two days earlier. Evidently the incident embarrassed Gates, for the day before he had urged that every Continental officer and soldier "show the utmost cordiality and brotherly affection" to the militia, who "deserve[d] every kindness" for having volunteered to defend their invaded country. Still, Marion and his militiamen were little more than bodyguards for Gates, so when the opportunity arose to dispatch them elsewhere, Gates jumped at the chance.

By happy coincidence a group of men forming a militia in South Carolina's Williamsburg Township, a Whig stronghold northeast of the Santee, had asked Gates to send them an experienced Continental officer to lead them. When their request arrived at Gates's camp, Marion offered himself for the job, and Gates was glad to oblige. On the morning of August 15, from his headquarters at Rugeley's Mills, South Carolina, twelve miles above Camden, he sent Marion and his men off to Williamsburg to the southeast. Gates gave them orders to watch the enemy's motions and to destroy any boats they found on the Santee River. In part that was a make-work assignment, but it also reflected Gates's supreme confidence: expecting total victory at Camden, he wanted to prevent Cornwallis from escaping to Charleston.

Marion's eagerness to take the field against the British made him a suitable match for the people of Williamsburg. Nearly all Scotch-Irish Presbyterians, they were fiercely independent and determined to live their lives unmolested by any external authority. They had held a public meeting at the old Williamsburg Presbyterian churchyard in the town of Kingstree and voted to take up arms. What they needed now was a leader.

Around August 17 Marion arrived at Witherspoon's Ferry on Lynches Creek in present-day Johnsonville, South Carolina, to assume command of the Williamsburg militia. He hardly looked the part of a dashing leader. Fifteen-year-old William Dobein James was there and later recorded his first impression of Francis Marion: "He was rather below the middle stature of men, lean and swarthy. His body was well set, but his knees and ankles were badly formed and he still limped upon one leg." Besides his eagle beak of a nose, his appearance was otherwise uninviting—a jutting chin and a large, high forehead. Yet he had "a countenance remarkably steady," young James noted, and possessed a wiry frame "capable of enduring fatigue and every privation necessary for a partisan." By now Marion had discarded his Continental blue uniform for a coarse crimson jacket—the hue of the enemy, yet about the only color of cloth Carolinians could obtain after the fall of Charleston. But he still wore the leather helmet (more like a skull cap) that composed part of the Continental uniform of the 2nd South Carolina Regiment. The cap featured a silver crescent sewn in front and was inscribed with the word *Liberty*.

Marion was a stranger to most of the approximately two hundred rank-and-file militiamen who had gathered at Witherspoon's. Technically he had no legal authority over any of them. They were pure volunteers operating independently of the now-dissolved state government and not as part of any regulated militia. As a practical matter they were free to come and go as they wished and fight for whomever they chose. Moreover, Marion held no formal militia command; he was a Continental officer, and in a regiment that no longer existed at that. He had come to Witherspoon's by invitation only, and if the men, after taking one look at him, had decided they were not going to follow him, that would have been their prerogative.

But Major John James (William Dobein James's father) vouched for Marion to the skeptics. A large, combative Irishman the same age as Marion, James had previously served with Marion under General Moultrie and had left Charleston during the recent British siege to help form a militia. An elder in the Presbyterian Church, James was strongly anti-British, and unlike many Whigs, he had refused to sign any oath of allegiance to the Crown after Charleston fell. His recommendation of Marion was seconded by the Horry brothers, Hugh and Peter, who, like Marion, were successful Lowcountry rice and indigo planters of French Huguenot descent. Close friends of Marion, Hugh and Peter Horry (pronounced oh-REE) would become two of his most trusted military confidantes.

Soon there were others: Major James's second cousin, Captain John James ("of the Lake"), and the major's twenty-three-year-old son, John James Jr., who had surrendered at Charleston then broke his parole to take up the fight.* Another recruit, Marion's cousin and best friend Captain Henry Mouzon, had a score to settle: Banastre Tarleton, a British cavalry officer, had recently burned his house to the ground, reportedly because of Mouzon's French Huguenot heritage. When Mouzon greeted the militia at Witherspoon's, he kissed Marion on both cheeks, per Huguenot tradition.

Although some of the soldiers, like young William Dobein James, were in their teens, most of the officers were in their twenties and thirties

---

*Under a parole, a captured enemy is released on a promise not to take up arms again unless and until exchanged for another prisoner. Taken from the French *parole* (word, promise), the practice goes back centuries and allows the capturing party to avoid the burden of feeding and caring for prisoners while preventing them from retaking the field of battle. Paroles were treated seriously in the eighteenth century, and violations of parole terms could lead to execution if the parolee were recaptured. The practice went out of favor by the twentieth century, and current US military policy prohibits US soldiers who are prisoners of war from accepting parole.

and primed for combat. From the area between the Great and Little Pee Dee Rivers came militia colonel Hugh Giles, a surveyor whose intimate knowledge of the area made him an especially valuable asset. Anxious to join the fray, Giles had already been planning offensive operations against the Tories and was collecting cattle and grain to feed Gates's army in anticipation of its arrival.

The Berkeley County militia supplied Captain William McCottry, an expert marksman whose company would gain renown as McCottry's Rifles. Several of the Witherspoons, whose Presbyterian family ran the ferry of the same name and were heralded for their courage and athleticism, reported for duty as well. John Ervin, a rabid and daring twenty-six-year-old patriot who had married a Witherspoon, answered the call and became one of the youngest colonels in the Revolution.

Twenty-year-old Thomas Waties had joined the Continental Army in 1775 out of the University of Pennsylvania, where he had headed a company formed by his fellow students. He was soon captured on a mission to England and, upon his release four years later, made his way to Paris, where he befriended Benjamin Franklin, who helped him get back to his native South Carolina. He joined Marion after the fall of Charleston and was made a captain. Then there were the Postell brothers, John and James, from the Georgetown area, who became known for taking on the most challenging assignments.

These men would form the nucleus of Marion's Brigade, a mixture of Huguenot plantation owners from the Santee region and Scotch-Irish small farmers of the Pee Dee. Major John James, who knew the character of his Scotch-Irish kinsmen, was astute in recommending Marion to lead them. Being a Huguenot and an outsider, Marion would arouse no jealousies on the part of the Scottish clan leaders, who had a habit of arguing with each other. Marion's taciturn nature also helped secure the men's respect; he was a doer, not a talker. Moreover, they would see him endure all they suffered, including sleeping unsheltered from the winter cold and rain and risking the malaria and yellow fever brought by swamp-dwelling mosquitoes each summer.

And so, from the day he took command, his brigade became a sort of spiritual fraternity that would be compared to Robin Hood of Sherwood Forest and his merry men. Like the outlaw band of legend, Marion and his men would use guerrilla tactics to attack the ruling order from secret hideaways before melting back into the forest or swamp.* They knew the terrain as the British did not, had an excellent spy network, and were by far the superior horsemen. Marion's highly mobile brigade would inflict losses on the enemy that were individually small but cumulatively a large drain on British resources and morale.

Immediately upon taking command Marion dispatched Peter Horry and three or four companies of men to the lower Santee River, with orders to burn all the boats and canoes there to prevent anyone from crossing. Meanwhile Marion took the rest of his men west from Witherspoon's to begin destroying boats along the upper Santee.

On August 19, while camped along the river, Marion received the shattering news that on August 16, the day after Gates had sent him off to Williamsburg, Gates's army had been routed by Cornwallis at Camden. During the battle almost twenty-five hundred Virginia and North Carolina militia, constituting the bulk of Gates's force that day, threw down their weapons and fled at the first sight of the British lines charging them with fixed bayonets. Gates had foolishly placed his greenest militia recruits—who had never stared down the approach of cold, shining steel—on the American left to face the British right, which by tradition consisted of its most highly trained, professional soldiers. It hadn't helped that Gates's men were half-starved; during the trek to Camden some had been reduced to using their hair powder to thicken soup. They had also marched all night before the battle after a hurried dinner of lean beef, half-baked bread, mush, and molasses. The inedible concoction brought on such diarrhea that the men broke ranks during their march to relieve themselves and went into the oppressively hot August conflict exhausted and dehydrated.

---

*Although Marion did not invent the guerrilla warfare style, references to which can be found in prebiblical writings, he was among the first Revolutionary War leaders to develop "irregular" fighting (currently referred to as "asymmetrical" warfare) into an art form. In later centuries revolutionaries, freedom fighters, and terrorists would use similar tactics: Cochise and the Apaches in the 1860s American West, Mao Tse-tung during the Chinese Civil War, the Viet Cong in Southeast Asia, the Afghan rebels against the Soviet Union in the 1980s, and in the years following the September 11, 2001, attacks against America, the Taliban in Afghanistan and insurgents and counterinsurgents in Iraq.

Among the casualties from the battle was Baron de Kalb, who was wounded eleven times and died three days later. There was one highly prominent survivor: Horatio Gates. Instead of falling on his sword, as honor might have suggested, Gates had exited the field in panic on a swift horse and galloped nearly two hundred miles in three days, barely pausing until he had reached safety in Hillsboro, North Carolina. Widely accused of cowardice, Gates saw his military career effectively come to an end.

The Battle of Camden marked the second time in three months that the Continental Army in the South was decimated. Then came more bad news: on August 18, two days after Gates's trouncing at Camden, Thomas Sumter's company of 800 partisans had been surprised and overwhelmed by Banastre Tarleton's smaller force of 160 at Fishing Creek, four miles above Camden. Sumter himself was literally caught napping and half-clothed before barely escaping on an unsaddled horse. Like Gates, he fled across the North Carolina border, his men scattering to the four winds. Although Sumter's and other partisan bands had won a series of skirmishes against the British and their Tory allies over the previous couple of months in the Carolina backcountry, the twin disasters at Camden and Fishing Creek largely dissipated those small gains.

For the Americans it was arguably the Revolution's darkest hour. The cause of independence in South Carolina—and maybe the entire revolution—lay in ruins.

For the second time Francis Marion had fortuitously missed being part of the destruction of the entire American southern army. But now he was alone. His was the only viable patriot fighting force left in South Carolina, the only organized resistance standing in the way of complete British subjugation of the colony. Instinctively Marion knew that if he told his newly formed brigade about Camden and Fishing Creek, the men might become so deflated that they would give up the fight before his campaign had even begun. So he kept the news to himself. But he also knew that unless the tide could somehow be turned quickly, the resistance effort might be over. He needed an opportunity to do something bold. He soon got one. South Carolina would shortly see the birth of a freedom fighter, one who would give new hope to the patriot cause.

1

A Most Uncivil War

The South Carolina that Francis Marion set out to liberate from British control in August 1780 was the key theater of operations in the American Revolution at that point. It was also in turmoil—a society riven by war and rooted in lawlessness, fear, violence, and oppression.

More battles, engagements, and skirmishes were fought in South Carolina during the Revolution than in any other colony. Conservative estimates place the number of combat actions in the state at more than two hundred, a third of all that took place in the entire war. No other colony had as many inches of its territory affected by battle; of the state's forty-six present-day counties, forty-five ended up seeing Revolutionary War actions. Nearly 20 percent of all Americans who died in battle in the Revolution died in South Carolina in the last two years of the war.

Ever since the shots were fired at Lexington and Concord in 1775, the South had been mostly untouched by the conflict, which was famously fought at places such as Bunker Hill, Fort Ticonderoga, Trenton, and Brandywine. But by 1779 the war in the North had reached a stalemate, with the British firmly in control of New York City under Sir Henry Clinton, and the Americans, led by George Washington, camped thirty miles away in Morristown, New Jersey, desperately hoping for help from a French navy anchored in the West Indies. The last significant engagement in the North had been in June 1778 at Monmouth Courthouse, where Washington and his most dependable officer, Nathanael Greene, battled Clinton and his lieutenant general, Charles Cornwallis, to a draw. But while the Americans remained hard-pressed, Britain had grown increasingly weary of war. Its coffers nearly bankrupt and its military stretched thin by an expanded conflict with France and Spain, Parliament agreed to finance one final effort to end the American rebellion.

It came to be known as Britain's "southern strategy." Jointly agreed on by Clinton, King George, and Lord Germain, the British secretary of state for America, the plan was elegant in both logic and economy. The British would begin by occupying and pacifying Georgia, where revolutionary sentiment was the weakest among the thirteen colonies. They would then subdue South Carolina, North Carolina, and Virginia while gathering men to confront Washington in the North.

The linchpin of the strategy was the belief, encouraged by American loyalist exiles in London, that the South, never as fervent for independence as New England to begin with, was teeming with loyalists who would rise up in arms against the rebels once the British army arrived to support them. Parliament saw a way to save money and British lives by having loyal colonial subjects do much of the fighting themselves, a plan to "Americanize" the war similar in concept to the Vietnamization policy adopted by the US government in Southeast Asia almost two hundred years later. At the very least, Britain figured, by conquering the South it would retain several valuable colonies even if it had to let the northern ones go.

And the British plan was working. Savannah fell easily in December 1778, allowing the British to quickly establish control over Georgia. Savannah, in turn, provided Clinton with a base for moving north by land on Charleston, which he had failed to capture in a brief, bungled land-and-sea operation in 1776. In the nearly four years since, Charleston had grown complacent, a place of balls, concerts, theater, taverns, and a general libertine spirit. But after the city's capitulation on May 12 the mood turned somber and defeatist. Much of the citizenry nearly tripped over themselves trying to prove their allegiance to Mother England. Two hundred Charlestonians signed a congratulatory address to Clinton and a British vice admiral, thanking them for restoring South Carolina's political connection to Great Britain. Merchants who had been ardent patriots abruptly shifted their loyalties to the Crown to position themselves for profitable wartime trade. The ringleaders of the rebellion were arrested and shipped off to St. Augustine, Florida. With Governor John Rutledge's flight in exile to North Carolina and later to Philadelphia, civil government in South Carolina ceased to exist. As one loyalist military officer observed, "The conquest of the Province was complete."

Believing the war in South Carolina to be at an end, thousands of its citizens swore oaths of allegiance to King George so as to secure protection as loyal subjects. Some voluntarily trekked to Charleston from fifty miles away to sign their pledges. Able-bodied men rushed to join the British forces, the better to ingratiate themselves with their conquerors. Patriot militia who did not wish to take up arms for the Crown nonetheless returned to their farms and plantations under a pledge of neutrality, agreeing to sit out the war quietly at home per the terms of their parole. Even prominent revolutionary statesmen, such as Henry Middleton, former president of the Continental Congress; Charles Pinckney, the first president of the South Carolina Senate; and Daniel Huger, a top member of Governor Rutledge's council, took British protection. The state seemed resigned to submission.

By June 4, a few weeks after Charleston's surrender, Clinton was able to report to Lord Germain that "there are few men in South Carolina who are not either our prisoners, or in arms with us." Confident that South Carolina had been pacified and that North Carolina was the next domino to fall, Clinton sailed back to New York to keep check on Washington, leaving the forty-two-year-old Cornwallis in charge of operations in the South.

Just before leaving Charleston, though, Clinton had issued a proclamation that exacerbated the division between South Carolina loyalists and patriots. Clinton had previously stipulated that so long as any civilian Whigs agreed to a parole, the British would grant them a full pardon and leave them in peace in their homes and property for the duration of the war. But almost immediately Clinton developed second thoughts, in part because vengeful Tories protested that the terms were too generous to their longtime antagonists. In part, too, Clinton concluded that the British needed more of a stick than a carrot approach to securing the citizenry's fidelity.

Accordingly, on June 3, 1780, Clinton announced that the prior paroles were null and void and that those previously on parole would be restored to their rights and duties as citizens of the Crown and were expected to actively assist the British government. Parolees had to sign an oath of allegiance by June 20 or be deemed still in rebellion and treated as enemies of the king. This edict, Clinton reasoned, would smoke out rebel agitators and prevent them from causing trouble while under the protection of parole.

But the proclamation ended up backfiring. Did the requirement to "actively assist" the British mean patriots actually had to take up arms with the British against their neighbors and fellow countrymen? That was the question the people of Williamsburg asked themselves. They sent a popular local representative and militia officer, Major John James, to Georgetown on the coast to seek clarification from the Royal Navy captain there. After opining that the rebels previously paroled were lucky they were not all hanged, the British captain told Major James that Clinton's new decree did indeed require those signing the oath to fight for the loyalist cause if called upon to do so.

In short, to the British, neutrality was no longer possible—the colonials were either for or against them. Many South Carolinians' hearts were already with the patriots, and reports of British raiders burning houses, plundering property, and committing other atrocities were driving them further into the rebel camp. One British officer told Cornwallis that after Clinton's revised proclamation, nine out of every ten backcountry inhabitants not previously in arms against the British had taken up the revolutionary cause. The countryside was suddenly awakened; the British had unwittingly let loose a hornet's nest of rebel sentiment. Forced to fight one way or the other, those with patriot sympathies chose to join the resistance.

As a result, South Carolina became the setting for a bona fide civil war—a conflict *within* the state far less "civil" than the one *between* the states eighty years later. It involved not merely a clash of professional armies, as was typical of European conflicts at the time, but also an insurgency and counterinsurgency that engaged much of the civilian population, more characteristic of the conflagrations of centuries to come.

What most distinguished the war in South Carolina was its vicious and personal nature. It pitted not only neighbor against neighbor and brother against brother but father against son. Unspeakable atrocities were committed, as men in their homes, sick with smallpox, were roused from their beds and executed; soldiers waving the white flag were mercilessly cut down with the sword; and captured enemies were summarily hanged for past crimes, real and imagined. And most of the brutality was visited not by British upon Americans or Americans upon British but Americans upon Americans. Rhode Island's General Nathanael Greene, a battle-hardened officer who came south to replace Horatio Gates as the commander of the southern Continental Army, had never seen anything like it. "The whole country is in danger of being laid waste by the Whigs and Tories, who pursue each other with as much relentless fury as beasts of prey," he was to observe.

Unlike many civil wars, this one was not based on geographic boundaries or even mainly on differences of political philosophy. South Carolina Whigs were not necessarily motivated by the lofty ideals expressed by Thomas Jefferson, nor were Tories inevitably inspired by devotion to King George. Instead, the decision whether to take up arms, and for which side, was frequently driven by private grievances and desires for revenge. A man's horse was once stolen by a Whig; he became a Tory. Another man, feeling slighted because the Tories passed him over for military promotion, might join forces with the Whigs. So indifferent were some to ideological issues that they switched sides during the war as many as three times or even more, depending on who was winning.

Old grudges resurfaced from the decade preceding the Revolution, when lawlessness reigned in the Carolina backcountry. In the 1760s vigilante groups, known as *Regulators*, had been organized to hunt down bandit gangs; the Regulators, in turn, were met by counter-vigilantes known as *Moderators*. The blood feuds generated among neighbors in the prerevolutionary period often determined whose side one was on during the Revolution.

Religious and ethnic resentments played a part as well. Presbyterian and Baptist dissenters resented discrimination by the established, tax-supported Anglican Church; the Presbyterians and Baptists detested each other; and the Scotch-Irish hated the English for having forcibly relocated their ancestors from Scotland to Ireland in the 1600s. Yet religious affiliations did not inexorably determine loyalties. Scottish Highlanders, for example, though Presbyterian, were mostly devoted to the

Crown because, unlike their Scotch-Irish brethren, they were recent immigrants to America who owed their land grants to King George. The
same was true of German Lutherans, whose Hessian brethren fought as
British mercenaries. Poor backcountry farmers generally preferred the
rule of the king to that of the elitist Charleston and Lowcountry merchants and plantation owners, who regarded backcountry folk as vulgar
rubes and denied them fair representation in the state assembly.

Adding fuel to the flame were animosities left over from the early
days of the war. In April 1775, when the first shots rang out at Lexington
and Concord, South Carolina's population was sharply divided in its attitude toward independence. Tensions were high as both Tories and
Whigs raised rival militia forces and vied for control of critical gunpow-
der stores. But the Whigs quickly won the propaganda war, seized control
of the militia and other machinery of government, and quashed a Tory
uprising in the backcountry. After gaining the upper hand, the Whigs
proceeded to suppress their Tory neighbors with forced loyalty oaths,
imprisonment or banishment of leaders, and physical intimidation, including tarring and feathering, burning, and scalping. This set the stage
for a cycle of retribution that accelerated when the British captured
Charleston. With the British at their backs, Tories took the opportunity
to settle old scores, all in the name of politics. Whigs responded in kind.
Meanwhile highway robbers, passing themselves off as soldiers for Whigs
or Tories as the situation suited them, plundered from both sides.

Finally, overlaying all was the white population's ever-present fear,
shared by Whigs and Tories alike, of Indian uprisings in the backcountry
and slave insurrections in the Lowcountry (where blacks outnumbered
whites by more than three to one). Fearful of antagonizing their Tory allies and in part because Cornwallis was reluctant to employ them, the
British never effectively mobilized their many Indian allies to fight the
Carolina rebels. For similar reasons, while thousands of slaves fled to
the British lines in search of their freedom or were forcibly taken from
Whig plantations, the British, with rare exception, chose not to arm
them as soldiers (they were mostly used as laborers or informers/messen-
gers). Had the British brought Tories, Native Americans, and slaves together in military operations against the patriots, they might have made

quick work of the rebellion; as it was, the war in South Carolina remained a free-for-all.

In short, when he ventured out on his one good leg to join the fight in South Carolina, Marion was wading into a maelstrom of violence and anarchy. Given that setting, one might expect that Marion, as the leader of a guerrilla brigade, would descend to the level of barbarism practiced by so many of his contemporaries. Yet he did not. When almost all around him were committing or at least condoning atrocities scarcely imaginable between fellow Americans, Marion refused to give in to passion or prejudice or vengeance. "Of all the men who ever drew the sword, Marion was one of the most humane," avowed his friend Peter Horry. "He not only prevented all cruelty, in his own presence, but strictly forbade it in his absence." He excoriated those serving under him who pursued what he termed the "abominable" enemy practice of burning private homes. He personally interceded a number of times to prevent vengeful patriot soldiers from brutalizing or hanging surrendering Tories. As the Revolution neared its end he adopted an almost Lincolnesque, "malice toward none" attitude, urging his fellow patriots to reconcile with their old Tory neighbors as quickly as possible and forsake overly punitive measures to confiscate the property of their former foes.

The question is how Marion came to be that way. As with any cipher, one must begin by searching for clues from his past. It reveals a man of moderation, equally covetous of liberty and order, in between the extremes of violence and passivity, neither a Charleston aristocrat nor a backcountry bumpkin, and ruthless in battle but averse to the shedding of needless blood, whether that of friend or foe. It begins with his ancestors, who weathered persecution in the Old World and sought freedom in a new one.

2

"A Spirit of Toleration"

*B*enjamin Marion, the grandfather of Francis Marion the revolutionary, was one of countless French Huguenots seeking to escape the tyranny of the French monarch in the late seventeenth century. Adherents of the Reformation teachings of John Calvin, these French Protestants had come to question the divine right of kings in favor of the sovereignty of the people and repeatedly had been oppressed for their beliefs.

Slaughtered by the thousands in the Saint Bartholomew's Day Massacre in 1572, the Huguenots had gained a measure of protection under the Edict of Nantes, issued in 1598. But in 1685 the "Sun King," Louis XIV, revoked the edict so as to make his rule absolute. All Protestant churches were demolished, meetings were banned, and Protestant schools were closed. Calvinists were given deadlines for renouncing their faith—in some cases as little as two hours—failing which the king's men would enter their homes to take them prisoner, confiscate their property, and cart their children off to Catholic institutions.

Many Huguenots found asylum in England, where they learned of an offer from a group known as the Lords Proprietor concerning a place across the ocean called Carolina. The lords, who owned the province, were granting land and religious freedom to anyone who promised to settle there, Huguenots included. One of these Huguenots, Benjamin Marion, originally from the town of La Chaume in Poitou on the French Atlantic coast, emigrated in 1690 with his wife and five servants. He received 350 acres about fifteen miles north of Charleston, on Goose Creek in St. James Parish.

Benjamin Marion (or M'Arion, as he signed his name) made good in his new country. Between his first wife, Judith Baluet, and, after her death, a second named Mary, he had eleven children. He became a naturalized citizen and taxpayer, started a plantation on Goose Creek, and acquired enough new land so that during his lifetime he was able to settle each of his marrying sons with a hundred or more acres with which to start their own estates. When he died in 1735 his inventory included thirty-two slaves, forty-six cattle, sixty-four sheep, horses, hogs, pewter and chinaware, guns, and "a parcel of French and English books."

Among Benjamin Marion's Goose Creek neighbors and a larger body of Huguenots who settled farther north on the banks of the Santee were native French families bearing names that would become well known in colonial South Carolina: Horry, Huger, Laurens, Lenud, Manigault, and Postell. Less identifiable are the names of two other groups who played important roles in the growth of the Huguenot population in South Carolina: Native Americans and African Americans. The former, whose identities are largely lost to history, befriended the newcomers and taught them frontier survival skills, including how to raise corn in place of wheat, barley, and other European crops (rice and indigo would come later).

Even more critical to the settlers' success were slaves from Africa and the West Indies, known only by their owners' last names or by first names or nicknames such as those identified in Benjamin Marion's inventory and will, written in French: Cabto, Gold, Monday, Primus, Sippeo, and Pappy Jenny. In 1720 approximately fifteen hundred slaves lived in Goose Creek as compared with eighty white families. Of the estate worth 6,800 British pounds sterling left by Benjamin Marion at his death, 5,400 pounds, or nearly 80 percent of the total, was attributable to the value of his slaves.

One other group had a seminal impact on the experience of Francis Marion's ancestors in the New World: the English. Although the first English settlement, at Charleston in 1670, preceded the arrival of the first Huguenots by less than ten years, the English Protestants had the advantage of taxpayer support for their Anglican Church. Resented at first by their English fellow colonists, the Huguenots maintained their distinct identity, speaking French and keeping their peculiar customs, manners, and forms of worship. But over time they assimilated into English society. They learned the English language, intermarried with English settlers, and anglicized their names. They even joined the Anglican Church, established as the official state church in 1706, after it agreed to translate its services into French.

The Huguenots were considered a "gentle race," given to humility, conciliation, and self-denial. Despite everything they had been through, these French immigrants did not become haters. Two centuries later a US senator and member of the Du Pont family would publicly boast of the "spirit of toleration which was a special characteristic of our Huguenot ancestors."

Benjamin Marion's eldest son, Gabriel, was born in South Carolina in about 1693. Around 1714 he married Esther Cordes, the Carolina-born daughter of a well-to-do Huguenot immigrant, Dr. Antoine Cordes of St. John's Parish. Gabriel and Esther had six children—one daughter (the oldest) and five sons, the youngest of whom was Francis.

Francis Marion came into the world in 1732, the same year as did George Washington. He was born at Goatfield Plantation, on the western branch of the Cooper River, about fourteen miles northeast of Goose Creek in present-day Berkeley County. Goatfield, where Gabriel and Esther had moved sometime after their marriage, was on lands called Chachan, belonging to Esther's politically connected Cordes family. As a result Francis was named for his uncle, Francis Cordes, thus becoming the only one of his siblings not given a biblical name. Upon Francis's birth his uncle Francis gifted him three African American slaves: a man named June, his wife, Chloe, and their son, Buddy, who would become Marion's childhood companion and later manservant.

Marion was tiny at birth, which may have been preterm. "I have it from good authority," wrote Parson Weems, his first biographer, that Marion "was not larger than a New England lobster, and might easily enough have been put into a quart pot." By the time of his birth the Marions were worshipping nearby at the new Anglican Church, known as

Biggin, where he was likely baptized and where his mother was eventually buried. The church would come to play a fateful role in one of Francis Marion's bloodiest Revolutionary War battles.

When Marion was just a child his father moved the family to Georgetown, a recently founded port town on the coast. The move seems to have been financially motivated. After changing occupations from planter to merchant, Gabriel became "embarrassed in his affairs"—a euphemism for bankruptcy—and by the time Francis was ten, Esther Marion was in "necessitous circumstances." Up until then Gabriel had been assigning portions of his estate to his three oldest sons—Isaac, Gabriel, and Benjamin—as they reached maturity. But by the time he got to his two youngest sons, Job and Francis, the money had run out, and they had to fend for themselves.

Gabriel Marion died when Francis was in his teens. Around that time Francis became a sailor aboard a Georgetown vessel bound for the West Indies. Perhaps he was driven by a restless desire for a seafaring life, but just as likely he saw it as a way of developing a career and making people take notice of him. His brothers Isaac and Benjamin as well as his sister, Esther, had each married into a wealthy English family of rice planters in Georgetown, the Allstons, and were settling into comfortable lives. But Francis had no money of his own, and lacking either good looks or an outgoing personality to compensate, he was without marital prospects. (Even Continental commander Henry Lee, an admirer of Marion, conceded that "his visage was not pleasing, and his manners not captivating.") A nautical voyage thus held some attraction for the young man. But the venture did not profit him: the ship foundered at sea, swept under by either wind or whale, and Francis, cast adrift for several days in an open boat, was one of four survivors among the crew of six. He returned to the welcoming arms of his mother in Georgetown.

Francis spent the next several years in Georgetown living with family, immersing himself in the town's English culture, and casting off the vestiges of Huguenot customs and habits. He hunted and fished the inland woods and swamps beyond the coast, gaining a knowledge of the local vegetation and terrain that one day would serve him well in battle. Sometime in his youth he obtained a rudimentary education, possibly at

home or from tutors hired by the Allstons. Although his later military
letters and orders will never be confused with literature, they were logical and coherent. They betrayed no French language influence, and if
they lacked uniformity of spelling and grammar, so did the English language while Francis was growing up. (Samuel Johnson's landmark dictionary, which set the standards, was not published until 1755, after Marion
had already obtained his common learning.)

In about 1755 Marion moved from Georgetown with his mother and
older brother Gabriel back to St. John's Parish, near the town of Monck's
Corner. Why they returned there is not known except that Esther Marion, then a sixty-year-old widow in declining health, may have wanted
to live out her final days in the parish of her birth. She would die less
than two years later, leaving the majority of her small estate to her two
youngest children, Job and Francis.

It was in St. John's Parish, soon after the move from Georgetown,
where Francis Marion had his first brush with military service. He and
his brother Gabriel were listed on the muster roll of the St. John's militia
company on January 31, 1756. No action was to be had at the time, but
by law every able-bodied man was expected to serve in the militia to
help defend the colony, primarily against Indian or slave uprisings. Responsible for supplying their own weapons and ammunition, typically
they would bring their muskets to church so they could drill after the
service.

The first real break in Francis Marion's life came indirectly, through
his brother Gabriel. Shortly after their mother died, Gabriel married
Catherine Taylor, a beautiful heiress whose wealthy landowner father
set the young couple up with his plantation, Belle Isle, in St. Stephens
Parish (present-day Pineville). Located just south of the Santee River,
St. Stephens was known as the English Santee, as distinguished from the
French Santee of St. James Parish, farther to the south, where Benjamin
Marion, the Huguenot emigrant, had first settled. By midcentury St. Stephens had become the "garden spot" of South Carolina, fertile and conducive not only to rice planting and livestock and poultry grazing but
also to growing the new and profitable crop of indigo. Francis Marion
went to live with Gabriel and Catherine at Belle Isle shortly after their

marriage and around 1759 was given an adjoining portion of the land, known as Hampton Hill, to cultivate himself. He became a farmer.

Whether through a knack of his own or the blessings of the soil, Francis almost immediately began producing profitable crops at Hampton Hill. A man of steady habits, he would have been content to live his life as a moderately successful gentleman planter along the Santee. Indeed, that is what he did, mostly without being heard from, for the next fifteen years. But the quiescence was twice interrupted during that period: first, at the outset, by a brutal Indian war on the western edge of the province and then again, at the end of those years, by the approaching fury of revolution. In the former case he would fight alongside British professional soldiers, trained by them as they would train their own. But later he would take up arms against them, applying the lessons he learned on the frontier.

3

Frontier Lessons

*I*n October 1759 Oconostota, the great Cherokee warrior, had come to Charleston in peace, but the British royal governor, William Lyttelton, would have none of it. The Cherokees had been loyal allies of Britain against France throughout the Seven Years' War, helping to procure the French abandonment of Fort Duquesne in the Ohio Valley in 1758. But on their way back home the Cherokees began to seethe. Believing the British had broken a promise to compensate them for the loss of horses during the campaign and feeling generally cheated by white traders and land grabbers, they decided to help themselves to some mounts belonging to colonists along the Virginia frontier. In retaliation the Virginians killed and scalped a number of Cherokees, who responded with murderous raids against settlers in the Carolina backcountry.

Upon hearing that Governor Lyttelton was preparing to raise a force to march against them, Oconostota led a delegation to Charleston and, laying deerskins at the governor's feet as a peace offering, proposed a treaty based on mutual forgiveness. But Lyttelton, an ambitious thirty-four-year-old politician, was in search of military laurels. He refused to pick up the deerskins, took the entire delegation hostage, and brought them along on his march west, claiming he was acting to protect their safety. In the meantime some thirteen hundred colonials had volunteered for the expedition.

Among the enlistees was twenty-seven-year-old Francis Marion. In the earliest known writing to bear his signature, on October 31, 1759, he

24

joined a number of prominent South Carolinians, including future revolutionary firebrand Christopher Gadsden, in pledging service in Lyttelton's expedition. Marion turned out as a captain in a troop of provincial cavalry headed by his brother Gabriel. This was a military unit of the British royal government, not a local militia, and thus Marion became exposed to British army training and methods.

Lyttelton's composite force consisted of British regulars, South Carolina provincial troops and militia, slaves, vagrants impressed into service, and assorted Native American foes of the Cherokees. In late 1759 they made their way to Fort Prince George in the far northwest corner of South Carolina near the border of the Cherokee Lower Towns. There, using the hostages as leverage, Lyttelton demanded the surrender of twenty-four other Indians, to be put to death as compensation for the same number of whites they allegedly had slain. The offended Cherokees refused and prepared to fight. Plagued by desertions from within the undisciplined, ill-equipped militia, Lyttelton was forced to quickly conclude a treaty, which he signed with Attakullakulla, the "First Beloved Man."

But the ink was barely dry on the agreement before smallpox broke out in the militia camp, prompting many of the remaining volunteers to desert. Returning to Charleston, Lyttelton claimed a victory and sailed to Jamaica to become governor there. He had achieved peace without firing a shot, but the expensive venture had accomplished little more than to further Native American resentments, guaranteeing future hostilities.

Although he saw no actual fighting, Marion witnessed for the first time a pair of phenomena he would contend with in later campaigns: the arrogance of British military commanders and the fickleness of the colonial militia. The colonials resented the haughtiness of the British officers, who enjoyed better accommodations and imposed severe discipline, such as flogging, causing them to desert in droves. When Marion obtained his own militia command in 1780 he would not make the same mistake.

No sooner had Lyttelton's expedition ended than word reached Charleston of a fresh outbreak of hostilities in Cherokee country. Egged on by their French allies, a Cherokee raiding party attacked South Carolina's frontier settlements, killing, scalping, and mutilating women and

children, among other settlers. At the request of panicked South Carolinians, England sent Colonel Archibald Montgomery, the dashing
leader of the 77th Highland Scots Regiment, down from Canada to lead
a second expedition against the Cherokees. In April 1760 Montgomery
set out with thirteen hundred British regulars, supplemented by some
colonials and friendly Indians. Although Marion's participation in this
campaign is undocumented, he likely was present because it followed
closely upon Lyttelton's expedition and had the same objective—to
eliminate the Cherokee threat on the western frontier.

Montgomery's force, which rose to seventeen hundred, managed to
surprise the Cherokees and destroy several of their villages near Fort
Prince George. But after moving deeper north into Cherokee territory,
his men were ambushed at a narrow pass near the Middle Town of Etchoe
in present-day North Carolina. Taking protection from the higher
ground on the adjacent hills, the Cherokees fired down upon the invaders, killing or wounding about a hundred of them. The Cherokees also
had the advantage of long rifles, which were accurate at a much greater
distance than British muskets. That lesson in weaponry was one that
Francis Marion would tuck away for future use.

Montgomery's expedition ended in retreat back to Charleston, and
his prompt departure for New York caused South Carolinians to question
the British commitment to their safety. Even more alarming was the
news out of Fort Loudoun, in the Tennessee Overhill Towns territory.
After capturing the fort, the Cherokees started to escort the garrison
prisoners toward Virginia. But angered upon learning that the whites
had hidden and destroyed ammunition—in breach of the surrender
terms—the captors massacred twenty-nine of the prisoners, three of
them women. The commanding officer was scalped alive and made to
dance until he died, after which the Indians "stuffed earth into his mouth
and said, 'Dog, since you are so hungry for land, eat your fill.'"

Having twice failed to rid the Carolina frontier of the Cherokee threat,
the British put together a much larger surge force for a third attempt.
Leading the contingent was a forty-year-old, hard-nosed Highland Scot,
Lieutenant Colonel James Grant. He took charge of an army of twenty-
eight hundred, split evenly between British regulars, South Carolina provincials, and specially trained rangers, plus fifty-seven Mohawk, Catawba,

Stockbridge, and Chickasaw Indians as well as eighty-one slaves. Francis Marion was commissioned a lieutenant in the provincial infantry, serving directly under Captain William Moultrie.

In June 1761 Grant marched his army into Cherokee territory. At night his Native Americans danced the War Dance around a bonfire, and as one British officer recalled, "The camp was a little alarmed one night by a vast howling of wolves—our Indians, screaming at the same time, making it impossible to judge for some time what it was." The Indians—and four dozen white woodsmen dressed and painted to look like them—were placed at the vanguard of Grant's force.

A few days later Grant's men passed a tree carving showing a British soldier being dragged away by hostile Indians, a warning not to go any farther, which they ignored. The next morning, on June 10, the two-mile-long army column entered a mountain ravine about a mile from the same pass where Montgomery had been ambushed the year before. There Grant was met by at least six hundred warriors, led by Oconostota, sounding the Cherokee "Yelp" that echoed down the line.

Again the Cherokees had formed an ambush, but after several hours of fighting they ran out of ammunition and were reduced to using bows and arrows. During the battle, as recorded by British captain Christopher French, a Cherokee warrior "was met by a relation of a Catawba Indian who was killed in the action, who knocked him down with a war club, tomahawked and scalped him, then blew out his brains, cut open his breast, and belly, and cut off his privy parts, and otherwise mangled him in a most shocking manner." Wanton killing was not limited to Native Americans; Captain French himself was under "orders to put every soul to death."

Grant's forces pushed through the pass and on to Etchoe, after which they burned fifteen settlements and thousands of acres of crops. Grant boasted to his superiors that his troops had managed "to demolish every eatable thing in the country" and had driven "5,000 people including men, women and children . . . into the woods and mountains to starve." The Cherokees were forced to sue for peace. Grant and Attakullakulla smoked a peace pipe and concluded a treaty. By the time the War of Independence came around, the Cherokees would be back fighting on the British side.

Marion's precise role in the 1761 expedition is uncertain. Weems paints a dramatic picture of Marion being chosen by Grant to lead a detachment of thirty men on a suicidal advance through the pass. In this telling, as deadly fire rained down upon Marion and his unit, only nine of the thirty made it through alive, but they opened the pass for the main column.

Weems's tale has some grounding in fact. Grant did send a platoon of William Moultrie's provincial light infantry across a ford to fire at the enemy and cover the river crossing by the rest of the line. Because Marion was Moultrie's first lieutenant in the provincial light infantry and was a small man of the type often used for light infantry operations, he was likely one of those chosen for the assignment.* It was no easy task. Describing the provincials' effort, Colonel Henry Laurens, a future South Carolina revolutionary leader, wrote, "Our men behaved bravely, returned their [the Cherokees'] fire, advanced briskly up the hills, and pushed with great intrepidity across the river."

But to call it a suicide mission would be an exaggeration. According to contemporaneous army accounts, the light infantry who were in front were fired at from a great distance and suffered only one slightly wounded private. Out of Grant's entire army of twenty-eight hundred that day, only eleven soldiers were killed (and only one of them a Carolina provincial)— barely half the number of dead that Weems ascribed to Marion's unit alone. Moultrie, whose 1802 memoirs preceded Weems's book by seven years, merely described Marion as "an active, brave and hardy soldier" during Grant's campaign. William Dobein James said he "distinguished himself . . . in a severe conflict between Colonel Grant and the Indians, near Etchoee" while acknowledging that the particulars were unknown.

More recently Marion's participation in the Cherokee campaign has been cited against him. In a backlash to the release of The Patriot in 2000 the British press asserted that Marion was not the virtuous gentleman farmer turned heroic fighter portrayed by Mel Gibson in the movie but rather a man given to "slaughtering Indians for fun." There is no proof

---

*Light infantry were agile, highly mobile soldiers used to skirmish with or harass the enemy and provide a screen ahead of the main army.

Marion personally committed any atrocities during the Cherokee War, at least as a matter of choice, although he participated in some by order. Weems quotes from a letter Marion wrote to a friend, in which he recalled the Cherokee campaign with sorrow. "We arrived at the Indian towns in the month of July," he wrote. "The next morning we proceeded by order of Colonel Grant, to burn down the Indians' cabins. Some of our men seemed to enjoy this cruel work, laughing very heartily at the curling flames, as they mounted loud crackling over the tops of the huts. But to me it appeared a shocking sight. Poor creatures!" He is then quoted as saying that when ordered to cut down the fields of corn, on which the Indians depended for their survival, and where their children so often played, he "could scarcely refrain from tears."

Marion may not have penned these exact words, which are written in a more florid style than he employed in his military writings, but precious few of his private writings exist, so it is possible that this highly personal message is in fact largely his own. In any event, the sentiments reflected in the letter are similar to those he would express twenty years later when he participated in a war just as vicious and brutal.

Marion's views toward Native Americans also may have softened over the years through close personal contact with them. One of his favorite slaves, Peggy, was the "mustee" daughter of an Indian man and an African American woman. And Joseph Willis, born a slave to his white, plantation-owning father and Native American or possibly mixed-race slave mother, claimed to have served with Marion during the Revolutionary War as a free person of color.

Whatever he did or saw during the Cherokee War of 1759 to 1761, Marion came away from the experience with a profound distaste for the cycle of vengeance that is set off when one side's atrocity is met with barbarism from the other. He also witnessed, firsthand, the ambush and hit-and-run style of warfare that would serve him so well when fighting the British and their Tory allies in the Revolution.

After the Cherokee War ended by treaty in late 1761, Marion returned to tilling the soil on the fertile western banks of the Santee and cultivating the increasingly profitable crops of rice and indigo. The next decade or so are his "lost" years, with little he did being recorded. He shows up on the grand jury and petit jury lists in St. Stephens Parish in

1767, the same year he acquired 350 acres of land in Berkeley County adjoining that of his brother Job. The following year he was granted and immediately conveyed another 450-acre plat in the Santee River Swamp. In his mid-thirties he seemed to be someone who had yet to find his place in the world. By this time, too, Francis was the only one of his siblings not to have married—and married well.

But Francis continued to acquire land and gradually prospered, with help from his brother Gabriel, who seemed to have the magic touch when it came to making money. (Gabriel would acquire 140 slaves and die with an estate worth 78,000 pounds.) By 1773 Francis was able to purchase a Santee River plantation of his own, called Pond Bluff, a relatively small, two-hundred-acre tract farther upriver in St. John's Parish. Now at the bottom of Lake Marion, it was located on the west bank of the Santee, about four miles east of present-day Eutawville and not far from Thomas Sumter's plantation. Marion's plantation manager was the man June, one of the slaves given to him at birth by his uncle Francis and the father of Francis's childhood slave companion and later manservant, Buddy.

Probably around 1773 as well Francis Marion felt sufficiently propertied that he made out a will. A curious document, it liberates and makes generous provision for certain favorite slaves—but not others—and leaves property to the children of his brother Gabriel, including one born out of wedlock, but not to any of his other nieces or nephews. Nonetheless it provides one of the best insights into Marion's character and is one of the few significant nonmilitary writings of his to be found. With original spellings and capitalizations maintained, the signed but undated will provides:

> 1st. I order all my Lawfull Debts paid out of the profits arising from my plantation.
>
> 2nd. I order my Negroes to be kept and not sold or disposed of till my Godson Robert Marion [a son of Gabriel] comes of the age of twenty-one years. . . . I give and bequeath to my niece Charlotte Marion [daughter of Gabriel] one negroe wench named Venus and her child Rachel and their increase, to her and her Hairs for ever.

2nd. I Enfrenchise and make free my faithfull Negroe man Named June, and my good old nurse Willoughby, I also make free the mustee Girl Peggy (the daughter of Phebey) these three slaves I declare are free from all bondage and slavery whatever.

3d. I give to my Enfrenchised slave June twenty pounds [sterling] per annum as long as he lives.

4th. I give and Bequeath to my Enfrenchised slave Willoughby one suit cloaths and twenty pounds per annum as long as she lives.

5th. I give and Bequeath to my Enfrenchised slave Peggy (the Daughter of Phebey) suitable cloathing, that is to say one Winters suite and one Summers suite of Cloathing Each to consist of one Gown, one petticoat and a shift, this Donation to be annuelly till she comes to the age of fifteen years—and I order that she shall be learned to Read and Wright to be paid out of my Estate, and that she shall have a living on my Plantation till she arrives at the age of fifteen.

6th. I give and Bequeath to my Godson William Marion [the "natu-ral son" of Gabriel] my Plantation on Santee, one Negro boy named tobey, and two thousand pounds currency, when he comes to the age of twenty-one years, after which period I give it to him and his hairs forever.

I also order and tis my will he should have Cloathing and Living, and be Educated, at charge of my Estate till he arrives to the age of twenty one years.

7th. I give and Bequeath to my Nephew Gabriel Marion my English horse.

Thus, the will frees the African American slave June but not his wife, Chloe, nor their son, Buddy. Buddy's sister, Phoebe, also remains a slave, but her daughter Peggy, the "mustee," is made free. The endowment for her education was in fact contrary to South Carolina law at the time, which made it a crime to teach slaves to write.

Why Marion made bequests to the children of Gabriel but not to those of any other siblings is unknown. Francis probably felt indebted to Gabriel, who lived nearby, for the financial help he had given him over the years. Another mystery is why Francis left the bulk of his estate to

William Marion, the illegitimate son of Gabriel. In his own will Gabriel made no provision for and did not even acknowledge William, whose birth mother was another member of the Marion family. Yet Francis Marion favored William as his godson.

As master of Pond Bluff, life had become good for Francis Marion. Being a Lowcountry planter, he was mercifully uninvolved in the backcountry quarrels among outlaws, Regulators, and Moderators. He had served ably in the Cherokee War, and the Native American threat to South Carolinians had abated. Other masters may have feared slave uprisings, but Marion's relations with his twenty slaves, from all that can be gathered, were stable. (A British newspaper's claim in 2000 that he was guilty of "regularly raping his female slaves" is totally fabricated.) He lacked a wife, but he was close to and derived satisfaction from his extended family, and given his improving financial lot, he might have looked forward to marrying at some point.

Although a comfortable man as he passed his fortieth year, Francis Marion was also a faceless man, someone destined to appear as a mere line entry in some genealogy compiled centuries later—that is, unless something happened to pluck him from obscurity.

On the morning of April 19, 1775, British redcoats fired upon a group of outnumbered patriot militia at Lexington Commons in Massachusetts. Later that day the Minute Men responded by inflicting major damage on the British at Concord's North Bridge. Emerson would describe it as the "shot heard round the world." For Francis Marion, his comfortable days were over.

4

Manning the Ramparts

*I*t was not inevitable that Francis Marion would become a patriot. He was conciliatory, not radical, by nature; he did not hate the English, who had provided asylum to his ancestors, granted land to his grandfather, and fought alongside him against the Cherokees; and he had long attended the Anglican Church. Unlike the Scotch-Irish of the Williamsburg district in the Pee Dee region, the Huguenots of the Santee did not universally align themselves with the Whigs; members of prominent French families who were neighbors or relatives of the Marions sided with and even fought for the Tories during the Revolution. And although the Marions, like their Huguenot neighbors, were generally well-to-do, slaveholding plantation owners, they were not part of the Charleston aristocracy from which the most rabid revolutionary faction of South Carolinians emerged.

Why, then, did Francis Marion so passionately take up the cause of independence? The simplest and best explanation is that he was influenced by his extended family. His older brothers had become respected members of their communities and served variously as church wardens, justices of the peace, and military officers. In December 1774, when the voters of St. John's Parish elected delegates to South Carolina's First Provincial Congress, they chose Job and Francis Marion to represent them. At the first session of the new congress, which convened in Charleston on January 11, 1775, Job and Francis were joined by their brother Gabriel, elected as a delegate from St. Stephens Parish.

The wealthy Allstons of Georgetown, heavily connected by intermarriage to the Marions, were staunch patriots; several of the Allston men would later serve in Marion's Brigade. So, too, would three of Francis's nephews—Gabriel Marion, the son of brother Gabriel, and Thomas and Edward Mitchell, sons of Francis's sister by her second husband. Isaac Marion, Francis's oldest brother, who married an Allston, was a member of the Committee of Correspondence and helped relay the news of Lexington and Concord by courier from his home on the North Carolina border down to Georgetown and Charleston.

In short the Marions were true believers, and it was natural that Francis Marion became one himself. Logically, as propertied slaveholders, they would have preferred maintaining the conservative status quo. And as growers of rice and indigo, they profited greatly by trade with Britain; it was not in their economic interest to sever that tie. But as self-made men in a new land, they placed a higher value on self-rule. They may have discarded their old French customs, but the Huguenots' historical antipathy toward unchecked monarchy lingered in their bosoms.

Thus, when Parliament, in the years following the French and Indian War, began taxing the colonies to replenish Britain's coffers and switched from a laissez-faire policy to one of heightened supervision and control, the Lowcountry "Rice Kings," the Marions included, rebelled. They had come to regard British rule as a form of tyranny. They did not appreciate, of course, the inherent contradiction pointed out by England's Dr. Johnson when he rhetorically asked, "How is it that we hear the loudest yelps for liberty among the drivers of negroes?" But that was the economic and social milieu in which the Marions lived.*

At its initial meeting in January 1775, which began in a Charleston tavern, South Carolina's Provincial Congress endorsed the Continental Association, a pledge to ban the import from and export to Britain of most goods. The Charleston assembly was largely made up of socially and politically connected Lowcountry citizens, such as the Marions and

---

*The British hardly came to this argument with clean hands. It was they who chiefly introduced slavery to South Carolina from their Caribbean colonies. Great Britain did not abolish the slave trade until 1807 or slavery itself until 1833.

Allstons, and read like a who's who of men who would play prominent roles in the Revolution: Henry Laurens, John Rutledge, Christopher Gadsden, Thomas Sumter, Andrew Williamson, and Charles Cotesworth Pinckney, among others. They voted to create committees to provide for the common safety and issued a statement that South Carolinians should be "diligently attentive in learning the use of arms."

It was not long before South Carolina took up those arms. On April 21, 1775, just two days after Lexington and before news of that battle could have reached them, Charleston rebels raided armories and British powder magazines to seize all the guns and ammunition they could. It was the first overt act of war in South Carolina. Within two weeks rumors spread that the British planned to incite Indians and slaves to rise up against the colonists, further inflaming passions. (The rumors were overblown, not that the idea hadn't occurred to the British: James Grant, Marion's commander in the 1761 Cherokee campaign, believed that "a few scalps taken by Indians" would do wonders in scaring off the rebels.)

Hastily the Provincial Congress called a second session, and the delegates reconvened in Charleston on June 1. The South Carolinians voted to raise three provincial army regiments—two infantry and one cavalry—of five hundred men each. They created a Council of Safety with supreme power over the defense of the province. Any citizen who refused to sign a pledge of loyalty was deemed an enemy of the state. Some of the unfortunate nonsigners ended up being stripped naked, tarred and feathered, or worse. Thomas Jeremiah, a free black man who had amassed considerable wealth as a harbor pilot, was hanged and then burned on flimsy allegations that he was planning to lead a slave revolt once the Crown's forces reached South Carolina.

Marion was not a speech maker, and there is nothing to indicate he took any active part in the Provincial Congress proceedings or other acts of rambunctiousness. But he was eager to serve in some military capacity. When the Provincial Congress took ballots for militia captains on June 12, Marion tied for third out of twenty, with 135 votes, behind only the 140 received by Charles Cotesworth Pinckney, a future US presidential candidate, and Barnard Elliot, a former member of the royal governor's council. The vote was an indication of how highly Marion was regarded even at that point. He was placed in the 2nd Regiment and, based on the prior vote, ranked second captain in that unit (Peter Horry was fifth captain). Marion's mentor, William Moultrie, was made colonel of the 2nd Regiment, with Isaac Motte as lieutenant colonel. Moultrie ordered his officers to provide themselves with blue cloth coats lined and cuffed in scarlet, with white buttons, waistcoats, and breeches; their black upturned caps would be plumed with a silver crescent insignia sewn in front. In time it would become the uniform of the 2nd Regiment.

Moultrie then directed his junior officers to go into the countryside on a recruiting mission, and Marion came back with sixty men from the Santee and Pee Dee River regions. He trained and disciplined them, seeing to it that they "keep themselves clean decent with their hair combed and dressed in a soldier-like manner." By September he had his men drilled and all dressed up, just needing a place to go.

His first mission was to capture British-held Fort Johnson, located at the east end of James Island at the entrance to Charleston's harbor. The Council of Safety suspected that the recently arrived—and decidedly unwelcome—British royal governor, William Campbell, was planning to reinforce the fort, encourage resistance by backcountry loyalists, or, worst of all, foment Indian or slave uprisings against the colonists. Fort Johnson was the principal fortification guarding the city's harbor, and the council ordered Moultrie to seize it. And so on September 14 a force of 150 men—50 under Marion's command and 50 each under Pinckney and Elliot—sailed at night from Gadsden's Wharf in downtown Charleston. They anchored a mile from James Island and prepared to storm the fort.

When they got there at dawn, though, they found the doors wide open with a small British guard of five men waiting to surrender the stronghold. During the night Campbell had ordered the fort dismantled and the garrison removed to the British warships *Tamar* and *Cherokee* anchored in the harbor. Marion's company, trailing those of Pinckney and Elliot, was still in the process of rowing ashore from their schooner when the surrender was made. But they made it in time to see a new American flag hoisted above the fort—the first such colors displayed in South Carolina, as no state or national flag existed at the time. Designed by Colonel Moultrie himself and later known as the Moultrie flag, it had a blue field and white crescent, in keeping with the 2nd Regiment's uniform.

Fearing for his life, Campbell left his house in Charleston and took refuge in a floating office on the *Tamar*, where he formally dissolved the moribund Royal Assembly. Never again would South Carolina be governed by a British civil administrator.

In November, Moultrie chose Marion, by now the ranking captain of the 2nd Regiment, for another important mission. Marion was ordered with about ninety men to defend an arsenal at Dorchester, a village twenty miles outside Charleston where the Tories were thought to be planning an attack. But the rumored Tory action failed to materialize, and within a month half of the troops left due to boredom or sickness. Called back to Charleston, Marion thanked the officers who had served under him, "except Capt. Wigfall," an indication that some friction marked the Dorchester tour of duty. But Marion was right to question his subordinate's commitment to the cause: a secret loyalist sympathizer, John Wigfall would later switch sides to the Tories and take the field against Marion.

Marion was recalled to help guard Charleston because so many Whig soldiers were away on an expedition to put down a Tory uprising in the backcountry. In November, while Marion was at Dorchester, the Revolution's first land battle south of New England took place at the trading post of Ninety-Six in the northwestern part of the state, where about nineteen hundred Tories besieged a fort under the command of patriot major Andrew Williamson. Each side had one man killed—the first bloodshed of the war in South Carolina. A siege-ending truce did not hold, and an enraged Council of Safety sent a force of three thousand—which later swelled to nearly five thousand—to go after the Tories. Just before Christmas, in the decisive battle of what would become known as the Snow Campaign due to a thirty-inch snowfall, Colonel Richard Richardson routed the Tories at Great Cane Break near the North Carolina border. The main loyalist leaders were either captured and taken prisoner to Charleston or escaped to Indian Territory. The battle effectively ended Tory resistance in the backcountry and placed the Whigs in control of the province for the next four years.

Back in Charleston, Marion had to be champing at the bit. The war in South Carolina was heating up, and he had yet to witness a single shot fired. Future partisan leaders Andrew Pickens, who had fought the Cherokees with Marion, and Marion's neighbor, Thomas Sumter, had each seen action in the Snow Campaign against backcountry loyalists, and ironically, unlike Marion, neither of them was a native South Carolinian (Pickens was born in Pennsylvania, Sumter in Virginia). But Marion's new assignments in Charleston were no more fulfilling: repairing Fort Johnson's walls and remounting its guns, then building a battery and fortifications across the way at Haddrell's Point. When the 2nd Regiment was ordered on March 1 to construct a fort on Sullivan's Island at the southeast entrance to the harbor, it sounded like more of the same. Except this time a sense of urgency and excitement was present: the British were coming to South Carolina.

By the summer of 1776 William Campbell had not gotten over the humiliation of being driven from his office as South Carolina's royal governor a year earlier. Ever since, he and North Carolina's ex-royal governor, who likewise had been deposed, had been lobbying Parliament to support an assault on their respective provinces. Commander William Howe was planning major operations against New York for that summer, but in the meantime he agreed to support a "mini" southern strategy less ambitious than the one that would be undertaken four years later. Henry Clinton and his second in command, Lord Cornwallis, together with naval squadron commander Commodore Sir Peter Parker, were to establish a temporary base of operations in the South from which loyalists could operate.

After forgoing their original objective of Cape Fear, North Carolina, due to a strong Whig presence there, the British set their sights on Sullivan's Island, at the mouth of Charleston Harbor. Clinton intended only to take the island as a base, with no plans to assault the city itself. But Charleston's residents did not know that. When word of the approach of fifty enemy warships and a landing force of three thousand troops reached the town, civilians began fleeing to the countryside. Men wrote letters to their wives asking them to kiss their young children good-bye for them.

Charlestonians braced for a defense as best they could, leveling stores and warehouses along the waterfront to give their cannon a clear shot at hostile vessels. Slaves were directed to strip lead ornaments from buildings for melting down into bullets and were stationed around the town to fight anticipated fires.

John Rutledge, the recently elected chief executive and commander in chief under a new state constitution adopted in March, summoned the militia to the defense of the town. Soon they came flocking in. The defenders' morale was boosted with the arrival from the north of hundreds of Continentals under Major General Charles Lee, the first commander of the Southern Department, bringing the total patriot forces to more than six thousand. Lee assumed overall responsibility for the safety of Charleston, while Colonel Moultrie and the 2nd Regiment, including Major Francis Marion (recently promoted from captain), were in charge of defending Sullivan's Island.

By early June, with the British armada in sight off the entrance to Charleston Harbor, Fort Sullivan was only about half-finished. (In part this was because the white soldiers objected to working alongside slaves.) The walls were being constructed of palmetto logs and sand—not based on engineering advice but because no stone or other masonry was available and those were the only materials that could be gathered. Of the fort's four sides only the two facing the sea were built up; the ones in back, guarding land, were exposed to attack.

When Lee, an experienced and brusque former British army officer, inspected the stronghold, he became convinced the enemy would destroy it in short order. Declaring it a "slaughter pen" for the men inside, he urged it be abandoned. He also sized up Moultrie as too easy of a commander to put up much of a fight. But Moultrie insisted it could be held, and Rutledge backed him up. "General Lee . . . wishes you to evacuate the fort," Rutledge wrote to Moultrie. "You will not, without [an] order from me; I would sooner cut off my hand than write one." Clinton issued an ultimatum calling for the rebels to surrender, but Rutledge promptly rejected it, leaving the fate of Charleston to Moultrie and his garrison of four hundred, including Marion, who were manning the ramparts.

The genial, forty-five-year-old Moultrie may have been an easygoing leader, but his St. John's Berkeley plantation neighbor, Francis Marion, was not. Never one to tolerate any nonsense, Marion had kept the enlistees busy toiling on the fort, whether they liked working with slaves or not. He ordered that no one sell beer or liquor without specific permission. He did not hesitate to court-martial disobeyers. He conducted surprise alarms in the middle of the night to keep the soldiers on their toes. But Marion showed solicitude for his men: per his order, no oak trees, which provided them shelter from the intense summer sun, were to be cut down.

On June 28, 1776, the British moved several of their frigates into the harbor and attacked the fort. It was no contest—but not in the way anyone could have predicted. Palmetto logs turned out to be the perfect material for the fort's walls, for the British cannonballs were absorbed into the spongy logs and did little damage. The only real strike the warships scored was to shred the fort's blue Moultrie flag—the same one hoisted above Fort Johnson a few months earlier. But an intrepid sergeant named William Jasper grabbed it, attached it to an improvised shaft, and waved it above to resounding cheers from his comrades. They were doubly inspired by the grog (rum and water) Moultrie served to them in buckets, which he drank from along with them, to alleviate the summer heat.

By contrast, nothing went right for the invaders. In their effort to get close to the fort, two of Peter Parker's warships ran into each other and then, along with another, became stuck in shallow water, where the defenders' eighteen-pounders blasted them with surprising accuracy.* One of the grounded British ships was abandoned and set on fire by her crew before blowing up.

Meanwhile an infantry force of twenty-two hundred under Clinton and Cornwallis ended up watching the action as spectators. They had camped on Long Island (now Isle of Palms), separated from the northeastern tip of Sullivan's Island only by a narrow marshy inlet, known as the Breach. In what was to be a land attack coordinated with Parker's naval assault, the infantry planned to wade across the inlet at low tide and swoop down upon the open backside of the fort. But instead of the

* In artillery terms *pounder* refers to the weight of the balls fired, not the weight of the cannon. Most movable field pieces in the southern theater were three- or six-pounders, whereas battery artillery might be twelve- or eighteen-pounders or more.

eighteen-inch depth that intelligence reports had indicated, the Breach was actually seven feet deep and unfordable. Clinton's force then tried an amphibious landing in boats, but riflemen and artillery rushed to the scene and barraged their small flotilla, and the British were repelled with heavy losses. Among those driven back was a young volunteer officer and law school dropout named Banastre Tarleton, then on his first mission in America.

The British abandoned the invasion and returned to New York. They had suffered more than two hundred casualties, including former royal governor Campbell, who had returned to participate in the operation only to be mortally wounded aboard Peter Parker's flagship man-of-war, the HMS *Bristol*. American losses were only ten killed, including "a mulatto boy," and thirty-four wounded. It was the most decisive victory of the war by either side to that early point.

Though a lackadaisical preparer, Moultrie had proved to be an inspirational battle commander. Even General Lee, who came over to offer encouragement during the fighting, admitted his presence was unnecessary because Moultrie's men, though mostly raw troops, were "cool to the last degree." The Continental Congress passed a resolution thanking Moultrie, promoted him to brigadier general, and absorbed his 2nd Regiment into the Continental Army for the remainder of the war.*

Francis Marion, who was manning artillery at Fort Sullivan, also distinguished himself that day. He did not, as Weems claimed, request to fire and then personally launch the final parting cannonball that ripped through the hull of the *Bristol*; that honor went to Captain Richard Shubrick. But Marion did perform a critical role during the heat of battle. As the Americans were running short of cannon ammunition, Moultrie sent Marion and a small party to remove the powder from the American schooner *Defense*, which was lying at a nearby creek. They returned with enough to allow the patriots to resume firing until a larger supply was brought in from the city. Marion's teenaged nephew Gabriel was with

---

* Fort Sullivan was soon renamed Fort Moultrie in his honor and was an active US Army post until the end of World War II. June 28 is still celebrated as Carolina Day each year, and the palmetto tree would give the state its nickname as well as a symbol for its official flag, added to the crescent image on the blue Moultrie flag.

him at Fort Sullivan that day and may have accompanied him on the mission.

Until the Battle of Fort Sullivan, South Carolinians had not been unified in their desire to break from the mother country. But the course of human events began overtaking the more reluctant revolutionaries. Unbeknownst to Charlestonians, on June 28, the same day as the climactic battle, Thomas Jefferson delivered the first draft of a declaration of independence to the Continental Congress in Philadelphia. A few weeks later word reached Charleston that in a document adopted on July 4 and signed by four South Carolina representatives, Congress declared that the thirteen colonies were free from all allegiance to the British Crown and that all political connection between them and Great Britain was "totally dissolved."

Euphoric from having staved off the most powerful military force on earth and now officially independent from the mother country, Charlestonians went back to their life of parties and concerts and balls. The British were now gone and would remain absent from South Carolina for quite some time. But they would be back.

5

Commander of
the 2nd Regiment

*F*rancis Marion was no longer a farmer; he was now a professional soldier, experienced in multiple phases of the military: infantry, cavalry, artillery, coastal engineering, and amphibious operations, not to mention the Indian-style warfare he had seen on the frontier. In November 1776 he became the lieutenant colonel of the 2nd Regiment on the Continental line when Isaac Motte, who held that commission previously, was promoted to colonel. Along with other officers, Marion took an oath to "renounce, refuse, and abjure any allegiance and obedience" to the king of England and "to the utmost of my power, support, maintain and defend the said United States against the said King George the Third." No less than the signers of the Declaration of Independence, he was wagering his very life on the success of the Revolution.

Maintaining the commitment of the men he commanded was another matter. With the departure of the British, the suppression of the Tories, and the squashing of another Cherokee uprising in the back-country in the summer of 1776, South Carolina was relatively quiet; almost all the fighting was taking place in the North. Boredom set in among the soldiers garrisoned at Charleston with Marion, leading to problems with recruitment and discipline. Men were frequently slovenly and drunk, and they misbehaved by stealing from each other, pillaging nearby plantations, exceeding leaves of absence, and even "runnin with one another intirely naked" about town.

Such conduct riled Marion, and he was quick to impose harsh discipline. Punishment could mean fifty to a hundred lashes on a bare back, orders to do double duty, or a couple of days' confinement with only bread and water, although often the penalties were remitted in whole or in part. Between 1775 and 1777 more than one out of four men in Marion's 2nd South Carolina Regiment received court-martial-ordered whippings. (One repeat offender, who was court-martialed six times, endured a total of 749 lashings.) Marion went so far as to threaten that any woman found bringing in or selling liquor contrary to orders would be "whipped and drummed out of the regiment."

Repellant as such measures may sound today, they were not considered cruel or unusual at the time. In 1776 Congress in fact raised the legal limit on military flogging from thirty-nine to one hundred lashes; the British army, where miscreants were brutally disciplined, was much harder on its soldiers.

Marion's military mindset was British—hardly surprising as he had been trained as an officer in the British regular service. He was a stickler for appearance and hygiene, insisting that the men comb their hair and wash their faces and hands and that they dress "clean and neat." He explained that because "long hairs gather much filth," every soldier should have his hair cut short or, if not, then braided or tied. (He even created the position of regimental barber to dress the men's heads and shave them daily.) If they appeared for parade with unkempt beards or hair, they would be shaved or dressed on the spot. At times, he lamented, his men appeared "more like wild savages than soldiers." He also decried the "filthy custom" of soldiers "doing their Occasions in and near the fort," which "made a disagreeable smell in garrison." Violators "guilty of such vile practices" were to be brought to court-martial.

Decorum was also important to him. On the first anniversary of the victory over the British at Fort Sullivan (since rechristened Fort Moultrie), the ladies of Charleston threw a "genteel dinner" for the men, to which the officers contributed a hogshead (sixty-three gallons) of wine and forty-two barrels of beer. Marion expressed hope that the men would "behave with sobriety and decency" and promised that anyone seen drunk or disorderly in the streets would be put quietly to bed in their barracks.

Nor were officers immune from his careful oversight. On one occasion he felt "obliged to take notice of the great neglect of most of the officers not attending their duty more punctually." Another time, lamenting the drunkenness of many soldiers, he criticized his officers for being "not sufficiently attentive to their men."

At times Marion must have seemed a martinet. But his rationale was simple: "Whenever any part of duty is neglected or done in a slovenly manner, though ever so minute, it [tends] to destroy discipline entirely." He thought a little education might help: when several soldiers petitioned him to allow one of their colleagues to teach them to "read, Wright & arithmitick," Marion readily granted the request. The chosen instructor was a chronically court-martialed sergeant who once had been sentenced to receive two hundred lashes for threatened desertion before Marion intervened to pardon him.

Given the absence of any serious military threat and the monotony of garrison life, it became increasingly difficult to recruit and keep common soldiers in the Continental regiments in Charleston. South Carolina's General Assembly, which had replaced the Council of Safety, offered bounties and land to volunteers and even resorted to drafting vagrants and petty criminals into service. Still it was not enough. By December 1778 Marion's 2nd Regiment was at less than half strength.

Shortly before the December muster roll Marion had become the commander of the 2nd Regiment (designated "lieutenant colonel commandant") when Isaac Motte resigned as colonel to serve on South Carolina's Privy Council (the governor's cabinet). In the ordinary course Marion should have become a full colonel, but to maintain equivalency in the exchange of prisoners with British lieutenant colonels, who were the commanders of their regiments, he remained a lieutenant colonel, with his next promised promotion to be brigadier general.

Marion's life was changing in other ways around this time as well. By the end of 1778 three of his four brothers had died, all of them since the Battle of Fort Sullivan. Isaac, the lone surviving brother, would live only another three years. Always close to his family, Francis assumed the role of guardian and provider for the children of various siblings even while he was out waging war against the British. He put two of his nephews through the University of Pennsylvania; one of them would become a US representative from South Carolina.

Another shift in circumstances occurred in December 1778, this one with more profound implications for Marion's future: the British came back to the South.

THE FALL OF SAVANNAH—the first leg in Britain's revised southern strategy—occurred on December 29, 1778, with hardly a shot fired. After General Robert Howe surrendered the city, loyalists overran much of Georgia. Major General Benjamin Lincoln, the new commander of the Continental Southern Department (having replaced Howe, who had replaced Charles Lee), moved out of Charleston and into Georgia in an effort to wrest back control of as much of that state as possible. But Lincoln's foray left Charleston dangerously exposed, and in April 1779 the British general Augustine Prévost (a Huguenot) decided to capitalize on that opportunity.

Although he had entered Georgia from Florida with no specific intention to attack the city, Prévost found himself, almost by accident, on the outskirts of Charleston by May 11. He brazenly issued a demand for its surrender. General Moultrie, who had been out on the venture with Lincoln, leaving Marion in charge of Charleston, hurried back to the city just before Prévost's arrival and was prepared to fight to the last.

But the civilian leadership—Governor John Rutledge and his Privy Council—had other ideas. Either because they suffered a loss of nerve or were peeved at what they considered a lack of northern support, they offered to capitulate. They told the British they could take possession of Charleston, provided that South Carolina be allowed to remain neutral for the duration of the war, its ultimate fate to be determined by treaty afterward. Prévost rejected the offer and prepared to lay siege or attack. But he was forced to retreat to Georgia when he learned that Lincoln was coming to the city's relief with a far superior force. On his way back, Prévost enraged Lowcountry Whigs by killing unarmed prisoners and burning and pillaging homes, including Rutledge's.

For the second time Charleston had managed to avoid what had looked to be all but certain capture. But the near success of Prévost's brief incursion highlighted the complacency prevailing in South Carolina since the victory at Fort Sullivan and the town's vulnerability to British attack. To Henry Clinton, who had failed so miserably in the assault three years earlier, Charleston now appeared to be there for the taking.

Recognizing that danger, John Laurens, the idealistic twenty-four-year-old son of Henry Laurens and an aide-de-camp to General Washington, proposed that South Carolina arm three thousand slaves to help defend itself. Those who faithfully served to the end of the war would be freed upon compensation to their masters. Laurens even offered personally to lead these African Americans in battle. But although Congress approved the plan, it was "blown up with contemptuous huzzas" by the South Carolina legislature. Christopher Gadsden, as radical a revolutionary as there was, told fellow patriot Sam Adams that South Carolina was "much disgusted" that Congress would suggest such a "dangerous and impolitic step." To a population constantly in fear of slave insurrections, the image of thousands of black men with weapons in their hands was too frightening to contemplate.

Instead, to help protect Charleston, General Lincoln decided to try to retake Savannah, the enemy's principal base of operations in the South. He was spurred to that plan when Admiral d'Estaing agreed to bring his French fleet from the West Indies, where he had defeated the British in August 1779, to assist the Americans in a joint attack upon Savannah. Erratic and restless, d'Estaing made it clear he would not stay long because he wanted to be back in the Caribbean by late October for another round against the British.

In Charleston, Lincoln ordered Lieutenant Colonel Marion, with the two-hundred-some men of his regiment, to stand ready to march at a moment's notice. Marion and Major Peter Horry were part of Lincoln's army of three thousand, along with a distinguished officer group that included Moultrie, John Laurens, Andrew Williamson, Isaac Huger, and Casimir Pulaski, a colorful Polish nobleman considered the father of the American cavalry. Just outside of Savannah the American forces united with d'Estaing's brightly uniformed French army of four thousand. In addition to French regulars (including Pierre L'Enfant, who one day would design Washington, DC) and various other European volunteers, d'Estaing's army was accompanied by a unit of five hundred free blacks from Haiti dressed in blue and green. One of them was Henry Christophe, the future "King of Haiti" and leader of the Haitian revolution against France.

When the Americans arrived at the French camp in mid-September they discovered, to Lincoln's consternation, that d'Estaing had already issued a demand for surrender to the British general Prévost, who had assumed command at Savannah. Omitting any mention of Lincoln's approaching army, d'Estaing asked the British to yield to "the arms of the King of France." Stalling for time, the wily Prévost requested twenty-four hours to consider the terms, which d'Estaing naively granted. Prévost used the postponement to bring in reinforcements and to continue strengthening his fortifications with the aid of hundreds of trench-digging slaves. By the time the combined French and patriot forces collected themselves, the British position was too secure for a direct assault. Marion reportedly was aghast at d'Estaing's blunder.

Still fully expecting victory, the allied forces commenced siege operations. The defense works consisted of a series of small, square, sand-built strongholds (redoubts) manned by battery gunners, surrounded by ditches and a row of thorny tree branches with sharpened tops pointing toward the enemy (abatis) that were the functional equivalent of barbed wire. In lieu of a direct attack, on October 3 the allies began bombarding the British with artillery fire. But the British and Tory defenders held firm, and d'Estaing grew impatient. His troops lacked bread and could not stomach the readily available rice. The sailors aboard the ships anchored off Savannah were dying of scurvy. It was also late hurricane season, and d'Estaing, who had been driven by storm from Newport earlier in the war, was unwilling to risk another such disaster for his fleet. Although standard siege operations, given time, likely would have succeeded, d'Estaing told Lincoln he would either abandon the siege or storm the town. Lincoln had little choice but to agree, and in the early morning of October 9 the two leaders prepared to launch their attack. As they lay waiting in the heavy predawn fog they could hear the melancholy strain of a single bagpiper pacing the walls of the British ramparts.

What followed was a bloodbath. The battle would last just an hour, but it was the most costly single day of fighting by combined American and French forces in the entire war, and it produced the greatest loss of life on one side since Bunker Hill. D'Estaing had planned a surprise attack on the weakest part of the enemy line, an earthen fort called Spring Hill Redoubt, manned principally by South Carolina loyalists. D'Estaing's plan was foiled by a deserter who informed Prévost of the point of attack, allowing him to prepare. The British gunners and grenadiers repulsed repeated assaults on Spring Hill by the allies—first by the French, who had claimed the honor of leading the vanguard, then by the Americans, including Marion's 2nd South Carolina Continentals and the Charleston militia, both under the command of Brigadier General Isaac Huger and young Colonel John Laurens.

At the height of the battle Marion led his men forward across the abatis and into a ditch in front of the redoubt. There they were sprayed with shot by Carolina loyalist riflemen under Thomas Brown, a Tory who had been tarred and feathered by the Whigs earlier in the war. As Marion's troops climbed forward, their standard bearer was wounded and fell. He passed the blue flag with the crescent symbol to Sergeant Jasper, the same man who had rescued the colors in the Battle of Fort Sullivan. But Jasper, too, was cut down and would die aboard a ship back to Charleston.

Under the heavy fire and after bitter, hand-to-hand fighting, the 2nd Regiment and the other colonials were forced to retreat. Of the 600 South Carolinians who charged uphill, 250 did not return. A British officer observed that "the ditch was choke full of their dead." Colonel Laurens, barely half Marion's age, drew his arms wide apart as if wanting to die with his men, but his time had not yet come. It had for Count Pulaski, who, in leading a literal last-ditch cavalry charge, was mortally wounded in the groin by cannon shot. He died at sea two days later.

The Franco-American forces suffered between one thousand and fifteen hundred killed or wounded during the entire siege, around 70 percent of them French. British casualties, by comparison, were light, with estimates between fifty and one hundred. Despite the lopsided defeat, Lincoln and Governor Rutledge pleaded with d'Estaing to continue the siege, but the Frenchman, himself wounded in the assault, had had enough. Blaming the Americans for the debacle, he sailed back to

France, where later, as a royalist sympathizer, he would meet the guillotine in 1794.

With Savannah now firmly in British hands, Clinton was cleared to come south for his long-awaited renewed effort to capture Charleston. Lincoln brought his army back to the city, leaving Marion at a plantation in Sheldon, South Carolina (near Beaufort). He was to watch the movements of Prévost and prevent him from pillaging on the Carolina side of the Savannah River. Marion's small force was involved in some minor skirmishing with raiding parties of African Americans; despite protests from white Georgians, including loyalists, Prévost had kept armed blacks in the field, finding them useful for plundering supplies across the South Carolina border.

It was a cold winter in Sheldon, and Marion's men, lacking shoes, blankets, and clothing, passed the time by growing mustaches. "When you see me," Marion wrote to Lincoln, "you will find I have a formidable . . . Mustassho, which all the regiment now ware and if you have not one you will be singular." (It is not known how long Marion kept his mustache.)

Marion remained at Sheldon until the end of January, when he returned to Charleston. The town had received word that on the day after Christmas Clinton had sailed south from New York with a large flotilla and an expedition force of eighty-five hundred. After a rough six-week journey during which the British fleet was forced to toss their horses overboard due to violent storms, Clinton dropped anchor on February 11 less than thirty miles from Charleston. From there he would rendezvous with the British forces heading north from Savannah. Unlike in 1776, this time the British would not conduct their assault mainly by sea but instead via an overland route. They planned to encircle the city, conduct a classic siege, cut off escape routes, and eventually squeeze Charleston into submission.

After a stint to guard Bacon's Bridge near Dorchester, where he reported his two hundred infantry men complaining that they had no rum, Marion was back in command in Charleston in mid-March. He worked feverishly to improve the city's fortifications, using slaves as laborers, although the legislature denied Lincoln's request to arm them. Lincoln also ordered the felling of trees and leveling of houses just outside Charleston to deny the British cover during a siege, but property owners managed to thwart the plan. Rural militia, unwilling to leave their farms and families and fearful of smallpox, largely ignored Governor Rutledge's request to come to the city's aid. In many ways South Carolinians were their own worst enemy.

On March 19 Marion attended an officers' party at the home of Alexander McQueen, General William Moultrie's adjutant general, at 106 Tradd Street at the corner of Orange and Tradd Streets. From a second-story window there he jumped to escape the endless drinking and shattered his ankle. By the first week of April the British had laid siege to Charleston, and on April 12 Lincoln, sensing doom, ordered all officers without an assigned command and any who were unfit for duty to leave the garrison and retire to the countryside.

By the next day Marion was gone from the city, as was Governor Rutledge, who had left to set up a government in exile. Peter Horry, furloughed after a consolidation of regiments in January, had already departed Charleston and was home at his plantation, awaiting further assignment. Lincoln considered evacuating his entire army, and given the eventual surrender of his more than five thousand men, it would have been wiser to try to save the army than the city. But the civilian leadership insisted that Charleston be defended to the last extremity, and Lincoln, an amiable man who suffered from peculiar bouts of narcolepsy, was not strong enough to stand up to them.

After April 14 it was probably too late to attempt an evacuation anyway. In the early morning that day Banastre Tarleton's cavalry surprised and routed a larger force of Americans under General Isaac Huger and Lieutenant Colonel William Washington (second cousin of the commander in chief) at Biggin Bridge near Monck's Corner, thirty miles north of Charleston. It had been the principal escape route from the city. Tarleton also managed to capture four hundred high-quality horses to help replace those lost on the voyage from New York. Huger, Washington, and most of the five hundred rebels stationed at Monck's managed to escape into the swamps, but the noose around Charleston had tightened. Lincoln proposed to Clinton that the British could occupy the city if the American army was allowed to leave with all its supplies, but Clinton was holding all the cards, and he promptly rejected the offer.

On May 6 Tarleton closed virtually the last way out. Some of the escapees from Monck's had re-formed with local militia and were resting at Lenud's Ferry, on the south side of the lower Santee River. They were waiting there for Virginia's Colonel Abraham Buford, who was supposed to be bringing boats for the crossing. Acting on a tip from Elias Ball, a hard-core Tory who happened to be related to Marion by marriage, Tarleton raced his cavalry to Lenud's and caught the two hundred Americans by surprise. Tarleton's men killed, wounded, or captured half the patriot force as Buford's men, just arrived on the north side of the Santee, could only watch the slaughter as it unfolded on the opposite bank. Lieutenant Colonel Anthony White, the American commander, and William Washington escaped by swimming across the dangerously swift river.

On May 7, British seamen took Fort Moultrie without resistance. Two days later Clinton began a general bombardment of the town, and the same civilians who had earlier threatened to "open the gates for the enemy" if Lincoln attempted to evacuate now pressed him to accept whatever terms Clinton offered. On May 11, 1780, the white flag was hoisted above Charleston, and the next day the richest town in America—and the entire Continental southern army—surrendered to the British.

One by one the British then established posts or accepted the surrender of existing garrisons as part of a semicircle of fortified towns stretching 140 miles from Savannah and Augusta, Georgia, up to Ninety-Six in northwest South Carolina, then down through Camden and on to Georgetown on the coast. Backcountry Whigs began accepting parole, including even such military stalwarts as Andrew Pickens and Andrew Williamson. Generals and politicians who were part of the surrendering force at Charleston were taken out of commission: William Moultrie became a prisoner of war in Charleston, while Benjamin Lincoln was forced to retire to his farm in New England. Christopher Gadsden was placed in solitary confinement in a dungeon in St. Augustine, Florida, and Henry Laurens was taken to England and imprisoned in the Tower of London.

Had he wished, Francis Marion could have come out of hiding along the Santee, limped back into Charleston, and accepted British protection for the duration of the war. He might have returned to Pond Bluff and lived comfortably there, unmolested by redcoat or Tory. But he had other ideas. He offered his services to Gates's Continental army and was sent off to head up the Williamsburg militia. Then came the calamities of Camden on August 16 and Fishing Creek on August 18, leaving Marion alone in South Carolina to resist the British occupation. As he camped with his men along the upper Santee, he was determined to do something to prove the contest was not over. And a week after their initial gathering at Witherspoon's Ferry, Marion's Brigade would make their first strike.

6

Birth of a Partisan

On August 23 Marion and his men drove off the British guard at Murray's Ferry (where modern US Route 52 crosses the Santee River), then moved upstream to camp near Nelson's Ferry, the major crossing point on the Santee between Charleston and Camden.

On the night of August 24 a Tory deserter walked into Marion's camp on the northeastern bank of the river with a tantalizing piece of news. Fearing that smallpox or malaria would break out among the American prisoners taken at Camden, Cornwallis was marching them off in groups of 150, under escort, down the road to Charleston to be put on prison ships. They consisted of Continentals from the Maryland and Delaware lines—the best-trained and, hence, most valuable soldiers in the American army. A convoy of about 150 of them was now being held at Thomas Sumter's abandoned plantation home on the Great Savannah six miles north of Nelson's Ferry.* They were being guarded by sixty troops under British army captain John Roberts—mostly veteran British regulars of the 63rd Regiment of Foot and loyalist provincials of the Prince of Wales Regiment,† plus a few Tory militia troops.

---

*Nelson's Ferry is now submerged under manmade Lake Marion that was created as part of a hydroelectric power project in the 1940s. Sumter's abandoned plantation on Great Savannah, also probably under water as well, is not to be confused with a different Sumter home that Tarleton had burned, which was located farther north in the High Hills of Santee in current Sumter County.

† *Provincials* were Americans loyal to the king who were recruited into units led by British army-trained officers and operated as adjuncts to the regular army. One

Marion had seventy men with him, as most of his brigade was still with Peter Horry, burning boats on the lower Santee. Determined to rescue the prisoners, he decided to attack in the dark, a tactic he would come to use many times. He roused his men and took them on a night ride toward Sumter's plantation, arriving just before daybreak. Marion sent sixteen men under the command of Colonel Hugh Horry to seize the pass over Horse Creek, which ran parallel to the Santee through a swamp just above the river. By taking hold of the Horse Creek pass, Marion could block possible enemy reinforcements from the guard at Nelson's Ferry, then under British control. Meanwhile the main body of men under Marion circled around behind Sumter's house, which stood on elevated ground above the swamp, to attack from the rear.

As is common in battle, things did not go exactly according to script. In the darkness Horry's men stumbled upon a British sentinel who fired at their shadows and alerted the rest of the guard. Their cover blown, Horry did the only thing he could: he immediately led a mounted charge down the lane that led to the front of the house. To his surprise and delight, he discovered that the enemy had left all of their muskets carelessly piled outside the front door. Horry's patrol seized the weapons and burst inside, soon joined by Marion. The fight was over in minutes. Before the astonished British even had time to react, two of their number were killed, five were wounded, and twenty were taken prisoner. (The rest apparently fled for their lives.) Marion had none killed and only two wounded. His men had retrieved all of the 150 American prisoners. The victory, though small, was complete.

Ironically, the freed prisoners included some of the same men who had snickered at Marion's "burlesque" little group in Gates's camp a few weeks before. Instead of gratefully joining the ranks of their liberators, these Continentals decided they'd had enough of fighting. They had spent a harsh winter in New Jersey before marching with scant provisions to the unbearably humid South, only to be whipped in a battle deserted by their field general. The defeat they'd suffered at Camden under

_____

source states that the British had more Americans in provincial units than Congress had in the Continental Army.

Gates had convinced them that their leadership was unreliable and the patriot cause hopeless. They saw no point in continuing to risk their lives for nothing. As a result, only 3 of the 147 retaken men accepted the offer to enlist in Marion's brigade. Some 85 were so demoralized that they insisted on continuing on to Charleston, preferring the safety of a prison ship to the peril of combat. The remainder, about 60, went to North Carolina to rejoin their original Continental units, but most of those ended up deserting.

Slender as the fruits of his victory may have been, Marion's daring predawn raid was the one piece of good news in an otherwise dismal picture for the Americans at that hour. General Gates, upon receiving Marion's account of the encounter, made his own report of it to Congress, briefly lifting its sagging spirits. Patriot newspapers included the name Francis Marion in their columns for the first time—though misspelling it as "Merien." A legend was in the making.

This was also the first time Cornwallis took notice of "a Colonel Marion." The British commander was irritated by what had happened at Great Savannah. It was, after all, *his* prisoners taken at Camden who had been freed and his program to have them conducted safely to Charleston that had been interfered with. He demanded an explanation and received one from Major James Wemyss (pronounced "Weems") of the 63rd Foot. "I am afraid negligence will mark the whole of it," was Wemyss's frank appraisal.

Clinton had left Cornwallis with instructions not to move into North Carolina until South Carolina was firmly secured. Anxious to get on with his planned northern invasion, Cornwallis was concerned that South Carolina was not quite as pacified as he had assumed. He expressed wonder that the "disaffection" of the people east of the Santee was so great that they had not allowed the defeat at Camden to stamp out their revolutionary ardor. Cornwallis also understood that he could not safely move his army north as long as Marion was strangling his supply line running from Charleston to Camden, chiefly through the choke point at busy Nelson's Ferry. Accordingly, on August 28 Cornwallis ordered Major Wemyss to sweep the area between the Santee and Pee Dee Rivers of any rebel forces. He also directed Wemyss to *"disarm in the most rigid*

manner all persons who cannot be depended on and punish the conceal-
ment of arms and ammunition with a *total demolition of the plantation.*" As
he reiterated to his outpost commanders:

> I have ordered in the most positive manner that every militia man who
> had borne arms with us and afterwards joined the enemy *should be im-
> mediately hanged.* I . . . desire that you will take the most *vigorous* mea-
> sures to *extinguish the rebellion* in the district in which you command
> and that you will obey in the strictest manner the directions I have
> given in this letter relative to the treatment of the country.

Despite his title, his Lordship was no mere genteel British nobleman
but instead a determined and at times ruthless adversary. No stranger to
brass-knuckle tactics, he had attended Eton academy, a rough place in
those days, and chose a military career at age seventeen over a life of lei-
sure. In his letter to Clinton he went on to boast, "*I have myself ordered
several militia men to be executed,* who had voluntarily enrolled themselves
and borne arms with us, and afterwards revolted to the enemy."

Just two months earlier Cornwallis had informed Clinton that British
operations had "put an end to all resistance in South Carolina." But now
he was starting to realize that the war in South Carolina was far from
over; indeed, as far as Francis Marion was concerned, it had only just
begun.

No longer a Continental officer except in name and virtually alone
in the field, Marion was embarking on a new career as a partisan leader.
There was no script telling him what to do or where to go. He knew he
wanted to inflict as much damage on the enemy as possible, but surely
Banastre Tarleton and others would be coming after him. To accomplish
anything useful Marion needed to keep another objective in mind—
staying alive.

7

Hitting and Running

After the victory at Nelson's Ferry on August 25 Marion marched his men and the freed prisoners back in the direction of Witherspoon's Ferry, where his brigade had formed just eight days earlier. Unable to care for the enemy prisoners he had taken at Sumter's plantation, Marion sent them off to a Continental camp in Wilmington, North Carolina.

After passing Witherspoon's, Marion camped a few miles away in the vicinity of Britton's Neck, a narrow strip of land between the junction of the Great and Little Pee Dee Rivers. Home to a close-knit Whig community and geographically isolated by rivers and swamps, the area would provide a frequent safe haven for Marion's partisans in the months to come.

On August 27 Marion wrote to Peter Horry, who was still burning boats on the lower Santee, to inform him of Gates's defeat and of his own success at Nelson's Ferry. As Marion explained, he had been forced to retreat in light of Gates's withdrawal to North Carolina. He ordered Horry to come up to meet him at Britton's Neck and to bring as many men as would follow him. But by the time they met, around September 1, Marion's militia numbered just over fifty, with many of the men having gone home. Citizens first and soldiers second, his rank-and-file would return to their farms at planting or harvest season to tend to their crops and families. Marion understood and acquiesced to the practice, but that does not mean he liked it.

Despite his inspiring victory at Nelson's Ferry, Marion was feeling very much alone. He had no logistical support from any government or military authority. On August 29 he wrote the first of several letters to Gates in which he asked, in effect, "Where is the army?" As he informed Gates, the lack of any news about the general's situation or even his whereabouts had dispirited the Whigs in South Carolina.

By now, too, the redcoats were coming. Major Wemyss had his August 28 orders from Cornwallis to "disarm in the most rigid manner" all rebels between the Santee and Pee Dee. From his position in the High Hills of Santee,* Wemyss was about to embark on that mission with the 63rd Foot. He was ordered to clear the Pee Dee region of opposition, then return by way of the Cheraws District, northeast of Camden and near North Carolina. The Cheraws had a fair number of Tories that Cornwallis expected Wemyss to recruit for an organized militia.

In fact, the Tories, too, were already coming after Marion. On September 3, while camped in the Britton's Neck area, Marion learned from spies that a large band of Tory militia from the Catfish Creek and Little Pee Dee regions to the north were on the march and planning to attack him by surprise the next day. They were led by Major Micajah Ganey, a hot-headed ex-patriot who had served under Marion in the 2nd South Carolina Regiment. Ganey had switched sides because a Whig had stolen some of his horses. Ganey's second in command was Captain Jesse Barefield, also a former 2nd Regiment member—he fought with Marion at Fort Sullivan—who joined the Tories because he felt he'd been insulted by a rebel officer. Now strident loyalists, Ganey and Barefield would remain nemeses of Marion for much of the war, posing an ongoing threat to Marion's dominance in the Pee Dee region north of Georgetown. Soon they would have their first encounter.

As Marion learned, Ganey was heading south toward him with a force of about 250, including mounted and foot soldiers. Marion had with him just 53 men, all mounted, "which is all I could get," he later wrote. Outnumbered five to one, Marion decided to strike first. According to one account Marion initially was hesitant to attack, but several

---

*The High Hills of Santee is a narrow range of sand hills north of the Santee and running east along the Wateree, where the current town of Stateburg sits. It was a haven for escaping the insufferable heat and malaria of the Lowcountry during the summer.

brothers persuaded him to try to rescue their father, who had been robbed and taken prisoner by Ganey's Tories. But sentimental as it may be to imagine Marion, against all odds, risking his brigade for the sake of one elderly man, it would have been out of character for him. If Marion decided to make a preemptive strike against a superior force, it was because he had concluded he had some military advantage, like the element of surprise, working in his favor.

In any event, at dawn on September 4 Marion set out on horseback from his camp on the east (north) side of the Pee Dee at Port's Ferry. As was becoming his custom, to prevent security leaks Marion told no one of his plans. Deserters and other volunteers came and went so frequently that one never knew for certain whose side they were on. In addition, loyalist and patriot militia were hard to tell apart because they both wore homespun. So that they might recognize each other in battle, Marion had his men place white feathers in their hats.

They headed north, along current South Carolina Highway 41, in search of the Tory militia. Later that morning they came upon an advance foraging party of forty-five of Ganey's horsemen, who were surprised to find their southward route impeded. As the frightened body of Tories broke, Marion's men killed or wounded all but fifteen of them, who escaped into the swamps.

Thus emboldened, Marion's men continued north on horseback for about three miles, where they quickly ran into the main body of Tory infantry in full march toward them near the Blue Savannah. The site was a swampy land indentation named for the bluish color of water that filled it and the bluish-gray mud that stuck to wagon wheels crossing it.* Accounts of the battle differ markedly. According to William Dobein James, whose father was there and who may have been there himself, Marion created a trap. Because he faced superior numbers and the Tories stood resolute in their ranks, he feigned retreat and led them into an ambush he had laid a ways back from the savannah. Marion's own report on

---

*The Blue Savannah was one of many inland South Carolina "bays"—swampy, sandy-rimmed depressions, elliptical or oval in shape, likely caused by ancient meteors. They are named for the bays (pine shrubs) frequently found in them, not for the water that collects in them.

the battle to Gates, however, does not mention any ambush but says he "directly attacked" the main body of Tories and "put them to flight." Under both versions, after the Tories got off a single volley that did little damage, they fled into a swamp just east of the road. From the swamp's edge Marion's men shouted curses and insults at their cowering foes, daring them to come out and fight. With a rare note of scorn, Marion would describe the gooey morass as "impassable . . . to all but Tories."

It was another stunning victory. That day, at a cost of four wounded and two dead horses, Marion had killed or wounded thirty Tories and scattered the rest. Ganey and Barefield trundled off to Georgetown. With their militia broken up, many of their men went back home, ending—for the time being—loyalist strength in the area east of the Pee Dee.

The next day Marion marched back to his camp at Britton's Neck, where sixty new volunteers from Colonel Hugh Giles's militia joined him, doubling the size of his yet small force. Two weeks earlier his name was unknown to the British, and now suddenly he was capable of operating behind Cornwallis's lines and harassing his right (eastern) flank. It was a vexation his Lordship needed to eliminate before he could launch his planned invasion of North Carolina. The success of Marion's hit-and-run tactics so infuriated the British high command that at least half a dozen death squads, beginning with Wemyss, were dispatched in sequence to go after him.

While at Britton's Neck, Marion threw up a small earthen fort on the east bank of the Pee Dee to guard the crossing at Port's Ferry. He managed to fortify it with two old iron artillery pieces the militia had brought him, which he thought would intimidate any Tories who tried to reassemble and threaten him. Then on September 7 he learned that a contingent of British regulars and Tories, said to number 150, were in the Williamsburg area burning the homes of men who had joined his brigade. He dispatched Major James to reconnoiter them.

Anxious for another chance to confront the enemy, Marion crossed the Pee Dee and Lynches Creek to the southwest with a hundred men, leaving fifty behind to protect his camp. He camped at Indiantown which, along with neighboring Kingstree, was perhaps the most solidly Whig area in all of South Carolina. At Indiantown he was met by Major James, who brought in a captured Tory straggler. From this prisoner

Marion learned that four hundred British redcoats and Tories under Wemyss were gathering that night in Kingstree, twenty miles west, with plans to eradicate Marion's resistance fighters.

Marion also had intelligence that two hundred more redcoats had arrived in Georgetown, a couple days' march away on the coast. With 600 enemy soldiers, the majority of them experienced redcoats, able to concentrate against his 150, he thought it prudent to fall back to his camp at Britton's Neck. But first he aired the issue with his officers, who dismounted and retired to consult. During a long and animated conference the rank-and-file sat on their horses and anxiously awaited the verdict. When the order was given to retreat back across Lynches Creek an audible groan could be heard along the line—the men knew their homes in Williamsburg were being left to the mercy of the pillaging enemy. Recognizing their disappointment, upon the brigade's retreat Marion left behind a number of men, including Major John James, to gather intelligence in the Williamsburg area and do what they could to comfort the distressed.

Back at camp on September 8 Marion received more distressing news: he was in danger of being surrounded on three sides. Wemyss had moved from Kingstree through Indiantown, crossed Lynches Creek at Witherspoon's Ferry, and was only a few miles away, coming up on him from the west. Tory militia out of the garrison at Georgetown, led by Colonels John Coming Ball and John Wigfall, had crossed the Black River to attack him from the south. And Ganey's Tories, who had just been dispersed, were collecting to the east of him. He had only one escape route, directly to the north, along the same road, unblocked for the time being, where he had defeated Ganey and Barefield. By now, too, he had released most of his men to go check on their families and homes. And so, at sunset on September 8 he took off with his remaining sixty men and the two field pieces and began retreating to North Carolina.

Marching day and night, he arrived at Ami's Mill on Drowning Creek near the North Carolina state line. Along the way he dumped the two field pieces into a swamp, finding that they impeded his progress. By mid-September he was camped at the Great White Marsh in eastern North Carolina, another thirty miles past the border. He would remain there, he wrote Gates on September 15, "until I hear from you or I have an oppertunity of doing something."

Wemyss, whose men had been suffering from malaria, pursued Marion for a day or two but broke off the chase to continue his other assignment from Cornwallis—to destroy rebel property. Upon his arrival in Indiantown around September 7 Wemyss burned the Presbyterian church there, calling it a "sedition shop." (Ironically, Wemyss was himself a Presbyterian.) Over the next few days he put the torch to several more homes, including that of Major James, allegedly because James's wife refused to provide information as to her husband's whereabouts.* He also hanged Adam Cusack, a local ferryman, in front of his wife and children as they pleaded for his life. According to American accounts, Cusack was executed either for refusing to ferry Wemyss's officers across a creek or because he fired a shot across the creek at a slave of Tory militia captain John Brockinton. When Dr. James Wilson tried to intercede on Cusack's behalf, Wemyss burned his house too.

Weems described Wemyss as "by birth, a Scotsman, but in principle and practice a Mohawk." In reality he was to emulate the malevolent Cherokee campaign of British colonel James Grant. On his march north from Kingstree to the town of Cheraw, Wemyss cut a path of destruction seventy miles long and five miles wide on both sides of the Pee Dee River, burning fifty houses and plantations along the way. He claimed that these "mostly" belonged to people who had broken their paroles or oaths of allegiance and were now in arms against the British. (He offered no justification for burning the others.) Wemyss also ordered his men to destroy blacksmith shops, looms, and mills and to shoot or bayonet any milk cows and sheep not taken by the British for themselves. The residents thus lost not only their shelter but also their means of livelihood, food, and clothing. Wemyss's scorched-earth policy would have echoes in Sherman's famous march through the South in the Civil War.

In a letter to Cornwallis on September 20 the thirty-two-year-old Wemyss wrote that he had done everything in his power to nab Marion and Colonel Hugh Giles but lamented that "I never could come up with

---

*Before burning the house Wemyss supposedly locked Mrs. James and her children in a bedroom for two days, during which they were given no food other than what a sympathetic British officer slipped to them through a window. This particular tale is probably an embellishment.

them." Nonetheless he boasted that he had broken up their band and forced their retreat into North Carolina. The rest of his report was, in Cornwallis's view, "not so agreeable." Wemyss had discovered that every inhabitant in that part of the country was deeply caught up in the rebel spirit, whereas the Tories were dispirited and apathetic. "It is impossible for me to give your Lordship an idea of the disaffection of this country," Wemyss wrote, ignoring that his house burnings had only fueled anti-British sentiment. Ten days later he repeated to Cornwallis his opinion that the Tory militia, without support from the main British army, were too weak to hold the countryside. In part, he said, they were intimidated by men like Marion and Giles, whom he accused, without a trace of irony, of "burning houses and distressing the well affected in a most severe manner."

Some men under Marion had indeed taken to house burning in retaliation for Wemyss's demolition policy. One of the homes Wemyss burned was that of Moses Murphy, a relation of Maurice Murphy, then a captain in Marion's brigade. Maurice Murphy needed little impetus to seek revenge; he was a patriot of "ungovernable passion, which was often inflamed by strong drink." He was the man who had stolen Micajah Ganey's horses, causing Ganey to become a Tory. Murphy had also shot to death his own cousin for chastising him for his harsh whipping of a Tory prisoner.

Realizing he would likely be blamed for Murphy's ravages, Marion sought to distance himself from his rogue officer. "I am sorry to acquaint you that Capt. Murphy's party have burnt a great number of houses on Little Peedee, and intend to go on in that abominable work—which I am apprehensive may be laid to me," Marion wrote to Gates. "But I assure you," he added, "there is not one house burnt by my orders, or by any of my people. It is what I detest to distress poor women and children."

Not long after, Marion wrote apologetically to Gates to say that Murphy was still burning houses and that another of Marion's top men, Lieutenant Colonel John Ervin, had adopted the practice as well. A staunch Presbyterian, Ervin may have been retaliating for Wemyss's torching of churches. But Marion would have none of it. Depredations of that sort, he told Gates, "will be the greatest hurt to our interest."

Miffed when Marion would not permit him to burn any more houses, Ervin left the brigade. Suitably chastised, he would return within a few months and serve capably for the rest of the war without further blemish. Murphy was allowed to stay, presumably with a stern warning by Marion, as there were no more reports of house burnings by him. Later promoted to militia major and then to colonel in Marion's brigade, he performed a valuable function by frequently engaging Ganey and Barefield in the Little Pee Dee region, keeping them occupied while Marion was attending to more urgent matters.

That two of Marion's officers committed what, today, would be considered war crimes goes to show that few commanders could claim a spotless record for their soldiers' atrocious conduct during South Carolina's civil war. No officer could completely control his men in that setting; the question is how hard one tried. Marion disclosed his men's transgressions to his superior, Horatio Gates, when it would have been easy to stay quiet about them. Lacking any legal authority over his volunteers, he nonetheless was anguished by their behavior, did what he could to change it, and for the most part succeeded.

By contrast, Cornwallis said not a discouraging word when Wemyss boasted of having laid waste to fifty houses and plantations; indeed, Wemyss had acted completely in accordance with Cornwallis's wishes. Cornwallis defended any brutalities committed on his watch as justified retaliation for rebel cruelties or punishment of parole breakers. "I have always endeavored to soften the horrors of war," his Lordship insisted just a few months after ordering the "total demolition" of private plantations and the immediate hanging of rebels formerly in British arms.

Back at Great White Marsh, camp life had turned grim for Marion's men. Food was scarce, mosquitoes prevalent, the mood downcast. Among those present was young William Dobein James, whose father and brother were still in Williamsburg Township assessing the situation there. The fifteen-year-old James found himself invited to dine with Colonel Marion and sat down to a spread set before them by Marion's manservant, partly on a pine log and partly on the ground. It consisted of lean beef, without salt, and sweet potatoes. James asked permission to send for a pot of boiled hominy (dried corn soaked in lye and wood ash), which had salt in it and provided them "a most acceptable repast." Marion said little beyond praising James's father, which gratified the boy. They had nothing to drink but bad water, and as James recalled, "all the company appeared to be rather grave."

Gravity—seriousness of purpose—was what gave Marion the intangible, almost mystical power he held over his men. Although he lacked physical presence or a magnetic personality, they regarded him with awe. Part of their reverence was due to his success, which naturally bred respect. But it was his steady, equable character that most caused them to follow where he led. "He had no uproarious humor," wrote one man who spoke with surviving members of Marion's Brigade. "At most a quiet smile lighted up his features." Although capable of sarcasm and sharp retorts and even playfulness among friends and military intimates, his demeanor was quiet and subdued. "He was singularly considerate of the sensibilities of others, and had his temper under rare control," the same chronicler wrote. "He yielded to few excitements, was seldom elevated by successes to imprudence—as seldom depressed by disappointments to despondency."

Conditions at White Marsh were nonetheless testing Marion's equanimity. Men started coming down with malaria from the unusually wet summer and the insects it had bred. Among those felled by the fever were young William James and Peter Horry. The others were starting to complain and become restless. Marion, who may have regretted going there in the first place, was looking for an excuse to return to South Carolina. He soon got one.

8

"My Little Excursions"

ot long after young William James's dinner with Marion, James's father, the major, arrived back in camp with infuriating news. He confirmed what Marion had suspected: Wemyss had stopped at nothing in pursuing his whirlwind of destruction. It was Major James who brought word that Wemyss had torched the major's house as well as the Indiantown Presbyterian Church, where James was an elder and many of Marion's men regularly worshiped. Other churches were either burned or turned into British army depots, and those that were not were closed by their congregations, as the people felt it was unsafe to gather in public. The men of Williamsburg, aroused as never before, were anxious to take the field again. And so on September 24, after two weeks at Great White Marsh, Marion decided to head back to South Carolina.

With his sixty men, Marion covered about fifty miles in two days before camping on the east side of the Little Pee Dee River on the afternoon of September 26. The next morning, seeking a suitable river crossing, they were guided through three miles of surrounding swamp by the Jenkins boys, Samuel and Britton, locals who had joined Marion's band in late August. Those who could swam across the Little Pee Dee; others, like Marion, floated across on their horses. By the night of September 27 they had made it to Port's Ferry, camping on the east side of the Pee Dee to keep the river between them and the British on the west side. With them now was Captain George Logan, who had stayed behind at Great White Marsh because he was too sick. Having recovered enough to travel, he rode sixty miles to catch up with Marion's party.

On September 28 Marion's men crossed the Pee Dee on flatboats, then rode several miles to Witherspoon's Ferry on Lynches Creek, arriving around sunset. On the far side of the creek they were met by Captain John James and about ten militiamen and, a little later, Captain Henry Mouzon and some additional volunteers. The arrivals had exciting news: a group of Tories under loyalist colonel John Coming Ball was camped about fifteen miles away at Patrick Dollard's Red Tavern on the bank of Black Mingo Creek near Sheppard's Ferry. His men in the mood for a fight, Marion decided they would attack Ball's unit that same night.

Marion knew these Tories. They were from St. James and St. Stephens Parishes, the French Santee and English Santee of Marion's family. John Coming Ball, a local rice planter, was a half-brother of Elias Ball, the Tory whose tip had helped Banastre Tarleton defeat the rebels at Lenud's Ferry in May. A Whig militiaman who switched sides after Charleston fell, Elias Ball was married to a Gaillard, whose sister married Marion's brother Job (his second marriage), with Marion serving as best man.

Peter Gaillard, another member of that prominent Huguenot family, was John Coming Ball's second in command. Although only a lukewarm Tory, Gaillard was under the influence of his rabidly loyalist father and had served on one of the early expeditions designed to hunt down Marion. John Peyre, whose family was related by marriage to the Gaillards, Balls, and Marions, had been neutral until the fall of Charleston, after which he took British protection and became a strong Tory. Captain John Brockinton, a resident of Black Mingo, was the man whose slave Adam Cusack allegedly shot at, leading to Cusack's hanging. Brockinton had been with Wemyss when they tried—and failed—to catch Marion during his retreat to North Carolina.

Although these neighbors and relatives were out to kill him, Marion took none of it personally. He would later describe the Tory militia at Black Mingo Creek as "men of family and fortune" who had shown themselves to be "good men" before the outbreak of civil war. He even hoped to convert some of them to his cause.

But first he would have to beat them. When he heard about the Tory gathering at Dollard's it was already nearing twilight, so he decided to let his men nap for a few hours in preparation for a night fight. He woke them from their slumber and led them south toward Black Mingo Creek, arriving close to midnight. They reached the Willtown Bridge, a wooden structure spanning the creek about a mile northwest of Dollard's. As they were crossing it they heard an alarm musket sound in the Tory camp. Under similar circumstances, at Nelson's Ferry, Marion's men had charged the enemy as soon as their attack was exposed, and they would do the same here.

Marion sent his men in a full gallop toward Dollard's, stopping on the main road about three hundred yards northwest of the tavern entrance. There they dismounted except for a small body of cavalry who stayed on their horses; believing that Ball's men were likely holed up inside the tavern, Marion reasoned that foot soldiers would be more effective than mounted ones in the impending battle.

Marion devised a three-pronged attack. Captain Thomas Waties, the one-time University of Pennsylvania student, was to lead an assault on the front of the tavern. Colonel Hugh Horry and his infantry would drive forward on Waties's right flank, while the cavalry would provide support on the left. Marion would sit back with a small reserve force and deploy as needed. In fact, due to his age and small size, he rarely engaged in personal combat; instead, like a modern general (and unlike the protagonist in *The Patriot*) he maintained command and control of the action from a secure position. Not immodestly, he also knew he was irreplaceable and the rebels could not afford to have him killed.

Ball, alerted to the patriots' approach, did not want to be trapped inside the tavern without an escape route. Unbeknownst to the patriots, he moved his men into an open field to the south-southwest of the tavern and lined them in formation to face their attackers approaching from the west. This had the effect of shifting the center of battle so that, from the patriots' viewpoint, Ball's Tories were to the right of the tavern. As a result, Hugh Horry's infantry, on Waties's right flank, now directly faced the enemy while Waties's men would be coming up on the Tories' right.

It was pitch black that night, with no illumination from the moon. As Horry's infantry moved east-southeast across the field, Ball's men held their musket fire. They could hear Horry's foot soldiers clomping toward them, but all they could make out in the blackness were a bunch of dark silhouettes.

When Horry's men came within thirty yards the Tory muskets suddenly burst out in flames, piercing the night like a clap of thunder and lightning. Horry's men were startled to be hit with direct fire, as they had been expecting to provide flanking support for Waties's frontal attack on the tavern. Horry's infantry fell back in confusion until Captain John James steadied and rallied them. Able to glimpse the Tories in the light of the muzzle flashes, James's company returned the volley in the enemy's direction. At this point Waties's men rushed forward, attacking the Tory right flank. The two sides traded a few more rounds of fire, but Ball's men, finding themselves in between two sets of volleys, gave way. After a fight that lasted about fifteen minutes, the Tories withdrew, taking refuge in Black Mingo Swamp to their rear.

Black Mingo, like so many engagements in the South during the Revolution, involved relatively few men on either side: Ball's Tories totaled only forty-seven, while Marion had perhaps seventy. (It was one of the few times he actually outnumbered his opponent, although it is not clear he knew this going into the encounter.) But because of the sharp exchange of fire at close range, the casualties were comparatively heavy. The Tories lost three killed and thirteen captured or wounded—a third of their unit—plus some unknown number later found dead or wounded in the swamp and adjoining woods.

Marion suffered two killed and eight wounded, but the psychological loss was greater—one of the dead was George Logan, who had left his sickbed and ridden miles to rejoin the brigade. The wounded included Marion's friend Henry Mouzon, who was shot up so badly that he never took the field again. Such was the nature of the many small actions and skirmishes in South Carolina, where the death or dismemberment of a few friends or relatives could have a greater impact on the participants' psyches than the loss of hundreds or thousands of strangers in full-scale army battles.

The significance of the engagement at Black Mingo was also greater than the numbers would imply. Marion's men captured all the guns, ammunition, baggage, and horses the Tories left behind. Marion took the Tory commander's steed for himself and, in a rare display of humor, renamed it "Ball." He would ride it the rest of the war.

Several Tories captured by Marion at Black Mingo took an oath of allegiance and joined his brigade. After escaping, Peter Gaillard, the Tory second in command, made it known that he too would like to enlist with Marion's band if they would have him without unduly humiliating him. Intermediaries (including Gaillard's brother-in-law, Job Marion) arranged an interview between him and Marion. The partisan commander cordially received his former foe, praised his bravery at Black Mingo, and personally escorted him into the patriot camp in front of the rest of the men so as to quash the bitterness many of them felt toward their Tory neighbor.

The victory at Black Mingo—Marion's third straight in a month— also brought Tory activity in the South Carolina Lowcountry to a virtual standstill. Ball, who managed to escape after the battle, refused to take the field again until late in the war. John Peyre and his brother Charles, both captured in the fighting and unrepentant, were sent off to prison in Philadelphia. With such prominent local men put out of commission, the Tories in the Santee region were in no mood to fight. As Marion explained in a letter to Gates in North Carolina a week after the engagement, "the Tories are so affrighted with my little excursions that many is moving off to Georgia."

Marion's victory reinforced the growing British belief that the loyalist militia was close to useless, at least without support from the regular British army. "I have found the militia to fail so totally when put to the trial in this province," Cornwallis wrote to Clinton a few days before Black Mingo. Indeed, before learning of the outcome of that action, Cornwallis predicted that Ball's militia would "meet with some disaster." Two days later one of Cornwallis's subordinate commanders wrote to him to say, "Depend upon it, [Tory] militia will never do any good without regular troops."

Cornwallis and other British officers were probably overstating the deficiencies of the Tory militia; Marion, for one, never underestimated their ability to rebound and cause him trouble. But overall the Whig partisans did deliver greater value to the revolutionary cause than the Tory militia provided to the loyalist side. It may be that the loyalists were simply too few in number or too uncommitted in their support of the Crown to constitute an effective counter to the patriot militia. An estimated one-fifth to one-third of the free population in South Carolina became loyalists during the Revolution, but those percentages are much lower than what the British had been led to believe—or had convinced themselves to believe—when they embarked upon their southern strategy.

Another factor may be even more important. With few exceptions the loyalist militia lacked the same high quality of leadership that partisan commanders such as Marion, Pickens, Sumter, and Elijah Clarke brought to the patriot side. When colonial militia elected their officers they usually chose men of property and standing in the community, and as the British were discovering, "all the leading men of property have been on the rebel side." Most of the Americans who had distinguished themselves in the Cherokee War also became patriots, creating a talent pool the Tories could not match. Many leading Tories had left or been banished from the province early in the Revolution, and Cornwallis found those who remained to be "dastardly and pusillanimous"—so weak-willed and incompetent in combating the patriots that he lost all sympathy for them.

Loyalist provincial commander Robert Gray, himself a Tory militia leader earlier in the war, admitted that Marion and Sumter "established a decided superiority" in the Whig militia over their Tory counterparts. This was true even though the two men had completely different styles. Sumter (nicknamed the "Gamecock" for his combative nature) was "bold and rash" and ran many risks, Gray wrote, whereas Marion was "timid and cautious and would risk nothing."

Marion was anything but timid—Cornwallis called him "cautious and vigilant"—and he often took risks, though they were always calculated ones. He would not jeopardize his men's lives by sending them into battle hopelessly outnumbered. He further sought to minimize the perils of war through a combination of intelligence operations, careful planning, and shrewd tactics. Among the latter were his attacks on lightly defended targets, ambush and surprise (often at night), use of rivers and creeks as a buffer against the enemy, and strategic retreat.

All of which raises a question about the operation at Black Mingo—namely, what went wrong such that Marion's approach set off the alarm and allowed the Tories to gain the initial advantage of surprise? Had the assault been undetected, Marion might well have routed the enemy, as at Nelson's Ferry and Blue Savannah, while suffering few if any casualties.

For more than two hundred years the answer to that question has rested on an account by Weems that has been repeated ever since. According to Weems, when Marion's men crossed the wooden bridge a mile above Dollard's Tavern, their horses' hooves loudly rattled on the loose planks, piercing the stillness of the night and alerting the enemy. From then on, under this telling, Marion made sure that whenever his men crossed a wooden bridge on horseback within the enemy's hearing distance, they placed blankets down to muffle the sound.

Although that innovation is usually cited as an example of Marion's ability to learn from tactical mistakes, it seems like something he should have thought about ahead of time. Marion was familiar with the Black Mingo area and knew he would need to cross the Willtown Bridge, which he had crossed any number of times. Either in planning the attack or at least when he arrived at the bridge, he would have known that dozens of horses trampling across the rickety boards in the dead of night would make a noise the enemy might hear. A truly attentive guerrilla commander would have anticipated the issue and found a way to deal with it.

As it turns out, he did.

At least four separate pension applications independently submitted under oath by veterans who fought with Marion at Black Mingo state that *before* crossing Willtown Bridge they spread blankets on it to prevent the Tories from hearing them cross. Parson Weems apparently decided it would make a better story if Marion did not think to lay down blankets on this occasion and then adopted the precaution from that point forward.

The question remains: How did Ball's Tories know Marion was about to attack? The answer is suggested in Marion's letter to Gates a week after the battle. "They had intelligence of our coming," Marion explained. That would indicate that it was not loud horse hooves a few moments before the battle that tipped off the Tories but rather some earlier advance warning. Marion was not the only person who had spies working for him. Plenty of Tories in the Black Mingo area would have been eager to spoil a patriot attack. Certainly that was true of Elias Ball. "He had about a hundred and fifty slaves, and he was a mean fella," one of his descendants recalled. Perhaps Elias Ball or another local Tory got wind of the action and told his brother John. But it was not enough to prevent Marion's triumph.

Immediately after Black Mingo, Marion wanted to go after Wigfall, who, along with Ball, had been sent into the Williamsburg area to keep the Whigs in check. Wigfall was now stationed with about fifty men at the Salem Black River Presbyterian Church upriver from Kingstree and was an especially enticing target for Marion. He had served under Marion earlier in the war, and Marion pointedly excluded him by name from the thanks he gave his officers at Dorchester. John Wigfall was one of those South Carolinians who blew with the prevailing winds, siding with whoever held the advantage. Marion wanted to pursue him but, as he told Gates, could not because "so many of my followers was so desirous to see their wifes and family, which have been burnt out." As a result, he withdrew in the first week of October to Britton's Ferry on the Pee Dee and then again to Ami's Mill. Even so, Wigfall, like Ball, feared Marion so much that he declined to come out and fight anymore.

Cornwallis's plan to secure South Carolina's countryside east of the Santee had failed. Wemyss had not swept the rebels from the area—the citizen population had been further inflamed, not pacified—and few Tory militia turned out in response to Wemyss's call for recruits. Those who did were men of "suspicious" character, Wemyss thought. By October 4 Wemyss had left Cheraw to return to Camden, while Cornwallis, who had moved up to Charlotte, North Carolina, just over the border, was planning to march farther north in the next two weeks to conquer that state. Still worried about Marion menacing his eastern flank, Cornwallis ordered Wemyss to try again: he was to return to the Williamsburg area as soon as possible "to prevent the enemy being thoroughly masters of the country you have left."

But Wemyss did not go back, and Cornwallis did not march north. On October 7, the same day Cornwallis gave Wemyss his orders, more than a thousand rebel frontiersmen annihilated an approximately equal number of loyalists at King's Mountain in the South Carolina backcountry next to the North Carolina border. The rebels were backwoods-men from North Carolina, "over mountain" men from present-day Tennessee, and militia groups from Virginia, Georgia, and South Carolina. They attacked up the mountain and surrounded the Tories, killing or wounding a third of their force and capturing more than six hundred. The inspirational British commander Patrick Ferguson (the sole non-American participant in the battle) was shot dead from his horse by a half dozen rifle balls, then dragged along the ground with his foot caught in his stirrup. His lifeless body, bones broken in several places, was then stripped naked. Shouting cries of revenge for atrocities they attributed to Tarleton, the patriot militia slaughtered the Tories who were trying to surrender until patriot commanders stopped the massacre. Afterward the rebels summarily tried and convicted thirty-six loyalists for treason and hanged nine of them before the rest were reprieved.

King's Mountain was a significant turning point in the war in the South. It destroyed Tory morale in the South Carolina backcountry just as Marion had done through his string of smaller victories in the Low-country. Cornwallis was now exposed on his western (left) flank to the ascendant backcountry patriot militia on South Carolina's northern frontier. Bad as that state of affairs was, he told Clinton that his situation on his eastern (right) flank—where his supply lines ran to Charleston—was even worse. He was still threatened on that front by Marion, who had so affected the minds of the people between the Santee and Pee Dee that, as Cornwallis lamented, "there was scarce an inhabitant" in that area "that was not in arms against us." Indeed, although Marion had not been at King's Mountain, his incursions east of Camden resulted in Wemyss not being there either. Cornwallis had planned to reinforce Ferguson's militia with Wemyss's 63rd Foot, and Wemyss would have been available to do so had he not been off chasing Marion.

With South Carolina decidedly unsecured, Cornwallis had to abandon for the time being his plan to invade North Carolina. Leaving Charlotte, where his army was constantly harassed by the locals, he retreated back across the border into South Carolina, setting up winter camp at Winnsboro, thirty miles west of Camden. By this time Cornwallis had come down with a feverish cold so severe he could not lift a pen and was forced to temporarily transfer command to twenty-five-year-old Francis Rawdon, the Irish-born head of the Volunteers of Ireland loyalist provincial regiment. A former aide to Clinton, Rawdon would prove to be the British army's most talented military leader in the South. As one of Cornwallis's last acts before turning over the reins to the younger man, his Lordship, feeling in need of reinforcements, recalled Wemyss to Camden, rescinding the order for him to return to the Williamsburg district.

Wemyss, the most hated man in Williamsburg, would never set foot there again. But his departure from the area created a vacuum the British decided had to be filled. They would raise a new force to replace the one commanded by Wemyss. It would provide Marion with his next big opportunity.

9

Dead Man's Hand

*W*ith the quieting of the Tory threat east of Camden, Marion sat at Ami's Mill pondering his next move. On October 4 he confessed to Gates that he had suffered many fatigues over the previous few weeks but had managed to surmount them. He had never had more than sixty or seventy men with him of all ranks, and sometimes as few as a dozen. In some cases he had been forced to fight against men who had left him to join the enemy; he regretted that he had no authority to punish them. If he had a hundred men from Gates's army, he thought, he could "certainly pay a visit to Georgetown" and attack the British garrison there. But Gates had answered none of his letters—besides which, Marion was not entirely sure where Gates even was at that point.

Marion decided to make a little probing incursion against Georgetown anyway. He heard that Micajah Ganey, the Tory whose force he had bested at the Blue Savannah, was in Georgetown to reinforce the British garrison there. On October 9 Marion entered the city unmolested with forty men on horse and, once inside, issued a rather audacious demand to the garrison commander to surrender. But after the predictable refusal, Marion withdrew, finding the fortifications too strong to storm. To have any chance at capturing the stronghold he would have needed artillery, which was impractical for his fast-moving guerrilla force to haul over long distances.

Before leaving, however, and to show the enemy he was a force to be reckoned with—or just to show off—he took his men on a little parade through the town. They made off with a few horses and some of the enemy's equipment and captured several notable Tory military men whom Marion immediately paroled to their homes. If nothing else, Marion served notice that if the British wanted to hold the second-largest population center in South Carolina, they would need to keep men and resources tied down there. "This damned Georgetown business," as the British called it, would prove an unwelcome distraction for months to come.

The Georgetown expedition had also scored another success. Two miles outside the city a separate advance guard of Marion's horsemen, led by Peter Horry, ran into some mounted Tories under Ganey's command and killed Ganey's lieutenant. Sergeant Allen McDonald, one of the three American prisoners rescued at Nelson's Ferry who had joined Marion's brigade, then set his sights on Ganey. McDonald ran down the Tory leader on horseback and bayoneted him, the knife dislodging from McDonald's musket and sticking in Ganey's back. Ganey rode that way all the way back to Georgetown, but despite Marion's assumption that he had been mortally wounded, he somehow managed to survive. Nonetheless the man Marion called one of "the most active persons against us" was put out of commission for several months.

Marion reported to Gates on his little foray, saying he wished to hear from him as soon as possible, for he had received no word from him in a month. As Marion explained, this lack of information forced him to act with extreme caution lest he fall into the enemy's hands. He closed by asking Gates to excuse his "scrawl," as he had no table to write on in "this wild woods." (Sometimes he lacked even paper to write on, which placed a premium on brevity.)

After Marion returned to Ami's Mill a letter showed up, finally, from Gates, sent from his headquarters in Hillsboro, North Carolina. Gates warmly congratulated Marion on his recent successes and asked him to continue his hostilities in the South Carolina Lowcountry to deflect attention from Gates's army. Marion was happy to receive an assignment directly from the Continental general who once had not known what to do with him.

Marion's initial thought was to seek out Major John Harrison, the head of a hundred-man loyalist provincial mounted unit known as the

South Carolina Rangers or Harrison's Corps. They operated at McCallum's Ferry on upper Lynches Creek in the Camden area. Although Harrison failed to raise the five hundred men Cornwallis was hoping for, his rangers often scouted and foraged for the regular British army. In particular, Harrison had helped guide Wemyss during his seventy-mile punitive expedition by pointing out the homes of rebel agitators to be burned. The Whigs considered him and his brothers Samuel and Robert, who served as captains in his regiment, to be among "the greatest banditti that ever infested the country." Even Wemyss described them as "if possible worse than militia, their whole desire being to plunder and steal and, when they have got as much as their horses will carry, to run home." He thought they were "not worth anything." They were also accused of having recently murdered three members of the Salem Black River Presbyterian Church, all upstanding citizens, in their homes.

As William James recalled, Marion wanted to "chastise" Harrison and his Tory band. But the militia was slow to respond to Marion's call. He understood his men's desire to spend time at home and to tend to their crops at planting and harvest season, but as a former Continental officer accustomed to having unquestioned authority over his soldiers, he was frustrated by the volunteer militia's constant coming and going. Despairing that they might not return this time, he considered taking a few of his most loyal officers with him to North Carolina to offer their services to General Gates, who now appeared to appreciate their value. But Hugh Horry, Marion's closest adviser, convinced him to stay. In time the militia began to saunter into camp, and Marion's spirits brightened. He moved back down into the Williamsburg district, camping at Port's Ferry, from where he sent out small patrols of five to ten men each night to gather intelligence on the enemy.

On October 24 one such patrol returned with a report that a sizeable group of Tory militia, which Marion later reported to number two hundred, was lazily camped in a field near Tearcoat Swamp, some fifty miles west. The Tories were under the command of Colonel Samuel Tynes, a man of some prominence in the High Hills of Santee who had been ordered to collect militia in that area to replace Wemyss's troops. A Virginia-born man of about thirty, Tynes joined the patriot militia in 1775 with his brother, but unlike Fleming Tynes, Samuel switched sides to the British after the fall of Charleston. Cornwallis called him a "weak, well intentioned man," and from a military standpoint it seems he had little to offer. Marion saw him as a ripe target because Tynes, in mustering his militia, had stocked up in Camden on guns, ammunition, and equipment, all of which Marion needed. Marion also believed it important to snuff out any new Tory muster in the area before loyalist sentiment was able to rekindle. He jettisoned the idea of pursuing Harrison's Corps—he would go after Tynes instead.

As he marched, first to Kingstree on October 24, then on toward Tearcoat the next day, Marion's force rose to 150, the largest it had ever been. Again he revealed his plans to no one. On the evening of October 25 Marion arrived near Tynes's camp at the fork of the Black River and sent out a couple of youths to reconnoiter it. They came back with confirmation that security there was lax and that most of the loyalists had gone to sleep; those still awake were playing cards. Just as at Black Mingo, Marion divided his brigade to attack from three directions— right, left, and center. After resting his men until midnight he fired his pistol to start the attack. The patriots rushed in, whooping and hollering like Cherokees as they overran the camp.

Most of the frightened Tories, including Tynes, abandoned their posts, left their guns behind, and fled into Tearcoat Swamp. Marion's men killed six, wounded fourteen, and captured twenty-three. Marion's losses were two horses and no men. Among the Tory dead was Amos Gaskens, a reputed thief who, like the Harrisons, had helped conduct Wemyss on his house-burning excursion. Legend holds that Gaskens, or another of Tynes's card players, was shot to death still clutching the ace, deuce, and jack of clubs in his hands. "He seemed to be in a fair way to do well," Parson Weems wrote, "but Marion came down upon him with a trump that spoiled his sport, and non-suited him forever."

The haul from the battle was substantial: eighty horses, with bridles and saddles, and all of the enemy's muskets, ammunition, food, and personal baggage. For the first time in a while Marion was able to equip his men. As after Black Mingo, a number of Tynes's men decided to join Marion's brigade and, according to William James, fought bravely for him thereafter.

To Marion's consternation, Tynes himself got away, just as several Tory leaders before him had managed to do after being routed by Marion's brigade. This time Marion decided to do something about it. He sent Captain William Clay Snipes, a zealous if uncontainable Tory-hater, with a party of men to the High Hills of Santee to seize all the militia and civil officials they could find. Snipes came back a week later with Tynes in custody, along with a few other militia officers and two justices of the peace. Marion sent the captured men to a patriot militia post in North Carolina and went into camp on Lynches Creek near Witherspoon's Ferry.

Marion's victory at Tearcoat Swamp left the British high command in a state of panic. With no effective enemy force in the field, Marion now had the ability to strike at will throughout the entire area of South Carolina east of the Wateree River and north of the Santee. As a result it had become almost impossible for the British to safely send supplies or communications from the coast to Cornwallis's army. The Santee, the major navigable river flowing through the heart of the state, did not connect directly to either Georgetown or Charleston. Therefore, to move supplies from the coast to Camden and Winnsboro, it was necessary to use both roads and waterways. Typically the British traveled either overland or by boat to Nelson's Ferry, where they crossed the Santee, then by wagon to Camden. But because of the threat Marion posed, the British were afraid to cross at Nelson's and began taking a longer, more circuitous route to the northwest over more difficult roads to Friday's Ferry on the Congaree River. From there they crossed the Congaree and traveled overland to Camden and Winnsboro.

Anxious for the fate of any supplies headed his way, Cornwallis was desperate to end Marion's dominance in the country between the Santee and Pee Dee Rivers. Nisbet Balfour, the commandant at Charleston, worried that unless further measures were taken, all communication between Charleston and Cornwallis's army would be "at an end." Marion was bleeding the British to death by a thousand cuts.

But what to do? George Turnbull, Cornwallis's commander at Camden, thought the answer was obvious: if you want to beat the enemy's best, you have to send your own best up against him. And Turnbull had just the man for the job.

10

The Swamp Fox

*I*n many ways Banastre Tarleton ("Ban," as he preferred) was the complete opposite of Francis Marion. Young (twenty-six in 1780), boyishly handsome, athletically built, a drinker, gambler, and womanizer, he cut the sort of dashing figure that some have mistakenly ascribed to Marion. His stock in trade was his ruthless pursuit of his quarry followed by a headlong, frontal cavalry attack, with sabers flashing and slashing when he inevitably caught up with them.

Son of a wealthy Liverpool slave-trading merchant, Tarleton attended Oxford and studied law at London's prestigious Middle Temple before quitting to follow his friend and fellow Oxfordian, Francis Rawdon, into the military. He purchased a "cornet," or commission, in the British cavalry in 1775 and voluntarily sailed to America to fight with the king's men. He was part of Clinton's first, unsuccessful attack on Charleston, saw action at Brandywine, and helped capture Charles Lee, the Continental commander, in a raid on a tavern in late 1776. During the British occupation of Philadelphia he gambled away his salary, nearly dueled an officer whose mistress he dallied with, and took part in a theatrical group formed by John André, who would later be hanged as Benedict Arnold's coconspirator.

In 1778 Tarleton, on the recommendation of Cornwallis, was promoted to lieutenant colonel in the British Legion, a loyalist provincial cavalry unit organized in New York. British in name only, its members were almost entirely American-born Tories recruited from New York and Pennsylvania. Like other "legions" during the Revolution, Tarleton's consisted of both traditional cavalry, who carried sabers and charged directly into battle, and dragoons—trained infantrymen who traveled on horseback but usually fought on foot, armed with pistols, swords, and sometimes short muskets called carbines. (During the Revolution, however, the term *dragoon* was used interchangeably with *cavalryman*.) Tarleton's soldiers wore short green coats and huge leather helmets with fur plumes to distinguish them from the red-coated British regulars. In a coincidence of history the dragoons took their name from the seventeenth-century French monarch's soldiers who entered the homes of Marion's Huguenot ancestors and "dragooned" or carried them off.*

Tarleton first gained prominence just before the fall of Charleston when his Legion routed the Americans at Monck's Corner and Lenud's Ferry and cut off the last escape routes from the city. In both cases he had been greatly outnumbered, but he was a risk taker going back to his student days in London, where he spent nights gambling at the fashionable Cocoa Tree club on St. James's Street.

Yet his greatest fame—or infamy, in patriot eyes—came from his follow-up to those encounters. In late May, Cornwallis had dispatched Tarleton and his Legion of 230, along with a company of 40 British army dragoons, to pursue Colonel Abraham Buford. Having arrived too late to reinforce Charleston, Buford and his 350 Virginia Continentals were then on the run toward North Carolina. With them were Governor John Rutledge and some members of his council, who had fled Charleston before it fell. Although the Americans had a ten-day head start on him, Tarleton drove his men relentlessly forward, covering 150 miles in fifty-four hours to catch up with them. Rutledge barely avoided capture by veering off from the main force hours ahead of the pursuers, but Tarleton overtook Buford just shy of the North Carolina border at a place called the Waxhaws.

---

*Like traditional dragoons, both patriot and Tory militia generally traveled on horse but dismounted to fight with whatever weapons they could bring to a battle, whether muskets, rifles, pistols, or swords. In practice the distinctions between "heavy" and "light" cavalry, "dragoons," mounted infantry, and "light" horse as well as "rangers" tended to blur. Especially in the South, where distances between engagements could be vast, almost all militiamen rode horses to and from battles and fought either on foot or from a mounted position, depending on circumstances.

There, in Tarleton's own words, "slaughter was commenced." Though outnumbered, Tarleton succeeded, as he boasted to Cornwallis immediately afterward, in cutting Buford's men "to pieces." The lopsided casualty figures bear out that characterization: as against 5 killed and 14 wounded on the British side, the Americans had about a 70 percent casualty rate: 113 killed, 150 wounded and captured (many of them "dreadfully mangled," one observer noted), and 53 others taken prisoner. Buford, who had refused relatively generous surrender terms before the conflict, managed to escape on horseback.

The patriot side claimed that after the fighting stopped, Tarleton's men were guilty of outright massacre, hacking Buford's men to death even as they lay down their arms and begged for quarter. "Tarleton's Quarter" (meaning take no prisoners) and "Buford's Massacre" became rallying cries for the patriots in later battles, notably King's Mountain. What is sometimes overlooked is that although the commander of the king's troops at both King's Mountain and the Waxhaws was a Briton, virtually all the slaughtering was done by Americans against Americans.

Some revisionists have argued that Tarleton's Legion committed no atrocities at the Waxhaws at all, that the entire patriot narrative was invented for propaganda purposes. Others allow that irregularities may have occurred but were brief in duration and resulted not from any bloodthirsty order by Tarleton but from confusion on the part of his men. Tarleton himself, who went down unhurt when his horse was shot from under him, claimed that his cavalry was influenced by a false report that he had been killed, even after the Americans raised the white flag. In his memoirs several years later he wrote that when his men heard they had lost their commanding officer, it "stimulated the soldiers to a vindictive asperity not easily restrained." By his own admission then, which likely was significantly understated, *something* atrocious happened after Buford's men tried to surrender.*

---

*Refusing quarter was hardly alien to Tarleton's Legion. At Monck's Corner, as recounted by Cornwallis's own surgeon, they had continued to slash and hack one of the patriot commanders who had given up the fight, mangling him in "the most shocking manner." And before the battle of Camden, Tarleton himself vowed to Cornwallis to "give these disturbers of the peace no quarter." They "don't deserve lenity. None shall they experience," he wrote.

Whatever the truth of what happened at the Waxhaws, to the patriots Tarleton became known as "Bloody Ban," the "Green Dragoon" who mercilessly slaughtered his foes. He has remained so in popular American history, even serving as the inspiration for the sadistic "Colonel Tavington" character in *The Patriot*.

What mattered to Turnbull, though, was that Tarleton had a perfect winning record. From Camden on November 1 Turnbull wrote to Tarleton at Winnsboro, imploring him to gather up his Legion to hunt down Marion. Tarleton rarely paid any compliments to his rebel adversaries, but he respected Marion, later writing that "Mr. Marion, by his zeal and abilities, shewed himself capable of the trust committed to his charge." Still, over the previous six months Tarleton had thrashed several more senior commanders—Isaac Huger, William Washington, Abraham Buford, and Thomas Sumter—and he had no reason to doubt he would do the same to Marion. He welcomed the opportunity to pursue him, and Cornwallis approved the operation, telling Tarleton, "I . . . most sincerely hope you will get at Mr. Marion."

On November 5, after conferring with Turnbull in Camden, Tarleton and his Legion, joined by Harrison's Rangers, the Tory "banditti," set out south after Marion. They heard a rumor he was at Singleton's Mills in the High Hills of Santee, but when they arrived, Marion was nowhere to be found. Instead, he was camped thirty miles farther south, just above Nelson's Ferry, where he planned to attack the British guard. He had arrived there with two hundred men on the evening of November 5 after a day-and-a-half ride west from Lynches Creek.

By November 7 Tarleton had moved down to the plantation of the recently widowed Dorothy Richardson, whose late husband, Brigadier General Richard Richardson, had been the victorious Whig commander in the Snow Campaign in 1775. From a local slave Tarleton learned that Marion was bivouacked sixteen miles south, near Nelson's Ferry. Marion had likewise detected Tarleton's presence in the vicinity. The two of them then engaged in a game of cat and mouse. Marion laid an ambush at Nelson's and waited until night, expecting Tarleton to cross there, but the Legion commander fell back a few miles in the other direction. Marion then came up to within three miles of Tarleton's camp, intending to surprise him.

But Tarleton was crafty as well: he spread the rumor that his main body had returned to Camden and sent out small patrols with instructions to show little signs of fear by leaving camps abruptly with food still cooking in order to draw Marion to attack. He lit bonfires at Richardson's Plantation designed to give the impression that he was burning the home of a revered patriot family. In the meantime he wheeled out two small artillery pieces capable of a kind of firepower Marion's men were not used to facing. Then, knowing Marion's penchant for making surprise attacks at night, Tarleton hid in the woods with his force of four hundred and waited for Marion to come to him.

Marion nearly took the bait. Seeing the light near Richardson's, he concluded that it was the plantation house on fire and that Tarleton was there. Not knowing the size of the enemy force, he crept forward, deliberating over his next move. Just then he was met by Richard Richardson Jr., son of the late general. He brought information that Tarleton was camped a couple of miles away with a hundred cavalry and three hundred dragoons. The junior Richardson, a thirty-nine-year-old militia major, had been taken prisoner at Charleston, paroled, and returned to service after being exchanged. By slipping away to alert Marion, he was risking his life. He also reported that Tarleton had two artillery pieces—a grasshopper (a light brass cannon, named for the way it jumped backward on firing) and a small field howitzer. He further informed Marion that one of his men had deserted to the enemy and was now serving as a guide for Tarleton.

Realizing that Tarleton held the advantage, including artillery, which his men had not yet faced, Marion decided he needed to depart the area at once. He took his men on a fast ride in darkness through a major swamp, not stopping until they were past Richbourg's Mill Dam on Jack's Creek six miles away. With a nearly impenetrable swamp and almost nine miles lying between him and Tarleton, Marion decided he was safe for the night.

The next morning, November 8, Tarleton was scratching his head over Marion's failure to attack, so he sent a few men to find out why. They brought back a prisoner who had managed to escape from Marion's brigade during the previous night's mad dash. He informed them that Marion would have attacked him had some "treacherous women" (the widow

Richardson and others) not smuggled out an emissary to warn Marion of Tarleton's actual number. Tarleton immediately ordered his men to their arms and mounts, but they soon discovered that Marion had already flown from his camp at Jack's Creek in the direction of Kingstree.

Tarleton then embarked on a seven-hour hunt for his intended victim, trudging through twenty-six miles of miserable swamps and narrow gorges. Marion in turn took his men on a thirty-five-mile jaunt, up to the head of one creek, down along a river and then across another, through woods and bogs, always staying beyond shouting distance of his pursuers. As Tarleton reported to Cornwallis, due to Marion's head start and "the difficulties of the country," he was unable to catch him. He abandoned the chase at Ox Swamp, outside of present-day Manning, which was wide, mucky, and without roads for passage. It was there Tarleton is said to have uttered the words that gave Marion his immortal nickname. "Come my boys! Let us go back, and we will soon find the Gamecock [Thomas Sumter]. But as for this damned old fox, the Devil himself could not catch him."*

At that point, the night of November 8, Marion was about twelve miles east at Benbow's Ferry, ten miles north of Kingstree. There he had established a strong defensive position with the Black River between him and his pursuers and swamps to his rear into which he could disappear if necessary. But Tarleton was giving up. He tried to put a good face on his excursion, telling Cornwallis that although he regretted not being able to bring Marion's rebels to a fight, he was happy to have broken them up. In his memoirs seven years later Tarleton would also claim that he would have caught up to Marion had he not received a message from Cornwallis ordering him immediately to return to Winnsboro. But although Cornwallis did issue that directive, it was not until after Tarleton had already

---

*Ironically, neither Tarleton nor anyone writing during Marion's lifetime is known to have referred to him as the *Swamp Fox*. In Weems's 1809 biography two young women in the company of British officers during the war supposedly called Marion a "vile swamp fox," expressing the colonial period view that swamps were dark, dank places fit only for lowly creatures. It was not until an 1829 poem and William Gilmore Simms's 1844 biography of Marion that the nickname Swamp Fox, as applied to Marion, took on a positive connotation.

ended his pursuit at Ox Swamp. Cornwallis's hope that Tarleton would "get at Mr. Marion" had gone unfulfilled.

Tarleton's frustration was evident from his actions immediately afterward. As he told Cornwallis, he "laid . . . waste" to all the houses and plantations of the rebels around Richardson's Plantation and Jack's Creek. (As usual, Cornwallis turned a blind eye to such depredations.) Tarleton paid a visit back to the widow Richardson's home and, as Marion reported to Gates, "beat" her to "make her tell where I was." Doing what he had earlier pretended to do in order to lure Marion to battle, Tarleton then burned Mrs. Richardson's home and some of her cattle, destroyed all her corn, and left her without so much as a change of clothes. From Nelson's Ferry to Camden he destroyed the homes and grain of thirty plantation owners. Worst of all, Marion reported, Tarleton had "behaved to the poor women he has distressed with great barbarity. . . . It is beyond measure distressing to see the women and children sitting in the open air round a fire without a blanket, or any clothing but what they had on, and women of family, and that had ample fortunes; for he spares neither Whig nor Tory."*

For the moment, however, Marion felt powerless to confront Tarleton. The patriots were low on ammunition, and the militia, afraid of the Legion cavalry, was reluctant to turn out. This gave Tarleton a temporary feeling of triumph. He laid down his torch and issued a proclamation from Singleton's Mills on November 11, offering pardons to any rebels who returned to their homes to live peaceably and promised to alert the Tory militia leaders to any future insurrections. "It is not the wish of Britons to be cruel or to destroy, but it is now obvious to all Carolina that treachery, perfidy, and perjury will be punished with instant fire and sword," his proclamation read. "The country seems now convinced of the error of insurrection," he boasted to Cornwallis. And if there had been even one local Tory not otherwise cowed by Marion who had given him any help, Tarleton maintained, he would have achieved

---

* The oft-repeated story that Tarleton dug up General Richardson's grave to gaze upon his face is almost certainly fanciful. But even Tarleton's defenders do not dispute that he harshly treated Richardson's wife and family, though one writer argues that "there is no record of humans being harmed beyond being left *homeless and hungry*."

"the total destruction of Mr. Marion." Yet Cornwallis was pleased with the results. He believed that by forcing Marion to take to the swamps, Tarleton had convinced the patriot citizenry that "there was a power superior to Marion" who could reward and punish them. Tarleton had "so far checked the insurrection," Cornwallis told Clinton, "that the greatest part of them have not dared openly to appear in arms against us since his expedition."

Even as the British were claiming to have subdued Marion, though, he was planning another offensive operation. Within a few days, as soon as he became satisfied that Tarleton was heading back to Winnsboro, Marion had gathered enough of a force to threaten Georgetown again. Nisbet Balfour, head of the garrison at Charleston, needled Cornwallis by reminding him that his favorite Tarleton had claimed to have ended the Marion threat. Despite Ban's claim, Marion had reappeared, which was "no joke to us," Balfour assured his Lordship. "I do not think that Tarleton flattered himself that he had done more than stopping his immediate progress and preventing the militia from joining him," Cornwallis coolly responded. Shortly thereafter Cornwallis acknowledged that Marion was still a problem. "We have lost two great plagues in Sumpter [sic] and [Elijah] Clarke," Cornwallis wrote to Balfour, based on a false report that those two partisan leaders had been killed. Then he added, "I wish your friend Marion was as quiet."

11

"I Must Drive Marion Out of That Country"

*M*arion's diversion of Tarleton had another positive—if indirect—repercussion that warmed patriot hearts: the disabling of the hated Major Wemyss. The direct credit for that achievement would belong to a reinvigorated Thomas Sumter, who remained very much alive.

Ever since his crushing loss to Tarleton at Fishing Creek in August, Sumter had been stirring about in the western part of South Carolina above Camden, looking for an opportunity to reenter the fray. But in three months he had done little. One of his militia regiments had participated in the battle of King's Mountain, but Sumter himself was absent, off angling for a promotion from South Carolina's exiled governor, John Rutledge, in Hillsboro, North Carolina. The day before King's Mountain, Rutledge commissioned Sumter as a brigadier general, making him the highest-ranking militia officer in the state.

Sumter's reputation had a way of staying elevated. Cornwallis considered him "our greatest plague in this country"—not so much for his battlefield prowess as for his ability to recruit large numbers of men quickly, even following defeat. Part of his recruiting talent was due to his willingness, unlike Marion, to indulge his men's desire for private plunder. In Sumter's defense, the line between arbitrary plunder and legitimate foraging was a blurry one. And Marion's scrupulous refusal to tolerate the practice marked him as a killjoy in the minds of some, making it more difficult for him to muster the rank-and-file. Marion preferred the loyalty of a few good men to the fickleness of many uncommitted ones.

While Tarleton was off chasing Marion, Sumter was gathering force and moving down from near the North Carolina border toward Winnsboro, where Cornwallis still had his winter headquarters. Wemyss, while patrolling and protecting the area in Tarleton's absence, learned that Sumter was just thirty miles away from the main British army. Not having been tested yet in actual battle in the southern theater, Wemyss asked Cornwallis for permission to engage Sumter. Although Cornwallis would have preferred Tarleton for the mission, he approved a dawn attack on Sumter's presumed camp on the Broad River. Wemyss enthusiastically went forward, even putting together a team of five men to kill or capture the Gamecock.

James Wemyss was good at burning plantations and hanging rebels when no enemy was around to stop him. But he was no battlefield tactician. Finding that Sumter had moved to Fish Dam Ford five miles downriver from where he was thought to be, Wemyss ordered an ill-advised, postmidnight cavalry assault. In his eagerness he had ignored Cornwallis's orders not to attack at night. The Americans repulsed the British and Tory horsemen and shot Wemyss through the arm and knee, unsaddling him from his horse and maiming him for life. Taken prisoner, Wemyss was paroled, then exchanged, but he never took the field again. He would be remembered in history mainly as the man who set fire to Presbyterian Church "sedition shops."

The one near success the British had at Fish Dam Ford came from the Sumter assassination squad. They burst into the sleeping militia commander's tent, from which he barely escaped, running half naked to hide in a briar patch while the fighting continued around him. He shivered all night until he climbed onto a bareback horse and hugged its neck for warmth.

Immediately after Fish Dam Ford, Sumter was bragging of his victory and reporting that his militia force had gone from three hundred to a thousand men overnight. Tarleton was to the south, burning houses and issuing his proclamation, when he received the summons from Cornwallis to return at once to address the Sumter threat. Thus, although the quote attributed to Tarleton—that he would leave the "damned old fox" and go find the "Gamecock"—undoubtedly is apocryphal, the essence of it is not far from the truth.

Tarleton succeeded in finding Sumter but failed to finish him off as hoped. To the contrary, it was the Green Dragoon who was routed this time. On November 20 Tarleton's force of three to four hundred met Sumter's thousand-man militia at Blackstock's plantation, seventy miles northwest of Winnsboro. Tarleton had with him his green-coated Legion and redcoats from Wemyss's old command, the 63rd Foot, mounted on horses they had stolen from the Pee Dee area during their burning spree. Tarleton had another 250 foot soldiers lagging behind him—the bagpipe-playing Scottish Highlanders—plus an artillery unit, but he decided not to wait for them before engaging Sumter's militia. Although Tarleton would falsely claim victory, in fact his men were mauled. About 60 percent of them were killed or wounded, while patriot casualties were minimal.

Among the patriot wounded was Thomas Sumter, who was hit with five buckshot in the chest and one in the shoulder. But he had just won his greatest victory of the war. The American militia had defeated not only Tories but also seasoned British regulars and had handed Tarleton the first battlefield loss of his career. Fighting from covered positions rather than in open fields, the militia even managed to beat back a bayonet charge by the 63rd Foot, which had dismounted to make the redcoats' usual bone-chilling thrust with cold steel.

It was Sumter's finest hour. But his injuries were so serious that they sidelined him for the next three months. In the meantime Francis Marion was again the sole patriot commander operating in South Carolina. And he was not happy about it.

THE DAY AFTER Sumter's victory at Blackstock's, Marion wrote to General Gates to report on his prior week's attempt on British-occupied Georgetown. Based on information that just fifty severely wounded soldiers ("invalids") garrisoned the town, Marion decided to enter it in search of sorely needed ammunition, clothing, and salt. He also knew that the capture of Georgetown would cause a heavy blow to British morale. But as it turned out, while Marion was busy evading Tarleton, a force of two hundred Tories under Jesse Barefield entered Georgetown to reinforce it. When Marion came near the town he sent out two separate reconnaissance parties, both of whom ran into bodies of Tories. Marion's men scattered one group of Tories and drove the other back into Georgetown, but as with Marion's first attempt to take the city, the enemy fortifications were too strong to permit an assault.

The expedition was not without success. In the skirmishing outside the city around November 13 Marion's horsemen killed a Tory captain and wounded the redoubtable Jesse Barefield on the head and body before he got away. The patriots also took twelve Tory prisoners. But Marion's men suffered a grievous loss of their own. In the scuffle with Barefield, Marion's nephew Gabriel Marion, a lieutenant in the brigade, was captured and then shot through the chest at point blank when the Tories learned his identity. Recently turned twenty-one at the time of his death, Gabriel was Marion's favorite nephew—the son of Marion's closest and late brother, Gabriel, who had done so much to help Marion financially over the years. Young Lieutenant Gabriel Marion must have realized how dangerous it was to be a member of his uncle's brigade: three weeks before he was killed he made out a will naming Francis Marion as a beneficiary.

Marion, childless himself, mourned young Gabriel's death as a father would a son. But his official report of the skirmish was typically laconic: "Our loss was Lt. Gabriel Marion and one private killed and three wounded." When, the day after the skirmish, one of Marion's soldiers put a bullet through the head of a captured mulatto man suspected—without evidence—of having killed his nephew, a furious Marion severely reprimanded the captain of the prisoner guard for failing to prevent it.

Marion concluded his November 21 letter to Gates on a desperate note. While camped at Britton's Ferry he learned that a force of two hundred Hessians and militia under Major Robert McLeroth had taken post at Kingstree. A loyalist provincial unit was also on its way there to drive off livestock and destroy provisions, à la Wemyss and Tarleton. Once again the British meant to challenge Whig supremacy in the

Williamsburg area. Marion wanted to come to the rescue of the locals, but
without more men and ammunition, he told Gates, he was unable to "do
anything effectual." Marion asked Brigadier General William Harrington,
head of the North Carolina militia, to send him some of his mounted
troops to help dislodge the enemy from Kingstree. But he did not really
expect Harrington—who had done nothing with the troops he had—to
part with any of them. Marion also told Gates that he was greatly in need
of a surgeon; one of his wounded had bled to death for lack of a doctor's
attention, and many others had returned home for lack of medicine.

But Marion's biggest complaint was that he still had no idea when—
or even if—the Continental Army was planning to return to South Carolina. "Many of my people has left me and gone over to the enemy, for
they think that we have no army coming on, and have been deceived,"
he informed Gates. "As we hear nothing from you a great while, I hope
to have a line from you in what manner to act, and some assurance to the
people of support." The next day he wrote Gates to reiterate the point. "I
seldom have the same [militia] set a fortnight," he lamented, "and until
the Grand Army is on the banks of Santee, it will be the same."

Marion was not overstating the difficulties he faced, but he was un-
derestimating the psychological impact his recent successes were having
on the enemy. The British chronically overestimated his numbers, partly
because of the many patrols he had spread out around the countryside,
creating an illusion that he was everywhere. In war the appearance of
strength can be as important as the reality in scaring the enemy.

After camping at the rebel stronghold of Kingstree for one night Major Robert McLeroth, unaware of Marion's whereabouts, became worried
that the partisan leader might swoop down upon him from out of nowhere at any moment. The Tory reinforcements McLeroth was expecting from Georgetown also had failed to show up; they had gone home
after their leader, Barefield, was wounded in the skirmish with Marion's
men. Believing his position too weak to stay at Kingstree, McLeroth
moved his 64th Regiment of Foot out of the patriot-infested Williamsburg area and down to Nelson's Ferry, where reinforcements brought his
total to about four hundred. There he set up camp around Sumter's plantation, the site of Marion's daring rescue mission in August. Unlike

Wemyss or Tarleton, though, McLeroth did not vent his frustration by laying waste to the countryside. A Scotsman by birth, he declined to burn the homes of his Scotch-Irish kinsmen, earning him the disdain of Cornwallis and other British officers.

To the British high command McLeroth lacked enterprise and vigor. Still, they grudgingly acknowledged that he was better off staying put on the Santee rather than conducting freelance operations through the Williamsburg region. "I think the sooner he can be put into a situation where he has not to act [for] himself the better—otherwise I fear some accident to him," Balfour wrote to Cornwallis from Charleston. Cornwallis expressed a similar concern to Rawdon, who had recently taken command at Camden after Turnbull, suffering from malaria, was granted leave to return home to New York. "I trust, my dear Lord, that you will have a constant eye to McLeroth, who by his letters requires much looking after," Cornwallis wrote on December 3, adding that "a blow to any British regiment cuts deep."

Deciding he was in no position to chase McLeroth from Kingstree to the Santee, Marion remained in hiding at the junction of Lynches Creek and the Pee Dee near Britton's Ferry. But events in the first week of December convinced the partisan leader it was time to strike the enemy again. He found out that a marauding band of Whigs had burst into the home of two brothers of Major John Harrison, the hated Tory bandit, and murdered them as they lay sick in their beds from smallpox. Marion expected that news of this atrocity would lead to a Tory uprising if left unchecked. He also received intelligence that Samuel Tynes, who had fled from Tearcoat Swamp only to be captured a week later by Marion's men, had escaped from General Harrington's camp in North Carolina and was again embodying the militia in the High Hills of Santee. Tynes reportedly was planning to join forces with McLeroth to give the British a superiority in the Pee Dee region that would force Marion to retreat from there. Determined to prevent that outcome, Marion left Lynches Creek and moved down to Indiantown in anticipation of another fight with Tynes. He enjoyed a sudden influx of volunteers who were motivated to defend the region from the invaders and, with harvest season over, had time on their hands.

But the Tynes threat was short lived. From Indiantown, Marion dispatched Peter Horry and a troop of horsemen to reconnoiter Tynes's position in the High Hills. Scared off by that movement and a false report that Harrington was marching from North Carolina to meet up with Horry, the Tories deserted their post. An "exceedingly frightened" Tynes rode into Camden and, explaining to Rawdon that he could do nothing with the militia, begged permission to resign. Rawdon accepted, and Tynes, who had fought initially as a patriot and then as a Tory, now would fight as neither.

In the meantime the British command had found a useful occupation for McLeroth. In Charleston two hundred raw recruits, earmarked for the British 7th Regiment of Foot (Royal Fusiliers), had just arrived from England and needed an escort to Cornwallis's army in Winnsboro. Cornwallis was anxious to have fresh manpower, as he was again preparing to invade North Carolina, having concluded—rather optimistically—that South Carolina was now sufficiently quiet for him to depart. To protect the new recruits' journey to the interior, though, Balfour wanted British regulars to accompany them. Marion, he told Cornwallis, was "too formidable" to oppose "without something better than militia." And so the plan was to march the recruits north from Charleston to Sumter's plantation at Nelson's Ferry through territory south of the Santee not controlled by Marion. From Sumter's, McLeroth and his 64th Foot would conduct them to the High Hills of Santee, where a cavalry unit from Camden would meet them.

By now Marion's brigade had swelled to about three hundred, enough to confront McLeroth's force. Thus, when he learned the Scottish major was leisurely marching the new recruits along the road from Nelson's Ferry to Camden, Marion decided to give them a rude baptism. Around December 13 he caught up with McLeroth's infantry at Halfway Swamp, about twenty miles north of Nelson's and a mile from the Richardson Plantation where Marion had nearly fallen into Tarleton's trap. Marion's riflemen fired upon the British pickets, driving them back in upon the main column. Then Marion's mounted troops swung around and attacked the enemy's flank and front, killing or wounding several men. McLeroth, who had the disadvantage of no cavalry, hurried his panicked recruits into an open field and took protection behind a rail fence. Marion drew up his horsemen on the road alongside the Elliott Millpond, a lime green, cypress-filled quagmire that to this day is among the most visually striking swamps in all of South Carolina.

After the two forces glared at each other for a time, McLeroth sent Marion a messenger under a flag of truce, protesting the shooting of his pickets. McLeroth also dared Marion to come out and fight like a gentleman in the open field. Marion replied that the British practice of burning houses was more egregious than his shooting of armed pickets, adding that as long as the British persisted in the former habit he would continue in the latter.*

As for McLeroth's defiant challenge to engage in open combat, Marion considered it an act of desperation, not chivalry. But then, according to William James, Marion issued a counterproposal that seems unprecedented in the annals of warfare—but actually dated to biblical times: he would not engage in a general combat, but if McLeroth agreed, each side could pick twenty "duelists" to meet on open ground and decide the contest that way. The British commander accepted, and the two sides selected a spot, south of an oak tree, to have their best marksmen square off.

Just what possessed Marion to make this unusual offer—if indeed he did—is difficult to imagine. As someone who prided himself in avoiding cruelty and barbarism, he may have been genuinely stung by McLeroth's accusations of uncivilized conduct. Or perhaps Marion simply figured that his riflemen were better sharpshooters than the British and were sure to prevail.

In any event, according to James, the men were picked and each side formed a line facing one another more than a hundred yards apart. Marion appointed Major John Vanderhorst to take command of the patriot team, and Vanderhorst asked Captain Gavin Witherspoon what distance

---

*Marion intuitively had the better of the argument. Under modern rules of warfare pickets and sentries are members of the armed forces of a party to the conflict and, not being religious or medical personnel, may be attacked as enemy combatants. But any destruction of private property by occupying forces is prohibited unless necessary as a military matter.

he would choose for firing the opening round of buckshot. Witherspoon replied "fifty yards," and Vanderhorst, explaining that he was not a good judge of distances, told Witherspoon to tap him on the shoulder once they were fifty yards from the enemy. The two opposing lines then marched forward, but when the British advanced to within a hundred yards, they shouldered their muskets and retreated back toward the main body. Marion's men let out a cheer, claiming a moral victory. Without a shot having been fired, both sides retired for the evening to plan the next day's operations.

In his typically cursory report on the encounter with McLeroth, Marion omitted any mention of an unorthodox duel, saying only that he had "skirmaged" with the enemy. Perhaps he was reluctant to admit that he had gone along with such a gimmick. Or maybe the whole story was made up. The source of it—not Weems, for once, but William Dobein James—appears to have gotten it years later from Gavin Witherspoon, who claimed to be the first man picked for the patriots' team. Witherspoon could have spun a tale for James that the author regarded as too good not to use.

Whatever the nature of the "skirmage," it turned out that McLeroth had been stalling for time. That night he kept his campfires burning to create appearances and before dawn slipped away toward Singleton's Mills, nearly fifteen miles north. It was one of the few times the Swamp Fox was himself outfoxed. McLeroth left his supply wagons and heavy baggage behind, a costly sacrifice that indicated how much he wanted to avoid a general engagement.

Upon discovering McLeroth's movement, Marion sent a detachment under Major John James, mounted on the swiftest horses, to take possession of the houses at Singleton's, which commanded a strong position atop a hill. James reached the buildings just as the British infantry arrived at the foot of the hill. But there he found a new enemy more dreaded than the British and Tories: the Singleton family had just come down with smallpox. James's men got off a single volley and killed a captain before fleeing the infected premises. McLeroth was reinforced there by 130 infantry (50 mounted, 80 on foot) under loyalist Captain John Coffin, and Marion elected not to pursue them.

After the patriots abandoned Singleton's, McLeroth and Coffin headed safely off toward Camden with the raw recruits. But the scare Marion had thrown into the newcomers would hamper their effectiveness at the critical battle of Cowpens a month later. As for McLeroth, his military career was effectively over. He asked leave to return to Charleston, and Rawdon, citing the Scotsman's lack of aggressiveness, granted his request. Yet Rawdon, a hardliner when it came to dealing with rebels, told Cornwallis that, in fairness, McLeroth's "mild and equitable behavior" toward civilians had been of great value. It was a lesson learned too late to save the victims of Wemyss's and Tarleton's excesses.

William Dobein James called McLeroth "the most humane of all the officers of the British army" and regretted that McLeroth and Marion, another man of moral principle, had been forced to war against each other. But regardless of McLeroth's humanity, his departure left the partisan leader in control of the Santee around Nelson's Ferry. "I must drive Marion out of that country," Rawdon declared to Cornwallis on December 15, "but I cannot yet say what steps I shall take to effect it." Cornwallis, who had bemoaned Marion's aggravations at the rate of almost a letter a week over the previous few months, was getting tired of hearing his name. He wrote Rawdon two days later, saying that he wanted Marion "disposed of."

12

"I Have Not the Honor of Your Acquaintance"

*N*ever one to tempt fate, Marion did not stay in place for long. After McLeroth left for Camden, Marion lingered about the Santee for a few days to burn enemy boats, but upon hearing that a British force was on its way, he retreated again to the Williamsburg district. Leaving some small parties behind to continue agitating the British between Nelson's and Singleton's, Marion took post on December 22 at Benbow's Ferry above Kingstree, where he had gone after the Tarleton chase.

Marion still had heard nothing from Horatio Gates. His last letter to him, written on December 6, was the tenth one he had sent the commanding general, only one of which Gates had bothered to answer. What Marion did not yet know when he sent the December 6 letter was that Gates was no longer head of the Continental army in the South. He had turned over that command on December 3 to the man George Washington had wanted for the position all along.

Nathanael Greene had what was probably the best military mind in the Continental Army. Yet he had no military training and little formal education. A lapsed Quaker, he was suspended from their meetings after being seen at a public alehouse in 1773; later he formally withdrew from the pacifistic sect. In 1774 he organized a militia in his native Rhode Island to oppose the British. His military learning was self-taught, gained from books among his 250-volume personal library. When the Revolution came in 1775 Greene was promoted from private to major general of the Rhode Island state army, and in June of that year Congress appointed him as a brigadier in the Continental Army. He was only thirty-two.

His meteoric rise continued a year later when he was made a major general and placed in charge of the army on Long Island. During his time in New York he commanded at Fort Lee in New Jersey and Fort Washington across the Hudson in Manhattan, but he was unable to hold either against the British. He crossed the Delaware with Washington on Christmas Day 1776 and led a column in the great victory over the Hessians at Trenton. He also fought ably under Washington at the losing battles of Brandywine and Germantown, then again in the standoff at Monmouth Courthouse, where Greene's Continental right wing held off a furious attack by Lord Cornwallis. It was the last major battle in the North before Clinton and Cornwallis sailed to take Charleston in 1780.

Greene was to become the fifth commander of the Continental southern army, following Charles Lee, Robert Howe, Benjamin Lincoln, and Horatio Gates. He received his appointment from Washington (who was finally allowed by Congress to pick his own man) in mid-October 1780 but did not arrive at Gates's headquarters in Charlotte, North Carolina, until December 2. There, in a little log cabin town, Greene found a starving, half-naked, dispirited army of twenty-three hundred men. Only fifteen hundred of them were fit for duty and eight hundred adequately clothed and equipped. On December 4, his first full day on the job, he sat down to write to several notables, including George Washington and Thomas Jefferson, to report on the deplorable condition of the army remnants he had inherited. One of his letters was to Francis Marion, who received it on December 22 at his camp at Benbow's Ferry. It was the first of more than dozens of letters Greene would write to Marion over the next two years.

"I have not the honor of your acquaintance," Greene began, "but am no stranger to your character and merit. Your services in the lower part of South Carolina in aiding the forces and preventing the enemy from extending their limits have been very important and it is my earnest desire that you continue where you are until further advice from me."

"I like your plan of frequently shifting your ground," Greene continued. "It frequently prevents a surprise and perhaps a total loss of your party." Having already perfected if not invented this method of operation, Marion hardly needed Greene to tell him how sensible it was. But after being ignored for so long by Gates, Marion would have welcomed a little flattery. Greene went on: "Until a more permanent army can be collected than is in the field at present, we must endeavor to keep up a partisan war and preserve the tide of sentiment among the people as much as possible in our favor."

Privately Greene often derided the partisan militia, likening it to "the garnish of a table" whose little "partisan strokes" merely kept the contest alive and, in comparison with the main army, provided no substantial national security. The goal of the war in the South, he wrote to Sumter around this time, was not to capture little outposts but to win the "contest for states," which only the army could accomplish. The British would never relinquish South Carolina, Greene added, until they saw a better barrier in the field than a volunteer militia who came and went as they pleased.

Too often, Greene told Sumter, the militia were more interested in pillage and plunder and placed their desire for private gain or personal glory above the cause. He also found that they demanded greater care and feeding than the Continentals, many of whom had endured the winters at Valley Forge and Morristown before coming south. The militia, Greene complained to a fellow Rhode Island general, were "like the locusts of Egypt [who] have eaten up every green thing." They were "of no more use than if they were in the moon."

Sumter, who had helped keep patriot hopes alive while risking his life the previous eight months, understandably took umbrage at Greene's stinging put-downs of the militia. Greene's disparaging attitude would strain his relationship with Sumter going forward. But Marion did not wholly disagree with Greene's comments. As a Continental colonel earlier in the war, he had promoted "good harmony" between the Continental troops and state militia and said he would not be "partial to either." But there were times during his Continental command when he found the militia to be "not of the least service." By now, having directly experienced what it was like to command them, he was just as frustrated with what he called the militia's "diffidence" as was Greene. And if anything he was even more intolerant of plunder, once going so far as to threaten execution of "any soldier of any denomination who is found taking any article from any plantation wither from white or black."

Much as Greene may have held the militia in low esteem, he would learn to use them cooperatively in a way that Gates never did. Greene knew he could not count on reinforcements from the North, where Washington was reduced to eyeing Clinton warily in New York and pleading for French help. To retake South Carolina, Greene would need the patriot militia's help. In time he would also come to view the "war of posts" as of signal importance.

Marion, too, understood that the Continental Army and the militia needed each other. Marion did like designing his own program and sometimes would chafe at instructions that differed from his own ideas on how best to engage the enemy. It was a natural reaction on the part of someone who had enjoyed considerable success trusting his own judgment and instincts. But unlike Sumter, who preferred flying solo, Marion was willing to subordinate himself to Greene if necessary for the greater good. Marion also favored the system of discipline and order that marked the regular army, as compared with the anarchy that prevailed within the militia. There was still much of the old Continental officer in the relatively new partisan leader.

To show he understood the militia's needs, Greene also responded to Marion's unanswered letters to Gates asking for various help. "Ammunition I am told is gone to you since you wrote [to Gates]," Greene assured him. Greene apologized that he could not supply Marion's men with any clothing because the army had none. Greene was too unfamiliar with the medical department to give Marion an answer regarding a surgeon but promised to send one if possible. "I am fully sensible your service is hard and sufferings great," he sympathized, "but how great the prize for which we contend!"

Greene had one immediate request of Marion, which was to provide badly needed intelligence regarding the enemy's operations. "Spies are the eyes of an army," Greene wrote, "and without them a general is always groping in the dark and can neither secure himself nor annoy his enemy." Again he was not telling Marion anything new. Greene was particularly interested in learning of any reinforcements arriving in Charleston who could march to join Cornwallis, and he asked Marion to "fix some plan for procuring such information and for conveying it to me with all possible dispatch." He promised that any money advanced to information couriers would be repaid.

Then Greene, who often lacked tact, presumed to tell Marion exactly how to carry out that mission. "The spy should be taught to be particular in his enquiries and to get the names of the corps, strength and commanding officer's name, place from whence they came and where they are going," he wrote. He told Marion to find someone who lived in Charleston to do this and to use a runner between the two of them because anyone who asked too many questions and lived out of town would be suspected. "The utmost secrecy will be necessary in this business," Greene emphasized. Over time, as he gained greater confidence in him, Greene would learn to leave it to Marion's discretion how to accomplish a particular goal.

Marion responded immediately to Greene's letter, writing on December 22 to say that he would "endeavor to procure intelligence as you desire." He explained, however, that spies required real money to do their job—gold or silver, not the IOUs Greene had offered. "The enemy is so suspicious they will not permit any men to pass on the south of Santee without the strictest examination and they have patroles along the river and guards at several passes," he added. The reinforced British guard at Nelson's now consisted of 80 Hessians and 150 new troops from Charleston. Marion also reported to Greene on his "skirmage" with McLeroth, but if it had involved the bizarre duel James described, Marion was not going to mention that in his very first communication with the new southern commander. He closed the letter by repeating what he had told Gates before: if he had a hundred Continental troops in addition to the militia with him, he would be able to accomplish much more.

At this point Marion went into camp for the winter. His brigade settled into a secret lair on Snow's Island, a triangular-shaped, three-mile-long by two-mile-wide swamp plateau at the confluence of the Pee Dee River and Lynches Creek. Located in the southeast corner of present-day

Florence County, it is surrounded by the Pee Dee on the northeast, Lynches Creek (now River) on the north, and Clark's Creek, a branch of Lynches, on the west and south. In Marion's time it lay within a few miles of each of Witherspoon's, Port's, and Britton's Ferries, familiar retreats for Marion's men over the previous four months. Marion or his fellow militia commander Hugh Giles, a surveyor and area landowner, had established the Snow's Island camp by mid-November 1780 and may have first stayed there somewhat earlier; by Christmas it had become Marion's main hideout and place of rendezvous from which his men ventured forth.

Snow's Island (named for local settlers) was to become the most famous and romanticized of all of Marion's various encampments. Neither here nor anywhere else did the Swamp Fox actually live in the swamps, which were breeding grounds for insects and disease. (Although that is not why no one dwelled in them; they thought that malaria and yellow fever were caused by poisonous vapors from the steamy morasses, not mosquito bites.) On Snow's the camp was on dry, higher ground toward the northern tip of the island above the marshy, flood-prone land stretching south. Inaccessible except by water, deep within a forest of cypress and pines, it was protected by tall canebrakes, briars, and vines.

To insulate themselves as much as possible, Marion's men felled trees and broke down bridges across creek fords and difficult passes. Sentries patrolled the area to warn of approaching danger or to signal the way clear for sallying out. To further guard against surprise attacks, they threw up a small earthworks, or redoubt, at Dunham's Bluff on the east side of the Pee Dee, opposite the island, and set up a camp there as well. In fact, recent archaeological findings suggest that rather than a single, permanent Snow's Island camp, there may have been multiple camps in the same vicinity, both on and off the island, and that Marion, like a classic guerrilla warrior, moved constantly from one to the other to maximize secrecy.

Here at Snow's was Marion's Sherwood Forest, his feudal fortress. As William Gilmore Simms, the most literary of Marion's early biographers, wrote, "The swamp was his moat; his bulwarks were the deep ravines, which, watched by sleepless rifles, were quite as impregnable as the castles on the Rhine." It was here, too, that the most famous of all Marion legends—the sweet potato dinner—has its setting. According to the oft-repeated story, a British officer arrived at Marion's camp from

Georgetown to negotiate a prisoner exchange. Marion offered him dinner, which consisted only of roasted sweet potatoes on pieces of bark
along with Marion's favorite drink of water and vinegar (the drink of the
Roman Legion, known for its mild antibiotic qualities).

"But surely, general," the officer inquired, "this cannot be your ordinary fare."

"Indeed it is, sir," Marion replied, "and we are fortunate on this occasion, entertaining company, to have more than our usual allowance."
The idealized story holds that the visiting Briton was so impressed that
when he returned to Georgetown he resigned his commission, saying
that the British had no chance of defeating men of such endurance and
sacrifice.

Although the particulars of the story are doubtful, attempts to substantiate it persist. True or not, the anecdote has proved valuable, for it
produced the only image of Francis Marion created by someone who
knew him during his lifetime —a painting by South Carolina artist John
Blake White that has hung in the US Senate since 1899. Also appearing in the painting is Marion's African American servant, Oscar (or
"Buddy"), whose contribution to the patriot cause was recognized by
presidential proclamation in 2006. A claimed descendant of the slave
describes him not only as a soldier but as Marion's "personal assistant,
sous chef, bugler, [and] oarsman." He also played the fiddle, as Marion
bought him one soon after the war.*

The Snow's Island community was dominated by Whigs, and they
furnished Marion's partisans with food and supplies to support the resistance effort. Even with many of the able-bodied men off fighting, women
and slaves kept the nearby farms and plantations running, with slaves
carrying salt and other necessities to Marion's brigade. The island became a beehive of activity. Peter Horry said the Whig neighbors played

---

*Even if the modest repast of legend did take place, it probably was not on Snow's
Island or the surrounding area. More likely, as some accounts hold, it took place
outside Georgetown, fifty miles to the south, during one of Marion's forays there.
The British officer was from Georgetown, and Marion's brigade, when traveling,
would live off provisions they brought with them. Furthermore, Snow's Island and
its environs had abundant supplies of livestock, fish, game, corn, and rice, and it is
unlikely that Marion's men were subsisting on sweet potatoes while camped there.

the dual role of "generous stewards and faithful spies, so that, while there, we lived at once in safety and plenty."

In return for supplies and information from the locals, Marion declined to plunder them. He took only what was necessary for his men's subsistence and gave patriot citizens receipts for supplies taken from them, many of which were redeemed for compensation from the government after the war. At least it was Marion's intent to make whole those citizens who provided his men with food and supplies. He apologized on one occasion to a man who had furnished an unusually large number of provisions and was given a receipt, explaining that "Some other damages has been made, but you well know the unruly militia which cannot be at all times restrained."

Marion also offered the citizens security and protection from Tory antagonists such as Ganey and Barefield, who lived a few hours' trek north of Snow's Island. Given that proximity, Marion and his men sometimes conducted foraging raids in the Tories' own backyard as a show of force. On one such sortie in late December, into the Waccamaw Neck region north of Georgetown, Captain (later Major) John Postell brought back 150 bushels of salt, the most precious commodity in the state. After satisfying his brigade's needs, Marion distributed the rest to the local Whigs, a bushel per family, further endearing himself to them.

Marion's cooperative relationship with the Snow's Island Whig community marked him as one of the earliest guerrilla warriors who understood the importance of moral, material, and intelligence support from the local civilian population. It was a principle applied by later guerrilla leaders such as Mao Tse-tung and continues to be endorsed as part of official US Army military doctrine. And it was one reason Marion gained the hearts and minds of his countrymen, whereas the British, with their threats and reprisals against the inhabitants, failed to do so.

Marion's living quarters on Snow's Island were the same as those of his men: crude lean-to huts that sheltered them from the wind and rain. It was the only home Marion had at the time, for the British had impounded his Pond Bluff plantation. In November, under the authority of Cornwallis, the British seized the plantations of Marion and several of his brigade members. William Moultrie, John Rutledge, Henry Laurens, and other prominent rebels had their homes taken as well. Anyone who tried to interfere with the property seizures was threatened with punishment for aiding and abetting the rebellion. The day after New Year's a Philadelphia Whig paper asked whether it was not "high time to think of retaliation or in future neither to give or take quarter from such an enemy?"

By New Year's Day, in addition to his new home, Marion had a new title. At the end of December, Governor Rutledge commissioned Marion as a brigadier general in the South Carolina militia with authority over the Lowcountry east of Camden above the Santee. Marion was now the senior-most militia commander in the state who was active in the field. Thomas Sumter, still laid up from the wounds suffered at Blackstock's, was in charge of the upcountry west of the Catawba River. Technically Sumter's earlier appointment as brigadier general gave him superior rank over Marion, which would lead to friction between them in later months. More important than their formal authority, though, was their practical ability to attract and retain men under their command, and their differing approaches to that challenge would separate them as well.

As the southern campaign of 1780 drew to a close, the patriots in South Carolina had to be encouraged that they remained in the fight at all. It was less than five months since Cornwallis's trouncing of Gates at Camden had all but sealed British domination of the state. And had it not been for Marion, things likely would have remained that way.

It had been a bloody year in South Carolina as well. Of the thousand patriots killed in action in the Revolution in 1780, 66 percent died in South Carolina. Even more startling, 90 percent of the two thousand patriots wounded in action in 1780 fell in that state. But 1781 would be bloodier still.

13

"Two Very Enterprising Officers"

*A*s he did with the Snow's Island community, Marion quickly established a symbiotic relationship with Nathanael Greene. It may not have seemed that way at first: unable to offer Marion much of what he needed, Greene did not hesitate to ask for this, that, or the other from the partisan leader. Greene wanted "a party of negroes" sent to him as soon as possible to assist the army with day-to-day chores and requested they bring with them corn and rice for the soldiers. Marion immediately complied by having John Postell collect fifty slaves from enemy territory above Georgetown ("taking care not to distress any family, but taking them where they can be best spared," he instructed Postell from Snow's Island). The slaves and provisions were sent up in boats to Greene's winter camp on the Pee Dee just below the South Carolina border, where Greene had moved because it was a more fertile forage area than Charlotte.

Greene also continued to press Marion for intelligence about the large body of British reinforcements under General Alexander Leslie reportedly making their way toward Winnsboro to join Cornwallis for his invasion of North Carolina. The information was of vital importance to Greene, who had split his already small, ill-equipped army by sending six hundred men under grizzled veteran general Daniel Morgan to the west of the Catawba River—Sumter territory—which put Morgan within striking distance of the British post at Ninety-Six. Greene's audacious move, against all conventional military thinking, was done as much out of necessity as choice: he could not feed his entire army in one place at one time. But the strategy also forced Cornwallis to divide his own force by detaching Tarleton west to defend Ninety-Six. Cornwallis himself could not chase Morgan, for Greene might link up with Marion to menace Camden or Charleston. So Cornwallis had to stay put. As soon as Leslie arrived, however, Cornwallis would be in position to strike offensively against Greene. He was convinced the rebels in South Carolina would not stop their harassment so long as Greene's army, shielded by friendly North Carolina territory above him, remained in the field. To subdue South Carolina, he needed to control North Carolina, and to control North Carolina, he needed to defeat Greene.

Marion was the first militia leader to learn of the arrival of Leslie's troops in Charleston in late December. He estimated their force at two thousand or fewer (the actual number was about fifteen hundred). He also was the first to learn of their departure for the interior, and he kept Greene up to date with regular reports of their strength and movements. He promised to keep his patrols constantly near the opposing forces to watch their movements and to notify Greene of "every particular respecting the enemy." In fact, throughout the war, despite the lack of hard money to pay spies, Marion informed Greene about everything significant happening in and around Charleston and Georgetown. He became, in effect, Greene's director of intelligence.

Greene also wanted Marion to harass the enemy; he obliged by sending Peter Horry from Snow's Island into the plantation-rich Waccamaw Neck region, from which the British garrison in Georgetown drew its subsistence, to remove rice and drive off cattle. Horry's mounted troops ended up engaging in some skirmishes with the British that Greene said "were clever and do them a great deal of honor."

What Greene wanted most, though, was horses. He understood, as Gates had not, that mounted forces were essential both to cover the vast open distances in the Carolinas and to navigate the often difficult terrain. "The war here is upon a very different scale to what it is to the Northward," he explained to Joseph Reed, the chief executive of Pennsylvania. "It is a plain business there. The geography of the country reduces its operations to two or three points. But here it is everywhere, and the country is so full of deep rivers and impassable creeks and swamps, that you are always liable to misfortunes of a capital nature." Greene, who had never set foot in the South before taking command there, learned its topography not only from on-the-ground experience but also from an intense, scientific study of maps. Within weeks of his arrival he knew the landscape as well as the British commanders, including Cornwallis, who had been there for half a year.

As Greene quickly discovered, roads in South Carolina were little more than dusty footpaths or wagon tracks, useless when the rains turned them to mud—and the winter of 1781 was an especially wet one. Bridges were few, and rivers were unfordable when flooded, as they often were. Not all men could swim, but horses could. Horses could negotiate most of these impediments better than men were able to, and where crossings were blocked, horses could more quickly get their riders to better passages elsewhere.

And so almost from the beginning of his arrival in South Carolina, Greene repeatedly requested that Marion find and send him as many horses as possible—preferably his best ones. When Marion was unresponsive, which was often, Greene was quick to remind him. "I hope you paid particular attention to the order sent you by Governor Rutledge for collecting the horses. Please to let me know what number you have and what addition you expect," Greene wrote on January 16. Later he would tell Marion to "get all the good dragoon horses you can to mount our cavalry. . . . This is a great object and I beg you pay particular attention to it."

When Marion did acknowledge Greene's requests on the subject, he replied that he had only enough horses for his own troops and that what few he might be able to collect were so "ordinary" that Greene probably wouldn't want them anyway. Before Greene arrived, Marion explained, the British had taken all the good horses, as a result of which his own brigade was now "badly mounted." The best he could promise was to send Greene "a few more [that] may be got."

Marion was not trying to be difficult, just realistic. His men, most of whom were farmers, were not going to give up their coveted horses to Greene's army. If Greene needed horses, they figured, let him get them from the Continental Congress, not from unpaid volunteers. In fact, the merest rumor that Greene was trying to take their horses from them prompted some of Marion's men to desert him.

Beyond this, Marion's militiamen, to be effective in the field, needed horses as much or more than Greene's army. True, it was important that the regular army have horses, as it was for everyone. But if horses were important to Greene, they were crucial to the militia. Militiamen could hardly scour the countryside for forage on foot. Greene wanted the militia to scout for his army and to serve, in part, as cowboys—driving cattle to the army and away from the enemy. And no cowboy was ever without a good horse.

Fast-moving steeds were also integral to the guerrilla tactics of hit-and-run and retreat. As an officer in Tarleton's Legion (and someone who ought to have known) explained,

> The crackers and militia in those parts of America are all mounted on horse-back, which renders it totally impossible to force them to an engagement with infantry *only*. When they choose to fight, they dismount, and fasten their horses to the fences and rails; but if not very confident in the superiority of their numbers, they remain on horse-back, give their fire, and retreat, which renders it useless to attack them without cavalry: for though you repulse them, and drive them from the field, you never can improve the advantage, or do them any material detriment.

Rawdon put it more succinctly, lamenting to Clinton that because Marion's and Sumter's militia were all mounted, "we have never been able to force them to a decisive action."

Marion needed horses for another reason. His men were chronically low on ammunition, often having no more than three or four rounds apiece available for battle. When out of musket balls and heavy buckshot (often loaded together as "buck and ball") they used bird shot. Swan or goose shot was effective at close range to disperse the enemy but not lethal beyond twenty or thirty yards. Marion's lack of firepower was a problem Greene was able to remedy only sporadically; the partisans' best chance of obtaining ammunition was to take it from a defeated foe, as

Marion had done at Black Mingo and Tearcoat Swamp. Due to the shortage of powder and ball, Marion converted as many infantry as he could to cavalry soldiers, arming them with sabers hammered by local blacksmiths from mill saws. And cavalrymen, by definition, had to have horses.

In time Greene would admit to Peter Horry, Marion's cavalry leader, that stripping the militia of horses to give to the Continental Army would be "like robbing Peter to pay Paul." But that realization would not come before the horses issue nearly ruptured the generally good working relationship between Greene and Marion.

In the meantime, as he organized his brigade on Snow's Island in January 1781, Marion was considering what the new southern commander could do for *him*. He would find that when it was within Greene's power to help, he readily did so. On January 14 Marion acknowledged receipt of the ammunition Greene had recently sent. He also reported his fear that without some reinforcements from the regular army he would be unable to stem the growing British/Tory threat in the Waccamaw Neck region above Georgetown. As Marion explained, he was exposed in that region because he had so many men out on detachments collecting supplies and gathering intelligence for the army, as Greene had requested. He was also concerned the Tories in the Drowning Creek area on the North Carolina border were planning to join forces with the British around Waccamaw Neck and gain control of the area's plentiful provisions. Greene immediately got the point and sent a hundred regulars and a hundred Virginia militia to disperse the Tories on Drowning Creek.

At the same time in early January, Greene granted Marion's fondest wish: he decided to send him an entire unit of Continentals. It was the mixed cavalry and infantry legion, some 250 strong, of Lieutenant Colonel Henry Lee, one of the Continental Army's most accomplished young officers. Nicknamed Light-Horse Harry after his daring cavalry strikes against the British in the northern theater, the flamboyant, twenty-five-year-old Lee was the Americans' answer to Banastre Tarleton. After graduating from Princeton in 1773 (then the College of New Jersey), he forsook studying law at Middle Temple in London, which Tarleton had attended, to become a cavalry captain in his native Virginia. He was promoted to a dragoon major in Washington's Continental Army and became lifelong friends with the man he would later eulogize as "First in war, first in peace, first in the hearts of his countrymen." Washington would be similarly idolized by Lee's son, future Confederate general Robert E. Lee, who married into the family of Washington's wife, Martha Custis.

Sent south by Washington in late 1780 to join Greene, Lieutenant Colonel Lee arrived at Greene's camp in early January and was promptly forwarded to link up with Marion at Snow's Island and conduct joint offensive operations. Marion was heartened by this development, although he made clear to Greene that he expected to hold rank above Lee, not on the basis of his brigadier generalship in the militia but because he was commissioned a lieutenant colonel in the Continental Army back in 1776, well before Lee's promotion to that position. Greene chose not to weigh in on that issue, leaving it to the two men to work it out between them.

They were an unlikely pair. Barely half Marion's age, Lee was an educated Virginia gentleman, articulate both orally and in writing, whereas Marion, who had scant formal learning, said little and was at best adequate with the pen. In comparison with the threadbare clothing worn by Marion and his brethren, Lee dressed elegantly and made sure his Legion was in full uniform. (They wore short green coats, similar to Tarleton's.) Lee was an egotist and self-promoter; Marion was modest and self-effacing. And yet, maybe because they were such opposites, they somehow hit it off.

Or perhaps it was because, in the areas that counted most, they were in fact quite similar: both were physically slight, relying more on speed, agility, and bold maneuvers for success; both were strong believers in discipline; and both were solicitous of the lives and safety of their men, gaining their loyalty by not needlessly exposing them to danger. Then, too, Marion was at heart a Continental officer who had morphed into a partisan militia commander out of necessity. He wanted to work with Continental professionals such as Greene and Lee. Lee wisely did not challenge Marion's claim of seniority, although he frequently offered his advice on strategy and tactics, and Marion always considered it and often accepted it. They would work together cooperatively in one of the most successful collaborations of regulars and militia during the war.

Henry Lee was a highly opinionated man who lashed out at anyone who criticized or crossed him. He would use his memoirs both to tout his own accomplishments and to settle scores with his bitter enemies, among them Thomas Jefferson. But he had only good things to say about Francis Marion. Lee's memoirs contain what probably is still the best and most frequently quoted assessment of Marion's character:

> He was reserved and silent, entering into conversation only when necessary, and then with modesty and good sense. He possessed a strong mind, improved by its own reflections and observations, not by books or travel. His dress was like his address—plain, regarding comfort and decency only. In his meals he was abstemious, eating generally of one dish, and drinking water mostly. He was sedulous and constant in his attention to the duties of his station, to which every other consideration yielded. Even the charms of the fair, like the luxuries of the table and the allurements of wealth, seemed to be lost upon him. The procurement of subsistence for his men, and the contrivance of annoyance for his enemy, engrossed his entire mind. He was virtuous all over; never, even in manner, much less in reality, did he trench upon right. Beloved by his friends, and respected by his enemies, he exhibited a luminous example of the beneficial effects to be produced by an individual who, with only small means at his command, possesses a virtuous heart, a strong head, and a mind directed to the common good.

Almost comically, Lee had a hard time finding Marion at first, stumbling around the Snow's Island vicinity until Marion's scouts guided him in. It seems that Marion, who tended to move his camp around every few days, could hide not only from his enemies but from his friends as well. In Lee's search for Marion it did not help that his men's dapper green jackets so resembled those of Tarleton's Legion that the Snow's Island–area Whigs refused to give him information as to Marion's location.

As soon as Lee arrived on January 22 they began planning their first operation, an attack on British-held Georgetown. Taking Georgetown had been a particular objective—indeed, almost an obsession—of Marion's for some time. Perhaps he was motivated by a desire to liberate his childhood home, where his sister still lived. But the reasons for his preoccupation with Georgetown were at least as strategic as sentimental. Georgetown was the main place where salt, that prized commodity, was manufactured along the coast. In addition, Georgetown commanded the rich rice-producing area to its north. And Georgetown was a transportation hub linking the areas below and above the Santee River.

The best explanation, however, comes from loyalist provincial commander Robert Gray, who observed that Georgetown supplied the Tories in the Little Pee Dee area with arms and ammunition, which they used to harass Marion's brigade. Because of Tory influence in that region, Marion was unable to draw volunteers from it and had to limit his recruiting mostly to the people of Williamsburg. Until Ganey and Barefield were disposed of, capturing Georgetown offered the best chance for Marion to neutralize them.

Marion was so intent on the mission succeeding this time that he skirted international law. He sent an officer to Georgetown under a flag of truce, supposedly to return some captured private correspondence and to discuss the terms of a prisoner exchange, when the real reason was to ascertain the strength of the enemy defenses. He and Lee then developed a creative but complicated plan of attack that Greene approved. It was an amphibious operation designed to approach the city from both land and sea. Lee's ninety-man infantry, guided by several of Marion's men with local knowledge, would float undetected on flat-bottomed boats down the Pee Dee to Georgetown and wait in the marshes south of the city. Lee's cavalry and Marion's militia would give the boats a day's head start before heading toward Georgetown on horse. Once they arrived, the two forces were to storm the town from different directions and converge inside to capture the garrison, which was manned by about three hundred British and Tories. Some of them were stationed inside a strong redoubt with cannon, but most of the defenders were in barracks, including a brick church.

Early on the morning of January 23 the flatboats, recently commandeered by John Postell from neighboring rivers, set off through the icy waters on their winding, ninety-mile journey. Marion sent Postell a short message that day ordering him immediately to join him at Kingstree with all the men who had been patrolling the countryside. In the month since being commissioned a brigadier general, Marion's written orders had become increasingly peremptory, and this one was no exception. "You must proceed by forced marches until you come up to me, for no time is to be lost," Marion wrote to Postell. "Leave your post as secretly as possible, without letting anyone know where you are going, or of your intention to leave it."

On January 24 the water-borne party reached Winyah Bay, which lay below the unguarded back of the town, and concealed themselves on a marshy island. That same day Marion and Lee's combined mounted contingent, numbering around 250, met Postell at Kingstree and galloped off down the road to Georgetown. They arrived in the early morning hours of January 25—later than expected—because the recent rains had turned the roads to mud. (Lee also blamed the blunders of guides for the delay.)

In the meantime Lee's infantry, after waiting all day, left their hiding place in Winyah Bay sometime past midnight and paddled ashore under cover of a poorly illuminated new moon. They landed on friendly ground, at the coastal rice plantation where Marion's sister lived. Upon reaching the undefended edge of town, with no word from the cavalry, they began to fear discovery from the approaching daylight and decided to attack around 4 a.m. They hoped to catch the men in barracks fleeing to the confines of the redoubt. But the Americans wasted the element of surprise on smaller objectives. They managed to capture the garrison's commander in bed in his quarters as well as two other officers, one of whom was found sleeping in a tavern where he had spent the night drinking. All three were immediately paroled. But rather than come out and fight, the rest of the alerted garrison stayed put, barricading themselves inside their housing or the sturdy fort.

By the time Lee and Marion arrived near dawn, conditions were not conducive to an assault. Once the sun came up they could be sniped at by enemy sharpshooters, and without artillery they could not breach the fort. They decided to withdraw and retreated to Murray's Ferry on the Santee. As Lee would later write, "Marion and Lee were singularly tender of the lives of their soldiers; and preferred moderate success, with little loss, to the most brilliant enterprise, with the destruction of many of their troops."

In a letter to Greene afterward Lee took credit for the operation, reporting that "I" completely surprised the garrison at Georgetown, with no mention of Marion. In his memoirs he would recall that the plan, although "conceived with ingenuity," was too complicated to succeed. In his own report to Greene, Marion explained that despite "the little success" he and Lee achieved, the attack had suffered from lack of artillery. Characteristically, he praised his co-commanding officer, writing that "Col. Lee's enterprising genius promises much." Britain's Balfour, for one, was impressed with both of them, calling them "two very enterprising officers" in a letter to Clinton.

Although the attack on Georgetown failed to accomplish its main objective, it nonetheless terrorized the British such that they were forced to continue devoting resources to protecting that town that Cornwallis might have used offensively elsewhere. The operation also proved that the militia and regulars could work together: Marion's men saw the virtue of discipline as exhibited by Lee's troops, and the Continentals were impressed with what the militia could accomplish based on their superior knowledge of the territory. The groundwork was laid for future mutual operations between the Swamp Fox and Light-Horse Harry.

When they settled back into camp Marion and Lee found waiting for them letters from Greene conveying the most thrilling news of the entire war for patriots in the South. On January 17, at a place called the Cowpens in northwestern South Carolina, Daniel Morgan, the "Old Waggoner," had delivered a crushing blow to the man he called "Benny" Tarleton. With a combined Continental and backcountry militia force, Morgan pulled off that rarest of military maneuvers—a double envelopment, or simultaneous pincer attack on both enemy flanks. (Its most famous use had been at the Battle of Cannae in 216 B.C., where Hannibal overwhelmed the Romans.)

Morgan deployed his one thousand men in three successive lines of defenders, each stronger than the last. He placed a row of militia sharpshooters up front, with instructions to fire two or three volleys before falling back. The idea was to lure the British into thinking that the militia was doing what they usually did—and what they had done at Camden: panic and flee at the first sight of approaching bayonets. The charging redcoats, believing they were commencing another rout, would then run into a second line, also militia, commanded by Andrew

Pickens.* The two militia lines were backed up by a third line of Continental infantry, with William Washington's cavalry in reserve.

The strategy—aided by a bit of luck—worked beyond measure: caught in a series of killing zones, Tarleton's force of 1,050 suffered 85 percent losses: 100 dead, 229 wounded, and 600 captured and missing along with two field cannon, 800 muskets, and 100 dragoon horses. Only Tarleton and some of his mounted officers and dragoons managed to escape. In an hour of fighting Cornwallis had lost a quarter of his army and all of his light infantry. "The late affair has almost broke my heart," he wrote to Rawdon afterward.

Among the poorest-performing British soldiers at Cowpens were the two hundred raw recruits for the 7th Regiment of Foot (Royal Fusiliers)—the ones Marion had so frightened in the engagement with McLeroth at Halfway Swamp a month earlier. Cornwallis had initially assigned them to protect Ninety-Six, then allowed Tarleton to take them with him to the Cowpens. But having panicked at Halfway Swamp, they had not yet learned how to fight. When faced with a counter-bayonet charge by the Continentals, the Fusiliers threw down their arms and begged for mercy. Remarkably, Morgan prevented his men from giving them "Tarleton's Quarter." The Americans were fortunate to have won, for Tarleton's officers and men went into battle that day with orders to give no quarter as they did not expect any for themselves.

Greene was of course elated at the news from Cowpens. "After this nothing will appear difficult," he wrote to Marion. He spoke a little too soon, for an infuriated Cornwallis, determined to recover the six hundred prisoners taken at Cowpens, set off to destroy Morgan's army before training his sights on Greene. But Morgan managed both to elude him and to reunite with Greene. The two American commanders then headed north toward Virginia for supplies and reinforcements, with Cornwallis, now joined by Leslie's fifteen hundred men, in hot pursuit. Burning his wagon train to lighten his load—including, to his men's chagrin, all of their

---

* Pickens, who took British protection after Charleston fell, had recently rejoined the patriot cause because he viewed the British as having violated the terms of his parole by destroying his property.

rum—Cornwallis would chase Greene through North Carolina in hopes of forcing a decisive battle he was sure he would win. It would become a race to see whether Greene, whose army still was too weak to risk a head-on engagement, could reach the Dan River separating North Carolina and Virginia before Cornwallis caught up with him. If so, Greene could cross it to safety; if not, Cornwallis might well end the war in the South.

For Marion the Americans' great victory at Cowpens was a mixed blessing. It resulted in Greene leaving South Carolina, which sent shudders through the Whig community around Snow's Island and along the Santee, complicating Marion's recruiting efforts. Adding to this unwelcome development, on January 31 Greene recalled Lee and his Legion from South Carolina to join him in his "race to the Dan." Marion was once again on his own.

There was at least some good news. On January 29, while at Cordes's Plantation on the Santee, Marion had sent another set of terse instructions to Captain John Postell:

> You will cross Santee river with twenty-five men, and make a forced march to Wadboo Bridge, there burn all the British stores of every kind. . . . After effecting my purpose at Wadboo, it will not be out of your way to come by Monck's Corner, and destroy any stores or wagons you may find there. . . . The destruction of all the British stores in the above-mentioned places is of the greatest consequence to us, and only requires boldness and expedition. Take care that your men do not get at liquor, or clog themselves with plunder so as to endanger their retreat.

Captain Postell and his brother, Major (later Colonel) James Postell, instantly carried off the mission without a hitch. Commanding separate companies of thirty-five men each, they burned large quantities of enemy supplies at Manigault's Ferry above Nelson's and at Wadboo Bridge and Keithfield Plantation, both near Monck's Corner. John Postell took thirty-three prisoners and destroyed twenty casks of the enemy's rum—rivaled only by salt as the staple most craved by the armies on both sides.

Whether Marion's men, who had not had any rations of rum for five months, adhered to his admonition not to indulge in any of the spirits is to be doubted.

Marion reported on the raids to Greene, who replied by asking that Marion "give my particular thanks to Major and Capt. Postell for the spirit and address with which they executed your orders over the Santee." It was no small matter to Greene, as the supplies the Postell brothers destroyed would otherwise have made their way to Cornwallis's army, which was being forced to live off a land already picked clean. As for the Postells, as William Dobein James would write, to them "nothing indeed appeared difficult."

Greene's letter, sent from North Carolina on February 11, included a more ominous note that did not sit well with Marion. General Thomas Sumter, Greene reported, had just returned to action and wished to call out the militia. Greene asked Marion to communicate with Sumter "and concert with him your future operations." In other words, the Swamp Fox now had to answer to the Gamecock.

14

Hound and Fox

Thomas Sumter had been absent at Cowpens and had with-held his men from the battle. He was miffed at Nathanael Greene for having placed Daniel Morgan—and not him—in command of the Catawba region in the run-up to the battle. Sumter had even gone so far as to tell his militia not to obey any order from Morgan un-less it came through him. A strong believer in the notion of "states' rights" before that phrase entered general usage, Sumter considered himself under the authority of only one man: South Carolina governor John Rutledge. If Sumter did not like the orders he received from Greene or any other Continental officer, then he felt no obligation to obey them.

From a strictly legal standpoint Sumter was on defensible ground, as the Articles of Confederation, formally ratified in March 1781, did not give the federal government clear power over the states' armed forces. Greene questioned that interpretation but felt constrained to recognize Sumter's seniority over Marion under South Carolina's military hierarchy (even though Marion still held a Continental commission and Sumter had resigned his in 1778). From a more practical standpoint Greene also needed to keep the influential Sumter happy, and he knew that Marion, as a dutiful soldier, would respect the chain of command. So would An-drew Pickens, promoted to brigadier general by Rutledge for his part in defeating Tarleton at Cowpens. And so Greene wrote flattering letters to Sumter praising his leadership qualities and placing Marion and Pickens at his disposal.

Sumter lost little time asserting his authority over Marion. With Cornwallis off chasing Greene through North Carolina, Sumter decided the time was right for attacking the smaller British outposts in South Carolina, and he asked for Marion's help. Sumter had his eyes on three particular posts: Fort Granby on the Congaree River above where it meets the Santee; William Thomson's plantation, known as Belleville, where the British had built a stockade thirty miles downriver from Fort Granby; and Fort Watson, a recently established outpost on Scott's Lake, ten miles above Nelson's Ferry. Sumter reckoned he could take them absent interference from Lord Rawdon's forces at Camden, so he asked Marion—politely, at first—to distract Rawdon from that design. "If you can, with propriety, advance southwardly so as to cooperate, or correspond with me, it might have the best of consequences," Sumter wrote on February 20 from near Fort Granby, to which he had laid siege the previous day.

Marion was then camped about twenty miles upstream from Snow's Island on Jeffries Creek at the confluence of the Pee Dee. Ironically, he had been driven there by Rawdon, the man Sumter was now asking Marion to distract. Marion's retreat to that location followed on the heels of his unsuccessful effort to enlist new militia west of the Santee, where he had ventured beyond his normal territory. Marion blamed the failure on Captain William Snipes, the man who had so valiantly captured Samuel Tynes. The hot-tempered, uncontrollable Snipes had been plundering the civilian population in that area, creating so many enemies that Marion's recruiting efforts there proved fruitless. What's more, Snipes, who was off on his own at this point, was claiming that he was acting under orders of Marion. An enraged Marion soon published a proclamation against looting, stating that certain unidentified parties not associated with his brigade were responsible and that once he published their names, anyone who found them was free to "put them to death" without being prosecuted. A few days later he issued another order stating that any persons who took provisions from a plantation without written authority from him would be deemed plunderers and would suffer accordingly.

His recruiting venture over, Marion headed back in the direction of Snow's Island. Along the way he was chased by Rawdon. Like Tarleton,

Rawdon narrowly missed catching the Swamp Fox, who this time escaped across Scape Ore Swamp southeast of Camden. And like Tarleton, Rawdon ended his chase to go after Sumter, whose presence to the west posed a threat to Ninety-Six. Rawdon reported Marion's strength as three hundred, all mounted, and boasted to Cornwallis, much as Tarleton had, that he was taking measures to "prevent Marion from troubling us much more." Rawdon did not specify what those measures were, but they would become apparent soon enough.

Moving from place to place at this point, Marion did not receive Sumter's summons for help until February 26. In the meantime the impatient Gamecock had gone forward with two abortive missions. On February 21 Sumter lifted his siege of Fort Granby, undertaken without artillery, when he heard that Rawdon was coming to its relief. The next day, after a failed attempt to storm the stockade at Belleville, Sumter withdrew, leaving behind a detachment to watch the site; they were quickly driven off as soon as a fresh British detachment arrived from Camden.

When Marion finally received Sumter's letter on February 26, he wrote back to say that the British position to the west was too strong for him to come to Sumter's aid just yet but that he would try to get as close as possible. In fact, Marion was not enthusiastic about cooperating with Sumter. He considered him a rash showboater and viewed his plan to attack the recently reinforced posts as a fool's errand. In addition, Marion's men did not like straying so far from their homes, which were many miles to the east. But Marion recognized an order when he saw one. He moved more than a hundred miles west toward Sumter, although without the same sense of urgency that had marked his earlier raids.

Again Sumter could not wait. He impetuously struck near Fort Watson on February 28 but had to call off the action after losing eighteen killed. It was his third consecutive failed attack on a British post in a week. Later that same day he wrote Marion from near the Great Savannah above Nelson's Ferry to reiterate his request to join him. "I shall wait impatiently for the happiness of an interview with you," he told Marion. But although they were less than a day's march from each other, the two partisan leaders failed to connect.

The next day, March 1, upon hearing that a British force was headed toward him, Sumter took flight north to the High Hills of Santee, grabbed his paralytic wife and their son, and rode another forty miles to Bradley's Plantation beyond the Black River. Marion had made his way to the same vicinity, but while Sumter was heading north, Marion moved south toward the Santee. They probably missed each other by a matter of hours and may have literally passed in the night.

Not realizing just how close they had been, Sumter wrote Marion again on March 4 from Bradley's to express disappointment that he was "so far out of the way of meeting with you at a time when there is the greatest occasion for it." But he still wanted Marion to link up with him. "I shall therefore remain at or near this place for that purpose," Sumter wrote, "and beg that you may come this way with all possible speed; if not convenient with all your men to facilitate an interview, please to come with a few."

Sumter waited another day, and when Marion did not come, he took his 250 men farther north, along with his wife and child. But along the way they stumbled upon a British force under Major Thomas Fraser that Rawdon had dispatched to intercept Sumter before he could join Marion. Fraser's unit inflicted heavy casualties on Sumter's group, which fled and continued their retreat north to the Waxhaws.

The Gamecock's campaign to capture British outposts had ended in failure. It had been reckless to attack the posts without cannon to bombard them. His men also believed they had been misled as to Rawdon's strength, for everywhere they turned, a large British detachment out of Camden seemed to appear. And they thought Sumter had used— or abused—them to rescue his family. Sumter was forced to explain himself in a long talk to his brigade, after which he released the militia to their homes for spring plowing. In a letter to Greene he made clear that he had received "no assistance from Genl. Marion," and later he would blame Marion directly for not helping in his failed attacks on the posts.

His shoulder still hurting from the buckshot that had struck him at Blackstock's in November, Sumter took his family up to the New Acquisition District just below Charlotte. There he would nurse his actual wounds, lick his figurative ones, and harbor a grudge against Francis Marion.

WITH SUMTER GONE, Marion was again the lone patriot military leader operating in South Carolina. Greene, who had successfully crossed the Dan River into Virginia ahead of Cornwallis, was now back in North Carolina, reinforced and resupplied, preparing to engage the British army in open battle. Lee, Pickens, and William Washington were all either with or assisting Greene, leaving Marion with no possibility of reinforcement. As a result, Lord Rawdon was now in a position to concentrate on Marion, and as he told Cornwallis on March 7, he intended to "press him to the utmost."

To carry out that task Rawdon chose a man who would prove to be Marion's most persistent and adept adversary among all the various British commanders he faced: the redundantly named John Watson Tadwell-Watson. The London-born, thirty-two-year-old Watson was a lieutenant colonel in the elite 3rd Regiment of Foot Guards (Scots). He enlisted in the war in America to escape his gambling debts. After serving three years in the North he arrived in Charleston in December 1780 to join Leslie's forces marching to reinforce Cornwallis. While on winter garrison in Philadelphia in 1778 he had run a fellow officer through the arm in a sword duel, and by the time he came south he had acquired a reputation of being difficult to work with.

It seems that none of the British high commanders wanted him. Rather than take him along to North Carolina with Leslie, Cornwallis assigned Watson to Rawdon in Camden, telling Rawdon, "I know I do not make you a great present in the person of Colonel Watson." When Rawdon agreed to take him, Cornwallis expressed relief to Tarleton that neither of them would have to deal with that "plague." Then Rawdon decided he didn't need Watson with him at Camden either and instead gave him the job of dealing with the rebel militia between Camden and Georgetown, meaning Marion.

Watson was, in effect, to lead the counterinsurgency. He did not relish the assignment, but Balfour told him that having an independent command was more prestigious than being a mere cog in the regular army. Unfamiliar with the southern terrain or guerrilla warfare, Watson asked a superior how to deal tactically with the irregular forces, to which the officer just shrugged his shoulders.

On his way to joining Cornwallis, Leslie dropped off Watson's men near Nelson's Ferry, where Watson joined them on Christmas Day. In taking post at Nelson's, Watson was replacing the hapless McLeroth, who had failed to deal aggressively enough with Marion. Watson made his first order of business the establishment of a new outpost overlooking the Santee River to serve as a base of operations. For his location he chose Wright's Bluff on Scott's Lake, ten miles upriver. There, atop an ancient Indian mound, he built a small fort and named it for himself.

It was Watson's force that successfully repelled Sumter's attack near the fort on February 28. After Sumter's departure north, Watson was ready to put into action the measures Rawdon had promised Cornwallis would "prevent Marion from troubling us much more." It was a closely guarded secret, as reflected in Balfour's note to a fellow officer on March 5, revealing that "a movement is intended against Marrion [*sic*], as little intelligence as is possible should be given of the movement."

The plan was for Watson to move south and east along the Santee in pursuit of Marion; meanwhile Lieutenant Colonel Welbore Ellis Doyle would bring his loyalist provincials from Camden in the direction of Snow's Island, where the British had a general idea of the location of Marion's camp. Watson would pursue Marion from the front and Doyle would attack from the rear in a lethal pincer movement that would trap the Swamp Fox in his lair. This time Rawdon was expecting Watson and Doyle to succeed where a long list of others had failed: Wemyss, Ganey, Tynes, Tarleton, McLeroth, and Rawdon himself.

On March 7 Watson moved out from his fort in search of Marion and arrived that day at Blakely's Plantation near Kingstree. It was a formidable force. He had with him at least 500 men, including his own battalion of more than 300 provincial light infantry, predominantly veterans from New York and New Jersey; remnants of McLeroth's old 64th Foot; 150 mounted loyalist militia under Lieutenant Colonel Henry Richbourg; and 20 dragoons from Harrison's South Carolina Rangers led by Major John and Captain Samuel Harrison. Watson also took with him two three-pounders (grasshoppers) Rawdon had given him. Watson left the fort to be guarded only by forty of his most incapacitated soldiers, an indication of how high a priority he placed on his search-and-destroy mission in the countryside.

When Watson moved out, Marion was not far away. He was camped along the Santee, probably at Mount Hope, the plantation of John Cantey, the brother-in-law of Thomas Sumter. Marion had learned of Watson's presence from one of his scouts, Captain Zach Cantey, of the same family, who spotted Watson's campfires near Nelson's Ferry and rushed to warn the partisan general. That information partially explains why Marion did not hurry to join Sumter at this time; Watson was coming after him in full force, and self-preservation was his main concern.

With three or four hundred horsemen, Marion had the cavalry advantage, which was important in the southern theater. Watson had greater total numbers, a higher percentage of veterans, and the benefit of artillery. On paper they were about evenly matched.

As usual Marion sought to compensate for his lack of numerical superiority with the element of surprise. On the morning of March 8 he took his brigade by rapid march to Wyboo (Wiboo) Swamp, about halfway between Murray's and Nelson's Ferries on the Santee, and set an ambush on a causeway passage there.* Watson was not fooled, as scouts (locals under Harrison or Richbourg) had informed him that the causeway was a likely spot for Marion to lie in wait.

When Watson arrived at the swamp, around 11 a.m., he and Marion sat atop their horses, staring at each other across the causeway. Behind them were, respectively, Watson's magnificently uniformed troops, among the world's finest, and Marion and his poorly equipped men in homespun. With the partisan commander were his stalwarts: the Horry brothers, Hugh Giles, Major John James, and others who had been there from the beginning. He was in familiar territory, not far from his Pond Bluff home. This was to be High Noon for Marion's brigade, the moment that would separate all that had come before from all that lay ahead. There would be no hit-and-run raid at Wyboo, no guerrilla ambush, and

---

*The site is now submerged under Lake Marion.

no turning back. The time had come for Marion's men to test their mettle in open battle.

Watson started the engagement by sending Colonel Richbourg and his Tory horsemen charging along the quarter-mile causeway toward the patriots. Richbourg had once served in South Carolina's Whig militia and was married to a member of the patriotic Cantey family of Sumter's wife. But he turned into a staunch Tory after the rebels plundered his home, and thus he welcomed the chance to lead the attack.

Although he had not gained the advantage of surprise, Marion still could not resist a little sleight of hand. He retreated with most of his men to the woods, several hundred yards back, to prepare, and he placed Peter Horry's cavalry in advance at the swamp. A few moments later, as described by an American participant in the action, the enemy "came dashing up, expecting to find us all in confusion and disorder, but to their astonishment we were ready for the attack, and perceiving this, they called a halt, at which time Marion and Horry ordered a charge." Horry's cavalry went hurtling forward to engage Richbourg's mounted militia and pushed them back toward the line of Watson's main body. Then they received what none of Marion's men had faced in a land battle before—cannon fire. Watson's two field pieces sprayed Horry's men with grapeshot, a cluster of small metal balls packed in a canvas bag or metal canister that spread out from the muzzle on firing, giving a devastating effect similar to a giant shotgun. It was especially effective when launched against men in a confined space, as the patriots were on the causeway. Horry's men were thrown back and dislodged, at which point Watson sent Harrison's dragoons in pursuit.

Private Gavin James, a second cousin of the major and a man of gigantic size, came forward to dispute their passage and slew two or three Tories with his musket and bayonet, dragging one of them fifty yards as the dying man clutched the barrel of James's gun. At that point Marion ordered another cavalry charge, led by Captains Daniel Conyers and James McCauley, and in hand-to-hand combat Conyers killed one of Harrison's officers.

His horsemen driven back by the patriot cavalry, Watson now sent his infantry racing with bayonets toward Marion's dismounted militia. A British bayonet charge, too, was something Marion's brigade had yet to experience. Marion realized his men could not withstand such an assault, so he ordered them to remount their horses and follow him in retreat back across the causeway, clearing it for Watson's passage.

Wyboo Swamp was the opening salvo in what would become a running, two-week battle between Watson's and Marion's forces—the first time Marion would stay engaged with the same adversary over an extended period. Watson would become to Marion as Cornwallis had been to Greene, and as Grant would be to Lee many decades later—a numerically superior force in relentless pursuit, determined to bring the enemy to a conclusive battle. It was to be known as Marion's Bridges Campaign and would mark his transition from a pure guerrilla warrior to an assayer of more conventional tactics.

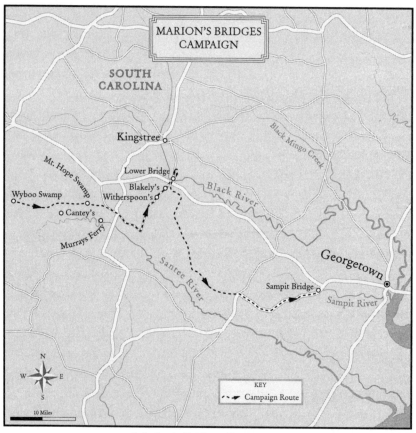

Marion's Bridges Campaign

Patriot and British assessments of the impact of the initial clash at Wyboo diverged widely, as they often did after battles that had mixed results. "Thus were the Tories intimidated at the outset," wrote William Dobein James. British soldier Henry Nase recorded it differently in his diary: "We had a skirmish with Marion and his gang of robbers, but they were soon dispersed, after which we marched peaceably to Cantey's Plantation." (Marion had moved from Cantey's to another location.) In reality Marion had merely checked Watson's progress, though Watson had failed to cut off the Swamp Fox's retreat, leaving him free to fight another day.

Before resuming their running battle, Watson returned to a running series of correspondence between the British command and Marion that was nearly as testy. It had begun a month or so prior when, in retaliation for the Postell brothers' raids on their supplies, the British seized the plantation of their father, John Postell Sr., who was on parole there, and carried him off to prison in Georgetown. On February 22 Marion wrote to propose a prisoner exchange to Captain John Saunders, who was installed as commandant of Georgetown after the capture of his predecessor in the combined Lee and Marion mission in January. Not being able to feed and care for the prisoners John Postell had taken at Monck's Corner at the end of January, who were being held at Snow's Island, Marion offered to exchange all thirty-three of them for four named rebels. Among them was Postell's father, then in his sixties and ailing. Marion told Saunders that he wanted to exchange Postell Sr. "on account of his age, and hope humanity will induce you to treat him like a gentleman."

Even as Marion was writing, the younger John Postell had begun taking matters into his own hands. On February 21, while Marion was off to the west, summoned by Sumter, Postell led a militia force east to reclaim the family plantation about twenty miles north of Georgetown. Through his knowledge of the grounds Postell avoided the sentinels, took possession of the kitchen, and demanded that the enemy commander, Captain James DePeyster, surrender. When he refused, Postell set fire to the kitchen and threatened to burn the whole house down, at which point DePeyster and his twenty-nine British soldiers surrendered unconditionally.

In response to Marion's letter of the 22nd, Saunders agreed to Marion's proposed exchange but said that given the recent capture of DePeyster (a member of a wealthy Tory family from New York and by reputation one of the handsomest men in the British army), he now had to be part of the deal. Saunders then promptly withdrew that offer, stating that he would not agree to a "partial" exchange, only a general one for all prisoners the two of them respectively held, except that he still wanted to exchange DePeyster for any patriot prisoner Marion wished to name. By that time, however, Marion had already shipped DePeyster north to a Continental prison camp.

Marion then made two major miscalculations. First, although Saunders had rejected a partial exchange, Marion went ahead and had four British prisoners fetched from Snow's Island and sent them to Georgetown to be exchanged for the four Americans named in his earlier letter. He told Saunders that he would think about a broader exchange. Marion was betting that Saunders would not refuse to make the more limited trade to which they had originally agreed once the four British prisoners were laid at his doorstep. He bet wrong.

A worse mistake was letting John Postell accompany the four British prisoners to Georgetown. During the first week of March, Postell went under a white flag of truce to negotiate a further exchange. But upon his arrival Saunders not only refused the prisoner exchange but seized Postell and took him prisoner. Saunders claimed that Postell had violated his parole by taking British protection after Charleston and then joining Marion's brigade.

As to the parole, Postell argued that he was justified in breaking it because the British or Tories had stripped him of all his property in contravention of the terms of the parole. And Marion contended that parole violation or not, the British were bound to honor the white flag. Nonetheless, given Postell's repeated, successful raids on British garrisons and his recent capture of the popular DePeyster, both he and Marion should have anticipated that the British would use any excuse to nab him.

A livid Marion protested to Saunders, but to no avail. Marion went over Saunders's head to Balfour, the commander at Charleston. But Balfour, with a reputation for severe treatment of rebels, backed up his subordinate officer. Marion also wrote to Watson on March 7, enclosing his correspondence with Saunders and Balfour and broadly hinting that, contrary to his inclinations, he would be forced to respond in kind to the violation of his flag as well as to the hanging of three of his men for supposed crimes. He sent the letters to Watson by another flag of truce, this time accompanied by an armed party—which, as Marion acknowledged, normally forfeits the white flag protection—but he regarded it as necessary because he could no longer trust the British to respect his flag.

On March 9, the day after the encounter at Wyboo Swamp, Watson was camped at Cantey's Plantation, where Marion had stayed two nights before. The British colonel sat down to pen a response to Marion, who had moved to another area plantation. Watson's lengthy letter, written to someone he clearly regarded as an untutored bumpkin, was dripping with condescension and sarcasm. He feigned surprise that Marion should send a letter under a flag of truce with an armed escort but said he was even more surprised to find Marion complaining of violations of international law. Watson wrote that it would be as difficult to find a single example of the British acting contrary to the rules of civilized warfare as it would be to find any instance in which the patriot side had properly observed those rules. As the most recent example he cited Thomas Sumter's men's refusal to give quarter to several British soldiers who had laid down their arms after surrendering their wagon train. "A few days after, we took six of his people," Watson wrote, then chillingly added, "Inquire how they were treated." Watson refused to apologize for hanging parole breakers or for the detention of Postell, claiming that both were justified by the law of nations. ("It seems the colonel had reference to the code of barbarous nations," William Dobein James would later quip.)

As for Marion's threat of retaliation, Watson said that as long as the Americans behaved with the same generosity that Britons could boast was characteristic of their nation, then they would receive benevolent treatment in return. "Men like his Majesty's troops, fighting from principle for the good of their country, with hearts full of conscious integrity, are fearless of any consequences," he intoned. "War itself bears with it calamities sufficient. Take care then, sir, that you do not, by improper behavior to our people who may from its chance of war become your prisoners, add to its natural horrors."

Marion made no immediate reply but ordered his nightly patrols to continue shooting at Watson's sentinels and pickets. Tensions were thus high going into the next engagement between the two commanders, which took place on March 9 or 10 at Mount Hope Swamp Bridge near Murray's Ferry. The bridge was east of Wyboo Swamp and on the way for Watson to either Kingstree or Georgetown. Marion arrived at the bridge first and tore it down, placing Hugh Horry's men on the opposite bank to contest Watson's passage. Again Watson's artillery and greater manpower allowed him to scatter the rebels and clear the way for him to cross the bridge after building it back up. Again Marion had forestalled Watson's progress and managed to scamper away with his brigade intact.

Still, all the momentum was with Watson at this point. He was moving his infantry slowly but inexorably after Marion. His firepower was proving to have the edge over Marion's cavalry. Marion could not risk a general engagement, yet he could not keep running forever. He needed somehow to turn the tide of the campaign.

His chance to do so would come at another bridge along the way, where he would finally be able to use one of his greatest—and hitherto unrecognized—assets.

15

Fox and Hound

*M*arion was not yet sure which way Watson was headed. The British were on the road to Georgetown, but they could well be going to Kingstree, where they would be within striking distance of Snow's Island. If left unattended at Kingstree, Watson would be in a position to wreak havoc on the Williamsburg and Snow's Island communities and their Whig inhabitants. Marion could be isolated and cut off from his support network. But maybe Watson would simply follow Marion wherever he went. On that hunch and to divert Watson from Kingstree, Marion decided to head east from Mount Hope Swamp, down the old Santee Road in the direction of Georgetown.

It was a calculated risk. But as Marion correctly guessed, Watson chased after him, passing right by the roads leading north to Kingstree to trail Marion east. Then, just as suddenly, Watson stopped his pursuit. On March 12 he halted along the Santee Road, near present-day Gourdin, turned back, and headed up toward Kingstree, less than twenty miles away. Once he crossed the Black River at Lower Bridge, five miles south of Kingstree, he would be free to overrun the Williamsburg area.

It looked as if Marion had miscalculated again. But he reacted quickly. Upon learning from scouts that Watson had turned around, he detached Major John James with seventy men, thirty of whom were McCottry's riflemen, to destroy the bridge and take post there. Marion was counting on James, aboard the brigade's swiftest horses, to outrace Watson's men, who were mostly on foot and encumbered by artillery. In the meantime Marion would get there with the rest of his men as soon as he could.

This was the pivotal moment of the Bridges Campaign. As James's son William wrote, "The pass of the Lower Bridge was now to decide the fate of Williamsburg." The men Marion chose for the mission were from the area and anxious to defend it. Major James and his men sped toward the bridge, taking shortcuts through the woods with the benefit of their local knowledge and arriving ahead of Watson. They dismantled the planks in the middle of the bridge and set fire to the supporting cords at the eastern end. McCottry's riflemen settled in on the east side of the Black River, nestling in the woods just beyond a low, marshy area.

Watson would be approaching the bridge from the west bank, fifty yards away, which was considerably elevated. With the bridge out of commission the best place for Watson to cross was a ford a short way below the bridge. Knowing this, the patriot sharpshooters placed themselves with a view across the bridge and of the ford. The men with muskets offered flanking protection for the sharpshooters as well as further defense of the ford. According to James, by the time the bridge work was done and the riflemen all deployed, Marion rode up with the rest of the brigade to take position in the rear. Then they waited for Watson.

Soon the Briton emerged, immediately grasping that the way across was via the shallow ford. But first he would need to clear the passage of enemy fire. He wheeled out his two artillery pieces and launched grapeshot down upon the riflemen on the opposite bank. At both Wyboo and Mount Hope Swamps cannon fire had allowed him to force crossings, but it would not work this time. Because the cannons were high on a hill, they could not be aimed low enough to strike the sunken eastern bank filled with American rifles. The grapeshot passed harmlessly over the heads of Marion's men, striking the tall pines across the river halfway up their trunks or falling with a thud. When Watson's artillerists tried to move the cannon lower down the bank for a more level shot McCottry's marksmen drove them off.

McCottry's unit was armed with the American long hunting rifles, which they personally owned. In England only the upper class hunted, but among American colonials hunting was more than a sport; it was a way of life. The long rifles had two disadvantages and one important

advantage compared with the smoothbore muskets the British used.*
Unlike muskets, rifles could not support a bayonet and took longer to
reload—a minute or two compared with fifteen seconds for a musket.
This made riflemen vulnerable to the customary British bayonet charge.
However, the American rifles were far more accurate at longer ranges,
owing to their spiral grooves that spun the ball as it left the muzzle. A
musket was accurate up to a maximum of only about fifty yards, whereas
a rifle was deadly at two hundred yards and could work at up to three or
four hundred. If a sharpshooter could fire his rifle from under cover of
woods, safe from the opponent's bayonets, he could be quite effective,
especially at picking off officers who easily stood out in battle. And in
irregular warfare the enemy's leaders are considered fair targets.

Determined yet to cross the river, Watson sent his men marching
toward the ford. An advance unit waded into the stream, led by an officer waving a sword. He was promptly shot in the chest. As others of
Watson's men tried to cross, they too were rained upon with rifle fire and
fled in disorder. Four men returned to carry off their wounded officer and
were cut down as well. Watson called off the effort. After collecting his
dead and wounded, he took up headquarters a mile or so south of the
bridge at the plantation of John Witherspoon, whose daughter was engaged to Marion's brigade captain Daniel Conyers. Either she or another
of the Witherspoon ladies, all devoted Whigs, overheard Watson say
that night that "he never saw such shooting in his life."

The shooting wasn't over. The next day, while camped on higher
ground below the ford, Marion sent McCottry's men back across the
river to harass Watson at Witherspoon's, where they recommenced firing
upon Watson's pickets and sentinels. Sergeant McDonald, the man who
had bayoneted Ganey outside Georgetown, climbed a tree and shot
British Lieutenant Torriano through the knee from a distance of three
hundred yards.

At the mercy of Marion's snipers, Watson withdrew half a mile north
to Blakely's Plantation, where he remained on the south (west) side of

---

*The British regular infantry generally was armed with the .75-caliber, British-
issue Brown Bess flintlock musket, whereas the American Continentals were issued the French .69-caliber Charleville musket, which many militia used as well.

the Black River. Blakely's was in an open field rather than among trees, so McCottry's riflemen no longer had a safe perch from which to shoot.

From Blakely's, on March 15 an annoyed Watson resumed his acerbic correspondence with Marion. Mocking the use of armed guards by which Marion had sent his last letter, Watson sent his through a "neutral person . . . a little boy of John Witherspoon's." He further chided Marion, saying that "the very extraordinary method you took of sending the letter I received from you makes it rather difficult to guess in what way you mean to carry on this war." Watson then asked Marion to grant Torriano and other wounded men safe passage to Charleston, where they could receive better care, to which Marion promptly agreed. As for Watson's snide comments, Marion responded matter-of-factly. "In answer to your letter, I wish to carry on this war as usual, with all civilized nations," he wrote, adding, "you may be assured that I will not act in any other way, than what I find is done by the British troops."

Seeking the last word, Watson wrote back immediately to complain of a series of recent alleged Whig atrocities. He made no apology for the British practice of burning enemy homes and property, telling Marion that it was "thought right and is customary in all countries."

At that point Marion stopped corresponding with Watson and the other British officers. He would entertain no complaints from them as long as John Postell remained a prisoner, threatened with execution. Marion did not necessarily disagree with the notion that parole breakers or others found to have switched sides were subject to being hanged; indeed, although he would not execute captured enemy combatants merely because they had committed heinous acts in the past, he was willing to hang persons viewed as having acted deceitfully, such as spies, patriots who had turned traitor, or civilians or slaves who had provided secret aid and comfort to the British. He was not unusual in that respect, as officers on both sides agreed that those engaged in treacherous behavior took their lives in their hands.

But Postell was different. Even if he broke his parole, Marion thought he had been unfairly captured, and lest the British think about executing him, Marion made clear that he was willing to retaliate in kind. He had his men detain and hold Cornet Thomas Merritt of the loyalist Queen's Rangers when he came to Marion's Dunham's Bluff camp near Snow's

Island under a flag of truce bearing a letter from Balfour regarding the Postell matter. Both Balfour and Saunders protested loudly, but Marion ignored them. And although his strategy did not succeed in getting Postell released, it did keep the British from executing him.

Meanwhile by March 18 Watson's position at Blakely's had become untenable. After pursuing Marion fruitlessly for nearly two weeks, his men were tired, sick, and hungry. Foraging the countryside was problematic, for when his men ventured out they were threatened by Marion's snipers and spied on by hostile civilians. Watson had heard nothing from Doyle, as no British messengers could get through the surrounding ring of Whigs. Watson decided he'd had enough. He weighted his bodies and sank them in an abandoned quarry in the Black River, loaded his wounded onto wagons, and headed south. Several miles below Blakely's he came to a boggy swamp where Marion had destroyed three bridges and felled trees across the causeway. In case he harbored any designs on Snow's Island at that point, Watson's way toward it was now impeded. He could either stay at the swamp and fight, or he could run. He ran. He took his men farther south, through open pine lands to the Santee Road, along which he had chased Marion ten days earlier.

Watson was now forty miles equidistant from Fort Watson and Georgetown. Marion, coming up on his rear, was between him and the fort, so returning there, over difficult terrain, was not an option. Georgetown also had what Watson's men needed most: rum, salt, shoes, and ammunition. He sent his infantry double-timing down the road toward Georgetown. As Watson's soldiers scurried away, Marion attacked them from behind while Peter Horry, with the cavalry and riflemen, harassed them in front and on their flanks. In this mad dash Marion and Watson had switched positions; the fox had become the hound.

On March 20 Watson reached the Sampit River Bridge, nine miles from Georgetown. Peter Horry's horsemen, sent ahead by Marion, had destroyed the span there too. Marion had spent the first part of the campaign tearing up bridges to impede his British pursuers; now he was doing the same to prevent them from escaping him.

Watson's desperate soldiers went plunging into the river. He was nothing if not resourceful—his artillerists blasted grapeshot to stem Marion's attack from the rear, and his veteran foot soldiers flashed their shiny bayonets at Horry's dragoons on the opposite bank, causing them to fall back when a frightened officer, John Scott, who was stationed with patriot riflemen, called for a retreat. (Years later Scott claimed he'd been "outflanked.") Still, before retreating, the American riflemen managed to inflict heavy damage on the enemy. Watson got his men across the river, but twenty of them were killed and nearly twice that number wounded. His own horse was shot out from under him.

Marion suffered a single killed. Watson left his dead where they lay, loaded up two wagons full of wounded, and limped back to Georgetown. Marion, his men exhausted as well, chose not to pursue Watson to the British-occupied town.

The Bridges Campaign was at an end. It had showcased Marion at his most brilliant, first in evading and then in demoralizing an enemy blessed with superior numbers and firepower. Watson's casualties in the campaign were in the dozens, whereas Marion's were minimal. On March 21, while camped at Trapier's Plantation just outside Georgetown, Watson complained about Marion's style of warfare. "They will not sleep and fight like gentlemen," Watson told the plantation owner, "but like savages are eternally firing and whooping around us by night, and by day waylaying and popping at us from behind every tree." Had he heard this indictment, Marion might have taken it as a compliment.

HOWEVER MUCH HE may have wanted to let his men rest on their laurels, Marion could not do so for long. After leaving the Georgetown area he headed back along the Pee Dee toward Snow's Island, stopping on the way in the Britton's Neck area to visit the homes of several of his men. But upon arriving at Britton's Ferry around March 26 to set up camp, or on the way there, he received alarming news: Colonel Doyle had found and destroyed Marion's Snow's Island base camp a few miles away.

A local Tory led the Irish-born Doyle and his New York Volunteers there, and they found easy pickings: Marion had left but a skeleton crew there, many of them sick or wounded, while he was out contending with Watson. Colonel Hugh Ervin, in charge of defending Snow's, could put up little of a fight before he dumped the rebels' arms and ammunition into Lynches Creek to keep the enemy from taking them. Ervin and some others escaped the island, leaving fifteen of their number, who were too sick to flee, to be taken prisoner. During the confusion Cornet Merritt, the flag bearer who had been detained a couple of weeks earlier, made his escape from the Bull Pen, the "small, nasty, dark place, made of logs," that Marion's men had constructed to hold prisoners. Marion's Sherwood Forest hiding place was history.

Although Marion did not mention the loss of his base camp in any of his writings, the loyalist press trumpeted it as a major victory. Within a week after the episode Charleston's *Royal Gazette* giddily reported the destruction of "Marion's repository of stores and plunder on Snow's Island" as well as Merritt's daring escape. Even if Marion sought to downplay the military significance of the episode, it was an embarrassment of the type he was more accustomed to inflicting than suffering.

Doyle, knowing Marion was near, did not linger at Snow's. As soon as he learned Doyle had moved upriver a few miles to Witherspoon's Ferry, Marion sent McCottry's mounted riflemen after him. They found him on the opposite (north) side of Lynches Creek, scuttling a ferry boat to slow Marion's expected pursuit. The patriot riflemen on the south bank fired across the river and struck a couple of soldiers; Doyle's musketeers returned the volley to little effect.

Doyle withdrew farther up the river, and Marion gave chase. With Lynches Creek flooded and no boats around, the patriots had to move five miles upstream from Witherspoon's, finally crossing at a shallower ford where they could swim their horses across. By now, around March 28, Doyle was off and running to the west, having received orders to return to Camden. Following the breadcrumb-like trail of baggage, which Doyle had discarded to move faster, Marion caught up with him by March 30 at Willow Grove, in present-day Lynchburg. There the two forces skirmished until nightfall. The next morning Doyle took off west toward Camden, thirty-five miles away, and was back there on April 1. Given Doyle's superior force, Marion did not pursue him further.

That day Marion camped at Burch's Mill on the west bank of the Pee Dee, about twenty-five miles above Snow's Island. From there a clearly

frustrated Marion issued an order that anyone who refused to join his
brigade if called to service would be branded an enemy of the state, with
their property subject to confiscation. But like similar decrees Marion
would issue from time to time, it was intended more as a deterrent than
as an edict to be enforced. As Marion told Peter Horry, a militia officer's
command was a "skulking position"—he dare not deal too severely with
his men for fear of them abandoning him—even worse, they might turn
Tory.

In the meantime Watson, refreshed and reinforced from Georgetown,
had marched north to resume his war with the Swamp Fox. In the first
week of April he reached the Snow's Island area. Emboldened by this
move, Micajah Ganey, recovered from his wounds, brought in two hundred Tories to help Watson crush their mutual foe. As word spread
among the locals that Marion's base camp on Snow's had been destroyed,
Marion's force dropped to 150 and was daily diminishing. Watson was
confident that loyalist supremacy could finally be restored in the Williamsburg area. Arriving at the home of the widow Elizabeth Jenkins
(mother of the Jenkins boys) near Snow's Island on April 7, he even
teased her that Marion had become so discouraged that he had gone over
to the other side and joined Lord Rawdon at Camden, which she refused
to believe.

Marion had not, of course, switched sides, but it was true he was becoming discouraged. He was now dangerously close to Watson, who was
only five miles away with much greater numbers. Marion's ammunition
was down to two rounds per man, most of it having been used up in the
Bridges Campaign and the rest destroyed in the raid on Snow's. He expected none from Greene, who was still in North Carolina. It seemed no
matter how ably his men performed, no matter how nimbly they eluded
their pursuers, the British would not let up until they achieved the total
destruction of his brigade.

Marion held a council of war among his most trusted officers to ask
whether they would follow him if he should decide to retreat over the
mountains into North Carolina, perhaps to join Greene's army. Marion
was not one for making speeches, but one brigade member recalled that
he "made an animated appeal to our patriotism and requested that we
would remain with him longer."

They unanimously resolved to follow wherever he led. The only dissenting vote came from Gavin Witherspoon, who wanted to stay and fight Watson before any more Tories joined him. Marion sympathized with his eager captain but said that without ammunition, fighting was not a viable option.

And then, just as suddenly, the mood in the camp turned joyous. Messengers came in with the electrifying news that General Greene had stymied Cornwallis at Guilford Courthouse in North Carolina. Even better, Greene was heading back to South Carolina with the goal of liberating the state. Then came the best news of all: Light-Horse Harry Lee was on his way to rejoin Marion.

16

"A War of Posts"

*W*ith the news of Greene's return and Lee's approach, Ganey's Tories, who had been so eager to help Watson finish off Marion, melted away in fear. Watson decided to retreat, hoping somehow to make his way to Camden to reinforce Rawdon, who was outnumbered almost two to one by Greene. To speed his flight, Watson dumped his two field pieces into a creek and discarded his heavy baggage. Then he headed back south to Georgetown, taking a circuitous route well out of the way of the American forces.

By April 14 Lee had arrived at Marion's camp at Benbow's Ferry on the Black River. Having been present at Guilford Courthouse, he was able to provide additional color on what happened there. In a classic set-piece battle that Greene called "long, obstinate, and bloody," both sides suffered heavy losses. (Tarleton had two fingers amputated afterward.) Cornwallis had kept the field and the honor of a technical victory. But the victory was Pyrrhic, for in chasing Greene through North Carolina he had far outrun his already precarious supply line to Charleston, and his sick, exhausted, and famished army could not go on. "They had the splendor, we the advantage," Greene wrote to Baron von Steuben.

Cornwallis withdrew his forces to Wilmington, North Carolina, on the coast to recuperate, and when Greene turned south to reenter South Carolina, Cornwallis elected not to follow him. Despairing of the "universal spirit of revolt" that prevailed southward and fearful of the patriot militia who lay between him and Camden, Cornwallis would not return to his former headquarters—he had had enough of South Carolina and its partisans. Leaving Rawdon in charge, Cornwallis abandoned the state forever and moved north to invade Virginia, where he would end up at a place called Yorktown.

Greene understood he needed to take back as much southern territory in British hands as possible because if a peace treaty were signed with Great Britain, then under international law the British could keep whatever ground they controlled. And even if they did not control the countryside due to interference from the partisans, the British still held Charleston as well as the chain of garrisons and forts they had established at Georgetown and throughout the interior of the state.

But with the departure of Cornwallis's army, the British position in South Carolina was more tenuous than appeared on the surface. Although they had eight thousand soldiers in South Carolina to Greene's army of fourteen hundred, most of the British force was concentrated in Charleston, with the rest spread thinly among the various outposts. With eight hundred men at Camden, Rawdon was not strong enough to take on Greene himself; in fact, that was why Doyle was abruptly called back to Camden after his raid on Snow's Island. But Rawdon dared not call in the defenders of the forts, as that would leave the outposts exposed to Marion, Sumter, and Pickens. The posts had become critical to the British hopes of holding the state, for they protected the supply lines from Charleston and kept Rawdon's army in Camden provisioned. Without them Rawdon would be forced to abandon the interior and retreat to Charleston.

Having once minimized the importance of the "war of posts," Greene now saw them as the key to regaining South Carolina. He would focus his army on the largest garrisons, first at Camden and then at Ninety-Six, the main British station in the northwest quadrant of South Carolina. The militia was responsible for recovering the smaller posts. Sumter was sent off to try again at Fort Granby as well as at the Orangeburg garrison south of Camden. Pickens would operate in the west and move down to the forts on the Georgia border around Augusta. To topple recently established Fort Watson and even newer Fort Motte upriver from it, Greene assigned the duo of Marion and Light-Horse Harry Lee.

Fort Watson was a tough nut to crack. Sumter had failed miserably in his attempt to take it, and although Greene had repeatedly asked Marion to attack it in January, Marion concluded it was impracticable because it was well protected and defended by 250 men under Colonel Watson. Marion had been willing to have a go at it in February with Lee, but then Greene called Lee back to join him, so the plan was dropped. Now that Lee, with his three-hundred-strong Legion, was back with Marion and Watson was gone from the fort, attacking it had become an option again.

Marion still needed convincing. He preferred chasing Watson toward Georgetown, either to overcome him in battle or prevent him from reinforcing Rawdon. Fort Watson was far from home for most of his men, and reducing it would require a siege—a mode of warfare with which Marion had little experience, and none of it good. The only offensive siege he had been part of was the disastrous one at Savannah in 1779. He had called off his prior attacks on Georgetown rather than laying siege to it. Harassing the enemy was what he was used to and good at. Sieges were tedious. And as Savannah had proved and as Sumter had recently shown, they tended to end with rash, near-suicidal assaults when the besiegers lost patience.

Henry Lee was a twenty-five-year-old second in command to the now forty-nine-year-old renowned Swamp Fox. Many men in Lee's position would have backed down. Lee did not. He argued that pursuing Watson would take their combined force too far from Greene's army; besides which, Greene had ordered them to cooperate in attacking the forts. They also lacked ammunition, which they could obtain by capturing the outpost garrisons. Lee further pointed out that from Fort Watson they would be able to intercept Colonel Watson on his way to Camden.

Never one to let his own ego get in the way of the right decision, Marion agreed. He had to see the merit to Lee's points, although later he was heard to regret that his orders did not allow him to pursue his nemesis Watson at that time. That Marion had only eighty men to Lee's three hundred and thus he lacked bargaining power also may have had something to do with his acquiescing.

On April 15 they arrived at Fort Watson and surrounded it. After they issued the customary demand to surrender, a reply came back that a British officer never timidly surrendered a fort and that "if they wanted it, they must come and take it."

The fort was small—under twenty yards on each side—but its position strong. It stood at the summit of a twenty-three-foot-high, pyramid-shaped Indian temple mound that Watson's builders had truncated and flattened at the top. Three rows of abatis surrounded the stockade. The enemy had cleared away all the trees and brush within shooting range of the fort so that patriot marksmen had no cover from which to fire on the fort. Inside the stockade were 114 defenders, a mix of British redcoats and loyalists, most of whom had recently arrived there. A provincial officer, British Lieutenant James McKay, commanded them in Watson's absence.

Lee and Marion initially thought they could reduce the fort by cutting off its water supply. They posted riflemen to pick off the occupants when they left to gather water from nearby Scott's Lake. But McKay sunk a deep well just outside the fort that his men could reach at night by a covered passage they had built. When the well struck water, four days into the siege, the patriots needed another plan.

The British had no cannon to ward off attackers, as the pair of three-pounders Watson had with him during the Bridges Campaign were now at the bottom of Catfish Creek. But the Americans were without artillery too, which Marion and Lee knew they would need to penetrate the fort's walls. Lee asked Greene for a field piece, saying that with one he could "finish the business" in "five minutes" and promising to return it immediately. Greene sent them a six-pounder, but the infantry carrying it got lost and returned to Camden.

The patriots had not counted on a long siege. They were starting to run out of ammunition for their long rifles. They also lacked such basic tools as picks and shovels with which to dig trenches. They managed to break ground a hundred yards from the enemy's works and kept digging with whatever utensils they had, but the process was slow. Morale was low. Marion's men, unlike Lee's Continentals from the North, had not been inoculated against smallpox, and some of them began coming down with the dreaded disease. Others, bored and restless, started going home. Marion published orders threatening capital punishment for deserters, but his troops had figured out that Marion rarely if ever put any of his own men to death.

Marion was burdened with other personnel issues as well. Captain Snipes, who had been freelancing and looting to the southwest of the Santee, was now bad-mouthing Marion to convince others not to augment his force at Fort Watson. According to Abel Kolb, a patriot militia colonel of Marion's in the Cheraws District, Snipes was taking all the men Kolb had ordered to join Marion and encouraging them to join Sumter, who promised they could hang and plunder Tories. When Kolb reminded Snipes of Marion's directive that no one leave his brigade without permission, Snipes responded that he had orders from Sumter to raise men wherever he could and that Marion's order meant nothing to him.

Informed of this exchange, Marion complained to Sumter and threatened to bring the matter to Governor Rutledge's attention. Sumter responded dismissively, saying that Snipes was not acting at any "particular direction" from him and adding that if he or Snipes had done anything wrong, it was up to Rutledge, not Marion, to say so.

Marion also voiced his disapproval of "Sumter's Law," the Gamecock's new solution to the problem of disappearing militiamen. Under the informal edict South Carolinians who enlisted in a regiment of state troops for ten months would be paid—not in cash, which the government lacked, but with horses, clothing, equipment, and slaves taken from Tories. (The pay scale was "one grown negro" for a private and up to "three grown negroes and one small negro" for a regimental commander.) Marion, who disliked plunder, doubted that men who needed such incentives would make better soldiers than volunteers, however transitory, whose only "pay" was fighting for the freedom of their country. But he was in the minority. Rutledge consented to Sumter's Law; Greene, despite some misgivings, enforced it; and Pickens raised a regiment under it.

Marion also received a letter from his mentor, the imprisoned William Moultrie, who had been informed by Balfour in Charleston that Marion's troops had been mistreating prisoners and had murdered three of them. Moultrie assured Balfour that such behavior was contrary to Marion's character, which was "generous and humane." But in writing to Marion, Moultrie issued what amounted to a reprimand. "I know you are acquainted with the customs of war, and that your disposition will not countenance such cruelties," he wrote his protégé. Appearing to credit Rawdon's allegations, Moultrie then ordered Marion to prevent his men from taking private revenges that only served "to disgrace the generous and the brave."

Peeved by the correspondence he had been receiving and with the attempt on Fort Watson seemingly going nowhere, Marion was feeling like the one under siege. He would have preferred to be off chasing Watson. Sensing Marion's frustration, Lee penned a note to Greene saying that Marion was feeling "neglected" and suggesting that Greene write a "long letter" to the partisan leader acknowledging his service and value.

Lee, himself unhappy that the field piece had not arrived, "despaired of success" as the siege dragged on into its sixth day. But a breakthrough was soon to come. After the fort's defenders solved their water issue a couple of days earlier, one of Marion's officers, Lieutenant Colonel Hezekiah Maham, had approached Lee and Marion with a bold idea. He proposed they build a log tower high enough to enable marksmen to fire down upon the fort's defenders inside. The concept dated to ancient times. It would be no small undertaking: with a stockade wall seven feet high atop the twenty-three-foot mound, this would mean constructing a tower more than thirty feet tall. But with nothing to lose, Marion and Lee gave Maham the go-ahead for his plan.

Grabbing every ax from neighboring plantations they could lay their hands on, the besiegers felled trees and cut logs from the nearby swamps. On the afternoon of April 21 they brought up a "wooden machine," as McKay called it, which they placed outside the fort beyond the firing range of British muskets. All that day and through the following night the patriots were busy piling the logs in crisscross fashion atop the base until the wood and earthen oblong structure rose above the height of the British fortification. They topped it off with a sniper's perch with portholes to poke guns through.

Under cover of darkness the prefabricated tower was finished on the night of April 22 and moved into place next to the fort. A party of Marion's riflemen took position in the perch. To guard the tower against enemy sallies from the fort, a contingent of Maryland Continentals was posted nearby on the ground behind a breastwork of logs. As dawn broke the American sharpshooters began raining fire down upon the helpless redcoats and Tories crammed inside the tiny fort. The defenders jumped into a ditch they had excavated with a protective earthen wall to shield them from sniper fire, but it was not good enough: Lieutenant McKay was wounded and two men were killed, with more deaths sure to come.

In the meantime, under protection from their marksmen, the patriots crept closer to the fort and obtained a foothold. From there they began ripping apart the abatis and taking axes to the stockade walls. Lee's infantrymen fixed bayonets and stood ready to charge the fort to finish off the work.

Marion issued another surrender request, and this time McKay raised the white flag. "We were reduced to the disagreeable necessity of capitulating, by the cowardly and mutinous behavior of a majority of the men, having grounded their arms and refused to defend the post any longer," McKay recorded in his journal. Marion and Lee granted generous terms: the British officers and regulars were paroled to Charleston to await exchange, with the officers allowed to keep their personal belongings and sidearms. The Tory irregulars were treated as prisoners of war.

It was the first time since the fall of Charleston that American troops had captured an entire enemy garrison. Lee and Marion had also acquired a rich supply of ammunition that would sustain them for some time. In his report to Greene on April 23 Marion commended Lee for his "advice and indefatigable diligence in every part of this tedious operation, against as strong a little post as could well be made on the most advantageous spot that could be wished for." Marion also gave credit to Maham, telling Greene it was Maham's innovation that "principally occasioned the reduction of the fort." It soon became known as the Maham Tower, and other combatants would come to copy it.

Lee, who rarely praised anyone's efforts but his own, was now convinced of Marion's merit as a leader. He wrote Greene to say that he would like to be formally under Marion's command "in some degree," as he knew that would please the militia general.

After the patriots razed the fort, Marion and Lee moved up to Bloom Hill Plantation in the High Hills of Santee to be closer to Greene's army and to await further orders. From the High Hills they were in position to block Watson's expected route to reinforce Rawdon's garrison at Camden, which Greene was preparing to attack. As Greene camped in battle formation outside the town he took time, per Lee's earlier suggestion, to assure Marion that he was, in fact, appreciated. "When I consider how much you have done and suffered and under what disadvantages you have maintained your ground, I am at a loss which to admire most, your courage and fortitude, or your address and management," Greene wrote to Marion on April 24. "Certain it is no man has a better claim to the public thanks, or is more generally admired than you are." He promised to make known Marion's merit to Congress, to General Washington, "and to the world in general."

Two days later Greene congratulated Marion on his success against Fort Watson and the "spirit, perseverance and good conduct" of the operation. In the same letter Greene also reported on his battle the day before with Rawdon at Hobkirk's Hill just north of Camden. Already outnumbered by Greene by about fifteen hundred to nine hundred and with no prospect of reinforcement from Watson anytime soon, Rawdon decided he had to strike offensively before Marion and Lee with their four hundred men could further enhance the Continental Army. Rawdon also had to worry that Sumter, with eight hundred militia not far away, would link up with Greene. (That fear proved unfounded; Sumter refused Greene's request to join him, leading a disgusted Greene to conclude that Sumter was interested only in plunder.)

Rawdon, a fearless, aristocratic, twenty-six-year-old, won a tactical victory at Hobkirk's Hill, driving Greene's soldiers from the field in a twenty-minute battle. This time the patriot militia could not be blamed—none of them had fought there. It was, instead, the 1st Maryland Continentals, the cream of Greene's army, who broke ranks and ran after being confused by an officer's order. In writing to Marion, Greene minimized the loss and asked him to quell the rumors spreading among the militia that the Americans had been routed at Hobkirk's. "By mistake we got a slight repulse," Greene maintained. "The injury is not great. The enemy suffered much more than we did." He tried to make the best of it, telling Lafayette, "We fight, get beat, rise and fight again."

Privately, though, Greene was crestfallen. He even briefly considered leaving South Carolina and going up to Virginia. But there was much truth to what he told Marion. Although both sides had suffered heavy casualties, Rawdon, who lost more than a quarter of his force, could ill afford such attrition, nor could he hold down the garrison in Camden any longer. He had hoped for reinforcements from Watson's 64th Regiment, and Watson said his men "would have crawled upon their hand and knees" to join Lord Rawdon. But delayed by the Bridges Campaign, Watson was unavailable to help. By the time he made his way to Camden on May 7 after crossing seven creeks and two nearly impassable swamps to get around Marion and Lee, it was too late to do any good. He arrived only to learn that his namesake fort, which he bypassed in his haste to come to Rawdon's aid, had been taken and destroyed.

The fall of Fort Watson was a major strategic blow to British hopes for holding South Carolina. It cut off Rawdon's communication and supply line to Nelson's Ferry and, thus, to Charleston. The lack of support from the local population and the absence of Cornwallis's army left Rawdon in an untenable position. To stay in Camden was to starve. And so on May 10, after destroying the fortifications and much of the town, Rawdon evacuated Camden, the site of Cornwallis's great victory over Gates nine months earlier. He marched south in the direction of Nelson's Ferry, intending to come to the relief of a post that Marion and Lee were hoping to make the next domino to fall. For a beleaguered Marion, it also threatened to become the last straw.

17

Ball of Fire

ort Motte, thirty miles upriver from Fort Watson, posed an
even more formidable challenge to the team of Marion and
Lee. When they arrived there on May 6, 1781, to plan their siege, they
found a virtual citadel that, as Marion described it, was "obstinate, and
strong."

The fortification was built on the plantation of Rebecca Motte, a
recently widowed aristocrat and rabid patriot who had previously used
female slaves to slip intelligence to Marion in Charleston. Just a few
months earlier the British had commandeered her three-story mansion,
building a wall, ditch, and abatis around it for protection. They had
moved there from the nearby Thomson plantation, Belleville, that Sumter tried and failed to overtake in February.

Although small by traditional fort standards, the enclosure was at
least double the size of Fort Watson, with about forty yards on each side.
The plantation house sat atop a 245-foot hill. The protective wall, just
outside the plantation house, was made of thick wooden stakes, almost
ten feet high, buttressed by an earthen rampart. The ditch was seven and
a half feet wide and six feet deep. At the corners of the fort were two
blockhouses with apertures for guns.

Inside, the fort was defended by a force of 184, consisting of 80 British
redcoats, 59 Hessians, and 45 loyalist militia. Their commander was
Lieutenant Donald McPherson of the highly regarded 84th Regiment of
Foot (Royal Highland Emigrants), a unit of Scottish immigrants who

had fought in Canada and were promoted from a provincial regiment into the regular army establishment.

Marion's 150 partisans spread themselves around the perimeter of the fort while Lee and his 250-man Legion camped on a hillside about a quarter-mile north. This time the Americans had an artillery piece, the six-pounder Greene had sent them at Fort Watson but was never delivered. Their plan was to dig zig-zagging trenches ever closer to the wall and then pound it with cannon fire. Marion's riflemen would provide cover for the excavators, and Lee's infantry would then storm the fort with bayonets. Lee figured that because the defenders were without artillery themselves, their defense would fail unless they were reinforced by Rawdon.

As THE SIEGE BEGAN, Marion was in another of his sour moods, this one the worst yet. To begin with, he had just learned that Abel Kolb, the respected Cheraws District militia colonel, had been murdered in cold blood by a band of Tory militia near the North Carolina border. Kolb had helped keep Ganey's Tories in the Little Pee Dee area in check and had sent men to assist Marion at Fort Watson. Late at night on April 28 a group of Tories surrounded Kolb's home, where they roused him and his family from their sleep. When the Tories threatened to burn the house down with everyone inside it if he refused to surrender, Kolb came out to lay down his arms. Outside his front door, in the presence of his wife and sisters, he was shot dead by a Tory private. The Tories then took a torch to Kolb's house.

Marion felt compelled to detach a party to chase after Kolb's killers, but they never caught up with them. Greene, writing to Marion, said he was sorry about Kolb's murder but he seemed even sorrier that Marion had to divert men from the important business at Fort Motte for a retaliatory mission.

Greene also raised another sore subject with Marion—horses. In a letter to Greene on May 2 Henry Lee had let slip—or, in his eagerness to curry favor with Greene, had volunteered—that Marion, if he were willing, could certainly spare at least 60 dragoon horses taken from Tories and maybe as many as 150. Sumter, always happy to disparage Marion behind his back to Greene, chimed in to say that Marion was "getting good horses" lately. Greene, believing Marion was holding out on him, immediately dashed off a letter to the partisan commander reminding him that he had written several times about dragoon horses without a satisfactory response. "I am told," Greene wrote, without naming his sources, that Marion's men had been impressing many high-quality steeds from Tories. Although he claimed to take a dim view of such plundering, Greene asked Marion to send him "sixty or eighty good dragoon horses."

Ever sensitive to criticism, this time Marion blew up. Responding on May 6, the day he arrived at Fort Motte, he began by noting that his men were weary and starting to drop away for lack of support. Then he addressed the horse issue. "I acknowledge that you have repeatedly mentioned the want of dragoon horses, and wish that it had been in my power to furnish them, but it is not, nor never had been," he wrote. "The few horses which has been taken from Tories has been kept for the service and never for private property," he asserted. Nonetheless, if Greene wanted the militia to donate their horses to the Continental Army, Marion said he would have it done—although he was "certain we shall never get their service in future."

Then came the punch line. Marion said it would not bother him if his militia never came back, as he had "for some time" determined to resign his militia command as soon as Greene arrived. He now proposed to do so as soon as Fort Motte was either taken or abandoned by the patriots. He would stick around long enough to help reduce the post there, but after Lee returned to Greene, Marion said, he would seek permission to go to Philadelphia, where he might apply to Congress for relief or reassignment within the Continental Army.

The stress and strain of war had caught up with Marion. For nearly nine months he had been doing his best to keep his brigade together under trying circumstances with little or no logistical support, all the while being hunted by one enemy death squad after the other. His flag had been disrespected by the British, who had treated him condescendingly in their correspondence, and even his friends, such as Moultrie and now Greene, were questioning his conduct. His secret base camp at Snow's Island had been discovered and destroyed, creating a sense of violation if not humiliation. His favorite nephew had been cruelly murdered. The wonder is that he had not snapped earlier.

After receiving Marion's letter Greene immediately backed off. He wrote to say he had no intention of taking horses from the militia if Marion thought it would adversely affect their morale or create problems for him in dealing with them. As for the threat to resign, Greene said he could not believe Marion meant it. Appealing to his conscience, Greene averred that if such a respected leader as Marion left "in the midst of our difficulties" to indulge in "more agreeable amusements," it would dampen the spirits of the rank-and-file. He also made clear that Marion had no monopoly on hardship; he himself, Greene wrote, had not had an hour's leave of absence or any private or family time since coming south. "Your state is invaded, your all is at stake," he emphasized. "What has been done will signify nothing unless we persevere to the end." He would say no more on the subject, he wrote in conclusion, until he and Marion had a chance to meet in person.

Marion pretended not to be mollified, but his tone began to soften. He assured Greene that he was serious about resigning but made clear that it was his frustration with the militia's comings and goings, more than Greene's request for horses, that had put him in such bad humor. He told Greene that he had just sent him a good quality horse for his personal use and would send more as soon as he was able to procure some. Then he went back to the business of besieging Fort Motte.

LEE THOUGHT THE trench operations were progressing with "rapidity," aided by slaves from neighboring plantations. But the digging was not fast enough. On May 10 McPherson learned that Rawdon had evacuated Camden and was on his way to the relief of the fort. By the following night the defenders could see the campfires of the British army burning in the distance. Rawdon was within forty-eight hours of Fort Motte. McPherson's men let out a loud cheer and resolved to hold out against the siege. When asked to surrender that day, McPherson vowed he would defend the fort to the last.

Conferring on May 11, Marion and Lee knew they needed to take the fort by the next day or else abandon the siege. But at the current pace of operations the fort was not going to fall that quickly. As at Fort Watson, they needed a bright idea. (A Maham Tower was not a practical option at Fort Motte.) Once again they found one—they would burn the British out.

With the recent hot, dry weather, the roof of Rebecca Motte's mansion made an enticing target for a ball of fire. The patriot trenches were now close enough that it was possible to launch a flaming projectile to the top of the house. But first the American commanders needed to secure permission from Mrs. Motte to destroy her property.

Accounts differ on who did the asking. According to Parson Weems, it was Marion who approached Rebecca Motte with this proposition. By contrast, a famous early nineteenth-century painting by John Blake White shows Marion and Lee making the request together. And Lee in his memoirs says it was he alone who spoke to her about it.

At the time Mrs. Motte was living in the overseer's log cabin on the plantation grounds, where the British had moved her, her mother, and two unmarried daughters when they took the mansion for themselves. At her request Lee's men had made her cabin their headquarters, where they enjoyed her hospitality, food, and what Lee praised as the "best wines of Europe" throughout the siege. According to Lee, when he gently proposed the idea of setting her main house on fire, she instantly agreed, saying it would be an honor to serve her country thusly. Lee recalled that she even supplied a special bow and arrow, imported from India, to substitute for the ones she saw being prepared, as she thought hers better suited the deed. But William Dobein James, who was also there, wrote that Sergeant Nathan Savage, whose house near Snow's Island was among those burned by Wemyss the previous year, set a ball of rosin and brimstone on fire and slung it to the top of the roof.

Whether the object was shot from a bow, fired from a musket, or flung by hand, it did the trick. After it landed, the roof was quickly aflame. McPherson sent some men to the roof to put out the fire, but they were driven off by canister shot from the Americans' six-pounder.

That same day, on May 12, the British garrison surrendered. The Americans doused the fire and saved the mansion, took possession of the enemy's guns and salt, then leveled the rest of the fortifications.

That night Mrs. Motte invited both the American and British officers to what Lee called a "sumptuous dinner" at her cabin. Lee recalled that the gracious hostess, though a confirmed patriot, treated everyone with such amiability that it was hard to tell the captors from the captured. As Peter Horry recalled, the wine was brought out, "we were all very gay," and "Britons and Americans mingled together in smiles and cheerful chat, like brothers."

At the formal surrender ceremony the redcoats laid down their arms to Lee's green-coated Continentals, while the loyalists surrendered to Marion's militia. Possibly this division reflected some friction within the American side. More likely it was a face-saving measure for McPherson. As the highest commanding officer of the victorious force, Marion was entitled by custom to receive McPherson's sword. But a British army officer would have considered it especially inglorious to surrender to a militia soldier. McPherson undoubtedly preferred surrendering to Lee, a "gentleman" who, in a further act of chivalry, returned some private British correspondence the Americans found in Mrs. Motte's home.

Little did McPherson know that Lee thought he deserved to be executed for needlessly prolonging the siege. Indeed, although Lee may have seemed more of a gentleman than Marion, he was far less punctilious about restraining the commission of atrocities. Three months earlier, while performing reconnaissance for Greene in North Carolina, Lee's Legion had surrounded and massacred a group of British soldiers just as mercilessly as Tarleton had cut down the Americans at the Waxhaws. And after the surrender of Fort Motte, Lee incurred Marion's wrath when the Legion troops began hanging some of the more notorious captured Tories. Three were executed—including Hugh Miscally, the man who had led Doyle to Snow's Island—before Marion, upon learning of the goings on, intervened to stop a fourth hanging, this one of the Tory militia commander. When the executioners told Marion it was Lee who had approved the death sentences, Marion thundered, "I will let you know that I command here, and not Colonel Lee." Lee later wrote that the man whose neck was saved thoroughly deserved the noose and that many of the American militia loudly demanded his punishment, but "the humanity of Marion could not be overcome."

Apart from the three hangings, the siege of Fort Motte was remarkably casualty-free. No British or Tories died, and the Americans lost only two men. One of them, though, was the storied sergeant (since made a lieutenant) Allen McDonald. He was the Zelig-like figure who was one of the three rescued prisoners from Marion's first partisan engagement to join Marion's brigade, went on to bayonet Ganey outside Georgetown, then climbed the tree to shoot Lieutenant Torriano through the knee at Witherspoon's Plantation. History does not record how he died at Fort Motte, but recent archaeological evidence consisting of clustered rifle balls suggests that Marion relied heavily on two particularly skilled sharpshooters at Fort Motte. Given McDonald's prowess, he may have been one of them.

As at Fort Watson, the cost to the British was again more strategic than human. Rawdon, who had hoped to get his hands on the provisions at Fort Motte, was chagrined to learn of its fall when he crossed Nelson's Ferry on May 14. "The stroke was heavy upon me," he told Cornwallis. Realizing that Nelson's Ferry, too, could no longer be held, Rawdon destroyed the fortifications there, headed south, and eventually pitched camp at Monck's Corner, thirty miles above Charleston.

After the surrender of Fort Motte, Greene went there to assess the situation and clear the air with Marion. It was the first time they met. Greene, a large, slightly rotund man, stood a full head taller than Marion. Like Marion, Greene had one bad leg, so the two of them would have limped to greet each other. Greene spoke with a Rhode Island accent, Marion with a southern twang, perhaps with a trace of French influence. What they said to each other is not recorded, but they must have smoothed things over because from that meeting forward Marion issued no more resignation threats.

It helped that Fort Motte had ended in success. Even George Washington was impressed, writing Greene from New York to say that the reduction of the fort "does honor to General Marian [sic] and Colonel Lee." Other good news was flowing in at the same time. On May 11 the garrison at Orangeburg had fallen to Sumter. Three days after Greene met Marion, Fort Granby surrendered as well. Sumter had started the siege there on May 2, but when he took his main force to Orangeburg, leaving a small detachment to continue the siege, Greene ordered Lee to Granby to finish the job. On May 15 Lee accepted the British commander's surrender terms, which stipulated that the British soldiers could keep their baggage, horses, and recently taken plunder. When Sumter returned, he was enraged beyond measure. Not only had he wanted the glory of taking Fort Granby himself, but he had planned to distribute the booty to his own men. But Lee had decided to grant the generous terms rather than prolong the siege because he was told that Rawdon was heading toward Granby with reinforcements.

Now Sumter took his turn in offering his resignation to Greene. But Greene would not accept it, and he managed to mollify the Gamecock by giving him some of the munitions and provisions captured at Granby as well as some slaves taken from loyalists there, which Sumter used to pay the men he had recruited under Sumter's Law.

Greene also reconfirmed to Sumter that he was the head of all militia in South Carolina, with authority to use Marion as he saw fit. To make sure Marion got the message, Greene had an aide send him a letter directing him to continue to harass the enemy "and to receive General Sumter's orders."

With that the American forces split off in different directions. Greene took his army to commence a siege at Ninety-Six, the only major garrison in the South Carolina interior still held by the British. Lee, acting in concert with Georgia militia leader Elijah Clarke, took Fort Galpin near Augusta on May 21, then moved to assist Pickens in reducing the remaining forts defending that key city. Sumter continued to patrol south and west of the Congaree.

And Marion set his sights once again on Georgetown.

An overly dramatized depiction of Marion leading his men through a pass against the Cherokees in 1761. Marion reportedly expressed regret about the subsequent atrocities committed by the British and colonials against the "poor creatures." *(c. 1844. New York Public Library)*

The British attack on Charleston's Fort Sullivan in 1776, in which Marion helped command South Carolina's 2nd Regiment in its successful defense of the fort. The British would return to Charleston four years later. *(Harper's Weekly, June 26, 1858)*

Colonel William Moultrie, Marion's mentor and overall commander of the defense of Fort Sullivan in 1776. The fort was soon renamed Fort Moultrie in his honor. (*Engraving, 1862, after a portrait by Alonzo Chappel*)

Replica of a soldier from Marion's South Carolina 2nd Regiment, in National Parks museum at Fort Moultrie. The inscription on the crescent reads "Liberty." (*author photo*)

The Battle of Savannah, 1779. Marion led an unsuccessful patriot assault on a British fortification in which nearly half the Americans did not return. A British officer observed that "the ditch was choke full of their Dead." (*Illustration by A. I. Keller, 1866–1924*)

106 Tradd Street in Charleston. According to legend, Marion jumped from a second-story window here in March 1780 to escape a drinking party where the host had locked the guests inside. It was a lucky quirk of history, as Marion broke his ankle and had retired to the countryside to recuperate when Charleston fell to the British and the American soldiers garrisoned there became prisoners of war. (*author photo*)

Sir Henry Clinton, commander in chief of British operations in North America, who directed the siege that led to Charleston's fall in May 1780. A proclamation that Clinton soon issued, requiring rebels to sign an oath of allegiance to the king and actively assist the British government, ended up backfiring. Citizens who had been neutral rallied to the patriot cause and formed a resistance movement that Marion, among other guerrilla leaders, would spearhead. (*John Smart, c. 1777. New York Public Library*)

General Horatio Gates, commander of the American southern army following the fall of Charleston. After Gates's disastrous defeat at the Battle of Camden in August 1780, Francis Marion's was the only viable patriot fighting force left in South Carolina. (*H. B. Hall, 1872. New York Public Library*)

Charles, Earl Cornwallis, commander of British southern operations from 1780 to 1782. Marion's constant harassment of British supply lines so infuriated Cornwallis that several "death squads" were dispatched in sequence to eliminate him as a threat. (*Engraving by George J. Stodart, from a painting by J. S. Copley*)

"Marion Crossing the Pee Dee." (*William Ranney, c. 1850*). Marion is likely the second horseman from left, wearing the blanket.

Banastre Tarleton, the dashing British cavalry leader reputed by legend to have given Marion his nickname. After pursuing Marion for seven hours through 26 miles of swamps, Tarleton called off the chase, saying, "as for this damned old fox, the Devil himself could not catch him." (*Portrait by Sir Joshua Reynolds*)

An idealized depiction of the "Swamp Fox" in action. *(Engraving, 1858, from a painting by Alonzo Chappel, c. 1856)*

"Revolutionary Militia Crossing a River." Marion is in front of the white flag. *(William Ranney, c. 1853–1854)*

Thomas Sumter, the "Gamecock," who led the patriot militia in the middle part of South Carolina, while Marion covered the eastern portion. The two leaders disliked each other; Sumter was considered "bold and rash," while Marion was "cautious and vigilant." (*Original portrait by Charles Wilson Peale. New York Public Library*)

Andrew Pickens, the third of the great triumvirate of "partisan" leaders in South Carolina, along with Marion and Sumter. Pickens led the militia in the northwest third of the state, closest to Indian Territory. (*Original portrait by Thomas Sully. New York Public Library*)

Modern day Halfway Swamp, much as it looked during Marion's engagement with the enemy there in December 1780. (*author photo*)

"General Marion Inviting a British Officer to Share His Meal." (*Engraving, c. 1840 by John Sartain, after a painting by John Blake White, c. 1810–1836*). In his imagining of the famous "sweet potato" dinner, White painted the only portrait of Marion by someone who knew him during his lifetime. Standing behind Marion is his faithful African American slave and personal valet, Oscar, or "Buddy." (*Library of Congress*)

General Nathanael Greene, who replaced Gates as the American Continental commander in the South in December 1780, and forged a close working relationship with Marion. (*Original portrait by Charles Wilson Peale. New York Public Library*)

Snow's Island, the location of Marion's secret base camp and place of rendezvous from which his men ventured forth to annoy the enemy. *(author photo)*

Henry "Light-Horse Harry" Lee, a young Continental cavalry commander, was sent by General Greene to join Marion at Snow's Island in January 1781 to begin conducting joint operations (but had trouble finding the secret lair). *(Original portrait by Gilbert Stuart. New York Public Library)*

Francis, Lord Rawdon, was left in charge of the British field army in South Carolina when Cornwallis left for Yorktown in Virginia. "I must drive Marion out of that country [South Carolina]," Rawdon had declared to Cornwallis, "but I cannot yet say what steps I shall take to effect it." *(Portrait by Joshua Reynolds)*

Marion's Brigade (right) prepares to engage John Watson's British force at Wyboo Swamp, South Carolina, in March 1781. (*painting by Terry Smith, 2006, courtesy of Swamp Fox Murals Trail Society, www.clarendonmurals.com*)

Fort Watson, a key British outpost Marion and Lee besieged in April 1781 and eventually captured, with the benefit of the hastily-constructed "Maham Tower" (shown at left). Patriot marksmen rained rifle fire from the tower's perch down upon the British defenders in the fort. (*Benson Lossing/Alice Barritt, c. 1850s*)

Opposite: Three weeks after the fall of Fort Watson, Marion and Lee forced the surrender of Fort Motte, another strategic British post, by setting the fort's roof on fire with flaming arrows. Here they are shown with patriot Rebecca Motte, who owned the mansion commandeered by the British for their fort; she willingly provided the bow and arrows with which to burn down her own house. (*John Blake White, c. 1850*)

A modern view of the Indian temple mound atop which the British built Fort Watson. The patriots built their tower more than 30 feet high to enable their sharpshooters to fire down into the fort. *(author photo)*

Peter Horry, Marion's longtime friend and subordinate commander, who provided a written manuscript that Mason L. "Parson" Weems turned into a highly fictionalized popular biography of Marion. *(John Szekes, 1976, after an original portrait by unknown artist, presented to Peter Horry Chapter of the Daughters of the American Revolution, Conway, South Carolina)*

Hezekiah Maham, who came up with the idea for the "Maham Tower" that toppled Fort Watson. Although a capable cavalry commander, Maham had a long-running dispute with Peter Horry over rank that created constant headaches for Marion, under whom both men served. *(South Carolina Historical Society)*

The ruins of Biggin Church, near Monck's Corner and Marion's birthplace, and where he likely was baptized. In July 1781 it played a crucial role in the lead-up to one of Marion's bloodiest battles. *(author photo)*

Marion's ambush of the enemy at Parker's Ferry in August 1781, perhaps his greatest victory as a partisan commander. One loyalist (Tory) officer caught in the surprise attack called it "the most galling fire ever troops experienced." *(c. 1844)*

A modern view of the Parker's Ferry causeway, where the British were wedged in so closely that they were forced to "run the gauntlet" of Marion's ambush. *(author photo)*

The Battle of Eutaw Springs, September 8, 1781, one of the bloodiest of the war, was the last major field engagement in the South. Marion was in charge of the front line of militia, which distinguished itself by firing 17 volleys per man. (*F. C. Yohn, 1903. New York Public Library*)

Marion, at Eutaw Springs. In typically understated fashion, he reported afterward, "My men behaved well." (*Engraving by Thomas Welch, c. 1836, from a drawing by James B. Longacre and portrait by Thomas Stothard, c. 1834*)

Marion, by an unknown artist c. 1847.

Marion's grave in Pineville, South Carolina. His marker describes him as "a soldier who lived without fear and died without reproach." His wife, Mary Videau, is buried alongside him. *(author photo)*

Francis Marion immortalized, in statues across South Carolina. Upper left: sculpture by Garland Weeks at Francis Marion University, Florence (*photo courtesy of Francis Marion University*). Upper right: sculpture by Robert Barinowski, displayed at 2014 Francis Marion/Swamp Fox Symposium, Manning (*author photo*). Bottom: sculpture by Alex Palkovich at Venters' Landing (formerly Witherspoon's Ferry) in Johnsonville, where Marion first took charge of a partisan guerrilla brigade. (*author photo*)

18

Winning by Losing

Almost as soon as Fort Motte fell, Marion began agitating for one more chance at taking Georgetown. "I beg leave to go and reduce that place," he wrote Greene on May 19, explaining that the garrison there was down to eighty men. Capturing Georgetown would quiet the Tories in the area, who were causing much trouble, Marion wrote. He hoped to hear from Greene as soon as possible lest the garrison "slip through" his hands. Even before hearing anything back, Marion wrote twice more to reiterate his request but said he would await Greene's orders.

Marion was now at Peyre's Plantation, a new hideout on Gaillard's Island along the Santee in St. Stephen's Parish, not far from his late brother Gabriel's Belle Isle estate. Like the camp on Snow's Island, this one lay deep within protective layers of marshes, cane brakes, and pines, with sentries posted to whistle their signals. Impatiently Marion waited there for the go-ahead from Greene to attack Georgetown.

But Nathanael Greene was not too interested in Francis Marion's designs on Georgetown. Although he had approved Lee and Marion's effort to capture it back in January, he now considered it an "inferior object." Greene's highest priority was taking the British post at Ninety-Six, northwest of Fort Motte, and he feared that Rawdon, despite having moved toward Charleston, might double back and interfere with his siege. He did not want Marion off in Georgetown, two hundred miles away, if Rawdon made the slightest move toward Ninety-Six. On May 26 he gave a half-hearted, conditional approval to the mission: he had no objection to Marion moving on Georgetown provided he did not leave Sumter exposed where he was and Rawdon did not head toward Ninety-Six.

Before Greene changed his mind or Sumter had a chance to say no, Marion chose to treat Greene's letter as a yes. On May 27, after gathering up the militia at Cantey's Plantation, he headed to Georgetown, arriving there the next day. Buoyed by the recent successes at Forts Watson and Motte, the militia had turned out in force. Having learned a few things at those forts, Marion proceeded to lay a standard siege by digging trenches. He again enlisted the help of local plantation slaves, one of whom allegedly furnished cattle and provisions to the British. According to one pension applicant, Marion had the "yellow man" (a term for a light-skinned mulatto) hanged.

Although lack of artillery had been a primary factor in his previous three attempts on Georgetown, Marion again had none with him. Perhaps he was waiting on some, but in the meantime he resorted to artifice. He wheeled in mounted, peeled logs and had them painted black to resemble cannon. Maybe with that bluff and his superior numbers he could induce the defenders into surrendering.

As it turned out, the enemy had no intention of putting up a fight. With their numbers greatly reduced, their commander, now the loyalist Robert Gray, was under orders to evacuate if seriously pressed. On the night of March 28, the same day Marion began the siege, the British spiked their cannons, boarded their ships, and left the city. They lingered in Winyah Bay outside town for a few days before sailing off to Charleston. Georgetown had fallen—finally—without a shot being fired.

Marion was exultant. Never one to care much about clothing, he treated himself to a change of wardrobe, fitting himself out in a new suit of regimentals. The successful mission carried an added bonus: cut off from their supply base in Georgetown, Ganey's Tories soon asked for a three-month ceasefire, later extended to a year, thus ridding Marion of a group who had been a thorn in his side for months. Ganey's men even pledged to restore all slaves and other plundered property they had taken from Whig civilians. Marion's euphoric mood was dampened only by the death of his last surviving brother, Isaac, in Georgetown on May 31.

Understanding how proud Marion was of his accomplishment, Greene wrote from Ninety-Six to say that he took "great pleasure" in the reduction of Georgetown and that it would be "attended with many good consequences to that part of the country." But he added that as soon as Marion was done dismantling the British fortifications there, he should swing back to the Monck's Corner area to keep watch on Rawdon and "act in conjunction" with Sumter. In particular Greene was worried that a new force of some two thousand British soldiers in Charleston, recently arrived from Ireland, would march on Ninety-Six with Rawdon to try to raise Greene's siege there. If they did, Greene told Marion, he should collect all the militia he could and join Sumter as soon as possible to stall the enemy's progress. With the fall of Augusta on June 5 to the trio of Pickens, Lee, and Clarke, Greene was now obsessed with toppling Ninety-Six.

Sumter was less effusive in complimenting Marion's success at Georgetown. He sent the Swamp Fox a terse congratulation and told Greene that Marion had proceeded against that object despite Sumter's request that he cover the countryside below the Santee and prevent the enemy from ravaging it. Sumter also informed Greene of some "unfavorable" information about Marion's force: due to the very success of the Georgetown expedition, Marion's men had begun to go home, considering their mission accomplished. As a result, Sumter believed Marion was "weak and badly armed" with very little ammunition. Sumter nonetheless assured Greene that he had given positive orders to Marion to march west with what he had and to collect more along the way.

The siege at Ninety-Six was going slowly. The post was heavily fortified and defended by 550 provincials and militia under Lieutenant Colonel John Harris Cruger, a wealthy New York Tory. The area around Ninety-Six was heavily loyalist in sympathy—the equivalent of Williamsburg for the Whigs. Although Cruger's defenders numbered only a third of Greene's besiegers, they were highly motivated, as they included many locals with long memories of the bloody struggles between Tories and Whigs during the Snow Campaign. The two hundred loyalist militia believed their rebel captors would grant them little mercy if they surrendered and thus were prepared to defend the fort to the last extremity.

Ironically, neither the defense nor siege should have even taken place. After abandoning Camden in March, Rawdon had ordered Cruger to evacuate Ninety-Six and head to the defense of Augusta. But the American militia intercepted Rawdon's orders and Cruger proceeded to fortify the post to the point where it stood nearly impregnable. The primary fortification was an eight-sided, star-shaped earthen redoubt, protected by a wall with pointed stakes and surrounded by ditches and abatis. Cruger also had the benefit of a trio of three-pounders, unlike at Forts Watson and Motte, where the defenders were without artillery.

Greene tried several shortcuts to overcome the defenses, none of them successful. He constructed a thirty-foot Maham Tower, but Cruger heightened the fort's walls with sandbags, neutralizing the maneuver. Borrowing a tactic from the siege of Fort Motte, Greene had his men shoot flaming arrows atop the buildings, but Cruger's men ripped the shingles off the buildings, eliminating their susceptibility to fire. Greene's engineer, the Polish Thaddeus Kosciusko, who had built the fortifications at West Point, had a mine tunnel dug underneath the fort, but the defenders discovered the diggers and drove them off with bayonets (killing the brother of Andrew Pickens). Greene was thus forced to rely on classic, trench-digging siege operations that might eventually succeed but would take time. In effect, he was in a race to complete the siege before Rawdon, moving toward him with two thousand effectives, could get to Ninety-Six—hence his orders to Sumter and Marion to do everything possible to retard Rawdon's advance.

They failed to do so. Rawdon, though suffering the effects of malaria, got past them unmolested, and by June 18 he was within a couple of days of Ninety-Six. Having run out of time, his entrenchers anxious to fight, and now reinforced by Lee and Pickens back from Augusta, Greene ordered a desperate assault on the fort that day. The Americans fought valiantly but were turned back with heavy casualties. The next day Greene lifted the siege—at twenty-eight days, the longest field siege of the Revolution—and withdrew to the east.

How had both Sumter and Marion so utterly failed to slow Rawdon's movement? In Sumter's case he was convinced that Rawdon was heading to Fort Granby to retake that outpost, so he stayed at Granby while

Rawdon, avoiding that place, marched by way of Orangeburg and made it past the Gamecock. When one of Sumter's detachments finally caught up with Rawdon's rear, the rebels were trounced and Sumter's militia deserted in droves.

Marion had his own reasons. Sumter kept changing his orders on him, telling him first to come quick, then to halt, then to resume marching, but not to hurry because Rawdon was moving slowly and Greene's siege was going well. On June 16, after the last of these fluctuating orders, Marion wrote Greene to say that although he was on his way to join Sumter, he feared that if he left the Nelson's Ferry area, where he was, the enemy would destroy all the provisions south of the Santee. These, he explained, were the only available supply for Greene's army until the crops north of the Santee could be harvested. In addition, he wrote, the British had augmented their force at Monck's Corner, and if he were allowed to stay there and given ammunition, he could keep the enemy hemmed in close to Charleston and prevent them from foraging for subsistence in the countryside.

Left unstated was perhaps the biggest reason for Marion's reluctance: his men had no desire to travel so far from their homes to be part of a difficult and protracted siege operation. Nor were they eager to confront a two-thousand-man enemy force along the way.

Greene was furious. A few days after ending the siege he wrote Marion to vent his frustration with the militia. Greene maintained that Ninety-Six had been on the verge of surrender and that if he had had Sumter and Marion to help him, the three of them could have defeated Rawdon instead of his having to abandon the operation. He told Marion it was a pity the militia would not turn out to join a united operation. He avowed that Sumter's and Marion's militia needed to join forces with him, not fly around the country here and there on inconsequential little forays. Clearly irritated, he instructed Marion in no uncertain terms to link up with Sumter and follow the Gamecock's orders.

Greene had a habit of blaming everyone but himself for his setbacks—at Guilford Courthouse the North Carolina militia failed him; at Hobkirk's Hill it was Sumter's absence and a subordinate Continental officer's order to retreat that were responsible for the loss. And thus he attributed the failed operation at Ninety-Six to the tardy South Carolina militia (and the absent Virginia militia, which Greene faulted Governor Thomas Jefferson for not sending). But Greene might also have looked in the mirror: inexperienced at siege operations, he failed to seize, early on, the small redoubt that protected the defenders' vulnerable water supply. Doing so would have made short work of things, but by the time the redoubt was taken it was too late to make a difference.

Marion did not respond to Greene, but given Marion's thin-skinned nature it is safe to assume he did not take kindly to Greene's criticisms. However, the debate over who lost Ninety-Six soon became moot, as the British ended up evacuating it a couple of weeks later. After briefly pursuing Greene, Rawdon had to call off the effort because his men were starving and too tired and sick to go on. They had just marched two hundred miles in two weeks in heavy woolen uniforms through 100-degree temperatures and humidity that the mostly Irish unit was not accustomed to suffering. Some of them carried parasols to shield themselves from the sun, to no avail—fifty died of heatstroke. Marion's intelligence network allowed him to assure Greene that Rawdon's soldiers were "so fatigued they cannot possibly move."

Returning to Ninety-Six, Rawdon found it so lacking in supplies that it could not be held. With the other outposts having fallen, the garrison there could not be resupplied. Rawdon had come to realize that winning battles did the British no good as long as the army could not be provisioned. He headed to Orangeburg to reestablish a position there, leaving orders for Cruger to abandon Ninety-Six, which he did on July 8. The loyalists in the area dared not stay to be persecuted by vengeful Whigs. After accepting Rawdon's offer to provide them safe haven near Charleston, a group of them began a long, depressing march to the Lowcountry, where they built themselves huts they called Rawdon Town.

Once again Greene had won by losing. Searching for a way to press his advantage, he called the triumvirate of Sumter, Lee, and Marion to a summit meeting. A few days after the fifth anniversary of the Declaration of Independence the four of them met for the first time as a group at Ancrum's Plantation on the Congaree, forty miles southwest of Camden. Greene wanted to draw Rawdon into battle at Orangeburg, but despite being reinforced by 350 men under Lieutenant Colonel Alexander Stewart up from Monck's Corner, Rawdon declined to come out and fight. His soldiers had had enough, as had the twenty-six-year-old Rawdon. Too sick to go on, he returned to Charleston and on August 21 sailed for England to recuperate. He would be captured on the voyage by privateers and turned over to the French; eventually he was exchanged for an American officer.

Greene had briefly considered an offensive attack on Rawdon and Stewart's combined force at Orangeburg, but when he rode out with Sumter and Marion to reconnoiter the British position on July 12 they concluded that the enemy was too well protected on favorable ground. By this time, too, the American army was exhausted by the heat and lack of provisions. The men from Virginia and northward, accustomed to corn and wheat bread, could not stomach the local rice. With no beef available, the soldiers were reduced to eating frogs and alligators. Satisfied that Rawdon had refused his offer of battle, Greene took his men to the cooler, breezier High Hills of Santee for the summer.

There would be no rest, though, for the Swamp Fox.

19

Dog Days

*I*t came to be known as the Dog Days campaign, named for the hottest part of the summer. And it ended with the final and total rift between Francis Marion and Thomas Sumter.

With the fall of Georgetown and Ninety-Six, the British in South Carolina were left holding only two significant outposts outside of Charleston—Monck's Corner, thirty miles north of the city, and Dorchester, twenty miles northwest of it. The only British army still in the field in the state was the one at Orangeburg, command of which passed from Rawdon to Stewart. Sumter persuaded Greene to let him lead an expedition to capture the two remaining outposts, thereby cutting off the British in Charleston from the army in Orangeburg.

To carry out this mission Sumter wanted command not only of his own regiments but also those of Lee and Marion. Greene agreed, his only stipulation being that Sumter make it a quick operation so his forces could return to assist the main army. Ultimately Greene's goal was to drive all of the British and loyalist forces back against the coast and confine them to the Charleston area; there they would be vulnerable to a land siege by the Americans and, as Greene later came to hope, a naval blockade from the French fleet.

Because he was with Sumter when Greene approved this expedition, Marion could no longer hide from the Gamecock. On the night of July 12, as directed by Sumter, Marion headed off toward Monck's Corner with his 180-man mounted force. Lee and his Legion, numbering 150, moved to secure Dorchester in cooperation with Colonel Wade

Hampton, who was leading a detachment of Sumter's cavalry. Sumter himself, with several hundred mounted infantry and a six-pounder, trailed behind the subordinate commanders. All told, the Americans were fielding upward of six hundred to seven hundred men.

Marion's unit had recently undergone several high-level personnel changes. Hugh Giles, as close as anyone to being Marion's co-commander, had retired to his estate near Snow's Island in late June. Twenty-seven-year-old John Ervin, who had curbed his previous house-burning appetite, replaced Giles as a full colonel.

Also in June, Greene commissioned as lieutenant colonels Peter Horry and Hezekiah Maham (of tower fame), each to raise an elite corps of dragoons who, like Lee's Continental Legion, would be elegantly dressed and well armed (except they would wear blue rather than green coats). Greene wanted a body of South Carolina horsemen more reliable and permanent than the mounted militia, and in exchange for being paid the same as Continentals, the new troops had to agree to serve at least a year. Greene allowed that the dragoon units could impress as many horses as they could find, not only from loyalists but even from Whigs if not already in service to the patriot cause, provided they gave receipts for their value for later reimbursement.

The idea, logical in concept, was plagued from the start by rivalries and ambiguities. Horry and Maham, though both Huguenots, had oil and water personalities—Horry was thoughtful and sensitive, Maham quick tempered and scornful of others' opinions. Horry, thirty-four, was a born aristocrat, son of a wealthy plantation owner, whereas the forty-two-year-old Maham had worked the fields as a plantation overseer in his youth before being granted land in St. Stephens Parish to start his own farm.

Complicating matters, their commissions from Greene were dated the same day, creating a conflict regarding which of them was the more senior. Maham considered himself at least equal in rank to Horry or even senior, as he had formed his state cavalry troop before Horry managed to raise his. Although Horry had an earlier Continental commission that was senior to Maham's, Maham viewed it as irrelevant, as Horry had been furloughed as a Continental officer before the fall of Charleston in

1780. Moreover, while Horry was on furlough Maham had been riding cavalry to harass the British invaders. When Horry asserted seniority and said he would take the matter to Greene, Maham suggested they draw lots to settle the issue. (They never did.)

Greene sided with Horry on the seniority question because Horry had never voluntarily resigned his senior Continental commission. Greene also told Horry that he could not believe Maham would seriously contest Horry's claim. But Maham refused to yield the point, and Greene did not step in to resolve the dispute.

There was also a question of to whom Horry and Maham reported. Although some thought was given to placing the new regiments on the Continental line, they were raised as state troops. Officially, then, Horry and Maham reported directly only to South Carolina governor Rutledge and on a "dotted line" basis to Greene.

So where did Marion fit in? He still considered Horry and Maham to be subordinate officers, subject to his orders in fact if not in law, and Greene (and later Rutledge) came to concur with that view. But Maham preferred to think of himself as an independent commander, answerable only to Greene. And Horry chafed at the restrictions Marion continued to impose. Horry wanted to employ Sumter's Law to promise bounties to enlistees in the form of confiscated slaves, but Marion would not allow it. Horry grudgingly told Greene he would continue to serve under Marion until he managed to recruit enough new men to act on his own. Unfortunately Greene's unwillingness to clarify matters at the outset would lead to poisonous relations among Horry, Maham, and Marion in the months ahead.

One of Marion's more nettlesome ex-brigadesmen also had his career terminated around this time. In early June, Captain William Snipes was the target of a surprise attack at his plantation fifty miles west of Charleston. The daring raid by the Queen's Rangers, an esteemed loyalist provincial cavalry unit, was led by John Saunders, the former Georgetown commandant who had imprisoned the flag-carrying John Postell in March. Saunders was accompanied by Thomas Merritt, who had been captured by Marion's men, despite carrying a flag of truce, in retaliation for the imprisonment of Postell, only to escape during Doyle's raid on

Snow's Island. Saunders's Rangers killed about twenty of Snipes's men and took one prisoner who, on Saunders's orders, was mercilessly hacked to death. Snipes managed to escape but fought no more.[*]

Marion did not miss having Snipes with him on his expedition to Monck's Corner; the man had been a hopeless plunderer. But he was glad for the time being that Horry and Maham were accompanying him, for he prized both of them as soldiers. The mission held particular significance for Marion, for he was, in effect, going home to oust the British invader from the area of his birth.

Lieutenant Colonel James Coates, who had just arrived in Charleston in June, led the British opposition at Monck's Corner. Coates had with him 500 to 600 British redcoats from the 19th Regiment of Foot—recent arrivals from Ireland who had yet to see combat. Added to this force were 100 to 150 provincial cavalry under the command of twenty-five-year-old Major Thomas Fraser of the South Carolina Royalists. Fraser's dragoons included remnants of John Harrison's South Carolina Rangers as well as members of the Queen's Rangers, the unit who had struck at Snipes's plantation. The loyalist cavalrymen, most of them from South Carolina, knew the territory as well as Sumter's and Marion's men.

Sumter's plan was to surround Coates at Monck's Corner and cut off his escape routes to Charleston as well as any reinforcements from Orangeburg. Lee, from the west, took Dorchester without opposition after the British abandoned the post there. Hampton seized control of the main route south from Monck's and thundered even at the gates of Charleston. The combined American forces then started closing in on Coates. Upon learning of their advance, Coates pulled up stakes at Monck's Corner and took his men five miles northeast to Biggin Church, a sturdy brick edifice with walls three feet thick. Marion knew it well; it had been his family's place of worship.[†] Coates moved all the supplies from the post at Monck's Corner to Biggin and hunkered down inside the church to await the patriot attack.

---

[*] Two years after the war ended, Snipes killed a man in a duel and was convicted of manslaughter, only to be pardoned by then governor William Moultrie.
[†] The church was founded in 1706, and the original structure, built around 1712, was destroyed by fire in 1755 and then restored.

From Biggin, Coates's only practical avenue of retreat toward Charleston was down the east side of the Cooper River. Going that way he would need to cross Wadboo Bridge, which straddled a creek a mile and a half south of the church. To head off that possibility, Maham was dispatched to the bridge with orders to destroy it. But the hero of Fort Watson proved to be better at building things up than tearing them down; preoccupied with burning two schooners he found at the crossing, he either neglected to break up the bridge or left it sufficiently undamaged so that Coates's men were able to repair it overnight. Maham's lapse would soon cost the patriots.

By the night of July 16, after some inconclusive skirmishing that day with Fraser's dragoons, the Americans had gathered their collective force and camped near Biggin Church. Around 4 a.m. they were awakened by a glowing light coming from the church—Coates had set the building aflame and was retreating toward Charleston down the east side of the Cooper. Sumter roused his men from sleep and immediately sent them after the elusive Coates, who had a significant head start. Lee and Hampton led the chase with their cavalry, followed by Marion's mounted militia, Lee's infantry (entrusted to Marion), and Sumter's mounted infantry. Maham's dragoons rode with Lee, while Peter Horry appears to have ridden separately. One of the patriot horsemen was Peter Gaillard, the ex-Tory who had joined his neighbor Marion's brigade after the engagement at Black Mingo.

When the American cavalry reached Wadboo Bridge on July 17, they discovered, to their consternation, that Coates had gotten across and demolished it behind him to impede their pursuit. They had to cross at a ford farther upstream, further slowing their progress. Soon they realized that at a fork in the road, Coates had split his force, sending Fraser's dragoons to the right while Coates, with the 19th Foot, swung left (east). Hampton's cavalry could not overtake Fraser's horsemen, who crossed the river at either Bonneau's or Strawberry Ferry and secured the boats on the other side. Lee continued his pursuit of Coates's infantry, who crossed over Quinby Creek, an eastern branch of the Cooper, at Quinby Bridge eighteen miles south of Biggin Church.

At daybreak on July 17 Coates and the 19th Foot linked up with Fraser's cavalry at the vacant plantation of patriot colonel Thomas

Shubrick. At Quinby Bridge, a half mile away, the British posted a how-itzer on the southern, or west, bank of the creek to guard the crossing. Coates also had his men pry up the planks on the bridge, which he intended to destroy once his rear guard, trailing with the unit's heavy baggage, made it across. But Lee and Hampton, along with some of Marion's militia horsemen, caught up with the slow-moving rear guard about three hundred yards north of the bridge and captured all hundred of the startled foot soldiers, together with their belongings.

While most of the 19th were still eating breakfast at the plantation, the first wave of Lee's green-uniformed cavalry swept across Quinby Bridge and drove off the artillerists manning the howitzer. But in charging across they so dislodged the loose planks that many fell into the creek, creating a gap in the middle of the bridge. A second group of dragoons jumped the dangerous chasm, but their action threw off more planks and further widened the gap. When Maham tried to negotiate the precarious span, his horse was shot out from under him. But Captain James McCauley, one of Marion's militia horsemen, was not to be deterred. McCauley had spearheaded a bold charge against Watson's redcoats at Wyboo Swamp, and here again he pressed forward, leading a group of horsemen safely to the other side of the creek.

Most of Lee's force was left stranded on the eastern, north bank of the creek. Lee later came under criticism for not ordering all of his men to make the crossing, but he maintained that the horses were too afraid to leap over the growing breach. And although Quinby Creek was only twenty-some yards wide, Lee explained that its muddy bottom was too soft for his men to gain a foothold to repair the bridge or to ford the stream. Nor could they find a firm enough spot on the soggy bank from which to swim their horses across.

On the other side of the creek it was chaos, with the opposing forces jammed in on a narrow causeway. Many of the green recruits of the 19th Foot threw down their weapons and fled, only to return when they saw how few Americans had made it across. In the meantime Coates and a group of his men, their backs against a wagon, drew their sabers and fought off the Americans in deadly hand-to-hand combat. After checking the patriot advance, the redcoats repaired to Shubrick's, taking the howitzer with them. At the plantation they took shelter in the two-story mansion on elevated ground as well as in a range of surrounding out-buildings (barns and slave quarters) protected by rail fences. Fraser's cavalry left for Charleston to seek reinforcements.

By now Marion had come up with the rest of his men. He and Lee assessed the enemy position and quickly concluded it was too strong to permit a direct assault. With Coates's soldiers fortified inside the various structures, the patriot cavalry was of little use, and an infantry attack would require an advance across an open field, exposing the rebels to enemy fire. The American infantry lacked bayonets and was without artillery, whereas Coates had a howitzer. Lee and Marion decided to wait for Sumter, who came up around 3 p.m. Unfortunately he was without the six-pounder that he had at Biggin Church, having left it behind with a subordinate commander so he could speed his chase of Coates.

Lee and Marion advised Sumter against attacking Coates and urged that they at least wait for the artillery to arrive. But at 4:30 p.m. Sumter, impatient for battle, ordered the infantry forward. He sent a South Carolina militia unit of forty-five men under his longtime, dutiful colonel Thomas Taylor to occupy a fence a short distance from the plantation house. Marion was directed across the open field, under heavy fire, to occupy a fence on the other side of the mansion, within fifty yards of it. Meanwhile Sumter moved his own brigade cautiously up the middle, where they took protection behind some of the slave quarters, out of shooting range. The patriot cavalry was kept in reserve; as it turned out, neither Lee's nor Hampton's men would see further action that day.

Taylor's militia came under a barrage of gunshot at the fence and, running low on ammunition, faced a spirited British bayonet charge. Marion, seeing Taylor's men in peril, took his brigade to their rescue. During their oblique movement to cover Taylor's retreat, a number of Marion's men were cut down by British fire. Yet Marion's militia checked and drove off the British bayonet attack, at the sight of which Taylor's men let out a lusty cheer. Marion's musket and riflemen fired from the slight protection of the rail fence, lying low on the ground except to re-load. Although the British shot at them from the house stoop, through doors and windows, and from around corners, Marion's men kept firing until they exhausted their ammunition. After a forty-minute battle Sumter called off the attack. Marion withdrew some three miles with the remainder of Sumter's combined force, and Coates soon retreated, un-molested, to Charleston.

Both Taylor and Marion suffered heavy casualties in the fight at Shu-brick's, with more than fifty killed and wounded, the bulk of them Mari-on's. One of his fallen soldiers was Francis Goddard, son of the widow Jenkins and half-brother to the Jenkins boys from Snow's Island. When news of Goddard's death arrived, his brother James considered it "like a dagger to my heart; and having heard that Sumter would go into battle, whether or not, live or die, I thought then, I could never forgive him. I was also informed that Marion was opposed to risk his men under cir-cumstances so forbidding; and, from what I have heard of his character, I am disposed to believe it."

Taylor loudly complained to Sumter that he had sent him on a forlorn mission without sufficient backup, and he vowed never to serve under the Gamecock again. No postbattle comments from Marion to Sumter are recorded, but Marion implied, in writing to Greene, that Sumter had or-dered him to assault an impregnable enemy position without a field piece or adequate ammunition while Sumter himself remained distant from the action. In his own letters to Greene, Sumter said nothing about Lee's and Marion's objections to making the attack and even suggested it was Mar-ion who had acted recklessly in coming to Taylor's aid. But Greene, likely having received details of the battle from Lee, wrote Marion to praise "the gallantry and good conduct of your men," adding, "I only lament that men who spilt their blood in such noble exertions to serve their country could not have met with more deserved success."

Most revealing of Marion's true feelings, he and Lee left during the night of the battle, rode fifteen miles, and pitched camp without inform-ing Sumter of their whereabouts. All but a hundred of Marion's men left him, angry that they had been endangered while Sumter's men stayed under cover. Whether he said it or not, Marion considered himself fin-ished with Sumter.

Just why Greene had placed Marion under Sumter's yoke is hard to fathom. Sumter had repeatedly failed to do what Greene wanted, whereas Marion had been of great assistance to him. Marion had not lost a sig-nificant engagement, while Sumter had been routed in several; Marion had proved himself the superior tactician. It may have come down to the notion that someone had to be in charge, and because Sumter was the more senior militia officer of the two, Greene considered that he had little choice.

Although Greene later told Lafayette that the Dog Days expedition was "far short of what it might have been," he acknowledged it had been "clever" and had achieved some advantages. The British evacuated their posts at Dorchester and Monck's Corner, although they would return in force to both areas in a few weeks. During the campaign the Americans captured some 140 prisoners, 200 horses, and wagonloads of baggage and ammunition. Among the valuables netted from Coates's rear guard was a pay chest containing 720 guineas (gold coins worth about a pound sterling each), which Sumter distributed to his own and some of Lee's men, one guinea apiece, as a reward for their bravery. Marion's men received none of it, which undoubtedly fueled their resentment of Sumter.

But Thomas Sumter's plundering days were coming to an end—along with his military career. His ten-month enlistees, not satisfied with their guineas, were demanding the bounties of slaves and other pay he had promised them. A week after the battle at Shubrick's, Sumter sent a detachment to Georgetown to seize the slaves, horses, indigo, salt, and medical supplies of the Tories living there. The British retaliated on August 1 by bombarding Georgetown from a warship anchored nearby, then sending sailors ashore to torch the town. Marion, sickened at the thought of so many homeless in a city he loved, hurried aid to alleviate their suffering.

Although Governor John Rutledge generally favored harsh treatment of Tories, he had begun to see that looting them was counterproductive. Having recently returned (at Greene's urging) to South Carolina from Philadelphia and with the patriot military back in control of most of the state, he was anxious to restore civil government. And plundering, he concluded, only served to exacerbate the tensions and unrest that hampered that goal. As a result, on August 5 he issued a proclamation strictly forbidding plundering for any purpose and requiring anyone holding stolen property to return it to the owners. It effectively nullified Sumter's Law.

Sumter took it personally. He resigned his commission in August and disbanded his brigade. Greene, who had not been consulted, was outraged that Sumter would so abruptly leave the patriots in the lurch. Lee offered his view that Sumter had become "universally odious." Greene persuaded Sumter to return to duty in the fall, but the defeat at Shubrick's turned out to be his last battle. He would resign a few months later, this time permanently, after serving a session in the new legislature.

Little more than twelve months earlier Francis Marion had scraped together a dozen followers to enlist in a seemingly hopeless cause. Now he was the supreme field commander of the entire South Carolina militia. And unlike Sumter, he would never willingly end his career on a losing note. But the war in the South was far from over, and winning it would remain, for Marion and the rest, a difficult and deadly proposition.

20

"The Most Galling Fire"

The hanging of Isaac Hayne showed that the British were not going away quietly.

Although many men on both sides were hanged during the Revolution, none, with the exception of Nathan Hale, would achieve the level of martyrdom of Isaac Hayne. A popular and influential Lowcountry planter and patriot militia officer, the thirty-five-year-old Hayne traveled from his plantation to Charleston in the summer of 1780 after its fall to the British to obtain a doctor and medical supplies for his gravely ill wife and children. The British would not allow him to return home unless he swore an oath of allegiance, which he did on the understanding that he would not have to take up arms against his countrymen. But with the American military successes in early 1781, the British pressured Hayne to enlist in the loyalist militia. At the same time, the patriot militia were courting him to rejoin their cause. Marion was told that if Hayne were to take the field for the Americans, another two hundred men would follow him. In the spring of 1781 Marion issued a commission by which Hayne became a lieutenant colonel in the South Carolina militia, and Hayne, after some hesitation, accepted.

In early July, Hayne led a party to suburban Charleston that captured the former patriot militia leader Andrew Williamson, the "Benedict Arnold of the South," who had taken British protection a year earlier. Fearing that the Americans would execute Williamson as a traitor, Balfour, from Charleston, dispatched Thomas Fraser and ninety of his cavalry to rescue him. Two days later Fraser's dragoons surprised Hayne's party at their camp, killed a dozen or so Whigs, retook and released Williamson, and took Hayne himself prisoner.* After a summary trial that he believed was just a preliminary inquiry and in which he was unrepresented by counsel and was unable to call any witnesses, Hayne was found guilty and condemned to death. Charles Fraser, the police chief of Charleston and brother of the man who had captured him, informed him of his sentence.

Despite pleas for Hayne's life by the ladies of Charleston and even some prominent loyalists, Balfour refused to remit the sentence. (Rawdon, in his last official act before sailing for England, concurred with the decision.) Hayne had argued that with the countryside now under Whig control, the British could not provide him the protection that had been a quid pro quo for his oath of allegiance. Consequently he considered himself no longer bound by his prior agreement. But if that argument were to prevail, it would open the floodgates to others looking for an excuse to break their paroles. The British needed to make an example of Hayne. And so on August 4, after being allowed a farewell session with his family, he was paraded through the streets of Charleston, past sobbing citizens, trailed by friends and well-wishers, and went to the gallows. A close acquaintance told Hayne he hoped he would show the world the proper way for an American in such circumstances to die, to which Hayne responded, "I will endeavor to do so." Then, according to a contemporary's account,

> He ascended the cart with a firm step and serene aspect. He enquired of the executioner, who was making an attempt to get the cap over his eyes, what he wanted? Upon being informed of his design, the colonel replied, "I will save you that trouble," and he pulled it over himself. He was afterwards asked whether he wished to say anything, to which he answered, "I will only take leave of my friends, and be ready." He then affectionately shook hands with three gentlemen—recommended his children to their care—and gave the signal for the cart to move.

---

*Williamson would later partially redeem himself in patriot eyes by providing valuable intelligence to the American forces.

Hayne's execution set off a storm of protest and cries for vengeance by southern patriots. The action was even condemned in Parliament, where a motion to censure Rawdon was voted down only after vigorous debate. Greene's officers petitioned him to retaliate in kind. Greene understood the popular reaction but also did not wish to prolong the cycle of violence he had witnessed ever since his arrival in the South. He cautioned Marion against hanging any Tory militia, assuring him that he intended to retaliate, instead, against any British officers equivalent to Hayne who fell into American hands. But other than temporarily suspending prisoner exchanges, Greene ended up doing nothing. When Balfour threatened retribution against American officers if Greene shed the blood of any captured British soldiers of rank—and especially after George Washington told him that sacrificing an innocent person for the guilt of another was considered inhumane—Greene let the matter drop.

Marion did not need to be warned against indiscriminately hanging Tories; that had never been his style. He would instead seek revenge by going after the man who had captured Hayne—Major Thomas Fraser.

IN THE LONG RUN the British decision to hang Hayne was counterproductive, as it created a potent rallying cry for patriots in the South. But in the short term it achieved exactly the desired effect. Intimidated into thinking they might be the next to face the executioner, the Whig militia in Hayne's home district, in the Lowcountry near Charleston, began quitting the field. Correspondingly the Tory militia became emboldened and turned out in force. The British capitalized on the situation, sending Fraser and others to raid the rice plantations in the fertile Lowcountry south and west of Charleston between the Combahee and Edisto Rivers.

For several months patriot militia colonel William Harden, an early member of Marion's brigade, had been commanding an independent partisan unit, with Marion's approval, to keep check on the Tories in that region. Despite a few setbacks, he had enjoyed some considerable success in harassing the British and disrupting their communications between Charleston and Savannah. But after Hayne's execution Harden's force was dwindling and the local population was discouraged to the point at which he asked Greene and Marion for help. With Greene's approval, Marion decided to go to the aid of his old partisan colleague.

At this time, in mid-August, Marion was at Peyre's Plantation on the Santee, where he had been for a few weeks. (With the British presence in that area diminished, he had less need to constantly move his camp.) He had two hundred men but figured he would need to pick up more along the way to be able to engage the enemy force to the south, which numbered upward of six hundred. He also wanted to take with him fifteen of Peter Horry's state dragoons and twenty of Hezekiah Maham's, but neither officer would agree without a direct order from Greene. After several back-and-forth letters, one of Greene's aides finally confirmed to Marion that he could tell Horry and Maham that Greene had ordered them to provide the requested troops. Marion was now ready to move out with an all-mounted force.

Heading out at night on August 22 to avoid detection, Marion took his men on a forced march, a hundred miles south, on a circuitous route that crossed over the main roads used by the British. By August 25 he had reached the Horseshoe, a swampy area around the Ashepoo River in modern Colleton County. The next night he was joined by 150 militia from the southernmost tip of the state and 80 men commanded by a Major Harden (possibly the colonel's son), as Colonel Harden was too sick to fight. Neither Peter Horry (who was left in command at Georgetown) nor Maham made the trip, although Peter's brother, Hugh, was present as usual.

Marion was now up to just over four hundred men. His intelligence reported that the enemy consisted of a mixed infantry and cavalry force under the overall command of a Hessian lieutenant colonel, Ferdinand Ludwig von Benning. Von Benning had 540 troops: 180 Hessians, 150 British redcoats, 130 Tories, and 80 provincial dragoons under Fraser.

The British were not looking for a fight; they were occupied with loading up boats with the rice and cattle they had gathered and sending the forage off to Charleston. But Marion was intent on bringing them to battle. He was not in a position to attack them directly; besides being outnumbered, he was without artillery, and von Benning had two field pieces. The situation instead called for an ambush.

On the night of August 27 Marion tried to ensnare the enemy along a causeway at Godfrey's Savannah, a grassy swamp west of the Ashepoo. He posted a small group there with orders to defend the pass until he could come up with his main body, which lay two miles away. But when the enemy came into sight the posted guards lost their nerve and left without firing a shot, allowing the British a clean passage. Marion aborted the attack.

After some sniping back and forth between the two sides, Marion tried again three days later. By this time, August 30, the British were camped, ironically, at Isaac Hayne's plantation, where his body had been buried just the day before. Marion, camped three miles away, figured the enemy would head northeast along the road to Parker's Ferry, where they would cross the Edisto on their way back to Charleston. In part his assumption was based on intelligence that a group of about a hundred Tories was camped on the east bank of the Edisto at the ferry crossing, waiting for von Benning. They were led by Brigadier General Robert Cunningham, the highest-ranking loyalist militia commander in South Carolina and cousin to the notorious "Bloody Bill" Cunningham.

Moving swiftly to get ahead of the British, Marion found a good spot for an ambush a mile southwest of Parker's Ferry along the road leading directly to it. On either side of the road (a narrow, barely elevated causeway) was a thick, jungle-like swamp. He formed his men in three groups. The main body of dismounted musket and riflemen, commanded by Marion, concealed themselves behind felled trees in the swamp, parallel to the causeway and within forty yards of it. The second group, the eighty men commanded by Major Harden, were ordered to retire a hundred yards from the line and to charge forward once the shooting began. A third group of sixty mounted swordsmen, under Major George Cooper, a subordinate of Colonel Harden, stayed back of Marion's line with orders to fall in the rear of the enemy once the firing became general and "to follow them whenever they moved, and to keep in fight . . . at all hazards."

It was near sunset on a steaming hot day when a party of Cunningham's Tories from the far side of the river crossed over to the west bank and began marching southwest down the causeway, apparently in search of von Benning's force. The Tories passed in front of Marion's line as the rebels waited in ambush. Marion intended to let the small group go by unmolested, and they had all but gotten past when they spotted one of Marion's men (by legend, due to a white feather in his cap). The Tories called out to him, and when he failed to answer they started shooting. Marion could restrain his men no longer, and when the patriots returned the fire the Tories scampered in fright back toward the ferry, in the same direction from which they had come. Marion sent a few horsemen after them who chased them back across the river.

Von Benning, being not far away, heard the shots and assumed it was just a few patriot militia skirmishing with Cunningham's Tories. Marching up front with the infantry and artillery, von Benning ordered Fraser and the cavalry, who were in back, to push down the road toward the ferry and disperse the rebels. As his dragoons came in front of Marion's ambush line Fraser saw Marion's horsemen on the causeway in the distance. Assuming them to be Harden's militia, he ordered his cavalry to charge them.

The next few minutes may have marked the supreme moment of Marion's career to that point. The twenty-five-year-old Fraser, a Scotsman who settled in New Jersey before the war, was very much in the Tarleton mold—a bold dragoon commander who had been antagonizing the patriots for months. He had routed Sumter in battle, eluded Lee at Monck's Corner, and captured Isaac Hayne. Lately he had been harassing Harden's militia and stealing rice from Whig plantation owners. And now he had fallen directly into Marion's carefully laid ambush.

As Fraser's men entered the killing zone, Marion's shooters let out the first barrage of buckshot, at which the front column of Fraser's horsemen raced forward. It was the only direction they could go. Wedged in together on the narrow causeway, they could not turn around and run into the horsemen charging up the road behind them, as it would have been like going the wrong way on a one-way street. Nor could they charge—or even see—the ambushers hidden in the heavy swamp behind the abatis they had formed. And so Fraser's dragoons continued moving forward, even though it exposed them to the rest of Marion's men, who shot them as they passed by. Fraser's riders were like people without umbrellas who try to outrun the rain, only to be drenched.

Both Marion and one of Fraser's cavalrymen, twenty-four-year-old Stephen Jarvis, used the identical phrase to describe what happened:

"running the gauntlet." That specific military term, together with Marion's statement that the enemy ran the gauntlet "through" his men, suggests Marion had placed riflemen on parallel sides of the road. Trapped on the causeway, Fraser's dragoons were forced to absorb the fire along the entire length of the ambush as they galloped toward Parker's Ferry. Jarvis, a loyalist from Connecticut, called it "the most galling fire ever troops experienced."

Fraser's cavalry was annihilated. Twenty of his men fell dead on the spot, with dozens more wounded. Horses quickly piled up on the road, around twenty dead and an equal number wounded, "all of them capital horses," Marion wrote. Fraser had his horse killed and was badly hurt when his cavalry rode over him. One disabled Tory soldier reported being "shot through the body, through the knee and in the head."

Marion's success would have been even greater had two of his commanders not failed him. As soon as the fighting broke out, Major Harden's eighty men retired without firing a shot, and Cooper's sixty swordsmen, who were supposed to hound the enemy cavalry's rear, were nowhere to be found. There may have been some loyalty issues; most of Harden's and Cooper's men were from Georgia or near the Georgia border and had not previously fought under the Swamp Fox. In any event Marion was deprived of a third of his entire force at a critical juncture, just as Fraser's horsemen were reeling and von Benning's infantry and artillery were coming up to join the battle.

Still, Marion's shooters managed to kill or wound almost all of the enemy artillerymen. Unfortunately at that point some of Harden's men ("villains," Marion called them) mistakenly cried out that the enemy was flanking them on the right, causing the patriots to break in confusion. As Marion tried to rally them, von Benning used the opportunity to retreat from the road, carrying off his field pieces and his wounded. Marion brought his men back to take possession of the road, where they stayed for three hours, but it was now dark, and neither side was anxious for further battle. As his men had not eaten for twenty-four hours, Marion took them two miles away to refresh them.

The next morning, August 31, Marion sent a small party to the causeway to bury the enemy dead, but they withdrew when they saw von Benning's superior infantry force coming up with two field pieces. The British buried their own dead, left twenty-seven horse corpses to rot under the scorching sun, and crossed the Edisto at Parker's Ferry uninterrupted. They then headed off to Dorchester to place rice on boats destined for Charleston, where they were headed as well.

All told, the British at Parker's Ferry suffered around twenty-five killed and another eighty to a hundred wounded. In addition, the British lost forty horses, almost all of which they previously had taken from the Continental Army. Marion had three privates wounded and one killed. It was the most lopsided victory of his career. In his report to Greene he singled out Hugh Horry and John Ervin for behaving like true "Sons of Liberty." Greene congratulated Marion on his success, saying it reflected "the highest honor upon your command." In a report to Congress, Greene praised Marion's "good conduct, judgment, and personal bravery."

Marion's trouncing of Fraser was a sweeter revenge for Hayne's execution than any retaliatory hanging would have been. It also served to allay the fears among the Whigs in that area that had caused militia strength to shrink. As Governor Rutledge told South Carolina's delegates to Congress, the victory had given "fresh spirits" to the militia.

Parker's Ferry was perhaps Marion's greatest triumph as a partisan commander. For all of a day he rested his men and horses, weary from their hundred-plus mile journey, then rode another hundred miles back to Peyre's Plantation to await his next assignment from Greene. It would be his most important one yet.

21

"At Eutaw Springs the Valiant Died"

*H*aving spent much of the summer resting his army, Nathanael Greene was ready to fight. But despite his many misgivings about the quality of the militia, he did not want to go into battle without them.

Just as Marion was heading south to go to Harden's aid, Greene decided to end his respite in the High Hills of Santee. Since mid-July he had been camped at John Singleton's Midway Plantation in the High Hills, barely fifteen miles north of the British army at William Thomson's Belleville plantation (next door to the site of the former Fort Motte). Ever since Alexander Stewart, Rawdon's replacement, had moved to Belleville with more than fifteen hundred men in early August, the two armies had been close enough to see each other's campfires. But they were separated by a large, impassable lake that had accumulated from the heavy rains that summer. By the last week of August, Greene had resolved to attack Stewart, but he would not be able to go directly at him.

Logically, to reach the enemy from his position in the High Hills, Greene would have marched south and crossed the Santee at Nelson's Ferry, then moved upriver to Stewart's camp just below the Congaree. But the approach to Nelson's was flooded. Thus, when he broke camp on August 23, Greene set out north, away from Stewart's army. For almost two weeks he marched in a counterclockwise direction that took him up, around, and then back down toward Stewart. He marched at a leisurely pace during the cooler morning and early evening hours to conserve his troops' strength and to give time to various militia commanders to respond to his orders to join him. With Cornwallis now at Yorktown, Virginia was no longer willing to send Greene the two thousand militia it had promised him, so he needed every militiaman from the Carolinas he could get. Greene's Continental army numbered about 1,250, and as he explained to Lee, he was confident that with the addition of six or eight hundred militia he could defeat Stewart with little loss to the regular army.

With his Continentals, including Lee's Legion, Greene headed north up the east side of the Wateree and ferried across at Camden on August 26. He picked up a group of 150 to 200 newly raised militia from North Carolina under French army officer François de Malmedy. From Camden he moved south to cross the Congaree at Howell's Ferry, where he camped on August 28. He was joined there by Pickens with 300 South Carolina militia (including members of Sumter's old brigade) and by Colonel William Henderson, Sumter's replacement, commanding about 150 to 200 South Carolina state troops. William Washington's Virginia Continental cavalry united with the army as well.

Greene was now within striking distance of Thomson's plantation, where he had planned to attack Stewart. But after learning of Greene's movement toward him, Stewart had moved almost forty miles southeast down the Santee to Eutaw Springs on the south side of the river a mile below Nelson's Ferry. He went there to meet a wagon train of supplies coming up from Charleston. At Eutaw Springs, Stewart now commanded an army of about two thousand.

Knowing Marion was busy far to the south, Greene had excused him from his orders to join him for the march against Stewart. But when Greene arrived at Fort Motte on September 2 he decided to wait there a few days to see if Marion's militia, estimated at 240, might be able to link up with him after all. Although he had not yet received Marion's report on the August 30 battle at Parker's Ferry, Greene had his aide-de-camp send the Swamp Fox a letter on September 4 saying he was collecting his force and intended to march the next day and attack the enemy. Greene, anxious to know Marion's whereabouts, wanted him to join him promptly because the army was moving in expectation of it.

It was the next day, September 5, when Greene received Marion's report on Parker's Ferry and realized Marion had already returned to the Santee and was only twenty miles below Eutaw Springs. Greene wrote Marion to tell him to come up as soon as possible, but he need not have worried about Marion's ability to move expeditiously. As soon as he received Greene's letter at his camp, Marion immediately ordered a night march in Greene's direction. To avoid being detected by the British army, which outnumbered him ten-to-one, Marion took his men on a clockwise route under cover of darkness below and around Stewart.

By September 6 Marion was at one of Henry Laurens's plantations, Mt. Tacitus, seventeen miles northwest of Eutaw Springs. He wrote Greene from Laurens's to say that his men and horses were exhausted and that he would remain there to await further orders.

The next day, September 7, Greene and his army met Marion at the Laurens farm and marched with him to Burdell's Tavern, just seven miles above Eutaw Springs. Greene's combined force now stood at over two thousand. At 8 p.m. that night he issued orders from Burdell's for the Americans to march at 4 a.m. the next morning to attack the enemy. He revised his order of battle to put Marion's brigade on the front line. Fighting on his home turf, just four miles from his Pond Bluff Plantation, Francis Marion was about to lead the first large-scale pitched battle of his career.

Eutaw Springs was a bucolic spot on forested land nestled along a creek that feeds into the Santee at Nelson's Ferry. The cold springs that bubbled up there were next to a handsome brick mansion with a walled garden overlooking a field cleared for crops. A small portion of the site near Nelson's Ferry, including the creek and springs itself, has since been submerged under manmade Lake Marion. Small houses and mobile homes as well as commercial establishments surround the area today. But most of the land is still there, and a key part of the battlefield is preserved in a small, peaceful park along the main road. It is hard to imagine that this quiet enclave was the scene of one of the bloodiest battles of the entire Revolution.

ALEXANDER STEWART, a forty-year-old Scot with a high opinion of himself, had entered the British army as a teenager and had many more years of military experience than Nathanael Greene. But at Eutaw Springs on the morning of September 8, 1781, he was nearly caught napping. Somehow unaware that Greene's entire army was only seven miles away, Stewart sent out an unarmed "rooting party" at 5 a.m., before the day's heat set in, to dig for sweet potatoes for his ill-fed troops. (Stewart would later blame his intelligence failure on the partisans having sealed off all the swamp passageways for his scouts, some of whom betrayed him by joining the rebels.) When a couple of American deserters came into the British camp to say that Greene was marching up from the west along the road from Burdell's, a disbelieving Stewart had them arrested as spies.

Just in case, Stewart dispatched cavalry commander John Coffin with both horse and foot soldiers to check out the report. When he ran into the American advance a couple of miles west, Coffin impetuously charged and was soon met by a superior force of Lee's and Henderson's men. The frightened potato diggers fled; many were taken prisoner. After a brief skirmish in which a number of Coffin's men were killed or captured, Coffin and the rest escaped and went back to alert Stewart to Greene's approach. Stewart sent some skirmishers ahead to slow the American advance, but they were quickly driven back by Lee's forward group with the help of two American field pieces brought up to reinforce him. During this skirmish the two main bodies of army formed and by 9 a.m. were ready to do battle.

Greene deployed his troops using a variation of the by-then-familiar Cowpens model, with the militia and state troops up front, the Continentals in a line behind them, and the cavalry on the flanks and in reserve. The soldiers set up in lines running north to south, directly facing the enemy to the east. The first patriot line, dismounted infantry, consisted of Pickens's South Carolina militia and Henderson's state troops on the left (north), Malmedy's North Carolinians in the middle, and Marion on the right, just south of the main River Road that ran east-west. As the senior officer, Marion had overall command of the entire militia force and would have decided on the configuration of the militia front line. To command the right of his own brigade, he chose Richard

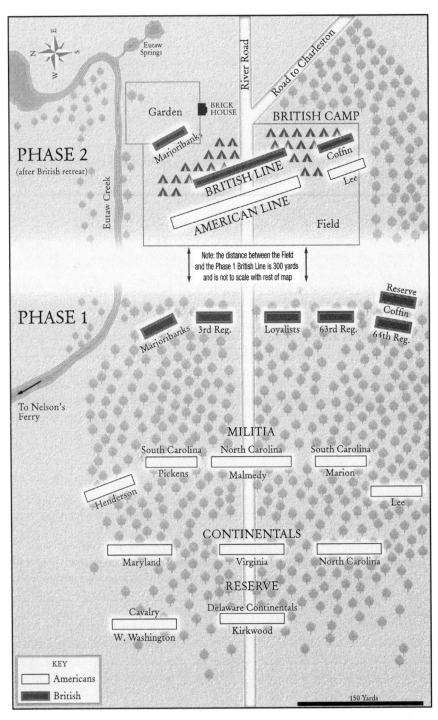

The Battle of Eutaw Springs, September 8, 1781

Richardson Jr., now a colonel, who a year earlier had risked his life to warn Marion of the trap Tarleton set for him at Richardson's Plantation.

The second American line comprised Continental infantry from Maryland, Virginia, and North Carolina, in that order, from left to right (north to south). The Marylanders and Virginians were battle-hardened veterans of such places as Camden, Cowpens, Guilford Courthouse, and Hobkirk's Hill. The North Carolina Continentals, by contrast, had only recently been re-formed and were untested in actual combat. They were led by Brigadier General Jethro Sumner, a dedicated and capable Continental commander who had been a wealthy tavern owner before joining the service.

In the third line were William Washington's eighty to one hundred Continental cavalrymen. Alongside them were sixty to eighty experienced Delaware Continental light infantry under Captain Robert Kirkwood, who had fought many northern battles under George Washington and had distinguished himself at the Battle of Cowpens.

Lee's Legion, including both mounted and foot soldiers, was posted off to Marion's right, protecting the far right flank of the front line. Guarding the extreme left flank was Henderson's South Carolina state cavalry, under the immediate command of Wade Hampton. Maham and his state dragoons apparently were present; Peter Horry, still at Georgetown and trying without much success to raise a cavalry regiment, was absent.

Greene also had four cannons—two three-pounders and two six-pounders—that were placed in the middle of the front and center lines, respectively.

Stewart's army was all British redcoats and loyalist provincials; no militia or Hessians fought with him that day. He posted a single main line of defense about three hundred yards west of the edge of the cleared crop field where the British were camped. Many of the British regulars were familiar to the Americans. Holding down Stewarts's left were remnants of the 63rd and 64th Regiments of Foot, who had served the entire war, first in the North and then variously under Wemyss, Tarleton, McLeroth, and Watson in their attempts to eliminate Marion. Here they looked directly across at their old adversary as he readied his militia on the patriot right.

On the British right were regulars of Stewart's own 3rd Regiment of Foot, the Buffs (named for the yellow-brown color of their decorative uniform coverings). Although they had arrived in the colonies just three months earlier, these mostly Irish soldiers were among the best trained in the British army.

In the center of Stewart's line were loyalist units from New York and New Jersey, including DeLancey's New York Brigade under John Harris Cruger, the defender of Ninety-Six during Greene's siege. (Cruger was married to a DeLancey, a prominent Tory family of New York Huguenots.) Although Cruger was not a British regular, Stewart put him in overall charge of the front line, making him Marion's counterpart that day.

Like the Americans, the British covered their flanks with soldiers of the highest order. The left was supported by the South Carolina Royalists—Thomas Fraser's loyalist cavalry unit, under the command of Major John Coffin. (Fraser, injured at Parker's Ferry, was absent.) The far right (north) was held down by Major John Marjoribanks (pronounced *Marshbanks*), who commanded flank companies of the 3rd, 19th, and 30th Regiments of Foot, recently arrived from Cork, Ireland, but eager for battle. They consisted of light infantry and elite assault forces of grenadiers (still called that, though they wielded no grenades). Marjoribanks's units would play a pivotal role on this day.

Stewart had four or five large artillery pieces at his disposal—at least two, possibly three six-pounders, plus a four-pounder. He also had some small, portable swivel guns that allowed a wide arc of movement.

Probably no two opposing armies in any large-scale engagement during the southern phase of the war were as evenly matched as these. Greene had perhaps a few hundred more men available for battle than Stewart did, partly because Stewart's original force of around two thousand was missing most or all of his rooting party, which had numbered anywhere from sixty to three hundred. Stewart was blessed with more experienced soldiers overall, but the bulk of the American force did not lack for seasoning. Several outstanding subordinate commanders led both sides. The British had more artillery power, but thanks to Marion's drubbing of Fraser's cavalry at Parker's Ferry the week before, Greene had a decided advantage in the number of mounted soldiers. Cavalry were of limited utility on the lightly wooded, brushy terrain, but they could play an important role in augmenting an assault or cutting off a retreat.

The biggest question mark was how the American militia, a third of Greene's total force, would perform. This was the first large pitched battle that Marion's irregulars were fighting under him. Other patriot militia had a spotty track record in such battles; under Gates at Camden they had cut and run, tossing aside their muskets the moment they saw the British bayonets charging at them. They had done surprisingly well at Cowpens, where Morgan asked only that they deliver two or three volleys before withdrawing. Guilford Courthouse, where Greene commanded, had been more of a mixed bag. How would they do under Marion on this day?

MARION'S SEVEN HUNDRED militiamen were the first to march forward through the open woods, squinting at the east-risen sun as it shone through the trees. Soon they would be fighting under sweltering, throat-parching conditions that had men feeling as if they might die from thirst if not from a sword or musket ball.

The British front line was about 150 yards away. When they came within firing range Marion's brigade on the right fired the first shots, followed down the line by Malmedy's North Carolinians and Pickens's troops. Shouting encouragement to each other as they surged forward, Marion's troops continued to fire volley after volley—an average of seventeen per man, he later estimated, an unheard of performance by patriot militia. It was a testament to their trust in Marion—and Pickens's men in their own leader—that the South Carolina militia kept pressing forward like veterans in the face of deadly fire.

Malmedy's North Carolinians were less disciplined. Never having fought under their French commander, they withdrew after three rounds, creating a hole in the middle of the line. Fortunately Sumner's North Carolina Continentals rushed up from the second line to plug the gap and protect Marion's left flank, allowing him to keep advancing with his comrades. But Sumner's Continentals eventually broke as well, and the militia's progress stalled.

After emerging from the protection of the woods into more open land, Marion's men became vulnerable to the British bayonets. Seeing an opportunity, the veterans of the British 63rd and 64th on the left excitedly charged the Americans with cold steel, forcing Marion to call a retreat. But when the redcoats pushed on with their counterattack, they ran headlong into the well-formed Maryland and Virginia Continentals from Greene's second line. The Americans gave the British a taste of their own medicine, firing a volley and then surging forward with bayonets. The 63rd and 64th ran in disorder back to their camp—the first and only time during the entire war in which those seasoned units made a full retreat with their backs to an American bayonet charge.

On the British right Lieutenant Colonel John Eager Howard's Marylanders broke the ranks of Stewart's Buffs in a clash of steel so close that some of the dead were found stuck in each other's bayonets. The Buffs, new to battle, fought with determination but retreated along with their more experienced colleagues. They left ankle-deep puddles of blood behind.

The British front line had collapsed. As part of the rout, the loyalists in the British middle also gave way and, in accordance with Stewart's contingency plan, took shelter in the brick house beyond the camp. Pursued by Lee's Legion infantry, who had flanked the British left, the provincial New York Volunteers barely managed to bar the door before the Americans could barge in on them.

During the British skedaddle, Marion set about to re-form his own brigade on the right. Meanwhile, on the American left, Henderson's South Carolinians were being pummeled on their flank by Marjoribanks's light infantry and grenadiers, the only British contingent that had held its ground. Henderson himself fell wounded, after which his command passed to Wade Hampton, who managed to steady the state troops.

With Marjoribanks now threatening the Marylanders' left flank, Greene ordered Washington's cavalry to drive him off. But Washington could not penetrate the scrubby thicket where Marjoribanks's men were posted with their backs to Eutaw Creek. In rashly trying to circle around them, Washington and his riders were exposed to dangerous fire, and all but two of his officers were killed or wounded. Washington fell under his dead horse and was bayoneted and taken prisoner. Hampton charged the British flank with his dragoons but was no more successful. Finally Kirkwood's Delaware Continentals, perhaps the cream of the American army, came up from their position in reserve and dislodged Marjoribanks, who withdrew in good order to a more secure position in the walled garden beside the mansion.

By now Stewart had retreated all the way through his camp, abandoning his tents and artillery to the pursuing Americans. Some of the British soldiers fled down the road toward Charleston. As Greene's army overran the enemy camp, the Americans appeared on the verge of a glorious victory. And then it began to unravel.

Greene's soldiers had been given swigs of rum before the battle to energize them, but when they came upon the British liquor barrels they could not resist getting into them to quench their thirst—and then some. They helped themselves to rum and other spoils. Although the officers (dwindling in number due to casualties) tried to stop the looting, the soldiers (mostly Virginia and Maryland Continentals) kept celebrating with food and spirits. As Maryland Continental commander Otho Williams wrote, the men became "utterly unmanageable."

Stewart in the meantime was busy re-forming his line in a diagonal running southeast just beyond the camp. Marjoribanks anchored the right from the garden while sharpshooters took up position from the windows of the mansion stronghold. Soon they began raining lethal gunshot on the drunk and disorderly Americans in the adjacent field as well as the artillerists who had brought up the Americans' heavy cannon. Marion was sent forward to assist, but his force and firepower were insufficient to stem the tide.

It was again Stewart's turn to counterattack. Marjoribanks assaulted the American left flank, and Coffin's cavalry, only defensively engaged to that point, swooped down upon the American right. Lee's cavalry, scattered over various parts of the battlefield, could not parry Coffin's assault. Lee himself was absent from his cavalry post at that critical moment, as he had been for much of the contest, preferring instead to roam about the field directing other units (for which he would be criticized afterward).*

It was left to Wade Hampton, who seemingly was everywhere that day, to cover the American retreat. Through sheer tenacity he managed to push Coffin back in hand-to-hand fighting but had to withdraw under heavy fire from the loyalists in the house and Marjoribanks in the garden. Marjoribanks then swept through the British camp and not only recovered two six-pounders left behind by Stewart but also captured the Americans' two six-pounders, abandoned during the flight of the intoxicated. With both of Greene's three-pounders having been put out of action earlier in the battle, he had no ability to batter the sturdy brick mansion.

After nearly four hours of fighting, Greene had little choice but to call a general retreat. He paused to collect his dead, then went in search of desperately needed fresh water for his men. With the enemy controlling access to the creek and springs, he withdrew several miles to Burdell's Tavern, where his soldiers came upon a filthy pond that the cavalry had tramped through earlier in the day. As William Dobein James later recorded, the men dove headlong into the puddle, over the shoulders of each other, and drank "with an avidity which seemed insatiable."

Greene called the Battle of Eutaw Springs "by far the most bloody and obstinate I ever saw." The casualties on both sides were frighteningly high. Officially Greene lost a quarter and Stewart at least a third of their respective forces, although both counts are probably understated. Some estimates place Stewart's killed, wounded, missing, or captured at just over 40 percent of his total, making it the greatest percentage loss of any field army during the war.

The Americans had an unusually high number of ranking officers killed or wounded—almost sixty. In addition to Henderson and William

---

*In his memoirs Lee claimed that his cavalry was hampered by an order for it to assist William Washington in his ill-fated attack on Marjoribanks and that absent that order, his mounted soldiers would have destroyed the British army during its retreat toward the brick plantation house.

Washington, Pickens was put out of commission by a musket ball to the chest that would have been fatal but for it striking the buckle of his sword belt. While discussing tactics with Lee, Lieutenant Colonel Richard Campbell, commander of the Virginia Continentals, fell wordless in his saddle from an enemy shot and died shortly thereafter. John Eager Howard, a heroic performer at many a previous southern battle, especially Cowpens, was speared by a bayonet but would live to become a governor and US senator from Maryland.

On the British side Stewart reported twenty-nine commissioned officers killed, wounded, or missing, but he failed to account for those who were among the several hundred British taken prisoners. Stewart was wounded on the elbow, although not severely, and had his horse shot in two places. The greatest loss was Major Marjoribanks, who more than anyone was responsible for snatching victory from the patriot grasp. Wounded while leading the final counterattack upon the Americans, he was taken on the British army's march toward Charleston and, after developing a severe fever, was left at the plantation of Huguenot patriot Daniel Ravenel, located a few miles above Biggin Church. Cared for in a slave hut, Marjoribanks died and was buried at Ravenel's Wantoot Plantation six weeks later. Before his gravesite was to be inundated by Lake Marion in the 1940s, he was reinterred on the battlefield at Eutaw Springs, to sleep forever near the garden spot from which he had so valiantly fought.

Marion's brigade was also hard hit that day. Marion listed five killed—two of them officers—and twenty-six wounded. Among the latter was Hugh Horry, who was wounded in the fleshy part of his leg. Private Jehu Kolb took a ball in the knee and was disabled for life. He was from a long line of military men: his father had been killed in the Cherokee campaign of 1759, fighting alongside Francis Marion, and his relative, militia colonel Abel Kolb, was the famous murder victim of vengeful Tories.

A further indication of the fierceness of the fighting comes from the pension application of Jim Capers, a free black man and former slave who long served as a drum major under Marion. Capers was wounded in four different places—once on the head and twice in the face with a sword and then once with a shot through the body that passed into the drummer behind him, killing the man instantly. A cook for Marion,

James Delaney, was among those wounded that day. One of the Snow's Island Jenkins clan who served under Marion was killed, and when his cousin, James Jenkins, visited the battlefield later, he counted thirteen bullet holes in a small tree that stood between the two armies.

Even Greene was impressed with the militia's comportment that day, later commenting that they fought with "a degree of firmness that reflects the highest honor upon this class of soldiers." In typically understated fashion, Marion reported to Peter Horry that "my Brigade behaved well." Congress agreed and awarded Marion special thanks for the "distinguished part" he took at Eutaw Springs as well as for his "prudent and intrepid attack" on the British at Parker's Ferry the month before.

As FOR WHICH side "won" at Eutaw Springs, that question would generate disagreement both in the days that followed and in years to come. Both commanding generals claimed an unequivocal victory. Stewart's contention rested on his having "held" the field at the end. But in reality he had been driven from the field to take refuge in and around the brick house from which place the Americans were repulsed, leaving neither side in total control of the battleground proper. Greene reported that he left behind a strong picket under Wade Hampton to watch the field when the main army went in search of water, and although Stewart heatedly denied this, he did not claim to have pursued the retreating Americans. Tactically the battle was more like a draw.

More telling, perhaps, is what happened the next day. Greene returned to the field, intending to offer battle to any British who remained there, but the rainy weather would have hampered the firing of weapons, so he gave up on the idea. Significantly, Stewart was already beginning to retreat down the road to Charleston. He burned his supplies, destroyed a thousand sets of small arms, and dumped casks of rum (what was left of it) into Eutaw Creek. He also left seventy wounded behind and his dead unburied—normally signs of losing. Greene buried both sides' dead and tended to the enemy's wounded, common indicators of victory in those days.

Although Greene had not scored a clear-cut victory in this—or, indeed, any other battle he fought in the South—he had achieved his overall strategic objective. Like Cornwallis's and Rawdon's armies before him, Stewart's was a spent force. The last substantial British field army in South Carolina withdrew to within the perimeter of Charleston and vicinity. "The more he is beaten," one British officer said of Greene, "the farther he advances in the end." Henry Lee, whose eloquence, unlike his battlefield judgment, was never questioned, summed it up as follows: "The honor of the day was claimed by both sides, while the benefits flowing from it were by both yielded to the Americans: the first belonged to neither and the last to us."

A few years after the battle the following opening stanza from an equally eloquent eulogy was penned by Philip Freneau, the romantic Huguenot poet of the American Revolution:

> At Eutaw Springs the valiant died;
> Their limbs with dust are covered o'er;
> Weep on, ye springs, your tearful tide;
> How many heroes are no more!

22

"Watchful Anxiety"

lthough Eutaw Springs had broken the back of British power in South Carolina, in many ways Francis Marion was just as busy after the battle as before it. Greene now looked to Marion to keep the enemy in check between the Santee and Charleston. Always fearing the worst, Greene also told Marion to be prepared at a moment's notice to join him should Cornwallis leave Virginia to return to South Carolina, as was frequently rumored. Governor John Rutledge, as part of his effort to restore civil government to the state, had a whole plateful of tasks he looked to Marion to carry out. Meanwhile the long-simmering dispute between Peter Horry and Hezekiah Maham over rank threatened to boil over with far more destructive consequences than before.

Immediately after the battle at Eutaw Springs, Greene had dispatched Marion's and Lee's forces, now including Maham, to cut off Stewart's retreat toward Charleston. Maham's dragoons managed to capture some British and Tory stragglers to the army's rear, but the Americans were unable to get behind Stewart's main force, as three or four hundred fresh British troops came up to Monck's Corner to cover his withdrawal. On September 12 the British received additional reinforcements from Charleston under Colonel Paston Gould, who took command of the army while Stewart, with his elbow wounded, retired to the city.

Upon his arrival in Charleston in June 1781, Gould had been placed in overall command of British forces in the Carolinas and Georgia, succeeding Balfour, who remained commandant of Charleston. But Gould, unfamiliar with the territory, had mostly stayed in Charleston, content to leave matters in the field to Stewart. He now would get a firsthand look at what the war in the South was like.

Passing Greenland Swamp near Eutaw Springs, he came upon a gruesome sight—the head of a black man placed on a stake beside the swamp as a warning to others. He was later identified as Harry, a slave owned by the Gaillard family of Tories. Frequently employed by Rawdon and Balfour to spy on partisan groups in the Lowcountry, Harry was near Monck's Corner, gathering intelligence on Marion, when he fell into the hands of a group of Whigs and was beheaded. A year later, in documenting the deaths of loyalists during the war, British officers attributed Harry's murder to an unidentified party of Marion's men. Marion did not hesitate to hang spies and at this time was under specific orders from Governor Rutledge to execute any slaves found to have spied for the enemy. So there is no reason to doubt the incident took place. But it is unlikely Marion would have approved of a grisly beheading.

After a brief maneuver in Greene's direction that took him as far as Laurens's plantation above Eutaw Springs, Gould turned back toward Charleston and stopped fifty miles from the city. He set up camp at Ravenel's Wantoot Plantation, where he and half the army were down with the seasonal fever and where Marjoribanks would die. Gould soon left for Charleston and was promptly succeeded in overall command by fifty-year-old General Alexander Leslie, who was better acquainted with the southern theater. Meanwhile Stewart resumed operational command at Wantoot, seven miles above Monck's Corner. From there his force of twelve hundred effectives raided neighboring plantations for food and collected slaves, including women and children, to send off to Charleston. There they could be used to strengthen the British fortifications, serve as domestics, and compensate loyalists for their abandoned property.

With the British below the Santee, Greene retired north again to the High Hills of Santee to rest his own tired and sickly army. Marion remained on the Santee near Murray's Ferry, fifty miles from Greene, low on troops and ammunition and—rare for him—slowed by the fever that had lately struck so many others. At least this one time, Marion's favorite vinegar-and-water concoction had failed to ward off illness.

Throughout the late summer and fall of 1781 Marion was in constant communication with Greene, providing him intelligence on the enemy's troop movements and strength. Marion was also being peppered with almost daily and sometimes twice-daily letters from Governor Rutledge issuing directives or seeking advice or favors on both military and civil matters. As head of the government-in-exile during the previous year and a half, Rutledge had been wielding virtual dictatorial power, limited only by what he chose to delegate. He put Marion in charge of appointing justices of the peace in each district and issuing passes for civilian travel to Charleston. Rutledge specified that women who went to town without leave were not to be allowed to return, while wives and children of Tories were to be sent off to the British lines in retaliation for the enemy practice of sending the families of Whigs out of the state. To make "severe examples" of them, Rutledge had ordered on September 2 that all slaves who took provisions or carried intelligence to the enemy were to be put to death—the fate that befell Harry.

Rutledge wanted the names of Marion's men who had switched sides to the Tories and details on the houses burned and Whigs hanged by the enemy. The governor also sought Marion's recommendations for administrators to process matters such as wills and property transfers that had lacked official sanction during the previous eighteen months of anarchy. That Rutledge, a London-educated, highly successful lawyer and politician, had brought Marion into his inner circle demonstrates how much trust and respect the partisan leader had earned.

Following the Battle of Eutaw Springs, Rutledge decided to offer all Tories, with certain exceptions, a pardon and permission to reunite with their families if they agreed to serve six months in the patriot militia. Those who declined to serve faced banishment and abandonment of their properties. Now that the British hold on the state was unfastened, Rutledge believed he could induce—or coerce—many men who had taken British protection after the fall of Charleston and even fought for the Tory side to return their allegiance to the patriot cause. It was the obverse of the original Clinton proclamation that offered pardons and paroles to Whigs who swore oaths of allegiance to the Crown and punishment for those who did not.

After seeking Marion's opinion on several points relating to the proposed amnesty, Rutledge issued a proclamation on September 27, 1781, and gave Marion responsibility for circulating it. It provided that those seeking pardons had to appear before a brigadier general of South Carolina within thirty days to swear oaths of allegiance and accept the terms of militia service. Marion therefore assumed the additional job of accepting the surrenders of the "six month" enlistees and keeping detailed lists of those who accepted pardons. Rutledge also kept him busy levying fines against men who shirked militia duty, finding places in the military for various prominent men or their relatives, selecting men fit to be magistrates, gathering up indigo and salt for public use, and performing sundry other assignments of an executive assistant nature, including finding the governor a printing press, paper, and ink.

Even as he was handling all of these tasks, Marion found time to attend to family matters. In October 1781 he sought to arrange for the shipment of indigo to Philadelphia for the support of his nephews in college there, adding that "I wish it could be soon as my boys are suffering from want of winter cloths."

In addition Marion had to deal with the growing insubordination of Peter Horry and Hezekiah Maham. Although Greene had previously directed both of them to follow Marion's orders, they continued to resist. Horry was also frustrated by his inability to find enough cavalrymen to satisfy Greene's earlier directive to raise state dragoons for extended service.

Perhaps perturbed at Horry for having been absent at both Parker's Ferry and Eutaw Springs, Marion gave his old friend a serious dressing down. On September 23 he wrote to say he had been informed that Horry or one of his officers had ordered a tar-kiln of John Brockinton, the Black Mingo Tory, to be set on fire to make coals for Horry's workmen. Marion told Horry that those responsible would have to pay the value of the destroyed property. Another of Horry's men allegedly tried to commandeer some property from a citizen; if true, Marion warned Horry, he would have the man arrested and court-martialed.

Marion added that he had heard that Horry's officers had taken a number of other liberties beyond their authority and that his infantry was full of men only pretending to do militia duty. (Three were performing the work of one, as Marion put it.) Marion also thought that many of Horry's officers seemed to be idle at that point. He sent Horry a list of the men he was allowed to keep and concluded with an icy brushoff: "The time is lost when your Horse would have been of service to me. You will therefore send your men to Gen. Greene, agreeably to his orders."

Rutledge followed up with a letter to Horry saying Marion had informed him that some of Horry's officers had "behaved very much amiss" in impressing citizens' horses that were not fit for dragoon service, including plow horses and breeding mares, which the governor ordered returned to their owners. Another letter from Rutledge accused Horry's men of taking "every step in their power to abuse, insult and exasperate the militia" and warned Horry that if he did not put a stop to the bad behavior, he (Rutledge) would.

Horry exploded. He sent a lengthy, point-by-point rebuttal to Rutledge in which he denied having countenanced any misconduct and complained that "Gen. Marion's charges always say 'your officers,' but do not name the officers in particular." Never in seven years of service, Horry added, had he received such a severe reprimand from a superior officer. He offered to submit to a court-martial trial to vindicate himself and silence Marion's complaints.

Then Horry separately wrote to Greene to label Marion's charges as groundless and to suggest he could no longer serve under him. "I used to submit to Gen. Marion's orders with pleasure," Horry said, "but at present I assure you it is disagreeable to me and all my officers who have experienced his late usage." Horry claimed to know what Marion's motives were for attacking him, but although they were "obvious" to him, he said he would not bother Greene with the details. Horry never did specify what he was referring to; possibly he thought Marion was envious that Horry had been commissioned to lead an elite cavalry unit, whereas Marion was still stuck with the lowly militia. Horry himself was still unclear whether he and his corps were on the Continental or state establishment, but if the former, he told Greene, "I shall receive orders from no other person but yourself." He concluded by asking how he was expected to complete his recruiting, as he had no money and Rutledge had ordered a stop to the practice of allowing men to buy their way out of military service by hiring substitutes.

Marion's relations with Maham were, if anything, worse. After Maham appropriated for his regiment the high-quality horse of one Mr. Oliver, the father of one of Maham's cavalrymen, Marion ordered him to return it. When Maham refused, Marion threatened to court-martial him. "It is high time, I think," Marion wrote to Maham on October 18, "that you and I should know whether I have the power of commanding you or not." Five days later Greene told Maham to mend his ways. "You will please to consider yourself under the command of General Marion," Greene wrote. To reassure Marion, Greene simultaneously wrote to him, enclosing his letter to Maham and a similar one to Horry, adding that "no man can command them better than yourself." Maham returned the horse.

No one had handled the conflict in command very well. Greene and Rutledge had failed to lay down clear lines of authority from the beginning. Marion had been cold and peremptory in his dealings with his more junior officers. And Horry and Maham exaggerated their own importance, fancying themselves as favored commanders on par with Light-Horse Harry Lee—while forgetting that Lee himself had acted co-operatively with Marion.

Although Maham would not be mollified, Horry and Marion managed to patch things up between them for the time being. Greene facilitated their reconciliation, writing Horry on November 6 to say that

> General Marion cannot wish to injure you after knowing how much you have done and suffered for the cause. It is your interest to be friends. . . . The General is a good man; few of us are without faults; let his virtues veil his if he has any. . . . Your bleeding country demands a sacrifice of little injuries and your own good sense will point out the best mode of avoiding them.

Marion, while stopping short of a formal apology, told Horry that he meant nothing personal; if he found fault with any officers for things he believed they had done wrong, he was not angry with them as individuals but with "the very action itself," especially if contrary to the

public good. At Marion's request he and Horry met in person during the
first week of November, and with Marion's promise to give Horry the
first opportunity to refute or redress any future complaints against him,
Horry pronounced himself satisfied.

These distractions aside, there was much cause for jubilation on the
part of Greene, Marion, and company at this time. Although it took a
couple of weeks for the official word to arrive, they learned that on October 19 Lord Cornwallis had surrendered his entire army to General
Washington and the French forces at Yorktown. Coupled with the vote
of thanks for his efforts at Eutaw Springs and Parker's Ferry, which he
received around the same time, the victory at Yorktown prompted Marion to take the unprecedented step—for him—of throwing a party. On
the evening of November 10 at John Cantey's plantation on the north
bank of the Santee, Marion hosted a ball for his officers and the area ladies. Reportedly he was subdued that night, but whether that was due to
a specific worry or his general nature is hard to know. "The general's
heart was not very susceptible of the gentler emotions," William Dobein
James explained. "His mind was principally absorbed by the love of country. . . . But if he did feel joy upon a few occasions, certain it is that
watchful anxiety was the daily inmate of his breast."

Weighing on his mind was the fate of two patriots languishing in
prison. One was John Postell, still being held in Georgetown despite
Marion's repeated pleas to Greene to arrange a release of him in exchange for one or more British prisoners. Marion believed Greene was
giving preference to other American prisoners over Postell, and said so,
but Greene explained that the execution of Isaac Hayne had suspended
all prisoner exchanges in the normal course. Marion asked Greene at
least to stop paroling various captured British officers until Postell was
freed, but Greene was not willing to go that far. Postell would remain in
jail for the duration of the war.

A more recent and urgent case was that of Peter Sinkler, a fifty-five-
year-old prominent patriot who owned a plantation adjacent to Eutaw
Springs. He had provided frequent service to Marion's brigade and had
other close connections to Marion: Sinkler's sister, Dorothy, was the
widow Richardson who had helped Marion escape Tarleton's clutches

(and paid dearly for it), and his first wife was the sister of Marion's cousin and best friend, Henry Mouzon. Shortly after the Battle of Eutaw Springs, while the British were still in the area, Sinkler's own brother-in-law betrayed him to the enemy by revealing his favorite hiding spot. The British captured the unarmed Sinkler and put him in irons in the basement of Charleston's dark, dank Exchange Building. Before being removed to that place he was forced to witness the destruction of his property and was denied a farewell visit with his wife and children.

Marion could not bear the thought of Sinkler wasting away in jail. Drawing on the goodwill he had developed with Rutledge, Marion prevailed upon the governor to take up Sinkler's case with Greene. Rutledge reported back to Marion to say that "between ourselves" Greene consented to Marion's exchanging any prisoner he already had or could "get" for Sinkler—as long as it were done without Greene's knowledge. Marion took that as a green light to seize some unarmed loyalists in hopes of exchanging them for Sinkler and some others of Marion's men being held by the British.

But the deal failed to materialize. Greene wrote Marion on October 30 to say that taking unarmed men to offer in exchange for prisoners was inappropriate. Greene released the Tory prisoners on parole. He was forced to take that position, having just written to Gould in Charleston to complain that the British were taking unarmed Americans. Sinkler remained in jail, contracted typhus fever as a result of the unsanitary conditions, and died soon thereafter.

DESPITE WHAT MOST history textbooks claim, Yorktown did not end the American Revolutionary War. Initially Greene hoped the victorious French fleet in the Chesapeake, under Comte de Grasse, would come south to Charleston to blockade the city from the sea, enabling Greene to attack by land and finish the British off in a siege similar to the one that trapped Cornwallis at Yorktown. Indeed, Henry Lee, who witnessed Cornwallis's surrender, went to Virginia at Greene's direction to lobby Lee's mentor, George Washington, for the French navy's help in reducing

Charleston. Lee also requested and Washington promised that Greene's field army would be reinforced by Continental troops freed up as a result of the capitulation of the British at Yorktown. When the British evacuated Wilmington, their last stronghold in North Carolina, on November 14, it also augured well for the American cause.

But the assistance Greene was hoping for failed to materialize. The French, in strategic alliance with Spain, sailed instead for the West Indies, where the British fleet soundly defeated de Grasse in his attempt to capture Jamaica. Washington did send some Continentals, but they ended up being too few and too late to make any real difference in South Carolina. The most valuable of them were the Pennsylvania regulars under General "Mad Anthony" Wayne, the hero of Stony Point, whom Greene sent to help liberate Georgia.

Greene did receive more substantial reinforcements in the form of three or four hundred "over mountain" men from what is now eastern Tennessee. They were under the command of militia colonels John Sevier and Isaac Shelby, heroes of King's Mountain. Greene assigned these buckskin-clad, tomahawk-wielding riflemen to help Marion patrol the areas outside Charleston. Arriving in Marion's camp at Cantey's Plantation by November 2, the mountaineers were expected to stay until the spring or the reduction of Charleston. But they left to go home to their native hills three weeks later, sticking around only long enough to steal some clothing and take part in one significant engagement. They preferred the mountains to the swamps and were bored by the long waits under hard living conditions the militia had to suffer between actions.

The final liberation of South Carolina was largely in the hands of Greene and Marion. Pickens had recovered from his wound at Eutaw Springs but was soon occupied on the western frontier keeping Indians and local loyalists under control. Sumter was back in charge of his brigades, and at Greene's request he established a post at Orangeburg, a hundred miles inland, to check the Tories there and prevent supplies from being sent to Charleston. His men were kept busy for a time defending backcountry raids by "Bloody Bill" Cunningham and other diehard Tory marauders bent on revenge. But Sumter, who regarded his remaining militia as "the worst men" in his brigade and his state troops as not of the quality he had expected, did not personally lead them in action. He did write to Marion, asking him to confer with him on a secret plan for expediting the war's end. But Greene, who no longer viewed Sumter as vital to the cause, had already told Marion he was free to coordinate with Sumter or not as he deemed appropriate. Needless to say, Marion ignored the Gamecock.

By now Greene had enough confidence in Marion to grant him discretion on how and where to deploy his troops. "As you are at liberty to act as you may think advisable, I have no particular instructions to give you, and only wish you to avoid a surprise," Greene wrote him on November 15. That same day, while at Peyre's Plantation, Marion sent Maham with 180 of his horsemen and 200 of Shelby's and Sevier's riflemen on a mission to stop British plundering along the Santee below Eutaw Springs. In a daring early morning raid on November 17 Maham and his riders slipped behind the main enemy lines at Wantoot and attacked the British post at Fairlawn Plantation seven miles south of Monck's Corner. The eleven-thousand-acre colonial barony, owned by the Colleton family, well-known Tories, featured a large mansion the British had converted into a hospital.* When Maham had the mountaineers dismount and move closer to fire their rifles upon the house, the inhabitants, given the choice of surrendering or having the mansion stormed by frontiersmen with scalping knives, surrendered without a struggle. An outnumbered British garrison of fifty manning a small fort half a mile away in sight of the house watched without intervening.

What happened next was and still is the subject of controversy. The British accused Maham's men of burning the hospital and "dragging away a number of dying people to expire in swamps," an act of "barbarity hitherto unknown in civilized nations." Marion's initial report to Greene

---

* Although the Colletons were loyalists, that had not stopped some of Tarleton's men from sexually assaulting some young Tory women, including Lady Colleton, at the Fairlawn mansion on April 14, 1780, after Tarleton's rout of the patriot force at Biggin Bridge. Patrick Ferguson, the British commander later killed at King's Mountain, had wanted the offenders immediately shot, but they were sent to Charleston for trial and afterward whipped.

said that Maham had burned the hospital because it was the only way to destroy the many arms and provisions housed there. Shelby later claimed it was the British who had burned the hospital after the Americans left.*

Within a matter of days the British abandoned their garrison at Fairlawn and evacuated their larger post at Wantoot. By the end of November the British had pulled their main body in even closer to Charleston, below Goose Creek, fifteen miles from the city. They were now camped where Marion's grandfather, Benjamin, had first settled nearly a century earlier.

These positive developments convinced Greene it was time to leave the High Hills with the main army and drive the enemy decisively back to Charleston. On December 1 Greene's advance party arrived outside Dorchester, which the British had recently reinvested. Mistaking the advance guard for Greene's entire army, the British hastily withdrew from the fort and brick church at Dorchester. They burned their supplies, dumped their cannons in the Ashley River, and abandoned the post, this time permanently. They pulled back to the Quarter House, a well-known tavern six miles north of Charleston, and withdrew the force at Goose Creek Bridge to there as well. The Americans now were in possession of all of South Carolina except Charleston and its upper peninsula, or "neck," and the adjacent islands. Greene's next step was to place the city under siege. Meanwhile, in Georgia, all but Savannah was back in patriot hands.

As the year 1781 drew to a close the British were in a "melancholy state" in the South, as Clinton put it, with "the whole country . . . against us except some helpless militia with a number of officers, women, children, Negroes, etc." who needed to be fed and cared for in Charleston.

---

*Maham, without addressing the hospital burning, put the attack in a far different light. In a letter to Greene, who had launched an inquiry into the matter, Maham described the hospital as primarily a military complex. He added that of the ninety-one prisoners he had captured, he took seventy-six who were fit for duty, placed them on horseback, and carried them off, even though they were capable of walking. He said he had ordered twelve who were too sick to be taken away as prisoners to be carried to the British fort half a mile away. He paroled two medical orderlies and a lieutenant and sent them to Charleston with their personal belongings. How the matter was resolved is not known.

And the expense of supporting the thousands of refugees who were daily driven into the British lines had become "almost intolerable."

Yet the Americans had serious problems of their own. Greene had no coats or blankets for his men going into the winter, and half of them were without shoes. Many were suffering from malaria. None of his soldiers had received a shilling of pay since coming south. He was practically out of ammunition, and what little he had he gave to Marion, figuring he could make better use of it. The British still had thousands of soldiers in Charleston and several armed galleys protecting the river approaches to the city, and although they had suspended offensive operations, they could forage the surrounding areas with impunity provided they marched out in force.

Greene lived in constant fear that General Leslie, the Charleston commandant, would be massively reinforced in preparation for a renewed incursion into the interior; as a result, he ran the nearly fifty-year-old Marion ragged. At the slightest rumor that the British were coming out of the city in increased numbers to attack him, Greene urgently ordered Marion hither and yon, forcing him to race fifty or more miles to the presumed enemy destination, only to discover it was a false alarm and he needed to return, just as quickly, to whence he came. Occasionally Greene would countermand his orders before they even reached Marion.

Although the threat of a renewed British offensive was perhaps more imagined than real, Greene still had some reason to fear one. Despite a growing peace movement in Parliament, neither King George nor Lord Germain was willing to give up the fight for the colonies. Given the British resolve and American material shortages, Marion told Greene that Charleston "will not be ours so soon" and predicted it would be another year before the Americans could retake it. Greene, who had formed a growing bond with the militia leader, commiserated with him. "If we are not supported and supplied with the means to defend the country," he wrote to Marion, then it was neither of their fault. "But be not discouraged," Greene concluded, "I look forward for better days."

23

"As Soon as
They Can Spare Me"

Although the American grasp on South Carolina was not entirely firm, Governor John Rutledge decided conditions were favorable enough for reestablishing the legislature, which had not met for almost two years. In late November 1781 he called for elections to be held in mid-December and asked Marion and other militia brigadier generals to appoint the election managers and supervise the voting in their militia districts. Marion, who feared the disruptions of war would prevent much of a turnout, was not thrilled with the idea. "I am sorry to see this business so soon entered on, as I am clear the elections cannot be full," he confided to Greene. Yet he would do what Rutledge asked of him.

After it became apparent that the British were not in fact reinforcing Charleston, Greene and Rutledge decided to convene the new General Assembly at Jacksonboro, a small, rustic village just thirty-six miles west of the city. Greene's army, camped near Parker's Ferry, was close enough to Jacksonboro to protect against loyalist raiders who might try to disrupt the gathering. Greene also wanted to demonstrate to the world the Americans' control of territory and confidence in their military prospects. But despite Greene's show of bravado, he told Marion five days before the Assembly was scheduled to convene that it was up to Marion to cover the area around Jacksonboro due to Greene's lack of ammunition and provisions.

212

Aside from Whig politicians, most of those elected to the legislature were military officers, former exiles, or exchanged prisoners of war. William Moultrie and Andrew Pickens took seats in the House of Representatives, and Thomas Sumter went to the Senate, where he was joined by Marion, chosen again by the voters of St. John's Berkeley Parish. Marion's own brigade supplied several Assembly members, including Hugh and Peter Horry, Hezekiah Maham, Major John James, Captain William McCottry (the fabled rifleman), and James Postell, whose brother John would enter the Senate in 1783 after his release from prison. So many military men were elected that some had to remain in the field, lest there be no one to defend the country.

As Marion had predicted, turnout was low. Many Whigs still in Charleston could not come out to vote in their parishes, and loyalists were ineligible to vote. The war also changed the composition of the Assembly, as many of the Charleston legislators were unable to reach Jacksonboro. As a result, the backcountry enjoyed a degree of representation it previously had been denied.

On January 11, from his plantation camp at Wambaw Creek by the Santee, Marion set out on an eighty-five-mile journey to Jacksonboro to take his legislative seat. Before leaving he placed Peter Horry at the head of his brigade until he could return from the Senate. He gave Horry strict orders to prevent anyone from entering or leaving Charleston without a pass from one or the other of them. It was an important directive, as most of the enemy's intelligence came from persons, especially women, going to or from town. Marion also ordered Maham's corps to Henry Laurens's Mepkin Plantation twenty-five miles north of Charleston (a comfortable distance from Horry's rival unit).

When he arrived in Jacksonboro a couple of days later Marion discovered that nothing was happening, as few of the new legislators had managed to make it there. After finally reaching a quorum, the Senate met on January 18 in Peter DuBose's tavern, where a partition was taken down to turn two rooms into one. The thirteen senators repaired to the larger Masonic Lodge, where the House had reached a quorum the day before, for a joint opening session with seventy-four members of the lower body (out of the nearly two hundred elected).

It was a dramatic scene, where the original revolutionary leaders were seen alongside a new group of heroes who had saved South Carolina in its darkest hour. There was Rutledge, the governor who had kept the faith, welcoming the Assembly and spectators with a stirring keynote speech, and Christopher Gadsden, the firebrand who had helped start it all. Also visible were living reminders of the devastating war: scarred and wounded soldiers, "emaciated victims of the prison ships," and "mutilated victims of Tory vengeance." According to one account,

> The hearts of the spectators throbbed as they saw them pass into the hall and take their seats on the long vacant benches. But especially on one short, slender man, of grave aspect, whose compressed lips told of indomitable will, as his light and wiry frame told of endurance and irrepressible energy, the eyes of all were fixed, as each pointed him out to the other, whispering in earnest admiration, "That is Marion."

Meeting even on Saturdays and Sundays, the Assembly debated and passed laws to repeal paper currency as legal tender, to reorganize the militia, and to raise and pay for Continental troops. Recognizing that many state troops had served for ten months in reliance on promised bounties of slaves, they ratified the terms of Sumter's Law. They elected a new governor, John Mathews, a lawyer and Continental Congress member, to succeed the term-limited Rutledge. (Gadsden was initially chosen but declined to serve, citing his age and health.) In appreciation of Nathanael Greene's service, the legislators bought him a Lowcountry rice plantation taken from the Tories.

But the issue that occupied the hearts and minds of the Assembly members as well as most of their time was the so-called Confiscation Act. The British had seized patriot properties and had exiled rebels earlier in the war; this legislation gave hearty expression to the notion that what goes around comes around. The act provided for the confiscation of the estates and personal property of various persons who, by their positions or conduct, had materially or actively aided the enemy.* Their

---

* The categories of persons targeted included British subjects who owned property in the state but lived abroad (absentee landlords), those who had fought for the

property was to be sold at public auction (although it was specified that in any sales of slaves, parents were not to be separated from their children, and slaves would be sold only as families). Persons whose estates were confiscated were to be banished from South Carolina upon pain of death without benefit of clergy if they should return. Those deemed guilty of lesser crimes were subjected to fines (amercement) amounting to 12 percent of the value of their estate.

The statements of individual legislators were not recorded, so Marion's precise views on the Confiscation Act are unknown. One story, originating with Weems, holds that when asked to give a toast at a dinner hosted by the new governor Mathews, Marion stood up and said, "Well, gentlemen, here's damnation to the Confiscation Act." That may well have reflected his general frame of mind, but there is no evidence he vocally opposed the act. Writing to Peter Horry, without commenting on the merits of the legislation, Marion noted that it would help raise needed revenue.

Voicing opposition would have been futile anyway, as the Confiscation Act garnered broad support from the Assembly. No doubt revenge was part of the motivation; the list of persons subject to confiscation included noted Tories Elias Ball, John Brockinton, and the Cunningham brothers. But necessity was also a major factor. The government was out of money; the ravages of war had impoverished the Whig citizenry. The legislators thought it appropriate that those who had been traitors to the patriot cause should be made to suffer along with those who had been true to it.

The bigger issue for consideration—over which there was endless debate and negotiation—was which individuals would have their estates confiscated. On that subject Marion aligned himself with the more dovish or conciliatory elements in the legislature (most of whom were from the Lowcountry, which had not witnessed the level of brutality seen in

British or Tories (unless they had later surrendered themselves and returned to the patriot cause), those who signed congratulatory addresses to Clinton after the fall of Charleston or to Cornwallis after the Battle of Camden, those holding British commissions in the Royal Militia or civil occupation administration, and those who by especially pernicious conduct had proved themselves to be "inveterate enemies of the state."

the backcountry). The original bill included more than 900 names of persons subject to confiscation, but was reduced to 238 in the final law plus 47 who were amerced. The list was further reduced over time, as 125 individuals were either moved from the "confiscation" to the "amercement" list or were dropped from the act altogether based on a showing of extenuating circumstances (or support from powerful friends).

Marion was on the Senate committee that reviewed the hundreds of petitions filed by loyalists seeking relief from confiscation. He became an ally of Christopher Gadsden, who, despite his radical leanings, was a peacemaker on this subject. Gadsden told Marion they needed to patiently seek ways to have the severities of the Confiscation Act "at least mitigated where there is room." Knowing Marion agreed with him, Gadsden wrote him to say that "he that forgets and forgives most . . . is the best citizen."

Marion was willing to forgive those who, although disloyal, had remained passive; many men who had sworn allegiance to the British had done so out of fear for their or their families' safety or to prevent their homes from being destroyed. Marion readily welcomed such men back to the patriot fold if they were willing to rejoin it and gave them passes to return to their estates. He even undertook to have John Brockinton removed from the confiscation and banishment list when he discovered that Brockinton, enlisting as a "six months man" after the deadline set by Rutledge, had joined Marion's brigade under Peter Horry a couple of days after Marion left for the legislature. (Others were less forgiving; although Brockinton's banishment was repealed, the confiscation remained.) Conversely, Marion would later testify against the petition of one James Gordon of Georgetown because he had acted "in conjunction to keep the Little Pee Dee men in arms against us" and had never entered the patriot service. (Gordon was nonetheless switched from the confiscation to the amercement list.)

Marion also served on a committee to devise ways of raising two new Continental regiments in South Carolina to meet the quota set by Congress. The plan the committee came up with, which the Assembly passed, was to give each man who enlisted a bounty for each year of service of "one sound negro" between the ages of ten and forty to be taken from the confiscated estates. At first blush Marion's support of this idea seems inconsistent with his opposition to Sumter's Law, but there was a significant difference. Sumter had allowed indiscriminate plunder for private gain from Whigs and Tories alike; this new program was to be regulated and administered by the state and was targeted at those deemed most guilty of disloyalty. Marion, who favored the rule of law over anarchy, appreciated the distinction. He and Charles Cotesworth Pinckney were selected to lead the two Continental regiments raised under this plan, but the units were never organized. Many enlisted men later complained that they never received their promised slaves.

Another proposal concerning slaves came from Nathanael Greene, who used Colonel John Laurens, recently elected to the House, as a local sponsor. Observing that "the natural strength of this country in point of numbers, appears to me to consist much more in the blacks, than the whites," Greene urged the Assembly to arm more than two thousand slaves to fight the British, with the promise of freedom for faithful service at war's end. "That they would make good soldiers I have not the least doubt," he wrote to John Rutledge. Greene recognized that his idea would be "opposed by common prejudices" but said it sprang from his "desire to secure this unfortunate country from a repetition of the calamity under which it has groaned for these two years past." Partly he was motivated by his fear that if the Americans did not arm masses of slaves, the British would.

Although the plan attracted some initial support, "people returned to their senses," as John Rutledge's brother, Edward, put it, and the House voted it down by one hundred to twelve or fifteen. "The Northern people," another House member observed, "regard the condition in which we hold our slaves in a light different from us. I am much deceived indeed, if they do not secretly *wish* for a general Emancipation." Because the measure died before coming up for a vote in the Senate, Marion did not have to take a position on it. And despite rumors that the British would place three thousand slaves in arms, the number ended up being only seven hundred, including two dragoon units operating around Savannah.

From the moment he arrived in Jacksonboro, Marion began receiving urgent messages from Peter Horry telling him he was needed back in the field. Horry was sick, and the militia was deserting him in great numbers ever since Marion's departure. Plus, the tensions between Horry and

Maham had reached a boiling point. A face-to-face meeting between Marion and the two of them in early January had failed to settle the dispute over rank, and despite Marion's orders to Maham to place himself under Horry's command, Maham refused.

Horry had not helped matters when, after Marion told him he could call on Maham for reinforcements but for no other purpose, Horry promptly instructed Maham to relieve a guard. Maham considered that militia work, beneath his unit, which he referred to as a Legion, the same as Henry Lee's outfit. Maham pointedly told Horry that "I . . . shall not obey any order that you may be pleased to send." Horry then complained to Marion that Maham was issuing passes to many ladies to go to town without Horry's permission and that Maham "interferes with my command so much that I can scarcely act."

Marion prevailed upon Greene to finally lay down the law to the "obstinate" Maham. Greene had just recently reaffirmed to Maham that, despite holding an "independent" command similar to Lee's, he was to act as directed by Marion. Now Greene told Maham that Horry also had "a just and unquestionable right to outrank you." At the same time, Greene emphasized to Maham that "rank is not what determines the character or consequence of an officer, it is actions." Greene then wrote Horry to advise him not to gloat but to be magnanimous in his dealings with Maham. "I esteem you both as men of merit," Greene told Horry, adding that "your triumph is great enough without upbraiding him of his folly."

In response to Horry's pleas for him to return, Marion said he was stuck in Jacksonboro until the Assembly finished its important business concerning the militia law, the raising of Continentals, and the Confiscation Act. He could not leave, he explained, because the Senate barely had a quorum most days. He had asked once for permission to leave and was told no because if he left, so would others. "As soon as they can spare me I will return," he told Horry. "I assure you I am tired of legislating and wish myself with you." Greene, too, was urging Marion to reassume command of his brigade as soon as possible, and Marion likewise told him that although he would like to return, if he left Jacksonboro it "would stop all business here."

Marion was not exaggerating the quorum issue; indeed, the Senate had to adjourn twice in February for lack of sufficient numbers. But his protestations about being tired of legislating may have been overstated. With all the feuding going on between Horry and Maham, the difficulties of keeping the militia together, and the chronic lack of supplies and ammunition, Marion probably welcomed a break from his brigade. Regardless, no one was going to keep him in Jacksonboro if a true emergency required his presence in the field.

That became clear when, after the session on February 20, six days before the Senate finished its work, Marion abruptly left his legislative duties behind and rushed off toward Monck's Corner. The British were suddenly back out in force again in that area. They had a bold new cavalry commander who was not afraid of the Swamp Fox. And he was looking for a fight.

24

"To Prevent the Effusion of Blood"

*T*he man spoiling for a fight with Francis Marion was a Massachusetts-born, future British physicist and inventor named Benjamin Thompson. He was as Tory as they came.

A New Hampshire schoolteacher who married into wealth, Thompson was arrested for loyalist sympathies early in the Revolution and fled to the British lines, leaving behind his wife and baby daughter, neither of whom he ever saw again. He served as a spy for the British general Gage in Boston (using invisible ink reports) and soon left for London, where he became a fellow of the Royal Society of scientists and an aide to Lord Germain. After Yorktown, despite Thompson's near-total lack of military experience, Germain made him a lieutenant colonel in a loyalist provincial cavalry unit. He sailed for New York, but a storm diverted him to Charleston, where General Leslie placed him in charge of the entire British cavalry in December 1781. With two hundred cavalry and five hundred infantry at his disposal—a mix of British redcoats, Hessians, and loyalists—his immediate assignment was to forage in the provision-rich area outside Charleston.

It did not take Thompson long to learn that the patriot forces in the vicinity and the cavalry in particular were in a vulnerable state. Peter Horry, incapacitated by illness, was resting at his plantation on the north side of the Santee near Georgetown, Marion was at the Assembly in Jacksonboro, and Maham was sulking. Uninterested in a field command

220

if he could not have his way, Maham rode to Jacksonboro and took his seat in the legislature on February 15.

Meanwhile Light-Horse Harry Lee, stung by continuing criticism of his behavior at Eutaw Springs and unhappy that Congress had passed him over for promotion to brigadier general in favor of men such as Alexander Hamilton and John Laurens, had asked for Greene's permission to leave the army. Greene, whose reports on Eutaw Springs had, in Lee's view, also slighted him, tried to talk him out of it. "I have the highest opinion of you as an officer, and you know, I love you as a friend," Greene assured him. But ultimately Greene did not stand in his way, and in mid-February Lee retired to his Virginia farm.

Taking advantage of the disarray, Thompson struck at Horry's position near Durant's Plantation on Wambaw Creek forty miles northeast of Charleston. When Horry went home to recuperate, he had left Marion's brigade and his own dragoons under the commands of Colonel Archibald McDonald and Major William Benison. A scout came to warn them that the British were approaching, but both McDonald and Benison, eating their afternoon dinners at separate camps, chose to disregard the report. McDonald did send Major John James to take command of the patriots at Wambaw Bridge. But when James arrived he was unable to prevent Horry's surprised dragoons from being routed by Thompson's cavalry, assisted by John Doyle's mounted Volunteers of Ireland and Thomas Fraser's South Carolina Royalists. Retreating across the bridge, many of Horry's men fled into the nearby swamps. Benison, who had doubted the enemy presence, was among the forty Americans killed. With sunset nearing, Thompson withdrew to Drake's Plantation eight miles away to reunite with his infantry.

Finding it easy to blame the dead, Horry reported afterward to Greene that the loss was due to Benison's "neglect of duty." Another likely factor was the makeup of the unit: most of Horry's dragoons were "reformed" Tories (also known as "new-made Whigs")—former loyalists who had recently enlisted with the patriots for six months to receive a pardon. It had not taken much to send them flying at the sight of their former allies.

The engagement at Wambaw Creek was on February 24. Marion, accompanied by Maham, had left Jacksonboro on the night of February 20

or the morning of February 21 based on reports that the enemy was planning a movement against Marion's brigade. When they reached Maham's
camp at Mepkin Plantation thirty miles west of Wambaw, they received
another report, this one false, that Thompson had returned to Charleston. Maham took the opportunity to visit his own plantation some
twenty-five miles north with plans, he would later claim, of returning
the next day. But within hours of Maham's departure Marion learned of
the defeat of his brigade at Wambaw Bridge. Taking Maham's dragoons
with him, he galloped off toward Wambaw that night and halted at the
widow Tidyman's Plantation, a few miles from the bridge. There, on the
morning of February 25, Marion rested his horses and men, including
the slender remains of Horry's unit who had escaped the night before.

Less than an hour after arriving at Tidyman's, while the horses were
still feeding, Marion's troops looked up to see the whole of Thompson's
cavalry emerge from the woods. They were a mere three hundred yards
away across a clear field. Thompson had been searching for Maham's
dragoons and had found them, but instead of Maham in command, it was
the small, unmistakable figure of the Swamp Fox himself.

Both sides were a bit startled to run into each other, but they quickly
formed for battle. With the Santee at their backs, the patriots could only
stand pat or charge; Marion ordered a charge. But Captain John Car-
raway Smith, leading Maham's dragoons, botched the assignment. At
the edge of a pond where it was necessary to maneuver left to reach the
enemy, he instead panicked and veered right, causing his men to fall into
confusion. Thompson countercharged and cut down a number of patriots, some of whom were killed before they could jump into the swamps
or river. Others were shot or drowned in attempting to swim to the opposite shore.

Adding to the Americans' humiliation, Thompson's forces captured
not only many horses and weapons but also Marion's own tent and can-
teens full of liquor. After Marion rallied his troops in the woods, Thompson elected not to press his advantage; nonetheless, he was able to boast
to Leslie that he had defeated a "chosen corps under the command of
General Marion, in person." The Tories in Charleston, elated with the
news that Marion was beaten, spent three days celebrating. Loyalist

newspapers even reported that Marion had drowned while trying to escape. That was wishful thinking on their part, but there was no disputing that Marion had, for the first time in his career, lost a battle in which he was the commanding officer.

Maham, livid that Marion had not waited for him before taking his Legion into battle, blamed Marion for the defeat. He told Greene that Marion had failed to order a charge, "which was the only thing that could possibly of saved our men." Instead, according to Maham, Marion had ordered them to file off to the right, which confused them into thinking they were to retreat. But Marion, writing to Greene, asserted that Smith had failed to charge as ordered, causing the patriots to lose "a glorious opportunity . . . of cutting up the British cavalry." That Smith resigned the next day would tend to support Marion's version over that of the absent Maham, who clearly had an axe to grind.

Peter Horry attributed the debacle to Marion's commitment to his legislative duties. "I repeatedly wrote him the necessity of his presence and urged as much as possible his return to his brigade and that I was fearful the enemy would take advantage of his absence," Horry explained to Greene. Had Marion been with the brigade, Horry believed, "the enemy would not have returned in triumph."

For his part, Greene shrugged off the setback, writing Marion to say that although he was sorry it would revive the enemy's "drooping spirits," there was "no guarding against so superior a force." In fact, despite the embarrassment Marion's brigade had suffered, the actions at Wambaw and Tidyman's were of little military significance. They did clear the area for British foraging for the next month, but after an abortive, harebrained scheme to capture Nathanael Greene, Thompson soon sailed for New York, having undertaken no further offensive actions. Although he would go on to a celebrated postwar career in Europe as Count Rumford, his tenure as a soldier in America would be remembered in England as "uneventful."

One consequence of the Thompson skirmishes was the final and painful resolution of the Horry/Maham dispute over rank. After the twin defeats and with Horry's and Maham's units each reduced to less than half strength, Marion suggested to Governor Mathews that the two cavalry regiments be combined into a single regiment. Mathews and Greene both agreed, leaving Marion to decide which of the two officers should command it. Marion made clear to Greene that he believed Maham to be the better cavalry commander (an opinion Greene shared), even if Horry was a better infantry officer. Marion also intimated that Maham was a more effective disciplinarian and organizer and commanded more loyalty from his officers and troops than did Horry, whose men were deserting for lack of pay and clothing.

To his credit, Marion made his judgment on the merits, despite his long friendship with Horry and often rocky relationship with Maham. But Marion recognized the delicacy of Horry's feelings and predicted he would expect to receive the command. Marion therefore tried, without success, to get Greene or Mathews to issue him a clear directive to appoint Maham as the commander of the combined cavalry unit. Both of them were too canny to get directly involved. As William Dobein James would write, "The preference appears to have been extorted from Marion."

Horry accused Marion of treachery. He now knew "to whom I am indebted for being turned out of service and Maham continued," he wrote to Marion on April 1. Marion admitted to Horry that he had proposed incorporating the two regiments, but denied, somewhat disingenuously, having said "which of the two officers was to be preferred." As Marion explained, it had simply come down to the fact that Maham was the best cavalry officer and Horry the best infantry officer. Marion had accordingly recommended that Horry's corps be dismounted and serve as infantry in Georgetown, with Horry remaining in command there.

The Georgetown assignment was an important one. The port had become the principal source of supplies for Greene's army. Trade was again flowing there, and as commandant, Horry had authority to set prices for virtually all necessities and luxury items (although to prevent profiteering, Marion instructed him that "salt must not be more than four hard dollars per bushel"). But Horry was not placated. Confessing to hurt feelings, he would remain in Georgetown another three months in name only to assist with administrative matters. In July he considered himself no longer necessary to the service and rode off to his plantation for the rest of the war. Nathanael Greene told him that he had aided his country "in the hour of her greatest distress" and that his efforts had "contributed to her deliverance."

As for Maham, he never did end up commanding any combined unit. On May 16, 1782, he was captured by a British raiding party at his plantation just as he was sitting down to supper with a doctor who was attending to his recent illness. Maham feared being tortured "in the most horrid manner," but because he was sick, he was allowed to remain at home on parole. The British commander left the written parole on the dining table, neglecting to take a copy with him, and Maham thought this might create a loophole that would allow him to ignore the pledge. But Greene told him that because he had signed the document, he was bound to honor it. Maham remained out of action for the duration of the war.*

MARION HAD ANOTHER festering problem to deal with in the spring of 1782. Loyalists from North Carolina were flouting the one-year truce with Ganey's Tories, set to expire on June 17. Although the former loyalist commandant at Georgetown, Robert Gray, admitted that Marion had adhered to the treaty "with great good faith," the same could not be said of the Tories. They did not consider the treaty binding in North Carolina and used the so-called neutral zone, between the Pee Dee and North Carolina line, as a haven for bloody raids across the border. The raiders also threatened the Snow's Island community that Marion held so dear to his heart.

Although Ganey may have tacitly approved of the treaty breaches, he told Marion he would personally try to put a stop to them. But he came

---

*Maham's cantankerous behavior continued after the war. In 1784 he refused to accept some writs for nonpayment of debts that a deputy sheriff was trying to serve on him, and he forced the deputy, upon threat of death, to swallow the papers. After eluding arrest and refusing to appear for trial, he was sentenced to three months in jail and fined one hundred pounds. But the punishments were later lifted based on Maham's claim that he acted out of passion because the creditor suing him was an ex-Tory.

under increasing pressure from diehard North Carolina loyalists to bring his South Carolina men back into the field against the patriots. The Tories were emboldened by their belief, shared by the ever-fretful Greene, that the British would any day mount a new offensive out of Charleston. The North Carolina loyalists' ringleader was the maniacal David Fanning, who had captured the former governor of that state in a daring raid the previous September. Fanning allegedly swore he would take Marion "dead or alive" and offered to bring the heads of Marion and Greene to General Leslie in Charleston "for a handsome reward."

By late May 1782 the uprisings in northeast South Carolina had reached the point at which Governor Mathews sent Marion to quell them. North Carolina governor Alexander Martin put 250 of his own state's troops under Marion's command to "act as you will judge most conducive to the service." He added that if Marion needed more North Carolinians, all he had to do was ask. Earlier in the war it had been next to impossible to get one state's troops to take orders from another state's militia commander; now Marion's name and reputation gave him that power.

Taking Maham's dragoons and his own militia brigade with him, Marion rode north from the Santee through the Williamsburg district, camping on June 3 at Burch's Mill, twenty-five miles above Snow's Island. He shared Greene's desire to resolve the crisis, if possible, without violence. British prime minister Lord North's prowar government had fallen in March, and the combative Lord Germain resigned, leading to rumors of an imminent end to hostilities. Marion reported to Peter Horry that, according to one British officer, "we shall very soon take one another by the hand in friendship. Some say there is a cessation of arms to take place, and that peace is actually on the carpet."

From near Snow's Island on June 2 Marion wrote Ganey to say he was coming to discuss a treaty to "prevent the effusion of blood and distresses of the women and children." The British were ready to make peace, he reported, which left Ganey no hope of being supported by them. Marion made clear that if Ganey did not agree to terms, the patriots would prosecute the war to the fullest after the existing truce expired. It was in Ganey's own interest, Marion concluded, to settle peaceably and avert "ill consequences from obstinacy which must terminate in your and your people's destruction."

The threats worked. Awed by the word that Marion was on his way, Ganey's Tories sought an armistice. A conference between the two sides to discuss terms broke down in acrimony, and after a brief skirmish Marion agreed to meet one-on-one with Ganey. Marion's men thought it beneath him to entertain such a "leader of banditti" in person, but he went forward with the meeting. At Burch's Mill on June 8 the two of them reached an agreement. A formal surrender ceremony took place a week or so later at Bowling Green, fifteen miles away.

Similar to the truce agreed to a year before and consistent with instructions Marion had received from Mathews, the new treaty required the Tories to lay down their arms except in support of the American cause, return any plundered property (including slaves), deliver up any American deserters who had joined them or any loyalists who persisted in rebellion against the state, and swear allegiance to the United States and South Carolina while renouncing loyalty to the Crown. In return the Tories would receive full pardons and could keep their personal property. Those who did not agree to be bound by the treaty were given safe conduct, along with their wives and children, to the British lines in Charleston, with the officers to keep their pistols and sidearms and one horse apiece. All in all, they were generous terms.

Marion even allowed Ganey to travel to Charleston to yield his British commission to General Leslie in person upon his word that he would return and enlist for six months in the patriot militia, which he did. Marion also warned his men that any Tories who received pardons for submitting, no matter how outrageous their prior conduct, were not to be molested; any patriots who took "private satisfaction" by taking revenge upon such "reformed" Tories would be punished to the full extent of the law. "It is recommended as Christians to forgive and forget all injuries which have been committed by such who have been led away by our enemies," he wrote. But he was not confident his men would spare the lives of those who had committed "so many enormities," even if they had a pardon on paper. For their own protection, Marion sent off a group of the most detested loyalists to the British lines in Charleston.

A few loyalists were considered so incorrigible or guilty of such atrocious crimes that they were excepted from the treaty. One of them was the Tory who had killed Abel Kolb in cold blood outside his home. Another was David Fanning, still hoping to kindle loyalist resistance, who took flight to Charleston to avoid capture. When he arrived he asked for safe passage for his new teenaged bride to go to the garrison there with some of their property. Marion granted a pass to her to meet him but, Fanning wrote later, did "not let her have any of our property, not even a Negro to wait on her." Needless to say, if Fanning had in fact vowed to bring the heads of Marion and Greene to Charleston with him, he showed up empty handed. He shortly left for Florida and eventually settled in Nova Scotia after being convicted in Canada, then pardoned, on a charge of rape.

As 1782 TURNED to summer the war was clearly winding down. The British evacuated Savannah on July 12, leaving Charleston as the only city north of Florida with any British troops. After those in Britain favoring a negotiated peace took power, Parliament replaced Clinton as the chief American commander with Sir Guy Carleton, the former defender of Quebec. Upon his arrival in New York in May, Carleton issued secret instructions to Leslie in Charleston to begin preparations to abandon the remaining southern posts. Yet the Americans would not learn of any evacuation order until August, and even then Greene distrusted the British, suspecting they would leave only to return after defeating the French. And so, with the support of Congress and the civilian authorities, Greene rejected several proposals from General Leslie for a ceasefire.

Leslie also requested permission for the British to buy rice and other provisions from farmers in the countryside rather than having to forcibly forage for them. But Greene rejected this overture as well, fearing the British would use the provisions to support their West Indies operations against the French. Although the Americans were weary of war and his own army's morale was low due to lack of pay and clothing, Greene preferred to keep the pressure on the enemy by starving them into submission. Given the absence of French naval support to besiege Charleston, that was the only way Greene could see to bring about a final surrender of the British southern force.

And so the British would continue to forage outside Charleston. Greene would continue to rely on Marion to oppose those sorties. Although Marion told Greene he was "much fatigued" and admitted he no longer had the energy he once did, Greene kept ordering him here, there, and everywhere at the drop of a hat, often changing his instructions. As Marion dryly noted to Peter Horry, Greene's custom was always to "keep . . . me between him and the enemy."

And the fighting would go on.

25

"An Affectionate Farewell"

*O*f all the combat deaths suffered during the Revolutionary War, that of John Laurens was the one Americans most mourned.

A devoted aide to Washington and cherished friend of Hamilton and Lafayette, Laurens had fought bravely—if recklessly—in every major northern battle. He had almost welcomed death at the disastrous Battle of Savannah in 1779, in which Marion participated. Educated in Geneva and London, where he studied law, Laurens went to Paris to help secure French financial and naval assistance. At Yorktown he was part of the "forlorn hope" of Hamilton's troops who successfully stormed the critical Redoubt #10, following which he helped negotiate the British surrender. After spearheading an aborted attack on British-held Johns Island outside Charleston in January 1782 he went to the Jacksonboro legislature where he pressed, unsuccessfully, for the bill to arm slaves. Greene then gave him command of the army's light infantry, including that of Light-Horse Harry's Legion, when Lee resigned his position. As always, Laurens would serve without pay.

The golden boy of the Revolution, Laurens had no faults, thought George Washington, "unless intrepidity bordering on rashness . . . excited by the purest motives" counted as one. It was totally in character, then, when he leapt from his sickbed in late August 1782 to lead his troops against a British foraging party on the Combahee River fifty miles west of Charleston. Tradition holds that he spent the night of August 26 at the Stock family plantation, where he regaled Mrs. Stock and her daughters with tales of a gallant cavalier and a preview of the next day's encounter, which he invited them to watch from a secure vantage point.

Before sunrise he was dead, caught in the first volley of an ambush that he impetuously tried to charge his men through. "Poor Laurens is fallen in a paltry little skirmish," Greene wrote to Otho Williams. "You knew his temper, and I predicted his fate. I wish his fall had been as glorious as his fate is much to be lamented. The love of military glory made him seek it upon occasions unworthy his rank. This state will feel his loss; and his father will hardly survive it."

John Laurens's death had been a needless effusion of blood in the late stages of the Revolution. Francis Marion did not want any of his men to be the last to die in the war, but they would continue to engage the enemy as necessary. Two days after Laurens met his fate a twelve-man scouting party under one of Marion's captains, George Sinclair Capers, surprised and routed a detachment of the so-called Black Dragoons—a volunteer unit of former slaves under the independent command of African American officers. Twenty-six of these dragoons were in the process of escorting a small group of American prisoners to Charleston when Capers's patrol fell upon them and "cut them to pieces."*

At the time of this encounter Marion lay camped forty miles north of Charleston at one of his favorite locations, the deserted plantation of loyalist John Colleton at Wadboo Barony. The twelve-thousand-acre estate, just three miles from Marion's place of birth, was near Wadboo Bridge, the span that Coates had crossed during his retreat from Biggin Church a year earlier.† Marion had his headquarters in the Colleton plantation house (described as a "castle"), while his men occupied the slave quarters and outbuildings. Marion's cavalry was out on patrol six

---

* Despite their defeat in this engagement, the Black Dragoons continued to be of service to the British for the duration of the war. As late as November 1782 they shot two German Hessian deserters and laid them beneath a gallows to serve as a warning to others.

† Wadboo Barony is not to be confused with the Colleton plantation known as Fairlawn, the site of the converted hospital that Maham and Shelby's mountaineers attacked in November 1781. Wadboo Barony was owned by John Colleton Esq., whereas Fairlawn, five miles west and across the Cooper River, belonged to his cousin Sir John Colleton.

miles away, and only a few of his men at the barony, including his officers, had horses. The rest were on foot, Governor Mathews having ordered most of the militia to be dismounted to save money as the war
wound down. With Marion was a group of his old Williamsburg militia
and forty reformed Tories who had laid down their arms at Bowling
Green, including their former leaders Micajah Ganey and Jesse Barefield.

Meanwhile Marion's old adversary Thomas Fraser was cruising the
area around Monck's Corner in search of beef cattle for the British in
Charleston. He had with him more than a hundred provincial cavalry,
including some of the Black Dragoons. Under the impression that Marion was in Georgetown, Fraser learned otherwise when he ran into and
captured some patriot sentinels at Biggin Church who told him Marion
was at Wadboo Plantation three miles away.

By this time Marion had learned of Fraser's presence and was preparing his men for battle. He posted them in and around three small out-
buildings and along a lane of cedars that ran from the castle to the
approaching road. With the owner living in London, the cedars had not
been trimmed for several years; as a result, their overgrown branches of
Spanish moss trailed almost to the ground, creating perfect cover for an
ambush. Marion then sent a party on horse under Captain Gavin Witherspoon to reconnoiter the enemy.

Fraser had decided to attack Marion from the rear of the mansion
across a large, open field. When he spotted Witherspoon's patrol he gave
chase at full gallop. Witherspoon turned back toward the plantation and
led Fraser's horsemen into the ambush zone. When Fraser's dragoons
came within thirty yards Marion's shooters let out a yell and opened a
deadly fire from behind the cedars and the buildings on the other side of
the road.

It was Parker's Ferry all over again. Twenty of Fraser's dragoons were
shot from their horses; four were killed, including the captain who had
led the charge, and more than a dozen were wounded. The British lost
seven horses killed and five captured. Marion had a few men wounded,
and a couple of his pickets were taken prisoner separate from the action.
The British also captured Marion's ammunition wagon during the battle
when the frightened driver drove off, contrary to orders. With the loss of
ammunition, the patriots had to leave the field, allowing the enemy to

take a mule team and Marion's tent and personal baggage. Fraser moved off to Huger's Bridge about ten miles away and collected cattle and sheep for the garrison in Charleston.

Writing to Greene from Wadboo on August 30—a year to the day since Parker's Ferry—Marion was lavish in his praise for his men. They had directed their ambush fire so well that the enemy broke and retreated in confusion; they then alertly shifted their positions to prevent Fraser from mounting an effective counterattack. And although Horry's re-formed Tories had not performed well at Wambaw Bridge in February, Ganey's men had stood the test at Wadboo. "The militia, though the greatest part was new made Whigs, behaved with great spirit," Marion reported to Greene. Refusing to yield their position, they wanted to pursue Fraser's men in the open field, but that would have given the enemy too great an advantage, Marion explained. William Gilmore Simms would later offer an explanation of the ex-Tories' bravery: "They fought with halters about their necks. Not a man of them, if taken, would have escaped the cord and tree."

Greene congratulated Marion for "the very honorable check you gave the enemy." He was particularly gratified that the British had been disappointed to find that despite Marion's embarrassing defeat at Tidyman's, the Swamp Fox had not lost his touch. Greene considered the action important enough to note in a letter to George Washington that "Fraser attempted a surprise upon General Marion but was repulsed."

The engagement at Wadboo Plantation, also known as Avenue of the Cedars, was to be Marion's last as a military commander. According to the conventions of the day, the patriots had "lost" because they abandoned the field to the enemy. But Marion had inflicted far greater damage on Fraser than the other way around. It was fitting that in his final military action Francis Marion, the Continental commander-turned-partisan, had won a Nathanael Greene–style victory.

MARION WOULD REMAIN at Wadboo for most of the next few months. He felt cut off from Greene, who was camped northwest of Charleston, fifty miles from Marion's location. Marion expressed a desire for more frequent communication and suggested Greene move his cavalry up to Goose Creek to be nearer the militia. He asked Greene to pardon this "hint," adding, "I wish not to exceed the station I am in and pay every deference to your superior judgment." Greene declined the suggestion but ordered Marion to keep himself "in the most perfect readiness for any operations."

Marion received sporadic reports of British threats upon Georgetown or elsewhere, but nothing ever came of any of them. In fact, with the exception of some minor clashes not involving Marion's men, the fighting was over. A treaty with the Cherokees in October 1782, after Pickens's campaign, ended the last hostilities of any significance in South Carolina.

The British were preparing to evacuate Charleston, and the loyalists had thrown in the towel. "It does not suit me to follow the English any more," wrote loyalist Robert Blair to Marion. After thanking Marion for the "great humanity" he had shown by protecting his wife when she was "in the greatest distress and persecution by some of her neighbors," Blair pleaded with Marion to espouse his case in a petition to remove his property from the confiscation list. Blair argued that his only sin was loyalty to a cause, that he now wished to "repent my folly," and that he hoped Marion would not "condemn that in me which you have done with so much honor to yourself and country." Citing Marion's "innate goodness," he begged for protection "for myself and what few negroes I have." He ended up being moved from the confiscation to the amercement list.

In November 1782 the Americans and Great Britain signed preliminary articles of peace in Paris. Although it would take almost another year to finalize the Treaty of Paris that formally ended the war, the British were ready to leave the South. In early November, Marion's informants sighted several large British frigates anchored in Charleston harbor, brought there to conduct the evacuation. Greene and Leslie agreed that the British could leave unmolested if they committed not to burn the town on their way out. (Ironically, the British negotiator of the deal was none other than James Wemyss, who had torched so many patriot homes two years earlier.)

On December 14 the great day finally arrived. That morning Leslie took his troops to Gadsden's Wharf and embarked them along with four thousand loyalists and five thousand slaves (many of whom would remain enslaved elsewhere). They set sail for various destinations, including Florida, Jamaica, New York, Nova Scotia, and England. The long British occupation was over.

The American army entered the city in triumph. Anthony Wayne's force followed a couple hundred yards behind the British rear guard as it marched down King Street to the sound of fife and drums. Later that day Nathanael Greene, William Moultrie, Governor Mathews, and their wives paraded in carriages ahead of a column of the Continental Army, and Greene escorted Mathews to the statehouse to assume the long-vacant governor's chair. That night the city was full of celebration, ushering in a return of the prewar Charleston of dances, concerts, and general merriment.

One group conspicuous by its absence was the militia. The reason has long been debated, but the simple and sad fact is that Governor Mathews—and Greene as well—did not want them there. Mathews ordered that no one was to enter Charleston for the British evacuation without his specific permission, and fearing that the militia's presence might lead to violence with the loyalists, he did not allow them into the city. Greene took pains to tell Marion it was Mathews, not he, who was keeping the militia away. But Greene did not protest the governor's order and shared the view that it was best they not attend the celebratory parade. "I wish you not to have the militia too near," Greene wrote Marion, on the pretext that some citizens might resent the militia's refusal to give them passes to go to Charleston as early as they might have wished.

Greene told Marion it was all right for him to enter the town with "three or four of your particular friends," and Mathews gave Marion permission to go into Charleston once the British had left. But Marion, recognizing a slight when he saw one, begged off with the excuse that he had never had smallpox and was afraid of catching it in Charleston. As for his men, he said they had no desire to go into town anyway. And so the militia, who for all of their shortcomings had been instrumental in liberating South Carolina, was not there to witness the historic and joyous occasion.

Marion had Greene's permission to dismiss the militia as soon as the enemy set sail. He gathered his men together for the last time, at

Wadboo Plantation alongside the cedar trees that had sheltered them in their final engagement. The discharge ceremony, recalled William Dobein James, "was conducted with republican simplicity." Marion "thanked his officers and men for their many and useful services, and bid them a friendly and affectionate farewell." With that he mounted his horse Ball, captured at Black Mingo, and rode off to his Pond Bluff plantation.

MARION HAD BEEN directly involved in about two dozen engagements or battles during the Revolution, most of them quite small. But his influence was to be measured by more than just the tallies of casualties inflicted and suffered. William Dobein James, who had first set eyes on the unlikely looking hero at Witherspoon's Ferry two and a half years earlier, summarized him as follows:

> His appearance was not prepossessing, his manners were distant, but not repulsive, yet few leaders have ever been so popular among their men; none ever had more of their confidence. . . . Cool and collected, he was always the general, never the common soldier. In short the whole bent of his soul was how he should best provide for his men, how he could most annoy the enemy, and how he could soonest achieve the independence of his country.

Few had done more to achieve those ends.

26

"The Purest Patriotism"

*P*ond Bluff was a place of desolation—overgrown with weeds and without provisions, livestock, furniture, clothing, or household goods. Marion had some money left over from family inheritances, but not enough to buy cattle and horses, which he would now need to purchase on credit. Inland rice production was down due to declining soil fertility and unpredictable water supply, not to mention the general devastation caused by war. And with British trade all but ended, the export market for rice and indigo evaporated. Cotton would not be introduced to the area for another few years. The value of slaves plummeted from prewar levels.

About half of Marion's twenty slaves had either been taken away by the British or had left of their own volition when Pond Bluff was confiscated earlier in the war. (At least one escaped to the British lines and settled in Nova Scotia.) Ten of his working slaves had moved over, apparently voluntarily, to Belle Isle, the Pineville plantation of Marion's late brother Gabriel. Marion, as executor, had placed Belle Isle under the management of a cousin while he was away at war. Also tending to Belle Isle were the slaves who had been singled out for favorable treatment in Marion's prewar will: overseer June and his wife, Chloe; their daughter Phoebe (sister of Buddy); and her daughter Peggy. These most faithful of Marion's servants, together with the ten field hands, went back with him to Pond Bluff.

Reelected to the Senate in November 1782, Marion was not able to stay long at his plantation before heading to Charleston—smallpox or

no—to attend the opening of the new legislative session that began on
January 6. Writing from there on January 18, 1783, he commiserated
with Peter Horry about their straightened financial circumstances and
the lack of government recognition of their efforts. His letter even bore
traces of eloquence not found in his military writings:

> I am much obliged to you for the favourable opinion of my endeavors to
> serve my country but had it not been assisted by such brave officers as
> the colonels Horry it would not have been in my power to do what I
> have done. I only regret that my country had not considered the merits
> of such officers and provided for them, instead of giving to strangers ten
> thousand guineas . . . but as the old saying is, "that kissed goes by
> favor."

Marion's mention of "ten thousand guineas" for "strangers" was an
obvious reference to the largesse bestowed on Rhode Islander Nathanael
Greene, who had received exactly that amount from the legislature with
which to buy a South Carolina plantation. As a subordinate commander,
Marion may have deferred to Greene's "superior judgment," as he had
recently called it, but the self-effacing Marion was apparently envious of
the man who was being hailed for having liberated the South despite
failing to win a single battle. Tellingly, although Marion and Greene had
corresponded almost constantly over the previous two years, they ceased
writing each other after the war. (Greene would die just three years later
at the age of forty-three.)

Marion, now fifty as he wrote Horry, lamented that he did not know
how he would procure what he needed to turn Pond Bluff into a viable
operation again. Like many Continental Army officers, he hoped for a
lifetime of half pay as promised by Congress, but that would not materialize; nearly fifty years would pass before pensions became widely available for veterans who were neither disabled nor destitute. "I have no
prospect that my country will so much as put me in a post of emolu-
ment," Marion added, because "idle spectators of the war" were in charge
of conferring such benefits. He also let Horry know that he had applied
for some clothing for him "but was told the supernumerary officers were

not to have any and if Col. Pinckney had not taken a few articles for me I should have gone without." Still, he insisted that all of this "neglect," as he termed it, could not diminish "my love for my country [and] my principles."

In early 1783 the South Carolina Senate did vote Marion a commendation for his "eminent and conspicuous service to his country" and a gold medal "for his great, glorious and meritorious conduct." In response Marion said that the honor "will be ever remembered with gratitude, and I shall be always ready to exert my abilities for the good of this State, and the liberties of her inhabitants." But it is not clear whether the medal was ever delivered. Two years later he would receive a 302-acre land grant from South Carolina for his service, although for reasons unknown he never applied for a 500-acre land bounty granted by Congress to Continental officers. (Eventually his heirs would claim it.)

In September 1783 Congress "promoted" Marion from a lieutenant colonel to full colonel in the Continental line. But it was not the brigadier generalship he had expected under prior congressional resolution. That twenty-six other lieutenant colonels were brevetted as brigadier generals at the same time suggests there was not enough money to go around. But the slight may have been partly intentional. Marion's lenity toward Tories had made him unpopular with powerful elements in South Carolina who believed that too many "obnoxious" individuals were being pardoned or removed from the confiscation lists. As one influential militia colonel had complained to Governor Mathews, various "villains" guilty of murdering and plundering Whigs had been "received by Gen. Marion as citizens" and had been restored to "equal privileges with the men who have suffered everything by them" and who had "borne the burden and heat of the day."

In March 1784 Marion received a sinecure in the form of the commandant post at Fort Johnson in Charleston Harbor, which he had helped take from the British (albeit without opposition) in 1775. The job, essentially that of a port collector, paid him five hundred British pounds sterling a year and required him to spend much of his time at the fort. Living in Charleston, a place of high society, did not much appeal to him, but the pay was decent and the work was not demanding. Four years later, though, budget cutters in the legislature decided to reduce his salary to five shillings a day, or about 20 percent of what he had been making. The pay was further conditioned on his living in the fort, a dreary, dungeon-like edifice. After a while the job no longer was worth it to him, and rather than swallow his pride, he resigned the position.

Marion was also too proud to accept another benefit South Carolina offered him. In early 1784 the legislature took up a bill to prevent lawsuits against any state or militia officers for taking private property from citizens for use in prosecuting the war. The intent was to give immunity to those who had plundered under Sumter's Law. According to one early postwar account, which gained acceptance through the years, Marion saw his name listed among those to be protected by the new law and nobly demanded it be removed. "For if," he is quoted as saying, "in the course of command, I have in a single instance departed from the strict line of propriety, or given the slightest cause of complaint to any individual whatever, justice requires that I should suffer for it."

The quotation is probably fanciful, but like so many Marion legends, this one has elements of truth. A bill did pass the Assembly in March 1784 specifically exempting Thomas Sumter and Andrew Pickens or any state or militia officer acting under their authority or command from liability for appropriating private property for public use. Marion was not named in the law—although arguably, as a subordinate militia officer to Sumter, he fell within the statute's protection. It may be that Sumter and Pickens had powerful friends who pushed the bill through for their benefit. Or, given that Marion had stridently refused to participate in Sumter's Law, some legislators may have felt he did not need or deserve specific legal protection. In any event no lawsuits were ever brought against him for alleged plunder.

If Marion was feeling underappreciated by the powers-that-be, he had at least one not-so-secret admirer. Mary Esther Videau, a spinster in her late forties, was Marion's first cousin and had known him since childhood. A Huguenot neighbor of his, she was a member of the influential

Cordes family, her mother being Anne Cordes Videau, a sister of Marion's mother, Esther. Over the years Mary Videau had inherited a considerable fortune in money and land from her deceased parents and brothers. She also kept up a correspondence with Marion, provided him with intelligence carried by slaves, and is said to have attended the ball at Cantey's Plantation that he threw to celebrate the victory at Yorktown. Yet she had never succeeded in getting the shy Marion to reciprocate her romantic feelings toward him.

But in that goal she had important allies in another pair of cousins: Marion's beloved niece, the widow Charlotte Ashby, a daughter of his late brother Gabriel, and her fiancé, Theodore Marion, son of Marion's deceased brother Job. Charlotte and Theodore prodded their uncle to pay a call on Mary Videau. He did; the two of them hit it off; and on April 20, 1786, a Thursday evening, the lifelong bachelor Francis Marion, now fifty-four, married forty-nine-year-old Mary Esther Videau. Apparently it was a double wedding, for that same day the cousins Theodore Marion and Charlotte Ashby were married as well.

The Marions made a sweet elderly couple and enjoyed a happy and loving marriage. Little is known about Mary's physical appearance, although William Dobein James wrote that she closely resembled him facially (not exactly a compliment). But they shared interests and heritage; traveled, camped, and fished together; played backgammon; and entertained dinner and overnight guests in their one-story, multibedroom home he rebuilt at Pond Bluff. Among his frequent visitors was Peter Horry, the two of them having repaired their long friendship.

As Mary was beyond her child-bearing years, they had no offspring, but they did each "adopt" a favorite child. For Mary, it was Charlotte Videau Ashby, daughter of Charlotte Ashby the matchmaker. The little girl's father, Anthony Ashby, a former member of the 2nd Regiment, had died around the time of her birth in 1784. For Marion's part, in a new will he executed in 1787, he adopted a grandnephew—ten-year-old Francis Marion Dwight, the grandson of Marion's brother Isaac. Marion provided that the income from his estate would pay for a college and professional education for the boy until he was twenty-one. His inheritance, however, was conditioned on him taking the name "Francis

Marion" and dropping the name "Dwight" entirely. Marion had no known antipathy toward Samuel Dwight, the boy's father; it was, rather, an effort to perpetuate his name in a direct line of succession.

Unfortunately it did not work. Although Francis Dwight did legally change his last name to Marion in 1799 after turning twenty-one, a subsequent marriage produced eight daughters and not a single son. When seven of those girls married, and the other one died childless, the Marion surname disappeared forever from the general's direct line. It would survive in collateral lines, and in the years to follow, thousands of Carolinians would give their sons the first and middle names "Francis Marion."*

As money generally begets money and land was cheap at the time, Marion was able to build a substantial estate from the property his wife brought to the marriage. He focused on raising cattle and hogs, and gradually the rice market improved. He hired out some of his slaves to do work at Fort Johnson while he was commandant there—in effect, paying himself for their services. Eventually his land holdings would total nearly six thousand acres. To the poorest of South Carolinians, Marion would have seemed rich, but he would more accurately be described as upper-middle class. He liberally extended loans to family members, comprising approximately a third of the value of his personal (non-real estate) assets.

Marion's postwar state Senate career bears few marks of distinction.† He was a "moderate Federalist" and thus a member of the same party as George Washington, to whom his character has often been compared. But he was not active in politics. He attended the South Carolina convention that ratified the US Constitution in 1788 but for reasons un-

---

* In addition more places have been named for Marion than any other revolutionary figure, excepting Washington. According to a current memorial project in the nation's capital, Marion has lent his name to twenty-nine cities and towns and seventeen counties across America, not to mention a four-year university, a national forest, and a small park on Capitol Hill that cries out for a monument in his honor.

† Marion represented St. John's Berkeley County in the Senate from 1782 to 1786 and from December 1791 to May 1794. The reasons for his hiatus from 1786 to December 1791 are unknown, although the period coincides with the first few years of his marriage.

known was absent for the final vote (as was Peter Horry). As a Federalist he probably favored ratification, along with William Moultrie, Henry Laurens, and former Marion brigade members Hezekiah Maham, James Postell, and Thomas Waties (by then a judge). States' rights advocates such as Thomas Sumter and Wade Hampton voted "nay," as did the irascible William Clay Snipes. The states' righters would have their day in 1860, when South Carolina voted to secede from the Union and shots were fired a few months later on the federal fort that bears Sumter's name.

In 1790 Marion was a member of the convention that drafted the new South Carolina Constitution, but his input, if any, is unrecorded. As a state senator, according to Peter Horry (as embellished by Weems), Marion urged legislation to establish free public schools to better educate the state's citizens. But if he did, no record of his involvement in any such debates or proceedings remains. Even less plausible is the rationale Weems attributed to Marion—namely, that it was lack of education and the resulting public ignorance that led so many South Carolinians, unlike the united New Englanders, to take up Toryism. Marion knew that for every Ganey or Brockinton or Harrison from South Carolina who was fighting him, there was a Fraser from New Jersey, or Thompson from Massachusetts, or New Yorkers under Tarleton, Watson, and Doyle who were equally zealous loyalists.

And yet, as evidenced by his early will and by his putting his nephews through college, Marion did place a high value on education. He may have envied the greater learning of men such as Henry Lee and Thomas Waties who fought alongside him. And he resented being patronized by Watson, Balfour, and other more cultivated Englishmen in their correspondence with him over prisoner exchanges. It would have been natural for him to have wished he had more formal schooling. Setting aside the flowery speeches Weems put in his mouth on the subject, Marion probably did favor free public education.

For many years Marion kept up command of a militia brigade, training and parading his men as in days gone by. He resigned in 1794 after a reorganization of the militia; both Marion and Sumter were nominated to be promoted to major general, but when the vote in the legislature deadlocked, their supporters agreed to Charles Cotesworth Pinckney as a compromise candidate. By that time Marion was in poor health and unable to serve anyway. Writing in November 1794 to his grandnephew Francis Dwight, away at college in Connecticut, Marion complained of a cramp in his fingers, "constant pain in my head for some time," and a "cold but ardent fever."

His decline was swift, and on February 27, 1795, "in his sixty-third year," according to his gravestone, he died at Pond Bluff. He was buried at Belle Isle, his brother Gabriel's plantation. Marion's estate, apart from his land, was appraised at 6,453 pounds sterling, roughly half a million dollars in today's money. More than half of that value was in the seventy-four slaves he owned. He willed to his wife all of the personal property she originally brought to the marriage, including her slaves and fine mahogany furniture. (By law it had all become his upon marriage.) He also left her all of his real and personal property for her use until she died or remarried. After her death or widowhood his entire estate was to go to his grandnephew Francis Dwight at age twenty-one, provided he took the name Francis Marion, which he did.

As it turned out, the will was invalid because it was not witnessed, and Mary Videau was limited to her one-half intestate share. The other half went by law to Marion's nieces and nephews, whom Mary promptly bought out. Marion's grandnephew Francis Dwight took no real estate, although written wills, even if void, were deemed valid to pass personal property, so he did end up inheriting Marion's slaves "and their increase" upon Mary Videau's death. She died in 1815 and Francis (Dwight) Marion died in 1833, leaving an estate with more than 150 slaves.

One unanswered question is why Francis Marion the general did not free any slaves in his final will—not even his lifelong faithful servant, Buddy, or the "mustee" girl Peggy, then in her late teens, who was to have been emancipated under his original will. He revised his will a year after his marriage and probably at that point felt he owed his greatest duty and loyalty to his new wife and adopted son. Then, too, manumission was not an unalloyed blessing in South Carolina—by law, an emancipated slave had to leave the colony within six months or face re-enslavement and sale at public auction, with consequent separation from family. Perhaps Marion also assumed that if Mary outlived him, she would free some favored slaves in her own will, but with the exception of one "Scipio," she did not. By the time of her death South Carolina had further discouraged manumissions, and five years later a new law would provide that enslaved African Americans could be freed only by an act of the legislature.

Also unknown are any details about how Francis Marion treated his slaves during his lifetime. By all evidence, his core family group—June, Chloe, Buddy, Phoebe, and Peggy—were well cared for, but what of his many field hands? Because he was a fair and humane man, as he demonstrated time and again during the war, it is safe to assume he was not a cruel master. Had he been so, moreover, it is doubtful any free persons of color would have joined his brigade, and some did. He also sympathized with the slave's condition, as evidenced by his recommendation as a member of a legislative committee that a slave named Antigua, who at the risk of his life had supplied valuable information about the enemy during the war, be freed as he had been promised. By act of the General Assembly, the man, his wife, and children were "forever delivered and discharged from the yoke of slavery" (an implicit rejection of the notion that even well-treated slaves would have preferred bondage to freedom).

Being a compassionate man, Marion likely treated his slaves better than most plantation owners did. But he was also a stern disciplinarian who from time to time ordered corporal punishment of his soldiers—at least when he was a Continental officer with authority to do so. As a militia commander he largely refrained from imposing harsh discipline, but that was because he was enough of a realist to know that his volunteers would not stand for it. It would not be surprising, then, if in dealing with slaves—over whom he had total control—he occasionally authorized physical punishment for what he considered bad behavior. Like other men of his planter class, he regarded his slaves as his property. Although African Americans fought under him, he, like so many of his contemporaries, could not see that the promise of the Declaration for which they fought could not be realized without a second American revolution and new birth of freedom some four-score-plus years later.

FRANCIS MARION WAS a man of his time and place, and there have been few more trying times and places in American history than from 1780 to 1782 in South Carolina. Marion emerged from that difficult period with a sterling reputation that took on added luster once Parson Weems created the romantic legend of the Swamp Fox.

But those who knew Marion best had long recognized that he deserved a place in the pantheon of American heroes. "History affords no instance wherein an officer has kept possession of a country under so many disadvantages as you have," Greene had written to Marion in 1781. He went on,

> Surrounded on every side with a superior force, hunted from every quarter with veteran troops, you have found means to elude all their attempts, and to keep alive the expiring hopes of an oppressed militia, when all succor seemed to be cut off. To fight the enemy with prospect of victory is nothing; but to fight with intrepidity under the constant impression of defeat, and inspire irregular troops to do it, is a talent peculiar to yourself.

In November 1794, a few months before his death, a delegation of Georgetown dignitaries was chosen to draw up an address to present to the aging Marion. It was written by William Dobein James, by then an esteemed judge, who, as the fifteen-year-old son of Major John James, had been an original member of the brigade formed at Witherspoon's Ferry in August 1780. The first signer on the list was Peter Horry.

"Your achievements may not have sufficiently swelled the historic page," the address read, its subscribers hardly anticipating that one day that assessment would be proved wrong. It went on,

> But this is of little moment. They remain recorded in such indelible characters upon our minds, that neither change of circumstances nor length of time can efface them. . . . Continue general in peace to till those acres which you once wrested from the hands of an enemy. Continue to enjoy dignity, accompanied with ease, and to lengthen out your days blessed with the consciousness of conduct unaccused of rapine or oppression, and of actions ever directed by the purest patriotism.

Unlike so many heroes with feet of clay, Francis Marion holds up to scrutiny. The more one learns about him, the more he inspires admiration. He has been called the "Washington of the South." Indeed, as even a casual drive across South Carolina reveals, he remains first in the hearts of those countrymen. And for reason. As the sign at his gravesite says, the legend may obscure the Swamp Fox, but the reality of what he did has never dimmed.

Acknowledgments

THIS BOOK WOULD not have been possible without the support and encouragement of the people who gather each year for the Francis Marion/Swamp Fox Symposium in Manning, South Carolina (www.francis marionsymposium.com). For the past thirteen years George and Carole Summers have provided a forum for historians, researchers, and other enthusiasts to share information and ideas on the southern campaign of the American Revolution in general and Marion in particular. Much of the learning that has emerged from the presentations and exchanges at those annual gatherings has found its way into these pages.

The Southern Campaigns of the American Revolution online magazine (www.southerncampaign.org/mag.php), published by Charles Baxley, has been another invaluable resource. Both Charles and David Neilan, his co-editor of the forthcoming *Francis Marion Papers*, provided me with ongoing guidance in my research, steering me in the right direction with their insights and wealth of knowledge and correcting common misconceptions. Dave also generously allowed me to review a draft of the Marion papers.

Karen MacNutt, a regular at the Swamp Fox symposia, was particularly helpful on the subjects of Marion's family, his Georgetown connections, and his participation in the Cherokee War of 1759–1761. Karen is also the leading expert on Marion images and offered many valuable thoughts about the actual look of the partisan hero.

I owe special thanks to two people for their careful reading of the entire manuscript: Christine Swager and Steve Smith. Chris is a self-described storyteller but has as firm a historical grasp on the Revolution in the South as anyone. Steve is the leading archaeologist of Marion battle sites as well as a prolific author of scholarly writings about Marion. Their comments on my draft were most helpful.

I also received helpful comments on portions of the manuscript from author Jack Buchanan and southern campaign experts Jack Parker and J. D. Lewis. As has become his custom, my former law partner, Larry Kamin, provided valuable editorial comments on the entire draft, as did David Aretha. Any errors in the book, of course, remain mine.

In addition, I benefited from conversations with the following individuals at the Marion symposia: Ben Rubin, Buddy and Bobbie McCutcheon, the late Joe Stukes, Peggy Pickett, and Tom Powers.

I am grateful to the following libraries, archives, and other institutions for their resources and assistance:

South Carolina: Harvin Clarendon County Library (Manning); Thomas Cooper Library (Brent Appling) and South Caroliniana Library, University of South Carolina (Columbia); Francis Marion University, Cauthen Educational Media Center (Bradley Wofford/Angie Bessenger) and Arundel Room, Special Collections (Florence); South Carolina Department of Archives and History (Columbia); South Carolina Historical Society (Charleston) (Lauren Nivens/Virginia Ellison); Horry County Historical Society; Orangeburg County Historical Society (Eric Powell); Swamp Fox Murals Trail Society (www.clarendonmurals.com) (George and Carole Summers); Fort Moultrie National Parks Museum (Charleston); Santee National Wildlife Refuge, Santee Indian Mound and Fort Watson Site (Summerton); Eutaw Springs Battlefield Park (Eutawville).

New York: New York Public Library (Stephen A. Schwartzman Building, Manuscripts and Archives Division, Mid-Manhattan Library, and Schomburg Center for Research in Black Culture).

Washington, DC: Library of Congress.

Massachusetts: Houghton Library, Harvard University (Leah Lefkowitz); Massachusetts Historical Society (Boston).

Canada: Harriet Irving Library, University of New Brunswick (Fredericton, New Brunswick) (Christine Jack).

I wish to thank Laura Galvin of Nomad Design House for her illustration work, Jim Legg and Chris Erichsen for their maps, and the following additional individuals for helping in various ways (alphabetically): Bob Barinowski (sculptor, Baron's Studio), Scott Butler (Brockington Cultural Resources Consulting), Gary Conlogue (Photos by Gary), Clay Tucker Mitchell (Francis Marion University), Brian O'Connor, Rob Oller, Alex Palkovich (sculptor), Terry Smith (artist, Terry Smith Studio), and Sue Sutton.

My agent, Jim Donovan, gave me the idea for this book and was helpful throughout, as usual.

I am, finally, indebted to Robert Pigeon and the rest of the team at Da Capo for their continued support.

Abbreviations

PEOPLE

FM Francis Marion
NG Nathanael Greene
PH Peter Horry

MANUSCRIPT COLLECTIONS

Bancroft Collection, NYPL George Bancroft Collection, Manuscripts and Archives Division, New York Public Library.
PCC Papers of the Continental Congress, National Archives.
Saunders Papers, UNB Saunders Papers, Loyalist Collection, Harriet Irving Library, University of New Brunswick, Fredericton, NB, Canada.
Sparks Collection, Harvard Jared Sparks Collection of American Manuscripts, 1560–1843 (MS Sparks 22), Houghton Library, Harvard University.

BOOKS AND OTHER PUBLICATIONS

Aiken Scott D. Aiken, *The Swamp Fox: Lessons in Leadership from the Partisan Campaigns of Francis Marion* (Annapolis, MD: Naval Institute Press, 2012).
Bass, Gamecock Robert D. Bass, *Gamecock: The Life and Campaigns of General Thomas Sumter* (New York: Holt, Rinehart and Winston, 1961).
Bass, Swamp Fox Robert D. Bass, *Swamp Fox: The Life and Campaigns of General Francis Marion* (1959; repr., Orangeburg, SC: Sandlapper, 1974).
Boddie, Traditions William Willis Boddie, *Traditions of the Swamp Fox: William W. Boddie's Francis Marion, with an Introduction by Steven D. Smith* (1938; repr., Spartanburg, SC: The Reprint Company, 2000).
Buchanan John Buchanan, *The Road to Guilford Courthouse: The American Revolution in the Carolinas* (New York: John Wiley & Sons, 1997).

CP   *The Cornwallis Papers: The Campaigns of 1780 and 1781 in the Southern Theatre of the American Revolutionary War*, ed. Ian Saberton, 6 vols. (Uckfield, East Sussex, UK: Naval & Military Press, 2010).

CSR   *Colonial and State Records of North Carolina*, vols. 14–17, in *Documenting the American South* (Chapel Hill: University Library, University of North Carolina, 2010), docsouth.unc.edu/csr.

Gibbes   Robert W. Gibbes, ed., *Documentary History of the American Revolution, Consisting of Letters and Papers Relating to the Contest for Liberty, Chiefly in South Carolina, in 1781 and 1782* (Columbia, SC, 1853).

Gibbes2   Robert W. Gibbes, ed., *Documentary History of the American Revolution, Consisting of Letters and Papers Relating to the Contest for Liberty, Chiefly in South Carolina . . . 1776–1782* (New York, 1857).

Huguenot Society   *Transactions of the Huguenot Society of South Carolina* (Charleston, SC: Walker, Evans, and Cogswell).

James   William Dobein James, *A Sketch of the Life of Brig. Gen. Francis Marion and a History of His Brigade from Its Rise in June 1780 until Disbanded in December, 1782* (1821; repr., Feather Trail Press, 2010).

Lumpkin   Henry Lumpkin, *From Savannah to Yorktown: The American Revolution in the South* (1981; repr., New York: Paragon House, 1981).

McCrady   Edward McCrady, *The History of South Carolina in the Revolution, 1780–1783* (New York: Macmillan, 1902).

NGP6   *The Papers of General Nathanael Greene*, ed. Richard K. Showman (Chapel Hill: University of North Carolina Press, 1991).

NGP7   *The Papers of General Nathanael Greene*, ed. Richard K. Showman and Dennis M. Conrad (Chapel Hill: University of North Carolina Press, 1994).

NGP8–12   *The Papers of General Nathanael Greene*, ed. Dennis M. Conrad (Chapel Hill: University of North Carolina Press, 1995–2002).

Parker   John C. Parker Jr., *Parker's Guide to the Revolutionary War in South Carolina*, 2nd ed. (West Conshohocken, PA: Infinity, 2013).

Pension   William T. Graves and C. Leon Harris, *Southern Campaigns Revolutionary War Pension Statements, Original Applications*, 2015, revwarapps.org (transcribed by William T. Graves unless otherwise indicated).

Rankin   Hugh F. Rankin, *Francis Marion: The Swamp Fox* (New York: Thomas Y. Crowell, 1973).

SCAR   *Southern Campaigns of the American Revolution* (Charles B. Baxley, publisher), www.southerncampaign.org.

SCHGM   *South Carolina Historical and Genealogical Magazine*.

SCHM   *South Carolina Historical Magazine*.

Simms   William Gilmore Simms, *The Life of Francis Marion: The True Story of South Carolina's Swamp Fox, with a New Introduction by Sean Busick* (1844; repr., Charleston, SC: History Press, 2007).

Weems   Peter Horry and M. L. Weems, *The Life of Gen. Francis Marion, a Celebrated Partisan Officer in the Revolutionary War, Against the British and Tories in South Carolina and Georgia* (1809; repr., Philadelphia, 1845).

Yeadon   Richard Yeadon, "The Marion Family," *Southern and Western Monthly Magazine and Review*, ed. W. Gilmore Simms, 2 vols., nos. 1–9 (March 1845–November 1845).

Notes

Author's Note

x   **"Parson" Weems:** Although Weems's *Life of Marion* ostensibly was based on a manuscript by Peter Horry, Marion's longtime friend and subordinate commander, Horry disavowed it upon publication, telling Weems it was "most certainly not my history . . . but your romance." Horry to Weems, February 4, 1811, Bancroft Collection, NYPL. Still, not everything Weems writes can be dismissed as fiction. Although much of the dialogue is invented, Weems did have access to Horry's original manuscript biography of Marion, from which he drew much factual and eyewitness material. In many cases Weems's history accords generally with the known record. In addition, Horry created an annotated copy of Weems's book in which he noted corrections in the margin. "Horry's Notes to Weems's 'Life of Marion,'" ed. Alexander S. Salley, *SCHM* 60, no. 3 (July 1959), 119–122.

Prologue: The Darkest Hour

3   **July 25 . . . Gates's camp:** "The Journal and Order Book of Captain Robert Kirkwood of the Delaware Regiment of the Continental Line, Part I: A Journal of the Southern Campaign, 1780–1782," ed. Joseph Brown Turner, *Papers of the Historical Society of Delaware* 56 (1910): 10; Horatio Gates to Richard Caswell, July 25, 1780, in "The Southern Campaign 1780: Letters of Major General Gates from 21st June to 31st August," ed. Thomas Addis Emmet, *Magazine of American History* 5, no. 4 (October 1880): 291; George F. Scheer and Hugh F. Rankin, *Rebels and Redcoats: The American Revolution Through the Eyes of Those Who Fought and Lived It* (1957; repr., Da Capo Press, 1987), 404.

3   **Some were white, some were black:** Otho Holland Williams, "A Narrative of the Campaign of 1780," Appendix B to William Johnson,

257

Sketches of the Life and Correspondence of Nathanael Greene (Charleston, SC, 1822), 1:488.

3   **Catawba Indian or two:** John W. Gordon, *South Carolina and the American Revolution: A Battlefield History* (Columbia: University of South Carolina Press, 2003), 108; Aiken, 6.

3   **A few . . . teens:** Williams, "Narrative," 488.

3   **"wretchedness . . . so burlesque":** Ibid.

3   **physique of a thirteen-year-old boy:** Karen MacNutt, "Images of Francis Marion," address at 8th Francis Marion/Swamp Fox Symposium, Manning, SC, October 16, 2010, DVD.

3   **knock knees . . . black eyes:** James, 26.

4   **he fractured it . . . light drinker:** Weems, 72–73; Rankin, 44–45.

4   **Oscar . . . Buddy:** Boddie, *Traditions*, 3, 13, 78–79; Yeadon 1, no. 1 (March 1845): 219; Joseph Johnson, *Traditions and Reminiscences, Chiefly of the American Revolution in the South* (Charleston, SC, 1851), 280–281; James, 31, 100. Johnson describes him as a "foster brother," giving rise to the name "Budde."

4   **"was so lame . . . ventured out":** William Moultrie, *Memoirs of the American Revolution, So Far as It Related to the States of North and South Carolina, and Georgia* (New York, 1802), 2:222.

4   **Cox's Mill . . . Johann Kalb:** Williams, "Narrative," 485–486; Buchanan, 126, 128–129; Warren Dixon, "Cox's Mill Encampment at Buffalo Ford on Deep River–July 1780," www.co.randolph.nc.us/hlpc/downloads/RaymondCoxMill.pdf.

5   **de Kalb sent them out:** de Kalb to Richard Caswell, July 10, 1780, Johann de Kalb Papers, 1780 July 10–1844 May 24, South Caroliniana Library, University of South Carolina, Columbia.

5   **Hollingsworth's Farm . . . to witness Gates's arrival:** "Journal of Kirkwood," 10; Scheer and Rankin, *Rebels and Redcoats*, 404.

5   **Gates was of the school . . . important role cavalry:** Buchanan, 144–145, 150; Lumpkin, 59, 70; Jim Piecuch, ed., *Cavalry of the American Revolution* (Yardley, PA: Westholme, 2012), xi; Williams, "Narrative," 506.

5   **July 27 . . . Gates allowed Marion:** Gates's After Orders, July 26, 1780, in "Orders Issued by Major Genl. Gates While Commanding the Southern Army, July 26th to August 31st 1780," ed. Thomas Addis Emmet, *Magazine of American History* 5, no. 4 (October 1880): 311.

5   **"show the utmost . . . every kindness":** Gates's Orders, July 26, 1780, in ibid., 310.

5   **bodyguards:** Charles Bracelen Flood, *Rise, and Fight Again: Perilous Times Along the Road to Independence* (New York: Dodd, Mead, 1976), 285.

5   **By happy coincidence . . . asked Gates to send them:** James, 25; Rankin, 55, 57.

5   **Marion offered himself:** Rankin, 57–58. Some sources claim that the Williamsburg militia asked for Marion by name. Simms, 69; Boddie, *Traditions*, 81. At some point a few weeks later a group of militia officers, including Hugh Giles and Peter and Hugh Horry, met and agreed that Marion should lead the area militia. Gilbert Johnstone to Susanna Barefield Johnstone, March 8, 1790, Johnstone Papers, Rogers Library, Francis Marion University, http://bccmws.coastal.edu/scbattlefields /doc/letter-gilbert-johnstone-susanna-barfield-johnston.

6   **August 15 . . . Rugeley's Mills:** Weems, 104; Salley, "Horry's Notes," 122.

6   **orders to watch . . . destroy any boats:** Williams, "Narrative," 488; FM to PH, August 17, 1780 (James, 108); Peter Horry, "Journal," ed. A. S. Salley, *SCHGM* 39, no. 3 (July 1938): 127.

6   **people of Williamsburg . . . voted to take up arms:** Boddie, *Traditions*, 47, 72–73; Cecil B. Hartley, *Heroes and Patriots of the South, Comprising Lives of General Francis Marion, General William Moultrie, General Andrew Pickens, and Governor John Rutledge* (Philadelphia, 1860), 124–125; James, 25.

6   **Around August 17:** Rankin, 59; Bass, *Swamp Fox*, 40–41.

6   **"He was rather . . . for a partisan":** James, 26.

6   **the only color:** Simms, 78; Boddie, *Traditions*, 89.

6   **leather helmet . . . Liberty:** James, 26. James inaccurately adds the words, "or death."

6   **Marion was a stranger . . . two hundred rank-and-file:** James, 25–26.

6   **no legal authority . . . free to come and go:** Bass, *Swamp Fox*, 41; McCrady, 73–74, 77; William T. Graves, "The South Carolina Backcountry Whig Militia: 1775–1781, an Overview," *SCAR* 2, no. 5 (May 2005): 9; William Thomas Sherman, *Calendar and Record of the Revolutionary War in the South, 1780–1781*, 9th ed. (Seattle: Gun Jones, 2014), 25, battleofcamden.org/sherman9.pdf; Thomas L. Powers, "Marion and his Commanders," address at 7th Francis Marion/ Swamp Fox Symposium, Manning, SC, October 17, 2009, DVD.

7   **Major John James:** Simms, 75–76; Boddie, *Traditions*, 141; William Willis Boddie, *History of Williamsburg: Something About the People of Williamsburg County, South Carolina, from the First Settlement by Europeans About 1705 until 1923* (Columbia, SC: The State Company, 1923), 49–50, 123–124; Daniel W. Barefoot, *Touring South Carolina's Revolutionary War Sites* (Winston-Salem, NC: John F. Blair, 1999), 19.

7   **Horry brothers:** James, 25–26; Simms, 112–113; Boddie, *Traditions*, 124–125.

7   **John James ("of the Lake") . . . John James Jr.:** James, 25, 43, 46n5; Rankin, 52, 77–78; Bass, *Swamp Fox*, 34; N. Louise Bailey, ed., *Biographical Dictionary of the South Carolina House of Representatives*, vol. 4,

1791–1815 (Columbia: University of South Carolina Press, 1984), 308–309; George Howe, *History of the Presbyterian Church in South Carolina* (Columbia, SC, 1870), 1:413, 490; "Family: James/McCalla," www.singletonfamily.org/familygroup.php?familyID=F4697&tree=1.

7   **Under a parole:** Ben Rubin, "The Rhetoric of Revenge: Atrocity and Identity in the Revolutionary Carolinas," *Journal of Backcountry Studies* 5, no. 2 (Fall 2010): 10, www.partnershipsjournal.org/index.php /jbc/article/viewFile/102/84; Patrick O'Kelley, *Unwaried Patience and Fortitude: Francis Marion's Orderly Book* (West Conshohocken, PA: Infinity, 2007), 672n903; *Code of Conduct for the Members of the United States Armed Forces*, Article III.

7   **Henry Mouzon:** Boddie, *Traditions*, 36–37, 81; Parker, 440. Although Boddie and many others have credited Mouzon with the definitive 1775 map of the Carolinas, it was Mouzon's cousin, also named Henry Mouzon Jr., who was the prominent surveyor and civil engineer. Wylma A. Wates, "Henry Mouzon," in "Henry Mouzon, Jr., or Henry Mouzon, Jr.—Which One Made the Map?" *North Carolina Map Blog*, William P. Cumming Map Society, July 23, 2013, blog.ncmaps.org /index.php/mouzon.

8   **Hugh Giles:** O'Kelley, *Unwaried Patience*, 695n1305; Saberton, CP2:214n11; Giles to Horatio Gates, August 12, 1780 (CP2:351); Clay Spivey, "Giles Family of SC, Col. Hugh Giles of Revolutionary War," *Genealogy.com*, February 7, 2011, genforum.genealogy.com /giles/messages/3407.html.

8   **William McCottry:** O'Kelley, *Unwaried Patience*, 694n1297; Bass, *Swamp Fox*, 34; Boddie, *History of Williamsburg*, 128–129; N. Louise Bailey and Elizabeth Ivey Coopers, eds., *Biographical Dictionary of the South Carolina House of Representatives*, vol. 3, *1775–1790* (Columbia: University of South Carolina Press, 1981), 453–454.

8   **Witherspoons:** Boddie, *History of Williamsburg*, 125–126; Steven D. Smith, "Archaeological Perspectives on Partisan Communities: Francis Marion at Snow's Island in History, Landscape, and Memory" (PhD diss., University of South Carolina, 2010), 117–120, ProQuest, search.proquest.com/docview/823439460.

8   **John Ervin:** Bass, *Swamp Fox*, 34–35, 48; Smith, "Archaeological Perspectives," 95–96; Sam J. Ervin Jr., "Entries in Colonel John Ervin's Bible," *SCHM* 79, no. 3 (July 1978): 219–222; O'Kelley, *Unwaried Patience*, 699n1405; Boddie, *History of Williamsburg*, 119.

8   **Thomas Waties:** H. D. Bull, "The Waties Family of South Carolina," *SCHGM* 45, no. 1 (January 1944): 17–18; James, 5.

8   **Postell brothers:** James, 52; O'Kelley, *Unwaried Patience*, 696n1323; William Dosite Postell, "Notes on the Postell Family," *SCHM* 54, no. 1 (January 1953): 48–53.

8   **a mixture of Huguenot plantation owners:** Henry Savage, *River of the Carolinas: The Santee* (Chapel Hill: University of North Carolina Press, 1968), 230; George C. Rogers Jr., *The History of Georgetown County, South Carolina* (Columbia: University of South Carolina Press, 1970), 134–135.

8   **James . . . was astute in recommending:** Boddie, *History of Williamsburg*, 98.

8   **compared to Robin Hood:** Simms, 108–109, 114; Smith, introduction to Boddie, *Traditions*, xi.

9   **Marion dispatched Peter Horry:** FM to PH, August 17, 1780 (James, 108).

9   **received the shattering news:** Rankin, 61.

9   **routed by Cornwallis . . . to thicken soup . . . dehydrated:** Williams, "Narrative," 486–487, 494–496; Buchanan, 161–170; James K. Swisher, *The Revolutionary War in the Southern Back Country* (2008; repr., Gretna, LA: Pelican, 2012), 161–166; Gates to President of the Continental Congress, August 20, 1780, in *Royal Gazette* (New York), September 20, 1780.

10   **de Kalb . . . died . . . Gates . . . reached safety:** Buchanan, 169–172; Swisher, *Southern Back Country*, 167. For a more sympathetic view of Gates's conduct, see Wayne Lynch, "Winner or Runner? Gates at Camden," *Journal of the American Revolution*, April 8, 2014, www.all thingsliberty.com/2014/04/winner-or-runner-gates-at-camden.

10   **Sumter's company . . . the four winds:** Swisher, *Southern Back Country*, 191–194; Bass, *Gamecock*, 82–85.

10   **series of skirmishes . . . largely dissipated:** Walter Edgar, *Partisans and Redcoats: The Southern Conflict That Turned the Tide of the American Revolution* (2001; repr., New York: Perennial, 2003), 101–107, 111–113; Lumpkin, 87; John S. Pancake, *This Destructive War: The British Campaign in the Carolinas, 1780–1782* (1985; repr., Tuscaloosa: University of Alabama Press, 2003), 111; Jim Piecuch, *Three Peoples, One King: Loyalists, Indians, and Slaves in the Revolutionary South, 1775–1782* (Columbia: University of South Carolina Press, 2008), 193–194; Saberton, CP2:5.

10   **kept the news to himself:** Rankin, 64.

CHAPTER 1: A MOST UNCIVIL WAR

11   **More battles, engagements, and skirmishes:** Gordon, *Battlefield History*, 1.

11   **at more than two hundred:** Buchanan, 105.

11   **a third of all that took place:** Gordon, *Battlefield History*, xvi.

11   **No other colony had as many inches:** McCrady, 734–736.

11   **forty-five ended up seeing:** Parker, viii.
11   **Nearly 20 percent:** Gordon, *Battlefield History*, 1.
12   **"southern strategy . . . Americanize":** McCrady, 711–715; Christine R. Swager, *The Valiant Died: The Battle of Eutaw Springs, September 8, 1781* (Westminster, MD: Heritage Books, 2007), 6, 8, 10; Ira D. Gruber, "Britain's Southern Strategy," in *The Revolutionary War in the South: Power, Conflict, and Leadership*, ed. W. Robert Higgins (Durham, NC: Duke University Press, 1979), 217–225; Pancake, *This Destructive War*, 9, 20, 56.
12   **Charleston had grown complacent:** Walter J. Fraser Jr., *Patriots, Pistols, and Petticoats: "Poor Sinful Charles Town" During the American Revolution* (1976; repr., Columbia: University of South Carolina Press, 1993), 20–24.
13   **"The conquest . . . complete":** Robert Gray, "Colonel Robert Gray's Observations on the War in Carolina," *SCHGM* 11, no. 3 (July 1910): 140.
13   **thousands . . . swore oaths:** Piecuch, *Three Peoples*, 179; Robert Stansbury Lambert, *South Carolina Loyalists in the American Revolution* (Columbia: University of South Carolina Press, 1987), 96.
13   **Some voluntarily trekked . . . their conquerors:** Gray, "Observations," 140–141.
13   **Patriot militia . . . returned to their farms:** Edgar, *Partisans and Redcoats*, 53–55; Simms, 73; Lambert, *South Carolina Loyalists*, 95–96.
13   **"there are few men . . . or in arms with us":** Clinton to Germain, June 4, 1780, in Pancake, *This Destructive War*, 72.
13   **Clinton had issued a proclamation . . . smoke out rebel agitators:** Lambert, *South Carolina Loyalists*, 97–98; Robert L. Tonsetic, *1781: The Decisive Year of the Revolutionary War* (Havertown, PA: Casemate, 2011), 29; Piecuch, *Three Peoples*, 178, 182–183.
14   **ended up backfiring:** James, 23–24, 29–30; Boddie, *Traditions*, 73–74.
14   **nine out of every ten:** Francis Rawdon to Cornwallis, July 7, 1780 (CP1:193).
15   **"The whole country . . . beasts of prey":** NG to Samuel Huntington, December 28, 1780 (NGP7:9).
15   **switched sides . . . three times or even more:** Edgar, *Partisans and Redcoats*, 125; Lambert, *South Carolina Loyalists*, 306.
15   **Old grudges . . . *Regulators* . . . *Moderators*:** Pancake, *This Destructive War*, 21, 94–95; Kristen E. Jacobsen, "Conduct of the Partisan War in the Revolutionary War South" (master's thesis, University of Rhode Island, 1999), 15–17, 40, www.dtic.mil/dtic/tr/fulltext/u2/a416929.pdf; Edgar, *Partisans and Redcoats*, 13–20, 24–25; Sherman, *Calendar*, 15.
15   **Religious and ethnic resentments:** Edgar, *Partisans and Redcoats*, 9–10, 30; Daniel J. Tortora, "The Alarm of War: Religion and the

American Revolution in South Carolina, 1774–1783," *SCAR* 5, no. 2 (2nd ed. 2008): 43–55; Sherman, *Calendar*, 15–16.

16 **Poor backcountry farmers . . . state assembly:** Gordon, *Battlefield History*, 18–19; Buchanan, 20, 90–98; McCrady, 708–710; Edgar, *Partisans and Redcoats*, xiii, 28–29.

16 **animosities left over . . . scalping:** John Alden, *The South in the Revolution, 1763 to 1789* (Baton Rouge: Louisiana State University Press, 1957), 198–201; Graves, "South Carolina Backcountry Whig Militia," 7–8; Edgar, *Partisans and Redcoats*, 29–33; Piecuch, *Three Peoples*, 44–57, 94–96; Jacobsen, "Conduct of the Partisan War," 34, 40–41; Pancake, *This Destructive War*, 73–76.

16 **cycle of retribution . . . highway robbers:** Pancake, *This Destructive War*, 81–85; Jacobsen, "Conduct of the Partisan War," 55–59; McCrady, 139. Historians continue to debate which side was "worse." For the view that the British were mostly to blame, see Edgar, *Partisans and Redcoats*. Jim Piecuch's *Three Peoples* argues that the Whigs were far more brutal than the British or Tories. Lambert concludes that both sides engaged in a "reign of terror" and that most atrocities were committed by those in control at the time. He also points out that Whig atrocities were more highly publicized, and Tory atrocities likely underreported because the only significant press in South Carolina was Charleston's *Royal Gazette*, a loyalist publication. Lambert, *South Carolina Loyalists*, 200–203, 210.

16 **Indian uprisings . . . slave insurrections:** Buchanan, 91; Jacobsen, "Conduct of the Partisan War," 19; Fraser, *Patriots*, 10; Piecuch, *Three Peoples*, 18, 70, 128.

16 **Fearful of antagonizing . . . slaves fled . . . chose not to arm:** Piecuch, *Three Peoples*, 42–43, 82–84, 159–161, 171, 175, 186, 204, 208–209, 219–222, 227, 332–333; Ray Raphael, *Founding Myths: Stories That Hide Our Patriotic Past* (New York: The New Press, 2004), 185–189, 319–320n30; M. Foster Farley, "The South Carolina Negro in the American Revolution, 1775–1783," *SCHM* 79, no. 2 (April 1978), 75, 82–84, 86.

17 **"Of all the men . . . forbade it in his absence":** Weems, 141.

17 **"abominable":** FM to Gates, October 4, 1780 (CSR14:666).

CHAPTER 2: "A SPIRIT OF TOLERATION"

18 **Slaughtered . . . Edict of Nantes . . . to Catholic institutions:** Arlette Jouanna, *The Saint Bartholomew's Day Massacre: The Mysteries of a Crime of State*, trans. Joseph Bergin (Manchester: Manchester University Press, 2013), 1–9, 170–173, 231–233; "Address of Col. H. A. Du Pont . . . April 13, 1917," *Huguenot Society* 23 (1917): 26–31; John

Wesley Brinsfield, *Religion and Politics in Colonial South Carolina* (Easley, SC: Southern Historical Press, 1983), 13.

18 **Many Huguenots . . . Benjamin Marion . . . 350 acres:** Du Pont, "Address," 29–34; Thomas Gaillard, "Copious Extracts by the Committee on Publication from the History of Huguenots of South Carolina, and Their Descendants," *Huguenot Society* 5 (1897): 7–18; Yeadon 1, no. 1 (March 1845): 213–215; no. 2 (April 1845): 270–271; Michael J. Heitzler, *Historic Goose Creek, South Carolina, 1670–1980*, ed. Richard N. Côté (Easley, SC: Southern Historical Press, 1983), 17–20. One source places Benjamin's arrival between 1692 and 1694. J. Russell Cross, *Historic Ramblin's Through Berkeley* (Columbia, SC: R. L. Bryan, 1985), 277.

19 **Benjamin Marion . . . made good . . . able to settle each:** Heitzler, *Historic Goose Creek*, 18–20; Yeadon 1, no. 1 (March 1845): 213–216; no. 2 (April 1845): 270–280; no. 3 (May 1845): 351–352; Thomas Gaillard, "Copious Extracts," 26, 38 (entry no. 114).

19 **his inventory . . . "a parcel . . . English books":** Yeadon 1, no. 2 (April 1845): 270–272; no. 3 (May 1845): 351–354.

19 **Native Americans:** Heitzler, *Historic Goose Creek*, 20; James, 6.

19 **slaves from Africa:** Heitzler, *Historic Goose Creek*, 20–21.

19 **Cabto . . . Pappy Jenny:** Yeadon 1, no. 3 (May 1845): 351–353.

19 **fifteen hundred slaves . . . eighty white families:** Heitzler, *Historic Goose Creek*, 21.

19 **nearly 80 percent:** Yeadon 1, no. 3 (May 1845): 352–354.

20 **Resented at first . . . assimilated:** Simms, 233–234n8; Robert Wilson, "The Huguenot Influence in Colonial South Carolina," *Huguenot Society* 4 (1897): 26, 28, 31; Thomas Gaillard, "Copious Extracts," 19–25, 52, 56–58, 72, 74–76; Daniel Ravenel, "Historical Sketch of the Huguenot Congregations of South Carolina," *Huguenot Society* 7 (1900): 12, 37–38, 46–48.

20 **"gentle race":** Simms, 9; Thomas Gaillard, "Copious Extracts," 56–57.

20 **"spirit of toleration . . . ancestors":** Du Pont, "Address," 35.

20 **eldest son, Gabriel . . . married Esther Cordes:** Yeadon 1, no. 2 (April 1845): 273; Thomas Gaillard, "Copious Extracts," 31 (entry no. 54), 38 (entry no. 114); John J. Simons III, "Descendants of Benjamin Marion," *Genealogy of the Simons Family of the South Carolina Low Country*, *Tripod.com*, April 4, 1998, members.tripod.com/~the_huguenot /mar.htm; John Simons, "Marion Family," *Rootsweb.com*, May 13, 2004, www.haygenealogy.com/hay/patriots/marion-descendants.html.

20 **1732 . . . Goatfield Plantation:** Boddie, *Traditions*, 1, 9; Yeadon 2, no. 6 (August 1845): 121–127; Samuel Gaillard Stoney, *Plantations of the Carolina Low Country*, ed. Albert Simons, 7th ed. (Charleston, SC:

Carolina Art Association, 1977), 65; Harriette Kershaw Leiding, *Historic Houses of South Carolina* (Philadelphia: J. B. Lippincott, 1921), 200. Marion's actual date of birth is unknown, but 1732 is the commonly accepted year. The Goatfield plantation no longer exists, but its approximate location is identified by a historical marker in present-day Cordesville at the intersection of Doctor Evans Road and Hard Pinch Road.

20   **named for his uncle . . . gifted him three:** Boddie, *Traditions*, 3. Boddie's recitation is somewhat at odds with a 1746 deed by which Marion's mother, Esther, was given three slaves—June, Willoughby, and Peter—in trust by her brother. Mabel Louise Webber, ed., "Historical Notes," *SCHGM* 15, no. 3 (July 1914): 145–147.

20   **"I have it . . . quart pot":** Weems, 20.

21   **Biggin:** Cross, *Historic Ramblin's*, 26, 143.

21   **father moved the family:** Boddie, *Traditions*, 13; Yeadon 2, no. 6 (August 1845): 123. Although many sources state that the move to Georgetown was to provide young Francis a public school education, the first public school did not open there for almost another twenty years. "Winyah Indigo School," *National Register of Historic Places Registration Form* (Washington, DC: US Dept. of Interior, National Park Service, October 3, 1988), www.nationalregister.sc.gov/georgetown/S108177 22032/S10817722032.pdf.

21   **After changing occupations:** Boddie, *Traditions*, 15; Yeadon 1, no. 2 (April 1845): 275.

21   **"embarrassed in his affairs":** Henry Lee, *Memoirs of the War in the Southern Department* (Philadelphia, 1812), 1:395.

21   **"necessitous circumstances":** Yeadon 1, no. 1 (March 1845): 219.

21   **fend for themselves:** Lee, *Memoirs*, 1:395.

21   **Gabriel Marion died . . . became a sailor:** Cross, *Historic Ramblin's*, 277; James, 9; Simms, 15; Boddie, *Traditions*, 18–19.

21   **had each married . . . the Allstons:** Yeadon 1, no. 4 (June 1845): 413, 420; Yeadon 2, no. 5 (July 1845): 51; Joseph A. Groves, *The Alstons and Allstons of North Carolina and South Carolina* (Atlanta: Franklin Printing, 1901), 42, 68, 320; Suzanne Cameron Linder and Marta Leslie Thacker, *Historical Atlas of the Rice Plantations of Georgetown County and the Santee River* (Columbia: South Carolina Dept. of Archives and History, 2001), 148, 181–182.

21   **"his visage . . . not captivating":** Lee, *Memoirs*, 1:396.

21   **ship foundered:** Weems, 20–21; James, 9; Simms, 16, 235n10; Boddie, *Traditions*, 19; Yeadon 2, no. 7 (September 1845): 202–203. Because the story originates with Weems, it may be considered apocryphal. There is, however, at least one newspaper report of a shipwreck in 1750 off the coast of Cape Lookout, North Carolina, in which "3 men

and a boy" were saved and a Bermuda vessel was driven ashore. *South Carolina Gazette*, October 29–November 5, 1750. Marion, at age eighteen, conceivably could have been the youth.

21 **returned to . . . his mother:** James, 9.

21 **Francis spent . . . rudimentary education:** Boddie, *Traditions*, 16–18, 39. I am also indebted to Karen MacNutt for these observations and in particular the following addresses: "After the Fox in Georgetown," 11th Francis Marion/Swamp Fox Symposium, Manning, SC, October 19, 2013, and "Francis Marion and Georgetown," 9th Francis Marion/Swamp Fox Symposium, October 15, 2011, DVDs.

22 **moved from Georgetown:** James, 10; Yeadon 1, no. 4 (June 1845): 412; Yeadon 2, no. 6 (August 1845): 126; no. 8 (October 1845): 265–266.

22 **declining health:** Boddie, *Traditions*, 22.

22 **She would die . . . Job and Francis:** Ibid., 23; Yeadon 1, no. 2 (April 1845): 275; Yeadon 2, no. 8 (October 1845): 266.

22 **listed on the muster roll:** Yeadon 2, no. 8 (October 1845): 265–266.

22 **every able-bodied man:** Jacobsen, "Conduct of the Partisan War," 34; Pancake, *This Destructive War*, 50–51; Clyde R. Ferguson, "Functions of the Partisan-Militia in the South During the American Revolution: An Interpretation," in Higgins, *Revolutionary War in the South*, 242.

22 **Gabriel married . . . heiress:** Yeadon 1, no. 4 (June 1845): 415–416.

22 **Belle Isle:** Ibid., 416; *Boddie*, Traditions, 23.

22 **English Santee . . . French Santee:** Thomas Gaillard, "Copious Extracts," 16; Yeadon 1, no. 4 (June 1845): 416n.

22 **"garden spot" . . . indigo:** Ravenel, "Historical Sketch," 39–41.

23 **profitable crops at Hampton Hill:** Boddie, *Traditions*, 24–25; Yeadon 2, no. 8 (October 1845): 267–268.

CHAPTER 3: FRONTIER LESSONS

24 **Oconostota . . . Lyttelton claimed a victory:** Alan Calmers, "The Lyttelton Expedition of 1759: Military Failures and Financial Successes," *SCHM* 77, no. 1 (January 1976): 10–26; John Oliphant, *Peace and War on the Anglo–Cherokee Frontier, 1756–1763* (Baton Rouge: Louisiana State University Press, 2001), 54–55, 69–72, 76, 102–104, 109–112; Tom Hatley, *The Dividing Paths: Cherokees and South Carolinians Through the Revolutionary Era* (New York: Oxford University Press, 1995), 113–125; Yeadon 1, no. 4 (June 1845): 418; Yeadon 2, no. 8 (October 1845): 268–272; Letter of Volunteers to Gov. William Henry Lyttelton, October 31, 1759, in *The Writings of Christopher Gadsden, 1746–1805*, ed. Richard Walsh (Columbia: University of South Carolina Press, 1966), 12–13. See generally Daniel J. Tortora, *Carolina in Crisis: Cherokees, Colonists, and Slaves in the American Southeast,*

1756–1763 (Chapel Hill: University of North Carolina Press, 2015), chaps. 3–4.

25   **The colonials resented:** John T. Schlotterbeck, *Daily Life in the Colonial South* (Santa Barbara, CA: Greenwood Press, 2013), 353.

25   **fresh outbreak of hostilities:** Oliphant, *Peace and War*, 110–111; Tortora, *Carolina in Crisis*, chaps. 6–7.

26   **Montgomery set out . . . British muskets:** Oliphant, *Peace and War*, 113–117, 123–132; Yeadon 2, no. 8 (October 1845): 274–275; Tortora, *Carolina in Crisis*, 118–128.

26   **Montgomery's expedition . . . caused South Carolinians to question:** Tortora, *Carolina in Crisis*, 128–129; Oliphant, *Peace and War*, 132–134; Hatley, *The Dividing Paths*, 132–133.

26   **the captors massacred:** Robert J. Conley, *The Cherokee Nation: A History* (Albuquerque: University of New Mexico Press, 2005), 49; Fred Anderson, *Crucible of War: The Seven Years' War and the Fate of Empire in British North America, 1754–1766* (New York: Knopf, 2000), 463–465; Tortora, *Carolina in Crisis*, 131–133.

26   **commanding officer was scalped alive:** Anderson, *Crucible of War*, 465.

26   **"stuffed earth . . . eat your fill'":** Ibid., 799n13.

26   **James Grant . . . Marion was commissioned:** Oliphant, *Peace and War*, 151; Anderson, *Crucible of War*, 466; Paul David Nelson, *General James Grant: Scottish Soldier and Royal Governor of East Florida* (Gainesville: University Press of Florida, 1993), 3–5, 33–35; Duane H. King, "A Powder Horn Commemorating the Grant Expedition Against the Cherokees," *Journal of Cherokee Studies* 1, no. 1 (Summer 1976): 23, 30; Yeadon 2, no. 9 (November 1845): 333–336; "Officers of the South Carolina Regiment in the Cherokee War, 1760–1761," *SCHGM* 3, no. 4 (October 1902): 202, 205.

27   **danced the War Dance . . . "The camp . . . what it was":** Christopher French, "Journal of an Expedition to South Carolina," *Journal of Cherokee Studies* 2, no. 3 (Summer 1977): 279–281 (May 16, 29).

27   **white woodsmen dressed and painted:** Tortora, *Carolina in Crisis*, 144, 148.

27   **Grant's men passed . . . after several hours of fighting:** Ibid., 148–149; French, "Journal," 283–284 (June 9, 10); "Journal of Lieutenant-Colonel James Grant, Commanding an Expedition Against the Cherokee Indians, June–July, 1761," *Florida Historical Quarterly* 12 (1933): 27–29; Oliphant, *Peace and War*, 158–163; Anderson, *Crucible of War*, 466.

27   **"was met . . . every soul to death":** French, "Journal," 283–284 (June 10).

27   **burned fifteen settlements . . . "to demolish . . . to starve":** "Journal of Grant," 30, 35.

27 **concluded a treaty:** Yeadon 2, no. 9 (November 1845): 337; Oliphant, *Peace and War*, 140, 171–188; Anderson, *Crucible of War*, 467–468.

28 **Weems paints . . . opened the pass:** Weems, 22–23. See also Simms, 29–30. Simms cites a written autobiography of Peter Horry that has since been lost.

28 **Grant did send . . . Moultrie's first lieutenant:** "Journal of Grant," 28; Tortora, *Carolina in Crisis*, 149; "Diary of Alexander Monypenny: March 20–May 31, 1761," *Journal of Cherokee Studies* 2, no. 3 (Summer 1977): 330 (May 31); *Pennsylvania Journal* (Philadelphia), July 9, 1761; Moultrie, *Memoirs*, 2:223.

28 **"Our men . . . across the river":** *The Papers of Henry Laurens*, vol. 3, *Jan. 1, 1759–Aug. 31, 1763*, ed. Philip M. Hamer and George C. Rogers Jr. (Columbia: University of South Carolina Press, 1972), 75.

28 **one slightly wounded private:** *Pennsylvania Gazette*, August 6, 1761 (quoting Grant headquarters report).

28 **eleven soldiers were killed:** "Journal of Grant," 28.

28 **only one of them a Carolina provincial:** French, "Journal," 285 (June 17).

28 **"an active . . . soldier":** Moultrie, *Memoirs*, 2:223.

28 **"distinguished himself . . . near Etchoee":** James, 10.

28 **"slaughtering Indians for fun":** "Mel Gibson's Latest Hero: A Rapist Who Hunted Indians for Fun," *The Guardian*, June 15, 2000, www .theguardian.com/film/2000/jun/15/news.melgibson.

29 **"We arrived . . . refrain from tears":** Weems, 24–25. In reviewing Weems's text Horry did not take issue with his rendition of the letter. Salley, "Horry's Notes."

29 **Peggy, was the "mustee" daughter:** Yeadon 2, no. 6 (August 1845): 124–126.

29 **Joseph Willis:** Scott Withrow, "Joseph Willis: Carolinian and Free Person of Color," in *Carolina Genesis: Beyond the Color Line*, ed. Scott Withrow (Palm Coast, FL: Backintyme, 2010), 148–153, 161–173; Randy Willis, "The Story of Joseph Willis," *Three Winds Blowing*, 2015, threewindsblowing.com/story-of-joseph-willis.html.

29 **grand jury and petit jury:** John D. Stemmons and E. Diane Stemmons, compilers, *South Carolina 1767 Jury List* (Sandy, UT: Census Publishing), 79.

30 **350 acres . . . continued to acquire:** Yeadon 2, no. 8 (October 1845): 267; Boddie, *Traditions*, 37.

30 **Gabriel . . . 140 slaves . . . 78,000 pounds:** Yeadon 1, no. 4 (June 1845): 418–419; Boddie, *Traditions*, 20–21.

30 **By 1773 . . . Pond Bluff:** Yeadon 2, no. 8 (October 1845): 267; F. M. Kirk, "Pond Bluff Plantation, Marion Family," c. 1930s, www.roots web.ancestry.com/~scbchs/pondbluff.htm.

30 **plantation manager was the man June:** Boddie, *Traditions*, 37.

30 **he made out a will:** Yeadon 2, no. 6 (August 1845): 126; Boddie, *Traditions*, 37–39.

31 **"natural son" of Gabriel:** Yeadon 1, no. 4 (June 1845): 419–420.

31 **crime to teach slaves:** David J. McCord, ed., *The Statutes at Large of South Carolina*, vol. 7, *Containing the Acts Relating to Charleston, Courts, Slaves, and Rivers* (Columbia, SC, 1840), 413, section XLV.

32 **Gabriel made no provision for . . . William:** Yeadon 1, no. 4 (June 1845): 419; Last Will and Testament of Gabriel Marion, February 29, 1776, Ancestry.com. William's mother was a Mary Marion, who was probably a first cousin of Gabriel and Francis. Last Will and Testament of Gabriel Marion [Jr.], October 21, 1780, Ancestry.com; Yeadon 1, no. 2 (April 1845): 276–277.

32 **"regularly raping his female slaves":** "Mel Gibson's Latest Hero."

CHAPTER 4: MANNING THE RAMPARTS

33 **prominent French families . . . fought for the Tories:** Johnson, *Traditions and Reminiscences*, 282–283; Frye Gaillard, *Lessons from the Big House: One Family's Passage Through the History of the South, A Memoir* (Asheboro, NC: Down Home Press, 1994), 12, 18–22; Lambert, *South Carolina Loyalists*, 7, 113–115, 123n22.

33 **His older brothers:** Yeadon 1, no. 4 (June 1845): 413–425; *Journal of the Provincial Congress of South Carolina, 1776* (Charleston, SC, 1776), 130, 132; MacNutt, "After the Fox in Georgetown"; MacNutt, "Francis Marion and Georgetown"; Cross, *Historic Ramblin's*, 215, 218; Groves, *Alstons and Allstons*, 68; Alexander S. Salley, compiler, *South Carolina Provincial Troops, Named in Papers of the First Council of Safety of the Revolutionary Party in South Carolina, June–November, 1775* (Baltimore: Genealogical Pub. Co., 1977), 76.

33 **First Provincial Congress . . . Job and Francis . . . Gabriel:** Moultrie, *Memoirs*, 1:14–16; Yeadon 1, no. 4 (June 1845): 418–419, 425.

34 **The wealthy Allstons . . . would later serve:** Rogers, *History of Georgetown County*, 134; James, 82; Groves, *Alstons and Allstons*, 53, 76, 320; Linder and Thacker, *Rice Plantations*, 183.

34 **Francis's nephews:** O'Kelley, *Unwaried Patience*, 38, 615n191; Rankin, 10; Charles J. Colcock, "The Marion Family," *Huguenot Society* 22 (1916): 46–47; Yeadon 2, no. 5 (July 1845): 55.

34 **Isaac Marion . . . helped relay:** Simms, 236n18; R. Howe to Isaac Marion, May 8, 1775; Isaac Marion to Dennis Hankins et al., May 9, 1775, in Robert W. Gibbes, ed., *Documentary History of the American Revolution . . . 1764–1776* (New York, 1855), 90.

34 **"Rice Kings":** Buchanan, 17–24.

34 **Provincial Congress endorsed:** Fraser, *Patriots*, 63–65; William R. Ryan, *The World of Thomas Jeremiah: Charleston on the Eve of the*

American Revolution (New York: Oxford University Press, 2010), 30–34; Moultrie, *Memoirs*, 1:12–18.

35 **"diligently attentive . . . arms":** Moultrie, *Memoirs*, 1:55.

35 **Charleston rebels raided:** Parker, 82, 87, 127.

35 **rumors spread that the British:** Fraser, *Patriots*, 67; Piecuch, *Three Peoples*, 64, 76–78.

35 **"a few scalps taken by Indians":** Piecuch, *Three Peoples*, 39.

35 **South Carolinians voted to raise . . . enemy of the state:** Rankin, 8; Fraser, *Patriots*, 67; Buchanan, 91–92.

35 **Thomas Jeremiah:** Piecuch, *Three Peoples*, 78–80; Farley, "The South Carolina Negro," 76–77; Ryan, *World of Thomas Jeremiah*, 19, 56.

35 **Marion tied for third . . . ranked second captain:** A. S. Salley, ed., "Miscellaneous Papers of the General Committee, Secret Committee, and Provincial Congress, 1775," SCHGM 8, no. 4 (October 1907): 190; Rankin, 9; O'Kelley, *Unwaried Patience*, 1, 601n10, 602n20.

36 **blue cloth coats:** O'Kelley, *Unwaried Patience*, 1; Fraser, *Patriots*, 74–75.

36 **recruiting mission:** Bass, *Swamp Fox*, 11.

36 **"keep themselves . . . soldier-like manner":** O'Kelley, *Unwaried Patience*, 11.

36 **His first mission . . . surrender was made:** Ibid., 14–15; Rankin, 10–11; Moultrie, *Memoirs*, 1:86–88; Ryan, *World of Thomas Jeremiah*, 46–48, 70–72; Parker, 103.

36 **new American flag:** Moultrie, *Memoirs*, 1:90–91.

37 **Campbell . . . dissolved:** Piecuch, *Three Peoples*, 17; Gordon, *Battlefield History*, 26.

37 **Moultrie chose Marion . . . arsenal at Dorchester:** O'Kelley, *Unwaried Patience*, 26; Moultrie, *Memoirs*, 1:109–110.

37 **Called back to Charleston . . . "except Capt. Wigfall":** O'Kelley, *Unwaried Patience*, 33, 36; Rankin, 13.

37 **John Wigfall would later switch sides:** Rankin, 73–74, 83, 87; Lambert, *South Carolina Loyalists*, 287, 292–293; Saberton, CP2:64n6; Frank Moore, *Diary of the American Revolution: From Newspapers and Original Documents*, vol. 2 (New York, 1859), 276–278. Some sources give his name as Joseph.

37 **Marion was recalled:** O'Kelley, *Unwaried Patience*, 33.

37 **first land battle . . . ended Tory resistance:** Ibid.; Parker, 247, 251; Edgar, *Partisans and Redcoats*, 33; Buchanan, 101–102.

38 **new assignments . . . ordered on March 1:** Rankin, 13–14; O'Kelley, *Unwaried Patience*, 47.

38 **William Campbell . . . had been lobbying Parliament:** Rankin, 14; Edgar, *Partisans and Redcoats*, 35–36; Gordon, *Battlefield History*, 32, 36.

38 **civilians began fleeing . . . defenders' morale was boosted:** Moultrie, *Memoirs*, 1:140–141; Fraser, *Patriots*, 84–86.

39   **Charles Lee . . . Colonel Moultrie:** Gordon, *Battlefield History*, 38–39; O'Kelley, *Unwaried Patience*, 61, 71.

39   **Marion . . . promoted from captain:** O'Kelley, *Unwaried Patience*, 47, 51.

39   **working alongside slaves:** Ibid., 618n219.

39   **palmetto logs . . . only materials:** Lumpkin, 13; Bill Izard, "The Palmetto State: Sullivan's Island, South Carolina," *PorterBriggs.com*, 2015, porterbriggs.com/the-palmetto-state-3.

39   **"slaughter pen" . . . too easy:** Moultrie, *Memoirs*, 1:141, 144.

39   **"General Lee . . . than write one":** Henry Flanders, *The Lives and Times of the Chief Justices of the Supreme Court of the United States* (New York, 1875), 540.

40   **no one sell beer . . . surprise alarms . . . no oak trees:** O'Kelley, *Unwaried Patience*, 47, 618nn219–220, 619n228.

40   **On June 28, 1776 . . . British were repelled with heavy losses:** Lumpkin, 14–17; Buchanan, 12–15; Gordon, *Battlefield History*, 40–44; Moultrie, *Memoirs*, 1:174–181.

41   **two hundred casualties:** Lumpkin, 281; Gordon, *Battlefield History*, 41, 43–44.

41   **American losses . . . "a mulatto boy";** O'Kelley, *Unwaried Patience*, 79.

41   **"cool to the last degree":** Charles Lee, *The Life and Memoirs of the Late Major General Lee* (1813; repr., Bedford, MA: Applewood Books, 2009), 313.

41   **passed a resolution . . . Continental Army:** Moultrie, *Memoirs*, 1:183.

41   **He did not . . . Shubrick:** Salley, "Horry's Notes," 120.

41   **Marion did perform a critical role:** O'Kelley, *Unwaried Patience*, 78; Rankin, 19.

41   **teenaged nephew Gabriel:** O'Kelley, *Unwaried Patience*, 615n191; Elmer O. Parker and Georgia Muldrow Gilmer, *American Revolution Roster Fort Sullivan (Later Fort Moultrie), 1776–1780: Events Leading to First Decisive Victory* (Charleston, SC: Fort Sullivan Chapter, Daughters of the American Revolution, 1976), 217.

Chapter 5: Commander of the 2nd Regiment

43   **lieutenant colonel of the 2nd Regiment:** O'Kelley, *Unwaried Patience*, 122–123, 185, 637n435; Gibbes2, 45.

43   **"renounce . . . George the Third":** O'Kelley, *Unwaried Patience*, 123.

43   **slovenly . . . exceeding leaves:** Ibid., 111, 202–203, 211, 307.

43   **"runnin . . . intirely naked":** Ibid., 216.

44   **Punishment could mean . . . remitted:** Ibid., 211, 262, 282, 288, 290, 318, 320, 622n267, 626n306, 630n358, 636nn417, 419, 648n563.

44   **more than one out of four men . . . 749 lashings:** John L. Frierson, "Discipline by the Lash: The Order Books of Gen. Francis Marion,"

Carologue: Bulletin of the South Carolina Historical Society 15, no. 4 (Winter 1999): 9, 12–13.

44   **"whipped . . . regiment":** O'Kelley, *Unwaried Patience,* 291.

44   **thirty-nine to one hundred:** Harry M. Ward, *George Washington's Enforcers: Policing the Continental Army* (Carbondale: Southern Illinois University Press, 2006), 160; Frierson, "Discipline by the Lash," 8.

44   **the British army . . . was much harder:** Buchanan, 158.

44   **men comb their hair . . . "clean and neat":** O'Kelley, *Unwaried Patience,* 277, 287.

44   **"long hairs gather much filth" . . . regimental barber . . . dressed on the spot:** Ibid., 284.

44   **"more like wild savages than soldiers":** Ibid.

44   **"filthy custom . . . vile practices":** Ibid., 283.

44   **"genteel dinner" . . . in their barracks:** Ibid., 207.

45   **"obliged to take notice . . . attentive to their men":** Ibid., 111, 172–173.

45   **"Whenever any part . . . entirely":** Ibid., 277.

45   **"read, Wright & arithmitick":** Ibid., 295.

45   **The chosen instructor:** Ibid., 97, 109, 131 (Howell Simmons).

45   **offered bounties . . . petty criminals:** Edgar, *Partisans and Redcoats,* 43; O'Kelley, *Unwaried Patience,* 345.

45   **less than half strength:** "Francis Marion's Regimental Muster Roll, 1778," *Thomas Cooper Library, University of South Carolina, Rare Books and Special Collections,* 2013, library.sc.edu/spcoll/marion/fmarion.html.

45   **"lieutenant colonel commandant":** Bass, *Swamp Fox,* 22; O'Kelley, *Unwaried Patience,* 344, 350, 672n904. In 1782 his commandant commission was backdated to September 1776. "The Francis Marion Congressional Military Commission," *Francis Marion University,* October 29, 2008, www.fmarion.edu/rogerslibrary/fmcommissiontext.htm.

45   **his four brothers had died:** Yeadon 1, no. 4 (June 1845): 413, 418–419, 421, 425.

45   **role of guardian . . . US representative:** Ibid., 418, 426; Boddie, *Traditions,* 42, 260, 269–270; Karen MacNutt, "Gen. and Mrs. Marion, Families of the Revolution," address at 7th Francis Marion/Swamp Fox Symposium, Manning, SC, October 17, 2009, DVD; "Robert Marion (1766–1811)," *Biographical Directory of the United States Congress,* bioguide.congress.gov/scripts/biodisplay.pl?index=M000130.

46   **The fall of Savannah . . . pillaging homes:** John C. Cavanaugh, "American Military Leadership in the Southern Campaign: Benjamin Lincoln," in Higgins, *Revolutionary War in the South,* 105–111; Edgar, *Partisans and Redcoats,* 44–47; Rankin, 29–32; Parker, 112; James Haw, *John and Edward Rutledge of South Carolina* (Athens: University of Georgia Press, 1997), 126–127; Gregory D. Massey, *John Laurens*

and the American Revolution (Columbia: University of South Carolina Press, 2000), 136–140.

47 **John Laurens . . . "blown up . . . huzzas":** David Duncan Wallace, *The Life of Henry Laurens, with a Sketch of the Life of Lieutenant-Colonel John Laurens* (New York: G. P. Putnam's, 1915), 448–450; Massey, *John Laurens*, 140–143.

47 **"much disgusted . . . impolitic step":** Massey, *John Laurens*, 140.

47 **General Lincoln . . . retake Savannah . . . Jasper, too, was cut down:** Cavanaugh, "Benjamin Lincoln," 118–119; Swisher, *Southern Back Country*, 90–105; Rankin, 34–39; O'Kelley, *Unwaried Patience*, 470–473.

49 **"the ditch . . . their dead":** O'Kelley, *Unwaried Patience*, 473.

49 **Colonel Laurens . . . Count Pulaski:** Ibid.; Massey, *John Laurens*, 147–148.

49 **Franco-American forces . . . British casualties:** O'Kelley, *Unwaried Patience*, 474; Swisher, *Southern Back Country*, 106–107.

49 **pleaded with d'Estaing:** Cavanaugh, "Benjamin Lincoln," 119; Haw, *John and Edward Rutledge*, 129.

50 **plantation in Sheldon . . . minor skirmishing . . . kept armed blacks:** Rankin, 39–42, O'Kelley, *Unwaried Patience*, 479–486; Piecuch, *Three Peoples*, 169–171.

50 **"When you see me . . . singular":** FM to Lincoln, January 26, 1780, South Carolina Historical Society, Charleston.

50 **Marion remained . . . returned to Charleston:** Rankin, 40, 43; Benjamin Lincoln to FM, January 31, 1780 (Gibbes, 9–10).

50 **Bacon's Bridge . . . no rum:** Carl P. Borick, *A Gallant Defense: The Siege of Charleston, 1780* (Columbia: University of South Carolina Press, 2003), 67–68, 87; O'Kelley, *Unwaried Patience*, 497–500.

50 **back in command . . . Rural militia:** Rankin, 44; Haw, *John and Edward Rutledge*, 131–132; Cavanaugh, "Benjamin Lincoln," 121; Fraser, *Patriots*, 117–119; Borick, *A Gallant Defense*, 56–59, 66–67.

51 **attended an officers' party:** Bass, *Swamp Fox*, 29; Buchanan, 151–152. Some sources say his ankle was sprained or dislocated rather than broken.

51 **on April 12 . . . Marion was gone . . . as was Governor Rutledge:** Borick, *A Gallant Defense*, 138–142; Sherman, *Calendar*, 134.

51 **Peter Horry:** Rankin, 40–41; Peter Horry, "Journal," ed. A. S. Salley, *SCHGM* 38, no. 2 (April 1937): 49–53; Rogers, *History of Georgetown County*, 146.

51 **Lincoln considered . . . was not strong enough:** Cavanaugh, "Benjamin Lincoln," 126; Buchanan, 49, 66.

51 **Tarleton's cavalry . . . managed to escape:** Gordon, *Battlefield History*, 82–83; Buchanan, 61–62; Cavanaugh, "Benjamin Lincoln," 126.

52 **Lenud's Ferry . . . Elias Ball:** Scott A. Miskimon, "Anthony Walton White, a Revolutionary Dragoon," in Piecuch, *Cavalry*, 120–126, 240n37; [Elizabeth Anne Poyas], *Our Forefathers: Their Homes and Their Churches* (Charleston, SC, 1860), 169–170; Edward Ball, *Slaves in the Family* (1998; repr., New York: Farrar, Straus and Giroux, 2014), 8–9, 15.

52 **"open the gates for the enemy":** Cavanaugh, "Benjamin Lincoln," 126.

Chapter 6: Birth of a Partisan

54 **On August 23 . . . Murray's Ferry:** FM to Horatio Gates, August 29, 1780, Sparks Collection, Harvard; Cornwallis to Germain, September 19, 1780 (CSR15:279–280).

54 **Tory deserter . . . best-trained . . . Sumter's abandoned plantation:** Aiken, 107; Pancake, *This Destructive War*, 49; Parker, 166, 412; Cornwallis to Germain, September 19, 1780 (CSR15:279–280). The exact location of Sumter's plantation remains uncertain. Steven D. Smith, with Tamara S. Wilson and James B. Legg, contributors, *The Search for Francis Marion: Archaeological Survey of 15 Camps and Battlefields Associated with Francis Marion* (Columbia: University of South Carolina, South Carolina Institute of Archaeology and Anthropology, July 2008), 18–22.

54 **guarded by sixty . . . a few Tory militia troops:** FM to Horatio Gates, August 29, 1780, Sparks Collection, Harvard; Cornwallis to Germain, September 19, 1780 (CSR15:279).

54n *Provincials* **. . . British had more Americans:** A. S. Salley, ed., *SCHGM* 2, no. 1 (January 1901): 248n.

55 **Marion had seventy:** FM to Gates, August 29, 1780, Sparks Collection, Harvard. Horry put Marion's force at 30 and the enemy guard at 90, whereas Cornwallis reported that Marion had 150 to 200 militia to only 36 or 38 prisoner guards. Weems, 116; Cornwallis to John Harris Cruger, August 27, 1780 (CP2:172); Cornwallis to Clinton, August 29, 1780 (CP2:41–42); Cornwallis to Germain, September 19, 1780 (CSR15:279). Throughout the Revolution each side tended to overstate the size of the enemy and understate its own force, particularly when it lost a battle.

55 **He roused his men . . . victory, though small, was complete:** Aiken, 34–35, 107–109; FM to PH, August 27, 1780 (Gibbes, 11–12); FM to Gates, August 29, 1780, Sparks Collection, Harvard; FM to Gates, September 15, 1780 (CSR14:617); Cornwallis to Clinton, August 29, 1780 (CP2:41–42); Cornwallis to Germain, September 19, 1780 (CSR15:280).

55   **the freed prisoners . . . about 60, went to North Carolina:** Rankin, 66; James Read to Jethro Sumner, September 12, 1780 (CSR14:771); Cornwallis to Cruger, August 27, 1780 (CP2:172); Cornwallis to Germain, September 19, 1780 (CSR15:280); Cornwallis to Clinton, August 29, 1780 (CP2:42); FM to Gates, August 29, 1780, Sparks Collection, Harvard; Otho Williams to Gov. Thomas Sim Lee, October 12, 1780, Calendar of Otho Holland Williams Papers, 1744–1839, MS 908, Maryland Historical Society; John Rutledge to South Carolina Delegates, September 20, 1780, in "Letters of John Rutledge," annotated by Joseph W. Barnwell, SCHGM 17, no. 4 (October 1916): 139.

56   **General Gates . . . made his own report . . . Patriot newspapers:** Bass, *Swamp Fox*, 46–47.

56   **"a Colonel Marion":** Cornwallis to Clinton, August 29, 1780 (CP2:41).

56   **"I am afraid . . . the whole of it":** Wemyss to Cornwallis, September 3, 1780 (CP2:213).

56   **"disaffection" . . . Santee was so great:** Cornwallis to Clinton, August 29, 1780 (CP2:41).

56   **"*disarm . . . the plantation*":** Cornwallis to Wemyss, August 28, 1780 (CP2:208) (emphasis added).

57   **"I have ordered . . . of the country":** Cornwallis to Cruger, August 18, 1780 (CP2:19) (first emphasis in text added).

57   **attended Eton academy, a rough place:** Franklin B. Wickwire and Mary Wickwire, *Cornwallis: The American Adventure* (Boston: Houghton Mifflin, 1970), 22–23.

57   **"*I have myself* . . . the enemy":** Cornwallis to Clinton, August 29, 1780 (CP2:41) (emphasis added).

57   **"put an end . . . South Carolina":** Cornwallis to Clinton, June 30, 1780 (CP1:161).

CHAPTER 7: HITTING AND RUNNING

58   **After the victory . . . numbered just over fifty:** FM to PH, August 27, 1780 (Gibbes, 11–12); FM to Gates, August 29, 1780, Sparks Collection, Harvard; FM to Gates, September 15, 1780 (CSR14:616–618).

59   **On August 29 . . . dispirited the Whigs:** FM to Gates, August 29, 1780, Sparks Collection, Harvard; FM to Gates, September 15, 1780 (CSR14:616).

59   **Wemyss was about to embark . . . expected Wemyss to recruit:** Saberton, CP2:26; Wemyss to Cornwallis, August 28, 1780 (CP2:209–210).

59   **Major Micajah Ganey:** Bass, *Swamp Fox*, 48; Micajah Ganey to FM, September 8, 1781 (Gibbes, 135–136); O'Kelley, *Unwaried Patience*, 505; Lorenzo Sabine, *Biographical Sketches of Loyalists of the American*

Revolution: With an Historical Essay (Boston, 1864), 1:458. His name is also frequently given as Gainey.

59 **Captain Jesse Barefield:** Bass, *Swamp Fox*, 48–49; O'Kelley, *Unwaried Patience*, 193, 505, 651n606; William Barfield Sr., "Twelve Generations of Barfields from Jon ('The Immigrant') Barfield," *Rootsweb.com*, November 12, 2004, under "Generation #4," archiver.rootsweb.ancestry .com/th/read/NCBLADEN/2004–11/1100288804; Alexander Gregg, *History of the Old Cheraws . . . and Sketches of Individuals* (New York, 1867), 334, 337–338. His name is also frequently given as Barfield.

59 **"which is all I could get":** FM to Gates, September 15, 1780 (CSR14:617).

59 **several brothers persuaded him:** Loftis R. Munnerlyn Pension, S18136. Munnerlyn made his pension application more than fifty years after the event, when he was in his eighties. He initially stated that Marion and thirty men rescued his parents from their home after it was "unroofed" by the Tories. In a second declaration four years after the original one he stated that his father was freed in the skirmish at Blue Savannah after he and his brothers told Marion they were determined to rescue him whether Marion helped them or not. Munnerlyn also claimed Marion agreed to attack with sixty men against five hundred Tories, which further undermines the plausibility of his account.

60 **told no one . . . feathers in their hats:** Bass, *Swamp Fox*, 49.

60 **came upon an advance foraging party . . . escaped into the swamps:** FM to Gates, September 15, 1780 (CSR14:617); James, 26; Francis Davis Pension, S8290; Rankin, 70–72. Most sources state that Ganey was with the advance party and that Major John James singled him out for pursuit. If the advance was merely a foraging party, as the Davis pension states, then Ganey probably was not with it.

60 **Blue Savannah . . . bluish color:** Parker, 322–323, 499n405 (citing address by Jo Church Dickerson). The engagement is believed to have taken place on the east side of present-day South Carolina Highway 41 about a quarter-mile south of its intersection with US 501. Parker, 322; Smith, *The Search for Francis Marion*, 27–29.

60n **many inland South Carolina "bays":** James, 47n14; "Carolina Bays," *South Carolina Department of Natural Resources*, 2014, www.dnr.sc.gov /wildlife/wetlands/carolinabays.html.

60 **William Dobein James . . . an ambush:** James, 26. See also Rankin, 71; Bass, *Swamp Fox*, 50–51; Aiken, 111–113. Some historians have read James to say that due to illness, he was absent for the entire early part of Marion's partisan campaign. In fact, he joined Marion's brigade at Witherspoon's Ferry in mid-August and was still with Marion at the Great White Marsh in North Carolina on September 24, when Marion returned to South Carolina and James stayed behind after

taking sick there. James, 5, 26, 31; Rankin, 75–76, 83. Even if James was not at Blue Savannah, his father, Major John James, was there.

61   **"directly attacked . . . put them to flight":** FM to Gates, September 15, 1780 (CSR14:617). The fact that Marion reported no Tories being killed suggests that there was no ambush, at least not in the manner described by James. John C. Parker Jr., email to the author, April 18, 2015. However, it seems unlikely that Marion would have plunged fifty-three men against two hundred in a headlong assault, especially at that early stage of his partisan campaign, when the loss of his brigade would have been disastrous for the patriot cause. He might have done so if he caught the enemy completely off guard, but James describes the Tories as being in formation, and Marion reported that they were on the march toward him. Like most of his cursory battle reports, Marion's letter to Gates probably omitted some details of the skirmish. Complicating matters, one pension application states it was Ganey's Tories, lying in ambush, who surprised and fired upon Marion's men in the second skirmish before retreating to the swamp. Francis Davis Pension, S8290.

61   **fled into a swamp:** FM to Gates, September 15, 1780 (CSR14:617); James, 26; Francis Davis Pension, S8290.

61   **shouted curses and insults:** Bass, *Swamp Fox*, 51.

61   **"impassable . . . to all but Tories":** FM to Gates, September 15, 1780 (CSR14:617).

61   **four wounded . . . sixty new volunteers:** Ibid.; George McCall Pension, R6598; Smith, "Archaeological Perspectives," 154.

61   **While at Britton's Neck . . . retreating to North Carolina:** FM to Gates, September 15, 1780 (CSR14:617); Rankin, 74–76; James, 31; Bass, *Swamp Fox*, 54; Sherman, *Calendar*, 252–254; *South-Carolina and American General Gazette* (Charleston), September 20, 1780.

62   **Ami's Mill . . . dumped the two field pieces:** Sherman, *Calendar*, 254 and n1271; James, 31.

62   **"until I hear . . . doing something":** FM to Gates, September 15, 1780 (CSR14:618).

63   **Wemyss . . . pursued Marion:** Wemyss to Cornwallis, September 20, 1780 (CP2:214–215); Bass, *Gamecock*, 89; Henry W. Harrington to Gates, September 17, 1780 (CSR14:624–625).

63   **burned the . . . "sedition shop":** James, 43.

63   **himself a Presbyterian:** Marg Baskin, *Oatmeal for the Foxhounds: Banastre Tarleton and the British Legion*, "Friends, Comrades, and Enemies: James Wemyss (1748–1833)," n30, January 2, 2011, home.golden.net /~marg/bansite/friends/wemyss.html.

63   **put the torch to several:** James, 31–32, 43; Parker, 189–190, 229, 324.

63n   **Wemyss supposedly locked:** James, 43.

63   **hanged Adam Cusack . . . John Brockinton:** James, 32; FM to Gates, October 4, 1780 (CSR14:666); Wemyss to Cornwallis, September 20, 1780 (CP2:215 and n12); Gregg, *Old Cheraws*, 303; Parker, 189, 223; Baskin, "James Wemyss," n41; Neil O. Myers, *Myers and Neighbors of Jeffries Creek, SC* (Aiken, SC: Lulu.com, 2007), 69–72.

63   **Dr. James Wilson:** Parker, 189; Bass, *Swamp Fox*, 58.

63   **"by birth . . . a Mohawk":** Weems, 128.

63   **cut a path of destruction:** James, 31; Parker, 229, 435.

63   **fifty houses . . . "mostly":** Wemyss to Cornwallis, September 20, 1780 (CP2:215).

63   **destroy blacksmith shops . . . cows and sheep:** James, 31–32, 43; Parker, 229; Buchanan, 185.

63   **"I never could come up with them" . . . boasted:** Wemyss to Cornwallis, September 20, 1780 (CP2:214–215).

64   **"not so agreeable":** Cornwallis to Wemyss, September 26, 1780 (CP2:216).

64   **"It is impossible . . . disaffection of this country":** Wemyss to Cornwallis, September 20, 1780 (CP2:215).

64   **Tory militia, without support . . . were too weak:** Wemyss to Cornwallis, September 30, 1780 (CP2:217).

64   **"burning houses . . . severe manner":** Ibid.

64   **Moses Murphy . . . Maurice Murphy:** Parker, 324; Gregg, *Old Cheraws*, 71–72, 246, 298, 303; O'Kelley, *Unwaried Patience*, 525, 532, 698n1376; Beverly White, "Malachi Murphy," *Rootsweb.com*, November 17, 2000, archiver.rootsweb.ancestry.com/th/read/MURPHY /2000–11/0974502591.

64   **"ungovernable passion . . . strong drink":** Gregg, *Old Cheraws*, 354.

64   **had stolen Micajah Ganey's horses:** Micajah Ganey to FM, September 8, 1781 (Gibbes, 136).

64   **Murphy had also shot . . . his own cousin:** Valentine Van Zee, "Gibson Family of Pee Dee, SC," *Rootsweb.com*, under "A-11, Gideon Gibson," freepages.genealogy.rootsweb.ancestry.com/~valvz/gibson_of _pee_dee.html; Gregg, *Old Cheraws*, 354.

64   **"I am sorry . . . women and children":** FM to Gates, October 4, 1780 (CSR14:666).

64   **Marion wrote apologetically . . . John Ervin:** FM to Gates, October 15, 1780 (CSR14:622). Some sources identify the miscreant as Colonel Hugh Ervin Sr., a senior militia officer of advanced age who, at least nominally, was Marion's second-in-command. Hugh Ervin Sr. was John Ervin's uncle and father-in-law. Rankin, 89, 148; Smith, "Archaeological Perspectives," 96, 158–159; Ervin, "Entries," 222. I agree with Jim Piecuch that John Ervin, who was younger and spent more time in the field than his father-in-law, is likely the person referred to in Marion's letter to Gates. Piecuch, *Three Peoples*, 230.

Unlike Piecuch, however, I do not read the letter to say that John Ervin had defected to the British and was burning Whigs' homes. In the letter Marion is lamenting the burning of Tory properties by men associated with his brigade.

64 **"will be the greatest hurt to our interest":** FM to Gates, October 15, 1780 (CSR14:622).

65 **Ervin left the brigade . . . would return:** Ibid.; O'Kelley, *Unwaried Patience*, 534, 699n1405.

65 **Murphy . . . Later promoted . . . keeping them occupied:** O'Kelley, *Unwaried Patience*, 525, 532; Sherman, *Calendar*, 65; Gregg, *Old Cheraws*, 374.

65 **Cornwallis defended any brutalities:** Cornwallis to Germain, August 21, 1780 (CP2:14); Cornwallis to Smallwood, November 17, 1780 (CP3:401–402).

65 **"I have always . . . horrors of war":** Cornwallis to Clinton, December 4, 1780 (CP3:28).

66 **"a most acceptable repast . . . rather grave":** James, 31.

66 **"He had no uproarious humor . . . his features":** Simms, 87.

66 **capable of sarcasm . . . playfulness among friends:** Ibid.; Alexander Garden, *Anecdotes of the Revolutionary War in America, with Sketches of Character of Persons the Most Distinguished, in the Southern States, for Civil and Military Service* (Charleston, SC, 1822), 28–29.

66 **"He was singularly . . . despondency":** Simms, 87.

66 **malaria . . . starting to complain:** James, 5; Bass, *Swamp Fox*, 61–62.

CHAPTER 8: "MY LITTLE EXCURSIONS"

67 **Not long after . . . back to South Carolina:** James, 31–32, 45.

67 **With his sixty men . . . Jenkins boys . . . would attack Ball's unit:** James, 31–32; Rankin, 67, 83–84.

68 **St. James and St. Stephens:** FM to Gates, October 4, 1780 (CSR14:665).

68 **John Coming Ball . . . Elias Ball:** Anne Simons Deas, *Recollections of the Ball Family of South Carolina and the Comingtee Plantation* (Summerville, SC, c. 1909), 97–101, 177–179; Ball, *Slaves in the Family*, 8–9; Pancake, *This Destructive War*, 79; Lambert, *South Carolina Loyalists*, 7, 113–115, 123n22.

68 **married Marion's brother Job:** Yeadon 1, no. 4 (June 1845): 424–425; Frye Gaillard, *Lessons from the Big House*, 18; Poyas, *Our Forefathers*, 169–170.

68 **Peter Gaillard:** Samuel Dubose, "Address at the 17th Anniversary of the Black Oak Agricultural Society, April 27, 1858," in Samuel Dubose and Frederick A. Porcher, *A Contribution to the History of the Huguenots of South Carolina, Consisting of Pamphlets*, ed. Theodore

Gaillard Thomas (New York, 1887): 14–19; Frye Gaillard, *Lessons from the Big House*, 17–22, 25.

68   **John Peyre:** Samuel Dubose, "Reminiscences of St. Stephens Parish, Craven County, and Notices of Her Old Homesteads," in Dubose and Porcher, *Contribution*, 49, 55, 60; Poyas, *Our Forefathers*, 168–171.

68   **Captain John Brockinton:** Josephine Lindsay Bass and Becky Bass Bonner, "My Southern Family, Capt. John Brockington II," *Rootsweb. com*, May 29, 2005, freepages.genealogy.rootsweb.ancestry.com/~my southernfamily/myff/d0006/g0000046.html; Smith, introduction to Boddie, *Traditions*, xxx, xliiin38.

68   **"men of family . . . good men":** FM to Gates, October 4, 1780 (CSR14:666).

68   **When he heard . . . cavalry would provide support:** James, 32; Rankin, 84–85; Aiken, 114–116, 278n20; Gordon, *Battlefield History*, 110–111.

69   **rarely engaged in personal combat:** Aiken, 46–47; James, 99; Simms, 6.

69   **Ball, alerted . . . Henry Mouzon . . . never took the field again:** James, 32–33; Rankin, 85–86; Aiken, 116; Smith, *The Search for Francis Marion*, 39–46. Whether the "Captain John James" involved at Black Mingo was John James of Lynches Lake or John James Jr. is uncertain. Boddie appears to confuse them with each other. Boddie, *History of Williamsburg*, 130; Boddie, *Traditions*, 236. Because James of the Lake was well advanced in years, John James Jr. probably was the combatant.

70   **relatives could have a greater impact:** Buchanan, 105.

70   **captured all the guns . . . renamed it "Ball":** Bass, *Swamp Fox*, 66–67. One source states that the horse may have been owned by Elias (Wambaw) Ball. Deas, *Ball Family*, 98.

71   **Several Tories . . . joined his brigade:** James, 33; Bass, *Swamp Fox*, 67.

71   **Peter Gaillard . . . enlist with Marion's band:** Dubose, "Address at the 17th Anniversary," 16–17; Frye Gaillard, *Lessons from the Big House*, 25–26.

71   **Ball . . . refused to take the field:** Bass, *Swamp Fox*, 71–72, 253; FM to Gates, October 15, 1780 (CSR14:622).

71   **John Peyre . . . off to prison:** Dubose, "Reminiscences of St. Stephens Parish," 55–56.

71   **"the Tories are so affrighted . . . off to Georgia":** FM to Gates, October 4, 1780 (CSR14:666).

71   **"I have found . . . in this province":** Cornwallis to Clinton, September 22–23, 1780 (CP2:46).

71   **"meet with some disaster":** Cornwallis to George Turnbull, October 2, 1780 (CP2:244).

71 **"Depend upon it . . . without regular troops":** Turnbull to Cornwallis, October 4, 1780 (CP2:250). Lieutenant Colonel George Turnbull, a Scotsman, was commander of the New York Volunteers, a loyalist provincial unit. Saberton, CP1:138n35.

72 **one-fifth:** Lambert, *South Carolina Loyalists*, 306.

72 **one-third:** Gray, "Observations," 140.

72 **lacked the same high quality:** Buchanan, 192; Sherman, *Calendar*, 30; Wickwire and Wickwire, *Cornwallis*, 185–186; Saberton, CP1:40.

72 **"all the leading men . . . rebel side":** Nisbet Balfour to Cornwallis, June 3 or 4, 1780, in Rogers, *History of Georgetown County*, 125.

72 **"dastardly and pusillanimous":** Cornwallis to Alexander Leslie, November 12, 1780 (CP3:40).

72 **lost all sympathy:** Cornwallis to Cruger, November 11, 1780 (CP3:269).

72 **"established a decided superiority":** Gray, "Observations," 144.

72 **"bold and rash . . . risk nothing":** Ibid.

72 **"cautious and vigilant":** Cornwallis to Tarleton, November 8, 1780 (CP3:334).

72 **shrewd tactics:** Aiken, 27–39.

73 **hooves loudly rattled . . . From then on:** Weems, 119.

73 **pension applications . . . spread blankets:** William Griffis Pension, R4320; John Booth Pension (transcribed by Sam West), W25258; David Watts Pension, S18267; Thomas Hitchcock Pension, R5057. To be sure, these applications were made many years after the Revolution by men in their seventies and eighties. But they were submitted at different times (sometimes three years apart) and in different states (North and South Carolina and Georgia). They do not repeat a Weems tale, as pension applicants sometimes did, but instead contradict one. It is unlikely that all of these applications, independently saying the same thing, could all be wrong.

73 **"They had intelligence of our coming":** FM to Gates, October 4, 1780 (CSR14:665).

74 **"He had about . . . mean fella":** Ball, *Slaves in the Family*, 8.

74 **wanted to go after Wigfall . . . Presbyterian Church:** FM to Gates, October 4, 1780 (CSR14:665); Bass, *Swamp Fox*, 62, 67.

74 **"so many of my followers . . . burnt out":** FM to Gates, October 4, 1780 (CSR14:665).

74 **Wigfall . . . declined to come out:** Rankin, 90; Saberton, CP2:64n6.

74 **few Tory militia turned out:** Wemyss to Cornwallis, September 20, 1780 (CP2:215); Cornwallis to Turnbull, September 27, 1780 (CP2:240).

74 **"suspicious":** Wemyss to Cornwallis, September 20, 1780 (CP2:215).

74 **Wemyss had left Cheraw . . . to Camden:** Wemyss to Cornwallis, October 4, 1780 (CP2:219).

74   **while Cornwallis . . . planning to march:** Cornwallis to Wemyss, October 7, 1780 (CP2:222).

74   **"to prevent . . . you have left":** Ibid.

74   **King's Mountain . . . rest were reprieved:** Gordon, *Battlefield History*, 112–117; Buchanan, 229–239; Piecuch, *Three Peoples*, 199. Another researcher has more recently estimated the rebel force at approximately 1,600 versus 1,125 loyalists under Ferguson. J. D. Lewis, "Kings Mountain: The Rest of the Story," address at 13th Francis Marion/ Swamp Fox Symposium, Manning, SC, October 24, 2015.

75   **"there was scarce . . . arms against us":** Cornwallis to Clinton, December 3, 1780 (CP3:24).

75   **Cornwallis had planned . . . would have been available:** Paul David Nelson, *Francis Rawdon-Hastings, Marquess of Hastings: Soldier, Peer of the Realm, Governor-General of India* (Madison, NJ: Fairleigh Dickinson University Press, 2005), 84.

75   **retreated back . . . feverish cold . . . Francis Rawdon:** Saberton, CP1:151–152; 2:31; Wickwire and Wickwire, *Cornwallis*, 221.

76   **recalled Wemyss to Camden:** John Money to Turnbull, October 12, 1780 (CP2:252).

CHAPTER 9: DEAD MAN'S HAND

77   **suffered many fatigues:** FM to Gates, October 4, 1780 (CSR14:666).

77   **sixty or seventy . . . few as a dozen . . . no authority to punish:** Ibid.; FM to Gates, October 15, 1780 (CSR14:622); FM to Gates, August 29, 1780, Sparks Collection, Harvard.

77   **"certainly pay a visit to Georgetown":** FM to Gates, October 4, 1780 (CSR14:666).

77   **probing incursion . . . immediately paroled:** Bass, *Gamecock*, 94; FM to Gates, October 15, 1780 (CSR14:621); Aiken, 182–185.

78   **"This damned Georgetown business":** Jethro Sumner to Gates and enclosed intercepted British correspondence, October 9, 1780 (CSR14:679–681).

78   **Allen McDonald . . . ran down:** James, 30, 53; Rankin, 66, 106–107; FM to Gates, October 15, 1780 (CSR14:621); James Craven Pension, R2457; William Shaw Pension, S19078; Daniel McDonald Johnson, *Blood on the Marsh: The Adventures of Brigadier William Mackintosh . . . Sergeant Allen McDonald and Alexander McDonald*, rev. ed. (Allendale, SC: CreateSpace, 2014), 439–440, 445–446, 559.

78   **"the most active persons against us":** FM to Gates, October 15, 1780 (CSR14:621).

78   **wished to hear . . . "scrawl . . . wild woods":** Ibid.

78   **lacked even paper:** James, 4; FM to NG, January 1, 1781 (NGP7:36).

78 **continue his hostilities:** Gates to FM, October 11, 1780, in Library of Congress, Thomas Jefferson Papers Series 2: Horatio Gates Letterbook Correspondence, 1780–81; Bass, *Swamp Fox*, 74.

78 **Marion's initial thought . . . Harrison:** James, 33; Lambert, *South Carolina Loyalists*, 115; Saberton, CP1:161n5; Robert D. Bass, "The South Carolina Rangers: A Forgotten Loyalist Regiment," *Proceedings of the South Carolina Historical Society* (1977): 65–68; Murtie June Clark, *Loyalists in the Southern Campaign of the Revolutionary War: Official Rolls of Loyalists Recruited from North and South Carolina, Georgia, Florida, Mississippi, and Louisiana* (Baltimore: Genealogical Pub. Co., 1981), 1:97–102.

79 **"the greatest banditti . . . country":** James, 25.

79 **"if possible worse . . . run home":** Wemyss to Cornwallis, September 30, 1780 (CP2:216).

79 **"not worth anything":** Turnbull to Cornwallis, October 4, 1780 (CP2:249).

79 **accused of having recently murdered:** James, 25; Parker, 417; Howe, *History of the Presbyterian Church*, 1:482.

79 **"chastise" . . . militia was slow . . . lazily camped:** James, 33 (quotation); Bass, *Swamp Fox*, 75; Rankin, 92, 103; FM to Gates, November 4, 1780 (CSR14:726). Tearcoat Swamp was also known as Tarcote or Tarcoat.

79 **Samuel Tynes . . . switched sides:** Saberton, CP2:92n64; T. Mark James, "Genealogy of the Tynes Family," *Rootsweb.com*, November 23, 2008, under "The Tynes Family of Granville, North Carolina," freepages.genealogy.rootsweb.ancestry.com/~tmark/Tynes.html; James Fred Patin Jr., page manager, "Robert Fleming Tynes, Jr.," March 27, 2015, www.geni.com/people/Robert-Tynes/6000000025566256975.

80 **"weak, well intentioned man":** Cornwallis to Frederick DePeyster, August 21, 1780 (CP2:211).

80 **a ripe target . . . Marion's losses were . . . no men:** James, 33; FM to Gates, November 4, 1780 (CSR14:726); Rankin, 103–104.

80 **Amos Gaskens . . . in his hands:** James, 33; Rankin, 77, 104.

80 **"He seemed to be . . . non-suited him forever":** Weems, 123.

80 **The haul from the battle:** FM to Gates, November 4, 1780 (CSR14:726).

80 **fought bravely for him:** James, 33.

81 **Tynes . . . got away . . . sent the captured men:** FM to Gates, November 4, 1780 (CSR14:726); Bass, *Swamp Fox*, 78–79.

81 **use both roads and waterways:** Pancake, *This Destructive War*, 122–123; McCrady, 100–101.

81 **longer, more circuitous route:** Bass, *Swamp Fox*, 79; Sherman, *Calendar*, 334.

81   **Anxious for the fate:** Rawdon to Balfour, October 31, 1780 (CP2:131).

81   **"at an end":** Balfour to Rawdon, November 1, 1780 (CP3:61).

CHAPTER 10: THE SWAMP FOX

82   **Banastre Tarleton . . . theatrical group:** Robert D. Bass, *The Green Dragoon: The Lives of Banastre Tarleton and Mary Robinson* (1957; repr., Columbia, SC: Sandlapper, 1973), 11–16, 19–20, 36–39; Holley Calmes, "Banastre Tarleton, A Biography, Part One: The Early Years," *Oatmeal for the Foxhounds: Banastre Tarleton and the British Legion*, January 2, 2011, home.golden.net/~marg/bansite/btbiog.html; Holley Calmes, "Banastre Tarleton and Mary Robinson," *Madame Guillotine*, October 7, 2012, madameguillotine.org.uk/2012/10/07/banastre -tarleton-and-mary-robinson.

82   **recommendation of Cornwallis:** Wickwire and Wickwire, *Cornwallis*, 257.

82   **British Legion . . . in name only:** Bass, *Green Dragoon*, 46–48; Lawrence E. Babits and Joshua B. Howard, "Continentals in Tarleton's British Legion: May 1780–October 1781," in Piecuch, *Cavalry*, 184–185.

82   **traditional cavalry . . . and dragoons:** Piecuch, *Cavalry*, xv; Pancake, *This Destructive War*, 40–41; O'Kelley, *Unwaried Patience*, 695n1302; Showman, *NGP6*:xlii.

83   **dragoons took their name:** Du Pont, "Address," 31.

83n   **Like traditional dragoons . . . tended to blur:** Michael C. Scoggins, "South Carolina's Back Country Rangers in the American Revolution: 'A Splendid Body of Men,'" in Piecuch, *Cavalry*, 159–161, 164–168; Pancake, *This Destructive War*, 40–41, 53; Sherman, *Calendar*, 70n274.

83   **Cornwallis had dispatched Tarleton . . . the Waxhaws:** Gordon, *Battlefield History*, 86–87; Buchanan, 80–82; Lumpkin, 50; Bass, *Green Dragoon*, 78–81.

84   **"slaughter was commenced":** Banastre Tarleton, *A History of the Campaigns of 1780 and 1781, in the Southern Provinces of North America* (London, 1787), 30.

84   **"to pieces":** Tarleton to Cornwallis, May 29, 1780, in Bass, *Green Dragoon*, 81–82.

84   **casualty figures:** Lumpkin, 50.

84   **"dreadfully mangled":** Ledstone Noland Pension, S16992.

84   **outright massacre:** Buchanan, 84–85; Edgar, *Partisans and Redcoats*, 56; James, 103–106 (letter of Robert Brownfield).

84   **Some revisionists:** Jim Piecuch, "Massacre or Myth? Banastre Tarleton at the Waxhaws, May 29, 1780," *SCAR* 1, no. 2 (October 2004):

4–10. See also Rubin, "Rhetoric of Revenge," 18–19. Another researcher has recently argued that evidence from sword and bayonet wounds at the Waxhaws supports the traditional massacre theory. C. Leon Harris, "Massacre at Waxhaws: The Evidence from Wounds," *SCAR* 11, no. 2.1 (June 2016): 1–4.

84   **"stimulated the soldiers . . . not easily restrained":** Tarleton, *Campaigns*, 31.

84n   **continued to slash . . . "the most shocking manner":** Charles Stedman, *The History of the Origin, Progress, and Termination of the American War* (London, 1794), 2:183.

84n   **"give these disturbers . . . None shall they experience":** Tarleton to Cornwallis, August 5, 1780 (CP1:365).

85   **imploring him to gather:** Bass, *Swamp Fox*, 79; Rankin, 110–111.

85   **"Mr. Marion . . . his charge":** Tarleton, *Campaigns*, 171.

85   **"I . . . get at Mr. Marion":** Cornwallis to Tarleton, November 5, 1780, in Bass, *Green Dragoon*, 110.

85   **Tarleton and his Legion . . . set out south . . . Marion . . . with two hundred men:** Turnbull to Cornwallis, November 5, 1781 (CP3:136–137); Bass, *Swamp Fox*, 79–80; Bass, "South Carolina Rangers," 68; Rankin, 111–112; Tarleton to Turnbull, November 5, 1780 (CP3:333); FM to Gates, November 4, 1780 (CSR14:726); FM to Gates, November 9, 1780, in PCC, Item No. 154, 2:334. Bass writes that Marion had four hundred men, but Marion's November 9 letter records his force as being no more than two hundred. Tarleton claimed Marion had five hundred militia, which is likely an exaggeration. Tarleton, *Campaigns*, 172.

85   **Tarleton had moved down . . . four hundred and waited:** FM to Gates, November 9, 1780, in PCC, Item No. 154, 2:334; Tarleton, *Campaigns*, 172; Tarleton to Turnbull, November 5, 1780 (CP3:333); Tarleton to Cornwallis, November 11, 1780 (CP3:337); Bass, *Swamp Fox*, 80–81. Bass and Rankin misidentify the widow as Mary (Cantey) Richardson. Bass, *Gamecock*, 99; Rankin, 112. Mary Cantey, Richardson's first wife, died in 1767, after which he married Dorothy Sinkler. Joseph S. Ames, *Six Generations of the Cantey Family of South Carolina* (Charleston, SC: Walker, Evans, and Cogswell, 1910), 23–24.

86   **nearly took the bait . . . Richard Richardson . . . safe for the night:** James, 34; FM to Gates, November 9, 1780, in PCC, Item No. 154, 2:334; Ames, *Cantey Family*, 45–46.

86   **scratching his head . . . "treacherous women":** Tarleton to Cornwallis, November 11, 1780 (CP3:337).

87   **Marion had already flown . . . seven-hour hunt:** James, 34; Tarleton, *Campaigns*, 172; Tarleton to Cornwallis, November 11, 1780 (CP3:337).

87   "the difficulties of the country": Tarleton to Cornwallis, November 11, 1780 (CP3:337).

87   abandoned the chase . . . "Come my boys . . . could not catch him": James, 34.

87n   referred to him . . . *Swamp Fox:* Steven D. Smith, "Imagining the Swamp Fox: William Gilmore Simms and the National Memory of Francis Marion," in *William Gilmore Simms's Unfinished Civil War: Consequences for a Southern Man of Letters,* ed. David Moltke-Hansen (Columbia: University of South Carolina Press, 2013), 36–37, 39.

87   at Benbow's Ferry . . . defensive position: James, 34–35; FM to Gates, November 9, 1780, in PCC, Item No. 154, 2:334.

87   tried to put a good face: Tarleton to Cornwallis, November 11, 1780 (CP3:337).

87   would have caught up . . . had already ended: Tarleton, *Campaigns,* 172. Tarleton misdated his pursuit of Marion to November 10. His seven-hour chase began on the morning of November 8, and Cornwallis's order to return was not sent from Winnsboro until November 9. Cornwallis to Tarleton, November 9, 1780 (CP3:335).

88   "laid . . . waste": Tarleton to Cornwallis, November 11, 1780 (CP3:337).

88   "beat . . . where I was": FM to Gates, November 9, 1780, in PCC, Item No. 154, 2:334.

88   "behaved to the poor women . . . Whig nor Tory": Ibid.

88n   "there is no record . . . *homeless and hungry*": Calmes, "Banastre Tarleton, Part Two: The Southern Campaign" (emphasis added). See also Marg Baskin, "Banecdotes: General Richardson's Grave or, the Power of Myth," *Oatmeal for the Foxhounds: Banastre Tarleton and the British Legion,* January 2, 2011, home.golden.net/~marg/bansite/banecdotes/85richardson.html.

88   low on ammunition . . . reluctant to turn out: FM to Gates, November 9, 1780, in PCC, Item No. 154, 2:334.

88   "It is not the wish . . . fire and sword": Tarleton Proclamation, November 11, 1780 (CP3:338).

88   "The country seems . . . total destruction of Mr. Marion": Tarleton to Cornwallis, November 11, 1780 (CP3:337).

89   "there was a power . . . since his expedition": Cornwallis to Clinton, December 3, 1780 (CP3:25).

89   threaten Georgetown: Aiken, 185–186.

89   "no joke to us": Balfour to Cornwallis, November 17, 1780 (CP3:85).

89   "I do not think . . . joining him": Cornwallis to Balfour, November 22, 1780 (CP3:87).

89   "We have lost . . . was as quiet": Cornwallis to Balfour, November 25, 1780 (CP3:89).

CHAPTER 11: "I MUST DRIVE
MARION OUT OF THAT COUNTRY"

90   angling for a promotion . . . commissioned Sumter: Sherman, *Calendar*, 276, 278.

90   "our greatest plague in this country": Cornwallis to Tarleton, November 23, 1780, in Tarleton, *Campaigns*, 203.

91   Wemyss asked Cornwallis . . . hugged its neck: Buchanan, 249–251; Lumpkin, 108–109; Bass, *Gamecock*, 96–99; Cornwallis to Tarleton, November 9, 1780 (CP3:335); Cornwallis to Balfour, November 10, 1780 (ibid., 68); Cornwallis to Clinton, December 3, 1780 (ibid., 25); Baskin, "James Wemyss."

91   Sumter was bragging: Bass, *Gamecock*, 101.

92   three to four hundred . . . beat back a bayonet charge: Buchanan, 251–257; Sherman, *Calendar*, 314–319; Lumpkin, 114; Wickwire and Wickwire, *Cornwallis*, 224–225; Bass, *Gamecock*, 102–107.

92   Marion wrote to General Gates: FM to Gates, November 21, 1780 (CSR14:746).

92   "invalids" . . . redoubtable Jesse Barefield . . . got away: Ibid.; O'Kelley, *Unwaried Patience*, 506–507; Rankin, 117–119; FM to William Harrington, November 17, 1780, in Gregg, *Old Cheraws*, 343–344; Parker, 233–234.

93   shot . . . point blank: James, 36; Parker, 234.

93   Gabriel Marion . . . made out a will: Last Will and Testament of Gabriel Marion, October 21, 1780, Ancestry.com.

93   mourned young Gabriel's death: James, 36.

93   "Our loss . . . three wounded": FM to Gates, November 21, 1780 (CSR14:746).

93   put a bullet . . . reprimanded: Weems, 142–143; James Jenkins, *Experience, Labours, and Sufferings of Rev. James Jenkins, of the South Carolina Conference* (Spartanburg, SC: 1842), 23–24.

94   "do anything effectual" . . . in need of a surgeon: FM to Gates, November 21, 1780 (CSR14:746–747).

94   "Many of my people . . . support": Ibid., 746.

94   "I seldom have . . . will be the same": FM to Gates, November 22, 1780, in Bass, *Swamp Fox*, 98.

94   Major Robert McLeroth . . . became worried . . . they had gone home: Ibid.

94   about four hundred . . . Sumter's plantation: Rankin, 124.

95   did not vent . . . lacked enterprise: James, 55; Saberton, CP3:77n31.

95   "I think the sooner . . . some accident to him": Balfour to Cornwallis, November 29, 1780 (CP3:98).

95   Turnbull . . . was granted leave: Sherman, *Calendar*, 311.

95 **"I trust . . . cuts deep":** Cornwallis to Rawdon, December 3, 1780 (CP3:191).

95 **Marion remained in hiding:** Bass, *Swamp Fox*, 104; Smith, "Archaeological Perspectives," 164–165, 168.

95 **marauding band . . . if left unchecked:** Rawdon to Cornwallis, December 5, 1780 (CP3:196); Bass, *Swamp Fox*, 105–106; Lambert, *South Carolina Loyalists*, 115, 200; "Memorial of Captain John Harrison Loyalist Claims—Public Records Office, London, England," transcribed by Houston Tracy Jr., *The Harrison Genealogy Repository*, Rootsweb.com, February 15, 2000, freepages.genealogy.rootsweb .ancestry.com/~harrisonrep/harrbios/captjohnharrisonSC.html. Another Harrison brother (or possibly their father), Robert, had been killed on October 14, 1780. Clark, *Loyalists in the Southern Campaign*, 1:101; Bass, "South Carolina Rangers," 69.

95 **Samuel Tynes . . . had escaped . . . time on their hands:** FM to Gates, December 6, 1780, Horatio Gates Papers, microfilm reel 13:67, Thomas Cooper Library, University of South Carolina; Coffin to Rawdon, November 23, 1780 (CP3:170); Bass, *Swamp Fox*, 101, 105–107.

96 **dispatched Peter Horry . . . Tories deserted . . . "exceedingly frightened":** Bass, *Swamp Fox*, 106–107; Rawdon to Cornwallis, December 8, 1780 (CP3:200) (quotation).

96 **two hundred raw recruits . . . preparing to invade:** Tarleton, *Campaigns*, 212; Sherman, *Calendar*, 326; Bass, *Swamp Fox*, 100; Rutledge, "Account," December 8, 1780, SCHGM 18, no. 2 (April 1917): 60.

96 **"too formidable . . . better than militia":** Balfour to Cornwallis, December 4, 1780 (CP3:104).

96 **the plan was . . . would meet them:** Balfour to Cornwallis, December 11, 1780 (CP3:111); Bass, *Swamp Fox*, 103, 107.

96 **swelled to about three hundred:** James, 53–54. Estimates of the opposing forces range from 300 to 700 for Marion, and 270 to 500 for McLeroth, depending on whether his 200 troops under escort are included. Sherman, *Calendar*, 333; FM to NG, December 22, 1780 (NGP6:605); Rawdon to Cornwallis, December 13, 15, 1780 (CP3:209–210, 214); Coffin to Rawdon, December 13, 1780 (CP3:211). The 700 figure for Marion would represent an unprecedented increase in his brigade in such a short time and is likely exaggerated. Rawdon reported to Cornwallis on December 2 that Marion's force was 300 and expressed disbelief at a later report that placed the number at 500. Rawdon to Cornwallis, December 2, 13, 1780 (CP3:190, 209–210). Another British report placed Marion's force, as of December 29, at 300 to 400. Filinghauzen, January 2, 1781 (CP3:419). On November 20 John Rutledge reported Marion with "perhaps 300" in the Kingston area. Rutledge to South Carolina

Delegates, November 20, 1780, *SCHGM* 17, no. 4 (October 1917): 143. James is probably correct that both forces were somewhere between three and four hundred.

96 **Around December 13 . . . Halfway Swamp:** James, 54. Halfway Swamp is located about a mile south of present-day Rimini, South Carolina, on either side of Highway 76. The actual date of the action is uncertain.

97n **modern rules of warfare:** Protocol Additional to the Geneva Conventions of 12 August 1949, and relating to the Protection of Victims of International Armed Conflicts (Protocol I, 8 June 1977), Article 43 (definition of combatants). Article 53 of the Geneva Convention Relative to the Protection of Civilian Persons in Time of War, of 12 August 1949, states that "any destruction by the occupying power of real or personal property belonging . . . to private persons . . . is prohibited, except where such destruction is rendered absolutely necessary by military operations."

At the time of the Revolution both the British and American Articles of War forbade any waste or malicious destruction of enemy civilian property other than by order of the commander in chief. A hostile power could destroy civilian property only if it gained some military advantage, weakened the enemy, or punished the enemy for an egregious violation of international law. John Loran Kiel Jr., "War Crimes in the American Revolution: Examining the Conduct of Lt. Col. Banastre Tarleton and the British Legion During the Southern Campaigns of 1780–1781," *Military Law Review* 213 (Fall 2012): 44, 50–51.

97 **best marksmen square off . . . "fifty yards" . . . both sides retired:** James, 54–55.

98 **"skirmaged":** FM to NG, December 22, 1780 (*NGP6*:605). Marion probably meant "skirmished," to convey an actual if small battle, but another intriguing possibility exists. The word "scrymmage," an alteration of "skyrmissh," meant "to fight with a sword, fence." Ernest Klein, *A Comprehensive Etymological Dictionary of the English Language* (Amsterdam: Elsevier Pub. Co., 1967), 2:1403, 1454. Could Marion have coyly signaled that the engagement involved a mere "scrimmage," that is, a pretend fight, like a fencing match?

98 **from Gavin Witherspoon:** James, 5, 54.

98 **stalling for time . . . fleeing the infected premises:** James, 55; Rankin, 132–133.

98 **130 infantry:** FM to NG, December 22, 1780 (*NGP6*:605).

99 **McLeroth and Coffin headed safely off:** Sherman, *Calendar*, 333.

99 **Rawdon . . . granted his request:** Rawdon to Cornwallis, December 16, 1780 (*CP3*:215).

99   **"mild and equitable behavior":** Rawdon to Cornwallis, December 18, 1780 (CP3:217).

99   **"the most humane . . . British army":** James, 55.

99   **"I must drive . . . to effect it":** Rawdon to Cornwallis, December 15, 1780 (CP3:214).

99   **"disposed of":** Cornwallis to Rawdon, December 17, 1780 (CP3:215).

CHAPTER 12: "I HAVE NOT THE
HONOR OF YOUR ACQUAINTANCE"

100   **lingered about . . . Benbow's Ferry:** FM to NG, December 22, 1780 (NGP6:605–606 and n4); Rawdon to Cornwallis, December 19, 1780 (CP3:218).

100   **Nathanael Greene:** Gerald M. Carbone, *Nathanael Greene: A Biography of the American Revolution* (New York: Palgrave Macmillan, 2008), 5–6, 11, 16, 19–21, 25, 32, 40–46, 53–56, 72–79, 94–96; Buchanan, 260–264, 269–271, 273–274; Terry Golway, *Washington's General: Nathanael Greene and the Triumph of the American Revolution* (2005; repr., New York: Owl Books, 2006), 39, 176–177.

101   **mid-October . . . December 2:** Buchanan, 275; Showman, (NGP6:xvi–xvii).

101   **Greene found:** Buchanan, 288; Carbone, *Nathanael Greene*, 153–154; NG to Ezekiel Cornell, December 29, 1780 (NGP7:21).

101   **"I have not the honor . . . in our favor":** NG to FM, December 4, 1780 (NGP6:519–520).

102   **"the garnish . . . partisan strokes . . . contest for states":** NG to Sumter, January 8, 1781 (NGP7:74–75).

102   **pillage and plunder:** Ibid., 75.

102   **"like the locusts . . . every green thing":** NG to Joseph Reed, January 9, 1781 (NGP7:85).

102   **"of no more use . . . in the moon":** NG to Ezekiel Cornell, December 29, 1780 (NGP7:21).

102   **Sumter . . . took umbrage:** Bass, *Gamecock*, 120.

102   **"good harmony . . . to either":** O'Kelley, *Unwaried Patience*, 431.

103   **"not of the least service":** FM to Benjamin Lincoln, December 23, 1779, Massachusetts Historical Society, Boston.

103   **"diffidence":** FM to NG, December 22, 1780 (NGP6:605).

103   **"any soldier . . . white or black":** O'Kelley, *Unwaried Patience*, 566.

103   **"Ammunition I am told . . . for which we contend!":** NG to FM, December 4, 1780 (NGP6:520).

103   **"Spies are the eyes . . . necessary in this business":** Ibid.

104   **"endeavor to procure . . . several passes":** FM to NG, December 22, 1780 (NGP6:605).

104   **80 Hessians . . . if he had a hundred:** Ibid.

105   **established the Snow's Island . . . main hideout:** James, 36–37; Bass, *Swamp Fox,* 104–105; Simms, 105; Weems, 189; Parker, 230; Smith, "Archaeological Perspectives," 165–166, 168–169; FM to NG, December 28, 1780 (*NGP*7:13 and n2).

105   **poisonous vapors:** Swager, *The Valiant Died,* 66–67.

105   **northern tip . . . vines:** James, 37; Bass, *Swamp Fox,* 104; Smith, "Archaeological Perspectives," 64, 283; Smith, introduction to Boddie, *Traditions,* xix.

105   **felled trees . . . redoubt, at Dunham's Bluff:** James, 38; Bass, *Swamp Fox,* 105; Smith, "Archaeological Perspectives," 170–173, 259–262, 279–281, 283, 317–318.

105   **recent archaeological findings:** Smith "Archaeological Perspectives," 257–295, 373. As Smith points out, the discovery of artifacts at Dunham's Bluff consistent with a militia site as well as other historical evidence suggests that Marion's principal camp may have been at Dunham's Bluff and not on Snow's Island itself, where no physical evidence of a militia camp has been found. Smith, "Archaeological Perspectives," 257–263, 284–286. But Smith notes that "an equally good argument can be made using the historic records that Marion's main depot was at the northern end of Snow's Island" (ibid., 283). A number of contemporaneous records referred to Marion's camp as being "on" Snow's Island. *Royal Gazette* (Charleston), March 31–April 4, 1781; Balfour to John Saunders, April 2, 1781, Saunders Papers, UNB.

        It is possible that *Snow's Island* was a catch-all term for various camps within the same general area. But in absence of definitive proof, it seems to this author that Marion had at least one camp and probably his main camp for some time on Snow's Island itself. Dunham's Bluff may have been the main camp at times or an adjunct camp that kept in close communication with the island camp across the river.

105   **"The swamp was his moat . . . the Rhine":** Simms, 109.

105   **sweet potato dinner . . . "But surely, general . . . our usual allowance":** Garden, *Anecdotes* (1822), 22. See also Simms, 114–117; Weems, 153–156; Benson J. Lossing, "Francis Marion," *Harpers Monthly* 17, no. 98 (July 1858): 159.

106   **attempts to substantiate it:** One writer points to a pension application by a member of Marion's brigade who claims that the dinner was actually a breakfast and that he was the one who cooked it. Nell Weaver Davies, "New Facts About an Old Story," *Carologue* 15, no. 4 (Winter 1999): 16, 20; Samuel Weaver Pension, W8993. A descendant of John Brockinton, the noted Tory from Black Mingo, claims that it was Brockinton, in the process of switching his allegiance to the patriot side, who invited Marion to the dinner and cooked it himself. James P. Truluck Jr., "The Legacy of Two Grandfathers," *Carologue* (Autumn 1989): 8.

106   **painting by . . . John Blake White:** "General Marion Inviting a Brit-
        ish Officer to Share His Meal," *United States Senate, Art and History*,
        www.senate.gov/artandhistory/art/artifact/Painting_33_00002.htm.
        White (1781–1859), a neighbor of Marion, was fourteen at Marion's
        death. He made several paintings of the same scene over a number of
        years, beginning as early as 1810. Davies, "New Facts," 16.

106   **Oscar (or "Buddy"):** Sue Anne Pressley Montes, "Post-Revolution-
        ary Recognition," *Washington Post*, December 16, 2006; Yeadon 1,
        no. 1 (March 1845): 219; Joseph Johnson, *Traditions and Reminis-
        cences*, 280–281. At the time of his recognition in 2006 Oscar/Buddy
        was assumed to be the African American kneeling behind the small
        table and roasting the sweet potatoes. Another researcher, however,
        maintains that the kneeling slave in the painting, clearly a field hand,
        is not Marion's body servant and that the real Buddy, as more befitting
        a personal valet, is the better-dressed African American man standing
        behind Marion and attending to him. MacNutt, "Images of Francis
        Marion."

106   **"personal assistant . . . oarsman":** Tina C. Jones, "Patriot Slave,"
        American Legion, July 1, 2008, www.legion.org/magazine/1562/patriot
        -slave.

106   **played the fiddle:** FM to M. T. Watson, February 22, 1785, Theodorus
        Bailey Myers Collection, New York Public Library.

106n   **More likely . . . Georgetown:** "A Yankee View, 1843," in *South Caro-
        lina: The Grand Tour, 1780–1865*, ed. Thomas D. Clark (Columbia:
        University of South Carolina Press, 1973), 210; Jesse Olney, *A History
        of the United States, on a New Plan* (New Haven, CT: 1836), 165;
        Weems, 147–156.

106n   **had abundant supplies:** James, 37; Smith, "Archaeological Perspec-
        tives," 62, 80, 277, 363.

106   **dominated by Whigs . . . furnished Marion's partisans:** Smith, "Ar-
        chaeological Perspectives," 14, 54, 223–224, 366.

106   **women and slaves . . . carrying salt:** Rogers, *History of Georgetown
        County*, 133–134.

107   **"generous stewards . . . safety and plenty":** Weems, 189.

107   **declined to plunder them:** O'Kelley, *Unwaried Patience*, 529; Jacob-
        sen, "Conduct of the Partisan War," 63.

107   **"Some other damages . . . restrained":** FM to James Cordes, February
        1, 1781, South Carolina Dept. of Archives and History.

107   **offered the citizens security:** Smith, "Archaeological Perspectives,"
        223–224, 366.

107   **Tories' own backyard:** James, 37.

107   **150 bushels of salt:** Ibid., 39, 109; FM to NG, January 1, 1781
        (*NGP*7:36); Rankin, 147.

107 **applied by later guerrilla leaders:** Mao Tse-tung, "Guerilla Warfare," in US Marine Corps, *Mao Tse-tung on Guerrilla Warfare, Fleet Marine Force Reference Publication 12–18* (Washington, DC, 1989), 43–44, 86, 104; Smith, "Archaeological Perspectives," 2, 11–13, 35–37.

107 **US Army military doctrine:** US Army, *Field Manual 3–24: Insurgencies and Countering Insurgencies* (Washington, DC, May 13, 2014). See also US Army, *Field Manual 21–31: Guerilla Warfare and Special Forces Operations* (Washington, DC, September 29, 1961), chap. 2.

107 **crude lean-to huts:** Bass, *Swamp Fox*, 104.

107 **British seized the plantations . . . "high time . . . such an enemy":** *Pennsylvania Packet*, January 2, 1781; Preliminary Sketch, September 16, 1780 (CP2:323–324); Balfour to John Cruden, November 20, 1780 (CP3:443); Lambert, *South Carolina Loyalists*, 235–237; Rebecca Nathan Brannon, "Reconciling the Revolution: Resolving Conflict and Rebuilding Community in the Wake of Civil War in South Carolina, 1775–1860" (PhD diss., University of Michigan, 2007), 81–82, deep blue.lib.umich.edu/bitstream/handle/2027.42/57715/brannonr_1.pdf.

108 **Rutledge commissioned Marion:** Rutledge to South Carolina Delegates, December 30, 1780, SCHGM 18, no. 2 (April 1917): 63.

108 **bloody year:** Edgar, *Partisans and Redcoats*, 137.

CHAPTER 13: "TWO VERY ENTERPRISING OFFICERS"

109 **"a party of negroes":** NG to FM, January 16, 1781 (*NGP7*:131).

109 **"taking care . . . best spared":** FM to John Postell, January 19, 1781 (James, 109).

109 **sent up . . . more fertile forage area:** FM to NG, January 20, 1781 (*NGP7*:165); Carbone, *Nathanael Greene*, 158–159.

109 **continued to press Marion:** NG to FM, January 4, 1781 (*NGP7*:47).

109 **split his . . . army . . . needed to defeat Greene:** Buchanan, 292–295; Carbone, *Nathanael Greene*, 156–157; Gordon, *Battlefield History*, 126–127; Wickwire and Wickwire, *Cornwallis*, 248–256.

110 **first militia leader . . . regular reports:** George W. Kyte, "Francis Marion as an Intelligence Officer," SCHM 77, no. 4 (October 1976): 217–218; FM to NG, December 27, 28, 1780 (*NGP7*:6, 13 and n1); FM to NG, January 1, 9, 1781 (*NGP7*:36, 86).

110 **He promised to keep:** FM to NG, December 28, 1780 (*NGP7*:13).

110 **"every particular respecting the enemy":** FM to NG, January 4, 1781 (*NGP7*:49).

110 **director of intelligence:** Simms, 124; Kyte, "Marion as an Intelligence Officer," 215–226.

110 **sending Peter Horry:** FM to NG, January 9, 14, 1781 (*NGP7*:86, 121); Bass, *Swamp Fox*, 128–130.

110   **"were clever . . . honor":** NG to FM, January 22, 1781 (*NGP7:168*).
110   **"The war here . . . a capital nature":** NG to Joseph Reed, May 4, 1781 (*NGP8:200*).
111   **learned its topography . . . unfordable when flooded:** Buchanan, 129–130, 288–289, 310–311; Carbone, *Nathanael Greene*, 153; Wickwire and Wickwire, *Cornwallis*, 253.
111   **Greene repeatedly requested:** NG to FM, January 4, 16, 22, 1781 (*NGP7:47*, 130–131, 168); NG to FM, April 27, May 4, 1781 (*NGP8:161*, 198–199).
111   **"I hope you paid . . . addition you expect":** NG to FM, January 16, 1781 (*NGP7:131*).
111   **"get all the good dragoon horses . . . pay particular attention to it":** NG to FM, April 27, 1781 (*NGP8:161*).
111   **"ordinary . . . badly mounted":** FM to NG, January 18, 20, 1781 (*NGP7:143*, 165).
111   **"a few more . . . be got":** FM to NG, January 9, 1781 (*NGP7:86*).
111   **If Greene needed horses . . . merest rumor:** Simms, 159–160; William Johnson, *Life of Greene*, 2:116.
112   **"The crackers . . . material detriment":** George Hanger, *An Address to the Army, in Reply to Strictures, by Roderick M'Kenzie . . . on Tarleton's History of the Campaigns of 1780 and 1781* (London, 1789), 82n.
112   **"we have never . . . decisive action":** Rawdon to Clinton, March 23, 1781, in *The American Rebellion: Sir Henry Clinton's Narrative of His Campaigns, 1775–1782, with an Appendix of Original Documents*, ed. William B. Willcox (New Haven, CT: Yale University Press, 1954), 501.
112   **heavy buckshot . . . bird shot:** FM to PH, August 17, 1780 (Gibbes, 11); James, 54, 70, 95; Lumpkin, 69.
113   **converted as many infantry:** James, 52; Moultrie, *Memoirs*, 2:223.
113   **"like robbing Peter to pay Paul":** NG to PH, October 23, 1781 (*NGP9:467*).
113   **On January 14 . . . reported his fear:** FM to NG, January 14, 1781 (*NGP7:121*).
113   **sent a hundred regulars:** NG to FM, January 19, 1781 (*NGP7:145*); McCrady, 86n1. Greene's action proved unnecessary, as the Tories were dispersed by a force of North Carolina militia before the regulars arrived. FM to NG, January 20, 1781 (*NGP7:164*).
113   **Lieutenant Colonel Henry Lee:** Charles Royster, *Light-Horse Harry Lee and the Legacy of the American Revolution* (1981; repr., Baton Rouge: Louisiana State University Press, 1994), 14, 16–17; Buchanan, 352–353.
114   **Lee arrived . . . Marion . . . expected to hold rank:** Sherman, *Calendar*, 349–350; Jim Piecuch and John Beakes, *"Light Horse Harry" Lee in the War for Independence: A Military Biography of Robert E. Lee's*

Father (Charleston, SC: Nautical and Aviation Pub. Co. of America, 2013), 83, 86; FM to NG, January 20, 1781 (*NGP7*:165).

114   **Greene chose not to weigh:** NG to FM, January 25, 1781 (*NGP7*:194–195).

114   **Lee dressed elegantly . . . solicitous of the lives:** Royster, *Light-Horse Harry Lee*, 18–23; Buchanan, 353.

115   **"He was reserved . . . common good":** Lee, *Memoirs*, 1:396.

115   **had a hard time finding Marion:** Ibid., 1:164.

115   **reasons . . . as strategic as sentimental:** Aiken, 177–178; Parker, 233; MacNutt, "Francis Marion and Georgetown."

116   **The best explanation:** Gray, "Observations," 149, 155.

116   **skirted international law:** Aiken, 188; Campbell to FM, January 21, 1781 (Gibbes, 15–16).

116   **plan of attack . . . January 23 . . . set off:** Lee, *Memoirs*, 1:248–250; Bass, *Swamp Fox*, 135; MacNutt, "Francis Marion and Georgetown."

117   **"You must proceed . . . leave it":** FM to John Postell, January 23, 1781 (James, 111).

117   **reached Winyah Bay . . . retreated to Murray's Ferry:** Lee, *Memoirs*, 1:250–251; James, 51; MacNutt, "After the Fox in Georgetown"; Bass, *Swamp Fox*, 135–137; Lee to NG, January 25, 1781 (*NGP7*:198); *Diary of Henry Nase, King's American Regiment*, January 25, 1781, transcribed by Todd Braisted from New Brunswick Museum, Archives Division, Nase Family Papers, lib.jrshelby.com/nase-diary.pdf. Marion's sister, Esther, lived at Greenwich Plantation near Georgetown, which she inherited from her second husband, Thomas Mitchell. Boddie, *Traditions*, 207; Suzanne Cameron Linder and Marta Leslie Thacker, *Historical Atlas of the Rice Plantations of Georgetown County and the Santee River* (Columbia: South Carolina Dept. of Archives and History, 2001), 69–70, 327, 523–524.

117   **"Marion and Lee . . . their troops":** Lee, *Memoirs*, 1:251.

117   **"I" completely surprised:** Lee to NG, January 25, 1781 (*NGP7*:197).

118   **"conceived with ingenuity":** Lee, *Memoirs*, 1:251.

118   **"the little success . . . promises much":** FM to NG, January 27, 1781 (*NGP7*:207).

118   **"two very enterprising officers":** Balfour to Clinton, January 31, 1781, Letterbook of Lt. Col. Nisbet Balfour, January 1–December 1, 1781, Society of the Cincinnati, Digitized Collections, 2012, societyofthecincinnati.org/collections/library/digitized_collections.

118   **letters from Greene conveying:** NG to FM, January 23, 25, 1781 (*NGP7*:173, 194–195).

118   **Cowpens . . . Cornwallis had lost:** Buchanan, 316–327; Swager, *The Valiant Died*, 36–44; Lumpkin, 132, 294–295; Patrick O'Kelley, *"Nothing but Blood and Slaughter": The Revolutionary War in the Carolinas, 1781* (Bradenton, FL: Booklocker.com, 2005), 3:34–49.

119   "The late affair . . . my heart": Cornwallis to Rawdon, January 21, 1781 (CP3:251).

119   7th Regiment of Foot: Bass, *Swamp Fox*, 134; Bass, *Gamecock*, 122; Saberton, CP3:7; Cornwallis to Rawdon, January 1, 1781 (CP3:237); Cornwallis to Clinton, January 18, 1781 (CP3:35); Sherman, *Calendar*, 93.

119   Morgan prevented his men: Buchanan, 325.

119   orders to give no quarter: Wickwire and Wickwire, *Cornwallis*, 265.

119   "After this nothing will appear difficult": NG to FM, January 25, 1781 (NGP7:194).

120   sent shudders through the Whig: Lee to NG, February 3, 1781 (NGP7:247–248).

120   Greene recalled Lee: Sherman, *Calendar*, 375; Bass, *Swamp Fox*, 138; Ichabod Burnet to Lee, February 2, 1781 (NGP7:234–235).

120   "You will cross . . . their retreat": FM to John Postell, January 29, 1781 (James, 112–113).

120   carried off the mission: James, 52; Parker, 57, 60, 375; *Memoirs of Tarleton Brown, a Captain in the Revolutionary Army* (New York, 1862), 37–38; FM to NG, January 31, February 2, 1781 (NGP7:229, 239).

121   who had not had any rations: FM to NG, January 1, 1781 (NGP7:36).

121   "give my particular thanks . . . over the Santee": NG to FM, February 11, 1781 (James, 113).

121   "nothing indeed appeared difficult": James, 52.

121   "and concert . . . operations": NG to FM, February 11, 1781 (James, 113).

CHAPTER 14: HOUND AND FOX

122   Sumter had been absent . . . Articles of Confederation . . . Sumter had resigned: Buchanan, 293, 304–305, 312, 315; Thomas L. Powers, "In Defense of General Thomas Sumter," SCAR 5, no. 2 (2nd ed. 2008): 33–34; Bass, *Gamecock*, 120–121; Conrad, NGP8:xv; O'Kelley, *Unwaried Patience*, 350.

122   flattering letters . . . at his disposal: Carbone, *Nathanael Greene*, 163; Bass, *Gamecock*, 127; NG to Sumter, February 3, 1781 (NGP7: 245–246).

123   "If you can . . . best of consequences": Sumter to FM, February 20, 1781 (Gibbes, 23).

123   Jeffries Creek . . . driven there by Rawdon: O'Kelley, *Unwaried Patience*, 513, 695n1311; Rawdon to Cornwallis, February 15, 1781 (CP4:50); Smith, "Archaeological Perspectives," 179–180.

123   effort to enlist . . . Captain William Snipes . . . under orders of Marion: FM to Isaac Huger, February 6, 1781 (NGP7:230n4); Huger to

FM, January 28, 1781 (Gibbes, 18–19); Rutledge to FM, January 28, 1781 (Gibbes, 19); Rankin, 160–161.

123   **proclamation . . . "put them to death":** O'Kelley, *Unwaried Patience,* 518.

123   **issued another order . . . took provisions:** Ibid., 521.

124   **Rawdon narrowly missed . . . three hundred:** Rawdon to Cornwallis, February 15, March 7, 1781 (CP4:47, 49, 50).

124   **"prevent Marion . . . much more":** Rawdon to Cornwallis, February 15, 1781 (CP4:50).

124   **Marion did not receive . . . until February 26:** FM to Sumter, February 26, 1781, reprinted in Bruce Gimelson, *Autographs/Paintings/Americana,* www.maineantiquedigest.com/adpage/4083); McCrady, 106.

124   **two abortive missions:** Bass, *Gamecock,* 129–130; McCrady, 106–107.

124   **too strong for him to come:** FM to Sumter, February 26, 1781 (Gimelson, *Autographs*).

124   **He moved . . . without the same sense of urgency:** Rankin, 163–165; Bass, *Gamecock,* 132.

124   **struck near Fort Watson:** Bass, *Gamecock,* 131–132; Parker, 172–173; McCrady, 108–109; Rawdon to Cornwallis, March 7, 1781 (CP4:48). The sources differ as to the precise date and nature of this attack. For a defense of Sumter's tactics, see Powers, "In Defense of Sumter," 32.

124   **"I shall wait . . . interview with you":** Sumter to FM, February 28, 1781 (Gibbes, 49).

124   **less than a day's march . . . Sumter took flight . . . Marion had made his way:** McCrady, 110; Bass, *Gamecock,* 132–134; O'Kelley, *Unwaried Patience,* 516–518.

125   **"so far out of the way . . . come with a few":** Sumter to FM, March 4, 1781 (Gibbes, 27–28).

125   **when Marion did not come . . . Major Thomas Fraser . . . to the Waxhaws:** Bass, *Gamecock,* 134–135; Rawdon to Cornwallis, March 7, 1781 (CP4:48–49).

125   **His men also believed . . . long talk:** Bass, *Gamecock,* 135; Gray, "Observations," 152.

125   **"no assistance from Genl. Marion":** Sumter to NG, March 9, 1781 (NGP7:417).

125   **blame Marion directly:** Sumter to FM, March 28, 1781 (Gibbes, 44–47).

126   **"press him to the utmost":** Rawdon to Cornwallis, March 7, 1781 (CP4:49).

126   **John Watson Tadwell-Watson:** Walter T. Dornfest, "John Watson Tadwell Watson and the Provincial Light Infantry, 1780–1781," *SCAR* 4, no. 2.1 (April–June 2007): 47–48; Marg Baskin, "John Watson Tadwell Watson (1748–1826)," ibid., 61–62; Robert D. Bass, "John

Tadwell-Watson, Builder of Fort Watson," *Independent Republic Quarterly* 12, no. 2 (Spring 1978): 10–11; Saberton, CP2:199–200n39.

126   **"I know I do not . . . Colonel Watson":** Cornwallis to Rawdon, December 13, 1780 (CP3:209).

126   **"plague":** Cornwallis to Tarleton, December 18, 1780 (CP3:352).

126   **He did not relish . . . shrugged his shoulders:** Dornfest, "John Watson," 48.

127   **Leslie dropped off . . . ancient Indian mound:** Ibid., 49.

127   **"a movement is intended . . . the movement":** Balfour to [Saunders], March 5, 1781, Saunders Papers, UNB.

127   **The plan . . . lethal pincer movement:** James, 55; Bass, *Swamp Fox*, 143. One Marion scholar has recently questioned the traditional view that Rawdon simultaneously ordered the two-pronged attack and has suggested that Doyle's movement, which began about two weeks later than Watson's, was perhaps an opportunistic afterthought based on fresh intelligence of the camp's location. Smith, "Archaeological Perspectives," 230n48. Although that is possible, the strong British desire to keep the plan secret from the outset seems more consistent with a creative, two-pronged pincer attack than with a movement by Watson alone. The British would not have expected a singular movement by Watson to remain hidden from Marion's scouts for long, and indeed, Marion discovered it fairly quickly.

   Another researcher offers a slight twist on the traditional view, suggesting that although Watson and Doyle did not coordinate their movements (due to Doyle's much later departure), Watson was carrying out a delaying action to keep Marion occupied while Doyle marched to Marion's base at Snow's Island. Parker, 174, 442, 504n516.

127   **On March 7 . . . Blakely's Plantation:** *Diary of Henry Nase*, March 6–7, 1781; Watson to FM, March 7, 1781 (Gibbes, 29). Most sources state that Watson left the fort on March 5 and that the ensuing engagement at Wyboo Swamp was on March 6. Nase's diary, however, is the most contemporaneous record of these events, and he places them at March 7 and 8, respectively.

127   **a formidable force:** Dornfest, "John Watson," 49; James, 55; Aiken, 126; Sherman, *Calendar*, 417; John Watson, "Narrative," transcribed by Donald J. Gara, SCAR 4, no. 2.1 (April–June 2007): 57–58; Clark, *Loyalists in the Southern Campaign*, 1:105; "Notes and Queries," *Pennsylvania Magazine of History and Biography* 36, no. 2 (April 1912): 256. Both Bass and Rankin identified Watson's own unit as the famed Buffs, the 3rd Regiment of Foot, but that crack outfit did not arrive in Charleston until June 1781. Bass, *Swamp Fox*, 117, 143; Rankin, 165; Sherman, *Calendar*, 93; Dornfest, "John Watson," 50. In a later article Bass corrected his earlier writings to point out that the forces Watson

commanded against Marion were brigades of Provincial Light Infantry. Bass, "John Tadwell-Watson," 11–12.

128 **camped along the Santee . . . Zach Cantey:** FM to Balfour, March 7, 1781 (Gibbes, 29); FM to Watson, March 7, 1781 (ibid., 30); Bass, *Swamp Fox*, 143, 200; Ames, *Cantey Family*, 15–16, 44; James, 5; Weems, 176.

128 **three or four hundred horsemen:** James, 56; Simms, 140; Watson, "Narrative," 58. One of Marion's soldiers put his force at two hundred. *Memoirs of Tarleton Brown*, 35–36. On March 7 Rawdon told Cornwallis that Marion's numbers "certainly do not amount to three hundred." Rawdon to Cornwallis, March 7, 1781 (CP4:49).

128 **March 8 . . . 11 a.m. . . . staring at each other:** *Diary of Henry Nase*, March 8, 1781; Bass, *Swamp Fox*, 144; *Memoirs of Tarleton Brown*, 34; Parker, 174, 493n235.

129 **sending Colonel Richbourg . . . staunch Tory:** Rankin, 165; *Memoirs of Tarleton Brown*, 34; Simms, 140; Lambert, *South Carolina Loyalists*, 156; O'Kelley, *Unwaried Patience*, 518; Rawdon to Cornwallis, December 15, 1780 (CP3:214); "Richbourg," *Blankenstein Genealogy, Heraldry, & DNA* (last entry under "Generation No. 3"), January 26, 2015, www .blankensteingenealogy.net/Richbourg.htm; Ames, *Cantey Family*, 21.

129 **"came dashing up . . . ordered a charge":** *Memoirs of Tarleton Brown*, 35.

129 **Horry's cavalry went hurtling . . . Watson's passage:** Ibid., 35–36; James, 56. James identifies the officer killed by Conyers as a Major Harrison, but both Major John and Captain Samuel Harrison were still in the field in late 1781. Clark, *Loyalists in the Southern Campaign*, 1:109. John Harrison went to Florida after the war, and Samuel Harrison lived in Jamaica until 1816, both on half-pay from the British army. Saberton, CP1:161n5; Bass, "John Tadwell-Watson," 13; Bass, "South Carolina Rangers," 70–71.

131 **"Thus were . . . the outset":** James, 56.

131 **"We had a skirmish . . . Cantey's Plantation":** *Diary of Henry Nase*, March 8, 1781.

131 **Marion had moved from Cantey's:** Marion's orderly book lists his location on March 8 as Cordes's Plantation, which is on the south side of the Santee. O'Kelley, *Unwaried Patience*, 521.

131 **the British seized . . . prison in Georgetown:** Jenkins, *Experience*, 20.

131 **Marion wrote to propose:** FM to Saunders, February 22, 1781 (Gibbes, 24).

131 **"on account of his age . . . like a gentleman":** Ibid.

131 **On February 21 . . . British soldiers surrendered:** Balfour to Clinton, February 24, 1781 (CP6:234); James, 52–53. James gives an erroneous date of January 18.

132   **Saunders agreed to Marion's proposed:** Saunders to FM, February 23, 1781 (Gibbes, 25).

132   **recent capture of DePeyster:** Sabine, *Biographical Sketches of Loyalists,* 1:372–376.

132   **would not agree to a "partial":** Saunders to FM, February 25, 1781 (Gibbes, 26).

132   **shipped DePeyster north:** FM to Saunders, February 26, 1781 (Gibbes, 26–27).

132   **had four British prisoners fetched . . . broader exchange:** Ibid.

132   **letting John Postell accompany:** FM to Balfour, March 7, 1781 (Gibbes, 29–30).

132   **seized Postell . . . violated his parole:** FM to Balfour, March 7, 1781 (Gibbes, 30); Saunders to Lt. Col. Irvin, March 6, 1781 (ibid., 29); FM to Saunders, March 7, 1781 (ibid., 31). Some sources state that Postell was armed when he arrived, but none of the British officers claimed this or cited it as a basis for taking him prisoner. "Irvin" is probably Hugh Ervin, in charge of prisoners at Snow's Island.

132   **Postell argued . . . justified in breaking:** James, 63, 85n10; Gibbes, 36 (ed. note).

132   **Marion protested . . . Balfour . . . backed up his subordinate:** FM to Saunders, March 7, 1781 (Gibbes, 31); FM to Balfour, March 7, 1781 (ibid., 29–30); Balfour to Saunders, March 12, 1781 (ibid., 35); Balfour to FM, March 12, 1781 (ibid., 36–37); Saberton, CP1:36.

132   **Marion also wrote to Watson . . . armed party:** FM to Watson, March 7, 1781 (Gibbes, 30–31).

133   **Watson's lengthy letter:** Watson to FM, March 9, 1781 (Gibbes, 33–35).

133   **"A few days after . . . how they were treated":** Ibid., 34.

133   **"It seems . . . barbarous nations":** James, 56.

133   **"Men like his Majesty's troops . . . natural horrors":** Watson to FM, March 9, 1781 (Gibbes, 34–35).

134   **ordered his nightly patrols:** James, 56.

134   **March 9 or 10 at Mount Hope Swamp Bridge:** Parker, 443, 469, 505n522; Sherman, *Calendar,* 427.

134   **tore it down . . . building it back up:** James, 56.

Chapter 15: Fox and Hound

135   **which way Watson . . . detached Major John James:** James, 56–57. Henry Nase records that on March 12 Watson "marched to one James, a rebel major on parole." *Diary of Henry Nase,* March 12, 1781.

136   **"The pass . . . fate of Williamsburg":** James, 57.

136   **The men Marion chose . . . McCottry's marksmen:** Ibid.; Weems, 176–177; *A Southern Sportsman: The Hunting Memoirs of Henry*

Edwards Davis, ed. Ben McC. Moïse (2010; e-book ed., Columbia: University of South Carolina Press, 2014), chap. 1. Although Weems and James both place Marion at Lower Bridge, it is not clear that he was there in time for the engagement. Henry Nase's diary notes an encounter with Major James on March 12 but does not mention Marion being there. By contrast, Nase specifically identified "Marion and his gang of robbers" as being at Wyboo Swamp on March 8. Marion's orderly book for March 11 lists his headquarters at Glover's Plantation on the Pee Dee, near Plantersville, about fifty miles east of Lower Bridge. O'Kelley, *Unwaried Patience*, 521, 696n1329; Linder and Thacker, *Rice Plantations*, 321; Smith, "Archaeological Perspectives," 230–231n52. It is unlikely that Marion could have reached Lower Bridge from Glover's ahead of Watson, who had to travel only about twelve miles to get there. However, sometimes aides recorded the entries in Marion's orderly book while he was in the field, so he may not have been physically present at the Glover's headquarters on March 11 while he was out dueling with Watson. It is also possible Marion reached Lower Bridge partway through the battle and the British soldiers, including Nase, did not notice him.

136   **long hunting rifles . . . smoothbore muskets:** Buchanan, 158–159, 213–214; Pancake, *This Destructive War*, 39, 51; Parker, 462–463; Stephen V. Grancsay, foreword to *Weapons of the American Revolution . . . and Accoutrements*, by Warren Moore (New York: Funk & Wagnalls, 1967), vi; Lumpkin, 92–93, 136–140.

137   **enemy's leaders are considered fair targets:** Stacey R. Whitacre, "An Analysis of Lead Shot from Fort Motte, 2004–2012: Assessing Combat Behavior in Terms of Agency" (master's thesis, University of South Carolina, 2013), 29.

137   **Watson sent his men:** James, 57.

137   **plantation of John Witherspoon, whose daughter was engaged:** James, 57–58, 85n5; Ree Herring Hendrick, *Lineage and Tradition of the Herring, Conyers . . . and Hilliard Families* (n.p., 1916), 62–63; Joseph G. Wardlaw, *Genealogy of the Witherspoon Family* (Yorkville, SC: printed at the Enquirer Office, 1910), 40, 62. Although James placed John Witherspoon's plantation "a mile above the bridge," it was a mile or so below the bridge, on the south (west) side of the Black River. Davis, *Hunting Memoirs*, chap. 1; James A. Wallace, *History of Williamsburg Church, a Discourse Delivered on Occasion of the 120th Anniversary of the Williamsburg Church, July 4th, 1856, Kingstree, SC* (Salisbury, NC, 1856), 64; Parker, 442. The location is near the well-known Cooper's Country Store in present-day Salters.

137   **"he never saw such shooting in his life":** James, 57.

137   **The next day . . . three hundred yards:** James, 57–58; Daniel Johnson, *Blood on the Marsh*, 477–478.

137 **Watson withdrew . . . to Blakely's:** James, 57; Davis, *Hunting Mem-oirs*, chap. 1. It is unclear whether this is the same Blakely's at which Watson camped a week earlier.

138 **"neutral person . . . carry on this war":** Watson to FM, March 15, 1781 (Gibbes, 38).

138 **Marion promptly agreed:** FM to Watson, March 16, 1781 (Gibbes, 41).

138 **"In answer to your letter . . . British troops":** FM to Watson, [March 15], 1781 (Gibbes, 38).

138 **Seeking the last word . . . Whig atrocities:** Watson to FM, March 15, 1781 (Gibbes, 39).

138 **"thought right . . . all countries":** Watson to FM, March 16, 1781 (Gibbes, 41).

138 **he was willing to hang:** O'Kelley, *Unwaried Patience*, 564–565; Loftis R. Munnerlyn Pension, S18136; Parker, 56; FM to NG, March 17, 1781 (*NGP*10:513).

138 **had his men detain . . . Cornet Thomas Merritt:** Jenkins, *Experience*, 18–19; John Graves Simcoe, *Simcoe's Military Journal: A History of the Operations of a Partisan Corps, Called the Queen's Rangers* (1787; repr., New York, 1844), 244–245.

139 **Balfour and Saunders protested:** Balfour to FM, March 21, 1781 (Gibbes, 42); Saunders to FM, March 24, 1781 (ibid., 42–43).

139 **by March 18 . . . "outflanked" . . . chose not to pursue Watson:** James, 58–59; Rankin, 173–174; Parker, 236, 469; Watson to Saunders, March 20, 1781, Bancroft Collection, NYPL; John Scott Pension, S32508 (quotation). Watson would later describe the engagement somewhat differently, saying his infantry managed to repair the bridge to facilitate a crossing. Watson, "Narrative," 58.

140 **On March 21 . . . Trapier's Plantation:** Smith, "Archaeological Perspectives," 186; O'Kelley, *Unwaried Patience*, 698n1373.

140 **"They will not . . . behind every tree":** Weems, 180. The source of this anecdote may have been Benjamin Trapier, a French Huguenot who provided Marion's men with corn, rations, and fresh horses during the Revolution. Lee G. Brockington, *Plantation Between the Waters: A Brief History of Hobcaw Barony* (Charleston, SC: History Press, 2006), 25; Linder and Thacker, *Rice Plantations*, 17. Possibly it was Paul Trapier, who took British protection in July 1780. Rogers, *History of Georgetown County*, 159.

140 **he headed back along the Pee Dee:** James, 59; Parker, 471.

140 **around March 26 . . . Doyle had found and destroyed:** Parker, 230, 471; Balfour to Saunders, April 2, 1781, Saunders Papers, UNB. For many years historians believed Marion called off his pursuit of Watson at Sampit Bridge on March 28 after learning of the destruction of the Snow's Island camp. The more recent consensus is that the Sampit

Bridge encounter was on or about March 20, before Doyle even left Camden for Snow's Island on March 22. This conclusion is based on the March 20 letter Watson wrote to Rawdon from Chovin's plantation, about ten miles from Sampit Bridge, saying he would be in Georgetown that afternoon. Doyle's raid on the Snow's Island camp was around March 25 or 26, a few days after Marion stopped chasing Watson. Parker, 236, 442, 469, 504n516; Smith, "Archaeological Perspectives," 230–231n52; *Diary of Henry Nase*, March 22, 1781.

140   **New York Volunteers . . . leaving fifteen:** Rankin, 175–176; Sherman, *Calendar*, 78, 450. One loyalist newspaper identified Doyle's force as the Volunteers of Ireland, another provincial unit, probably because he had commanded it earlier or because his brother, Major John Doyle, succeeded to that command around the same time. *Royal Gazette* (Charleston), March 31–April 4, 1781; Sherman, *Calendar*, 81; Saberton, CP1:185n5; 2:119n126; *Diary of Henry Nase*, March 15, 22, 1781.

141   **Merritt . . . made his escape:** Rankin, 176. According to Saunders Merritt escaped on his own just before Doyle's raid. *Simcoe's Military Journal*, 240, 245–246.

141   **Bull Pen . . . "made of logs":** *Simcoe's Military Journal*, 245.

141   **"Marion's repository . . . on Snow's Island":** *Royal Gazette* (Charleston), March 31–April 4, 1781.

141   **Doyle . . . did not linger . . . Marion did not pursue:** Rankin, 175–177; James, 59; Parker, 227–228, 309; *Diary of Henry Nase*, April 1, 1781. As Smith points out, that Doyle withdrew to Witherspoon's Ferry is support for the view that the base camp was located on the island itself rather than at Dunham's Bluff. Smith, "Archaeological Perspectives," 263.

141   **Burch's Mill . . . issued an order:** O'Kelley, *Unwaried Patience*, 525.

142   **"skulking position":** Horry, "Journal," *SCHGM* 38, no. 3 (July 1937): 82.

142   **Watson, refreshed . . . was confident:** Watson, "Narrative," 58; Smith, "Archaeological Perspectives," 190–191. James puts Marion's force at five hundred and Watson's at nine hundred, both of which seem inflated. James, 59–60.

142   **Elizabeth Jenkins . . . refused to believe:** Jenkins, *Experience*, 25–27.

142   **only five miles away:** James, 60.

142   **two rounds per man . . . council of war:** James, 60.

142   **"made an animated appeal . . . remain with him longer":** Samuel McGaughy Pension, W9981.

143   **They unanimously resolved . . . not a viable option:** James, 60.

143   **Messengers came in . . . Lee was on his way:** James, 60; Rankin, 183–184; NG to Lee, April 4, 1781 (*NGP*8:46); NG to FM, April 4, 1781 (*NGP*8:47).

CHAPTER 16: "A WAR OF POSTS"

144 **Ganey's Tories . . . back south to Georgetown:** James, 60–61; Watson, "Narrative," 58; Bass, *Swamp Fox*, 168.

144 **By April 14 Lee had arrived:** FM to NG, April 23, 1781 (*NGP*8:139).

144 **"long, obstinate, and bloody":** NG to Joseph Reed, March 18, 1781 (*NGP*7:450).

144 **heavy losses . . . could not go on:** Buchanan, 378–383; Carbone, *Nathanael Greene*, 182–184.

144 **"They had the splendor, we the advantage":** NG to von Steuben, April 2, 1781 (*NGP*8:25).

144 **Cornwallis withdrew . . . elected not to follow:** Buchanan, 383.

144 **"universal spirit of revolt":** Cornwallis to William Phillips, April 24, 1781 (*CP*4:116).

145 **under international law:** Swager, *The Valiant Died*, 51; Carbone, *Nathanael Greene*, 200.

145 **eight thousand soldiers . . . would leave the outposts exposed:** Pancake, *This Destructive War*, 190, 203; Aiken, 162.

145 **Greene had repeatedly asked . . . plan was dropped:** NG to Lee, January 15, 1781 (*NGP*7:123); NG to FM, January 19, 25, 1781 (ibid., 145, 194–195); FM to NG, January 20, 27, 31, 1781 (ibid., 164, 207, 229).

146 **three-hundred-strong Legion:** Lee, *Memoirs*, 2:53.

146 **Lee . . . argued . . . eighty men:** James, 61.

146 **On April 15 they arrived:** FM to NG, April 23, 1781 (Gibbes, 57).

146 **"if they wanted . . . take it":** James McKay, Robert Robinson, and Thomas B. Campbell, "Journal of the Blockade at Scott's Lake, [SC] Fort Watson, 15–23 April 1781," *SCAR* 4, no. 2.1 (April–June 2007): 52 (entry under April 15).

147 **The fort was small . . . 114 defenders:** Leland G. Ferguson, "Exploratory Archeology at the Scott's Lake Site (38CR1) Santee Indian Mound—Ft. Watson Summer 1972," *Research Manuscript Series*, Book 30 (Columbia: University of South Carolina, South Carolina Institute of Archeology and Anthropology, 1973), 9, 15, 38, scholarcommons .sc.edu/archanth_books; James, 61; Watson, "Narrative," 57; FM to NG, April 23, 1781 (Gibbes, 57); Balfour to Clinton, May 6, 1781 (*CP*6:244 and n79).

147 **Lee and Marion initially thought . . . well struck water:** FM to NG, April 23, 1781 (Gibbes, 57); Lee, *Memoirs*, 2:51; McKay, "Journal of the Blockade," April 17, 18, 19, 20, 22, 1781; Ferguson, "Exploratory Archeology," 43–44.

147 **"finish the business" in "five minutes":** Lee to NG, April 18, 1781 (*NGP*8:113).

147 **starting to run out of ammunition . . . threatening capital punishment:** FM to NG, April 21, 1781 (*NGP*8:129); FM to NG, April 23,

1781 (Gibbes, 57); Lee, *Memoirs*, 2:51–52; McKay, "Journal of the Blockade," April 18, 19, 1781; Jenkins, *Experience*, 24; Rankin, 187–188; O'Kelley, *Unwaried Patience*, 527.

148 **Captain Snipes . . . Marion's order meant nothing:** Abel Kolb to Snipes, April 1781 (Gibbes, 52); Snipes to Kolb, April 16, 1781 (ibid., 52–53); Kolb to FM, April 18, 1781 (ibid., 55–56); John L. Frierson, "Col. Abel Kolb–SC Patriot Militia," *SCAR* 3, no. 5 (May 2006): 28.

148 **Marion complained . . . Sumter responded dismissively:** Sumter to FM, April 30, 1781 (Gibbes, 64–65).

148 **"particular direction":** Ibid., 65.

148 **"Sumter's Law":** Bass, *Gamecock*, 144–145; Haw, *John and Edward Rutledge*, 158; Powers, "In Defense of Sumter," 32–33.

148 **"one grown negro . . . one small negro":** Richard Hampton to John Hampton, April 2, 1781 (Gibbes, 48).

148 **he was in the minority:** Carbone, *Nathanael Greene*, 194–195; Bass, *Gamecock*, 146, 178. Greene urged Marion to support Sumter's Law. NG to FM, May 17, 1781 (*NGP*8:276–277).

148 **Marion also received . . . "generous and humane":** Balfour to Moultrie, March 1781 (Moultrie, *Memoirs*, 2:171–172); Moultrie to Balfour, March 31, 1781 (ibid., 174).

148 **"I know . . . generous and the brave":** Moultrie to FM, April 16, 1781 (Gibbes, 52). Of the three alleged murders details can be found for only one. The unarmed John Inglis was shot, apparently by mistake, by Simon Fraser, a soldier under William Harden, an early member of Marion's brigade who was operating independently in the Lowcountry at the time. To retaliate some loyalists took Fraser prisoner in September 1781 while he was bearing a flag of truce for a prisoner exchange. Harden to NG, November 7, 1781 (*NGP*9:543–544 and nn1, 4); Gould to NG, November 8, 1781, 546 (*NGP*9:546); Alexander Garden, *Anecdotes of the Revolutionary War in America, with Sketches of Character Illustrative of the Talents and Virtues of the Heroes and Patriots, Who Acted the Most Conspicuous Parts Therein* (Charleston, SC, 1828), 145–147.

149 **"neglected . . . long letter":** Lee to NG, April 20, 1781 (*NGP*8:125).

149 **Lee, himself unhappy . . . "despaired of success":** Ibid.; Lee, *Memoirs*, 2:51 (quotation).

149 **Colonel Hezekiah Maham . . . "wooden machine" . . . McKay raised the white flag:** FM to NG, April 23, 1781 (Gibbes, 57); Lee, *Memoirs*, 2:51–52; McKay, "Journal of the Blockade," April 21, 23, 1781 (quotation at April 21); Ferguson, "Exploratory Archeology," 17, 29; James, 61; John Thomas Scharf, *History of Maryland, from the Earliest Period to the Present Day* (Baltimore, 1879), 2:417.

150 **"We were reduced . . . any longer":** McKay, "Journal of the Blockade," April 23, 1781.

150   **generous terms:** "Terms of Capitulation Proposed by Lieutenant McKay, Commandant of Fort Watson," *SCAR* 4, no. 2.1 (April–June 2007): 52.

150   **"advice . . . reduction of the fort":** FM to NG, April 23, 1781 (Gibbes, 57).

150   **"in some degree":** Lee to NG, April 23, 1781 (*NGP*8:139).

150   **After the patriots razed . . . Bloom Hill:** Ibid., 58; Lumpkin, 179; McCrady, 175–176; Rawdon to Cornwallis, April 26, 1781 (CP4:180).

151   **"When I consider . . . world in general":** NG to FM, April 24, 1781 (*NGP*8:144).

151   **"spirit, perseverance and good conduct":** NG to FM, April 26, 1781 (*NGP*8:150–151).

151   **Rawdon at Hobkirk's . . . had to strike:** Bass, *Gamecock*, 157; Carbone, *Nathanael Greene*, 186; Rawdon to Cornwallis, April 25, 1781 (CP4:179).

151   **Sumter refused . . . disgusted Greene:** Bass, *Gamecock*, 158–160; Pancake, *This Destructive War*, 199.

151   **tactical victory . . . confused by an officer's order:** Carbone, *Nathanael Greene*, 186–188; Gordon, *Battlefield History*, 149–151; Lumpkin, 182–183; Parker, 278–279.

151   **"By mistake . . . more than we did":** NG to FM, April 27, 1781 (*NGP*8:160).

151   **"We fight . . . fight again":** NG to Lafayette, May 1, 1781 (*NGP*8:183).

152   **Greene was crestfallen . . . both sides had suffered:** Carbone, *Nathanael Greene*, 188; Golway, *Washington's General*, 270; McCrady, 205, 221–224; Gordon, *Battlefield History*, 151.

152   **"would have crawled . . . hand and knees":** Watson, "Narrative," 58.

152   **on May 7 . . . get around Marion and Lee:** Rawdon to Cornwallis, May 24, 1781 (CSR17:1031); FM to NG, May 6, 1781 (*NGP*8:215); Watson, "Narrative," 58–59; Dornfest, "John Watson," 49–50; Lee, *Memoirs*, 2:67–71.

152   **The fall of Fort Watson . . . Rawdon evacuated Camden:** McCrady, 227–228; Gray, "Observations," 157–158; Lee, *Memoirs*, 2:72–73; Rawdon to Cornwallis, May 24, 1781 (CSR17:1032–1033); Parker, 278.

152   **He marched south . . . to the relief:** Lee, *Memoirs*, 2:73.

CHAPTER 17: BALL OF FIRE

153   **on May 6 . . . "obstinate, and strong":** FM to NG, May 6, 1781 (*NGP*8:214); FM to NG, May 12, 1781 (ibid., 246) (quotation).

153   **Rebecca Motte . . . intelligence to Marion:** Steven D. Smith et al., *"Obstinate and Strong": The History and Archaeology of the Siege of Fort Motte* (Columbia: University of South Carolina, South Carolina Institute of Archaeology and Anthropology, 2007), 12–13, scholar

commons.sc.edu/cgi/viewcontent.cgi?article=1052&context=anth
_facpub.

153   **three-story mansion . . . apertures for guns:** Ibid., 21–22, 50; Lee,
       Memoirs, 2:73–74.

153   **force of 184 . . . Lieutenant Donald McPherson:** Smith et al., *"Ob-
       stinate and Strong,"* 22 and nn51, 53; Rawdon to Cornwallis, May 24,
       1781 (CSR17:1033); Balfour to McPherson, January 21, 1781, in
       SCHGM 17, no. 1 (January 1916): 3–4; Lee, *Memoirs*, 2:74; Rankin,
       201; O'Kelley, *Unwaried Patience*, 529; *Royal Gazette* (Charleston),
       May 26–30, June 2–6, 1781. Although most contemporaneous sources
       refer to the commander as a "Lieutenant" McPherson (with no first
       name), the Tory militia commander at Fort Motte, Levi Smith, iden-
       tifies him as Captain Charles McPherson of the DeLancey Corps.
       Royal Gazette (Charleston), April 13–17, 1781.

153   **84th Regiment of Foot:** Gavin K. Watt, *I Am Heartily Ashamed*,
       vol. 2, *The Revolutionary War's Final Campaign as Waged from Canada
       in 1782* (Toronto: Dundurn Press, 2010), 429n12.

154   **150 partisans . . . Lee figured:** FM to NG, May 6, 1781 (NGP8:214);
       Smith et al., *"Obstinate and Strong,"* 23; Piecuch and Beakes, *Lee*, 163;
       Lee, *Memoirs*, 2:74; James, 66.

154   **Abel Kolb . . . Tories then took a torch:** Gregg, *Old Cheraws*, 357–
       361; Frierson, "Col. Abel Kolb," 28–29; Marika Ann Manuel-Kolb,
       "Descendants of Dielman Kolb" (no. 119), *Genealogy.com*, August 25,
       2005, www.genealogy.com/ftm/k/o/l/Marika-A-Kolb/GENE3-0011
       .html.

154   **Marion felt compelled . . . Greene . . . was sorry:** NG to FM, May 6,
       1781 (NGP8:211); Gregg, *Old Cheraws*, 360, 367.

154   **Lee had let slip:** Lee to NG, May 2, 1781 (NGP8:192).

155   **"getting good horses":** Sumter to NG, May 2, 1781
       (NGP8:193–194).

155   **"I am told":** NG to FM, May 4, 1781 (NGP8:198–199).

155   **"sixty or eighty good dragoon horses":** NG to FM, May 6, 1781
       (NGP8:211).

155   **"I acknowledge . . . for some time":** FM to NG, May 6, 1781
       (NGP8:214–215).

156   **Greene immediately backed off . . . "in the midst . . . to the end":**
       NG to FM, May 9, 1781 (NGP8:230–231).

156   **Marion pretended . . . would send more:** FM to NG, May 11, 1781
       (NGP8:242).

156   **"rapidity" . . . to the last:** Lee, *Memoirs*, 2:75.

157   **it was Marion who approached:** Weems, 220.

157   **Lee . . . alone who spoke to her:** Lee, *Memoirs*, 2:77.

157   **Mrs. Motte was living:** Ibid., 74; James, 66; Bass, *Swamp Fox*, 189;
       Smith et al., *"Obstinate and Strong,"* 14, 16.

157   **"best wines of Europe":** Lee, *Memoirs*, 2:77.

157   **she instantly agreed . . . thought hers better suited:** Ibid.

157   **Nathan Savage . . . slung it:** James, 67; Parker, 229.

157   **bow . . . musket . . . by hand:** Lee, *Memoirs*, 2:78–79; James, 67; Smith et al., *"Obstinate and Strong,"* 25–26. Rawdon told Cornwallis that the house was "set in flames by fire arrows." Rawdon to Cornwallis, May 24, 1781 (CSR17:1033).

157   **men to the roof . . . May 12 . . . leveled:** James, 67; Smith et al., *"Obstinate and Strong,"* 26, 34, 52; Conrad, NGP8:253n8; Greene to Samuel Huntington, May 14, 1781 (Gibbes, 71).

158   **"sumptuous dinner":** Lee, *Memoirs*, 2:80.

158   **wine was brought out, "we were all . . . like brothers":** Weems, 221–223.

158   **formal surrender ceremony:** Rankin, 206.

158   **returned some private British correspondence:** Rawdon to Lee, May 14, 1781 (Gibbes, 70).

158   **Lee thought he deserved:** Lee, *Memoirs*, 2:79–80.

158   **Legion had surrounded and massacred:** Royster, *Light-Horse Harry Lee*, 37–38; Jim Piecuch, "'Light Horse Harry' Lee and Pyle's Massacre," *Journal of the American Revolution*, June 19, 2013, allthingsliberty.com/tag/pyles-massacre; Buchanan, 363–364.

158   **Three were executed . . . Hugh Miscally:** Smith et al., *"Obstinate and Strong,"* 28–29; Smith, "Archaeological Perspectives," 186; Weems, 223; *Royal Gazette* (Charleston), April 13–17, 1782.

158   **"I will let you know . . . not Colonel Lee":** *Royal Gazette* (Charleston), April 13–17, 1782.

159   **"the humanity of Marion could not be overcome":** Lee, *Memoirs*, 2:79.

159   **the Americans lost . . . Allen McDonald:** Rankin, 206; James, 67; Daniel Johnson, *Blood on the Marsh*, 485, 559. McDonald had also carried the regimental colors at the assault on Savannah in 1779.

159   **archaeological evidence . . . two particularly skilled sharpshooters:** Whitacre, "An Analysis of Lead Shot," 132–133, 136.

159   **"The stroke was heavy upon me":** Rawdon to Cornwallis, May 24, 1781 (CSR17:1033).

159   **Rawdon destroyed . . . headed south:** Ibid., 1033–1034; Smith et al., *"Obstinate and Strong,"* 29–30; Bass, *Swamp Fox*, 197–198; FM to NG, May 16, 1781 (NGP8:274).

159   **After the surrender . . . Greene went there:** Rankin, 208.

159   **"does honor . . . Colonel Lee":** George Washington to NG, June 1, 1781 (NGP8:336).

159   **Fort Granby surrendered . . . Sumter used to pay the men:** Parker, 311–312; Bass, *Gamecock*, 172–178.

160   **Greene also reconfirmed:** Bass, *Gamecock*, 177–178; NG to Sumter, May 17, 1781 (*NGP8:278*).

160   **"and to receive General Sumter's orders":** J. Burnet to FM, May 18, 1781 (Gibbes, 74).

CHAPTER 18: WINNING BY LOSING

161   **"I beg leave . . . slip through":** FM to NG, May 19, 1781 (*NGP8:285*).

161   **Marion wrote twice more:** FM to NG, May 20, 22, 1781 (*NGP8:287, 294*).

161   **Peyre's Plantation:** Bass, *Swamp Fox*, 3, 198; James, 69, 76; Savage, *River of the Carolinas*, 230–232; Simms, 110; Boddie, *Traditions*, 90, 224.

161   **"inferior object":** NG to FM, May 26, 1781 (Gibbes, 81).

162   **On May 27 . . . headed to Georgetown . . . digging trenches:** FM to NG, May 29, 1781 (*NGP8:329*); Bass, *Swamp Fox*, 199; O'Kelley, *Unwaried Patience*, 530.

162   **plantation slaves . . . "yellow man" . . . hanged:** Loftis R. Munnerlyn Pension, S18136.

162   **peeled logs . . . painted black:** Ibid.

162   **numbers greatly reduced . . . under orders . . . if seriously pressed:** Sherman, *Calendar*, 90–91; Balfour to Robert Gray, May 20, 1781, Letterbook of Lt. Col. Nisbet Balfour, January 1–December 1, 1781, Society of the Cincinnati, Digitized Collections, 2012, societyofthe cincinnati.org/collections/library/digitized_collections.

162   **change of wardrobe:** James, 67.

162   **three-month ceasefire . . . extended . . . pledged to restore:** Articles of Agreement and Treaty, June 17, 1781 (Gibbes, 98–99); Ganey to FM, August 25, 1781 (ibid., 130).

162   **death of . . . Isaac:** Yeadon 1, no. 4 (June 1845): 413.

163   **"great pleasure . . . act in conjunction":** NG to FM, June 10, 1781 (*NGP8:373*).

163   **Greene was worried . . . stall the enemy's progress:** NG to FM, June 10, 1781, second letter (*NGP8:374*).

163   **Sumter was less effusive . . . told Greene:** Sumter to FM, June 9, 1781 (Gibbes, 93); Sumter to NG, June 7, 1781 (*NGP8:360*).

163   **"unfavorable" information . . . mission accomplished:** Sumter to NG, June 8, 1781 (*NGP8:361*); O'Kelley, *Unwaried Patience*, 531.

163   **"weak and badly armed":** Sumter to NG, June 14, 1781 (*NGP8:390*).

163   **positive orders to Marion:** Sumter to NG, June 15, 1781 (*NGP8:393*).

163   **550 provincials . . . John Harris Cruger . . . a trio of three-pounders:** Lumpkin, 192–200, 300–301; Carbone, *Nathanael Greene*, 193; Gordon, *Battlefield History*, 155–156.

164   **Greene tried several shortcuts:** Gordon, *Battlefield History*, 157; Carbone, *Nathanael Greene*, 194; R. L. Barbour, *South Carolina's Revolutionary War Battlefields: A Tour Guide* (Gretna, LA: Pelican, 2002), 97.

164   **They failed . . . lifted the siege:** Pancake, *This Destructive War*, 212–213; Carbone, *Nathanael Greene*, 196–197; Gordon, *Battlefield History*, 156–157; William Johnson, *Life of Greene*, 2:148–154; Lee, *Memoirs*, 2:128–129.

164   **Sumter's case . . . militia deserted:** Pancake, *This Destructive War*, 212–213; William Johnson, *Life of Greene*, 2:153–154; Bass, *Gamecock*, 183–187.

165   **Sumter kept changing his orders:** Sumter to FM, June 13, 14, 15, 16, 1781 (Gibbes, 95–97).

165   **On June 16 . . . prevent them from foraging:** FM to NG, June 16, 1781 (NGP8:394).

165   **Greene was furious . . . wrote Marion to vent:** NG to FM, June 25, 1781 (NGP8:457–458).

165   **blaming everyone . . . Thomas Jefferson:** McCrady, 303.

166   **might also have looked in the mirror:** Pancake, *This Destructive War*, 212; Buchanan, 398; Lee, *Memoirs*, 2:98, 119n.

166   **men were starving . . . heatstroke:** Swager, *The Valiant Died*, 63, 96; Sherman, *Calendar*, 527; Tarleton, *Campaigns*, 507.

166   **"so fatigued they cannot possibly move":** FM to NG, July 1, 1781 (NGP8:505).

166   **Rawdon found it . . . Rawdon Town:** Nelson, *Francis Rawdon-Hastings*, 99–100; Gordon, *Battlefield History*, 157–158; Tonsetic, *1781: The Decisive Year*, 114–115; Swager, *The Valiant Died*, 63; Moultrie, *Memoirs*, 2:279; Conrad, NGP9:590n5.

166   **Marion to a summit meeting:** Bass, *Swamp Fox*, 205; Lee, *Memoirs*, 2:141–142.

167   **Rawdon declined . . . was exchanged:** Swager, *The Valiant Died*, 63; Carbone, *Nathanael Greene*, 198, 202, 207; Sherman, *Calendar*, 598–599n3551; Nelson, *Francis Rawdon-Hastings*, 101–105.

167   **Greene had briefly considered . . . High Hills of Santee:** Carbone, *Nathanael Greene*, 198–199; Kyte, "Marion as an Intelligence Officer," 222; Pancake, *This Destructive War*, 215; Bass, *Swamp Fox*, 205; Lee, *Memoirs*, 2:145.

CHAPTER 19: DOG DAYS

168   **Sumter persuaded Greene . . . Greene's goal:** Bass, *Gamecock*, 195–196; Sherman, *Calendar*, 565; Smith, "Archaeological Perspectives," 199; Tonsetic, *1781: The Decisive Year*, 146; Carbone, *Nathanael Greene*, 201–202; Nelson, *Francis Rawdon-Hastings*, 102; NG to Thomas McKean, July 17, 1781 (NGP9:29); William Pierce to

St. George Tucker, July 20, 1781, Coleman-Tucker Papers, 1664–1945, College of William & Mary, Earl Gregg Swem Library, Special Collections Database, Item 1004.

168 **night of July 12 . . . six hundred to seven hundred men:** Aiken, 225–226; Lumpkin, 206–207, 302–303; William Johnson, *Life of Greene*, 2:167; Lee, *Memoirs*, 2:146–147; O'Kelley, *Unwaried Patience*, 536; Sherman, *Calendar*, 565–566, 571.

169 **Hugh Giles . . . retired . . . John Ervin:** O'Kelley, *Unwaried Patience*, 534, 699n1405.

169 **Greene commissioned . . . impress as many horses:** NG to Maham, June 21, 1781 (*NGP*8:433 and Hezekiah Maham Orderly Book, Manuscripts and Archives Division, New York Public Library); FM to NG, January 15, 1782 (*NGP*10:196); Rankin, 219–220; Scoggins, "South Carolina's Back Country Rangers," 172–173; NG to FM, January 16, 1782 (*NGP*10:202); FM to PH, September 17, 1781, March 20, 1782 (Gibbes, 168, 277–278); PH to FM, June 29, 1782 (Gibbes2, 196).

169 **Horry and Maham . . . start his own farm:** Cross, *Historic Ramblin's*, 274; Joseph Johnson, *Traditions and Reminiscences*, 286–287; O'Kelley, *Unwaried Patience*, 602n25, 624n294; David Neilan, "Marion and the Trials and Tribulations of Peter Horry," address at 11th Francis Marion/Swamp Fox Symposium, Manning, SC, October 19, 2013, DVD. Some sources state Horry was born in 1743 or 1744, not 1747. Either way he was younger than Maham.

169 **dated the same day . . . answerable only to Greene:** Rankin, 220–221; NG to Maham, June 21, 1781 (*NGP*8:433); NG to PH, July 30, 1781 (*NGP*9:107 and n2); Maham to PH, January 20, 1782 (Gibbes, 238); Borick, *A Gallant Defense*, 55–56; PH to NG, July 19, 1781, in Mabel Louise Webber, ed., "Revolutionary Letters," *SCHGM* 38, no. 1 (January 1937): 5–6; Neilan, "Marion and the Trials and Tribulations of Peter Horry." The "dotted line" phrase, common in today's corporate world, is Neilan's.

170 **Horry grudgingly told Greene:** PH to NG, June 28, 1781 (*NGP*8:471).

170 **Captain William Snipes . . . managed to escape:** O'Kelley, *"Nothing but Blood and Slaughter,"* 3:269–272; *Simcoe's Military Journal*, 247; Sherman, *Calendar*, 526–527; Weems, 163–167. According to Weems Snipes hid in the bushes nearby, and his black overseer refused to disclose his master's whereabouts to the British, despite being nearly hanged to death by them.

171n **Snipes killed a man . . . pardoned:** Mary Harrell-Sesniak, *Five Hundred Plus Revolutionary War Obituaries and Death Notices* (Houston, TX: Lulu.com, 2010), 186, 192; *The Papers of Henry Laurens*, vol. 16, *September 1, 1782–December 17, 1792*, ed. David R. Chesnutt and C. James Taylor (Columbia: University of South Carolina Press,

2003), 609n1; Mabel Louise Webber, ed., "Historical Notes," *SCHGM* 12, no. 3 (July 1911): 160–162.

171   **James Coates . . . Thomas Fraser . . . knew the territory:** Sherman, *Calendar*, 77, 82, 93, 96–97, 527, 566; Saberton, CP1:243n11; Gordon, *Battlefield History*, 160.

171   **Sumter's plan . . . Coates pulled up stakes . . . Biggin Church:** Lumpkin, 207; Rankin, 224–225; Lee, *Memoirs*, 2:146–147; McCrady, 325–330; Bass, *Gamecock*, 195–197; Sumter to NG, July 15, 1781 (*NGP*9:17–18).

172   **Maham was dispatched . . . sufficiently undamaged:** Bass, *Gamecock*, 197; Lumpkin, 207; Rankin, 225; Sherman, *Calendar*, 567–568; Parker, 58; Sumter to NG, July 18, 1781 (*NGP*9:52, 53n6).

172   **night of July 16 . . . crossed over Quinby Creek:** Lumpkin, 207–208; James, 69, 86n16; Rankin, 226–227; Bass, *Gamecock*, 198; Aiken, 228, 294n15; Sumter to NG, July 17, 1781 (*NGP*9:50); NG to Thomas McKean, July 26, 1781 (ibid., 84); Frye Gaillard, *Lessons from the Big House*, 27.

172   **At daybreak . . . vacant plantation:** Stephen Jarvis, "An American's Experience in the British Army," *Journal of American History* 1, no. 3 (1907): 463–464. Most sources state the British did not take refuge at Shubrick's until after a skirmish at Quinby Bridge, but these accounts are largely secondhand, and Jarvis, who was present, makes clear that Coates and Fraser were at the plantation before any fighting at Quinby Bridge took place.

172   **Thomas Shubrick:** "Col. Thomas Shubrick," *Find a Grave*, March 25, 2009, www.findagrave.com/cgi-bin/fg.cgi?page=gr&GRid=35118052; Thomas Burbage Pension, S17868.

173   **posted a howitzer . . . Lee's force was left stranded:** Lee, *Memoirs*, 2:149–152; Jarvis, "An American's Experience," 463; FM to NG, July 19, 1781 (*NGP*9:47); D. John Brailsford to "Charles," August 11, 1781, in PCC, Item No. 51, 1:659–661; McCrady, 332–335; William Johnson, *Life of Greene*, 2:169–172.

173   **Lee later came under criticism:** Joseph Johnson, *Traditions and Reminiscences*, 541; William Johnson, *Life of Greene*, 2:171–172. Joseph Johnson went so far as to claim that *none* of Lee's horsemen crossed the river because Lee was too fearful of losing some of his own dragoons and preferred to let the South Carolina militia take the risk. According to Johnson, "It was a common remark among the Carolinians, that Lee would rather a dozen militia men should be killed, than one of his government horses." Joseph Johnson, *Traditions and Reminiscences*, 406.

173   **horses were too afraid . . . Nor could they find:** Lee, *Memoirs*, 2:152–153.

173   it was chaos . . . **Marion withdrew:** Lumpkin, 208–211; Rankin, 227–229; William Johnson, *Life of Greene*, 2:172–175; Jarvis, "An American's Experience," 464; FM to NG, July 19, 1781 (*NGP9*:48); Sumter to NG, July 18, 22, 25, 1781 (*NGP9*:51–52, 63, 81); D. John Brailsford to "Charles," August 11, 1781, in PCC, Item No. 51, 1:661; Aiken, 229–230; Joseph Johnson, *Traditions and Reminiscences*, 541–542; James Harbison Pension, W17039. Although many secondary sources say the battle lasted three hours, the firsthand accounts indicate a duration of forty minutes to an hour.

175   **Coates soon retreated . . . to Charleston:** Tonsetic, *1781: The Decisive Year*, 147; Swager, *The Valiant Died*, 69.

175   **heavy casualties . . . bulk of them Marion's:** James, 69; Aiken, 230, 294n22; FM to NG, July 19, 1781 (*NGP9*:48); Sherman, *Calendar*, 573; O'Kelley, *Unwaried Patience*, 540.

175   **"like a dagger . . . believe it":** Jenkins, *Experience*, 27–28.

175   **Taylor loudly complained:** Joseph Johnson, *Traditions and Reminiscences*, 541–542.

175   **Marion implied . . . Sumter had ordered:** FM to NG, July 19, 1781 (*NGP9*:47–48).

175   **Sumter said nothing . . . it was Marion:** Sumter to NG, July 17–19, 25, 1781 (*NGP9*:50–53, 80–82); Rankin, 230–231.

175   **"the gallantry . . . more deserved success":** NG to FM, July 21, 1781 (*NGP9*:54).

175   **Most revealing . . . All but a hundred:** Rankin, 229–230; Bass, *Gamecock*, 200; Sumter to NG, July 19, 1781 (*NGP9*:52).

176   **"far short . . . clever":** NG to Lafayette, July 24, 1781 (*NGP9*:72).

176   **the Americans captured:** Sherman, *Calendar*, 572–573.

176   **a pay chest . . . Marion's men received none:** NG to Thomas McKean, July 26, 1781 (*NGP9*:85); Sherman, *Calendar*, 573; "General Thomas Sumter's Accounting of Public Money," transcribed by William T. Graves, SCAR 2, no. 4 (April 2005): 12; Lee, *Memoirs*, 2:156–157.

176   **Sumter sent a detachment:** Lee to NG, July 29, 1781 (*NGP9*:102 and n2).

176   **The British retaliated . . . torch the town:** FM to Rutledge, August 6, 1781, quoted in *New Jersey Gazette*, September 19, 1781; NG to Thomas McKean, August 25, 1781 (*NGP9*:241 and 243–244n4); Bass, *Swamp Fox*, 209. Others suggest Balfour ordered Georgetown destroyed to prevent it from being used to supply Greene's army. James, 77; William Johnson, *Life of Greene*, 2:215–216.

176   **Marion, sickened . . . hurried aid to alleviate:** FM to Rutledge, August 6, 1781, quoted in *New Jersey Gazette*, September 19, 1781; Rutledge to FM, August 7, 1781 (Gibbes, 124); Bass, *Swamp Fox*, 209.

176   **Governor John Rutledge . . . issued a proclamation:** Haw, *John and Edward Rutledge,* 136, 158; Moultrie, *Memoirs,* 2:407–409.

176   **Sumter took it personally . . . resigned:** NG to Henderson, August 12, 16, 1781 (*NGP*9:169, 188); Bass, *Gamecock,* 204–205, 210–216; Conrad, *NGP*10:169n5.

177   **"universally odious":** Lee to NG, August 20, 1781 (*NGP*9:216).

Chapter 20: "The Most Galling Fire"

178   **Isaac Hayne . . . went to the gallows:** David K. Bowden, *The Execution of Isaac Hayne* (Orangeburg, SC: Sandlapper, 1977), 15–34; Lee, *Memoirs,* 2:252–264; Mabel Louise Webber, ed., "Death Notices," *SCHGM* 17, no. 4 (October 1916): 159; William Harden to FM, April 7, 18, 1781 (Gibbes, 50, 55); Bass, *Swamp Fox,* 175–176, 212–213; James, 71–73; McCrady, 382–398, 409; Ladies' Petition (Gibbes, 112–114); Saberton, *CP*5:236n23.

179   **"I will endeavor to do so":** McCrady, 398.

179   **"He ascended . . . cart to move":** Ibid.

180   **storm of protest . . . let the matter drop:** Rubin, "Rhetoric of Revenge," 11–13; McCrady, 402–403, 407; Bowden, *Execution of Isaac Hayne,* 49–58; Officers of the Army to NG, August 20, 1781 (Gibbes, 128–130); NG to FM, August 10, 1781 (ibid., 125); Balfour to NG, September 3, 1781 (*NGP*9:283–284); Conrad, *NGP*9:252–253n2.

180   **the desired effect . . . The British capitalized:** Bass, *Swamp Fox,* 213; Bowden, *Execution of Isaac Hayne,* 47; Sherman, *Calendar,* 587, 592; Charles B. Baxley, "Marion at Parker's Ferry," address at 9th Francis Marion/Swamp Fox Symposium, Manning, SC, October 15, 2011, DVD; NG to FM, August 10, 1781 (*NGP*9:158–159); NG to Henderson, August 12, 1781 (*NGP*9:169).

180   **William Harden . . . considerable success:** Sherman, *Calendar,* 62, 454; McCrady, 434, 438; Balfour to Cornwallis, April 26, 1781 (*CP*4:177n50).

181   **asked Greene . . . Marion decided to go:** NG to FM, August 10, 20, 1781 (*NGP*9:158–159, 208); FM to NG, August 13, 16, 18, 1781 (ibid., 179, 191, 204 and n3); Edmund Hyrne to FM, August 18, 1781 (ibid., 199).

181   **at Peyre's Plantation on the Santee:** James, 69; O'Kelley, *Unwaried Patience,* 541.

181   **had two hundred men . . . ready to move out:** FM to NG, August 16, 18, 20, 1781 (*NGP*9:191, 204, 216–217); Hyrne to FM, August 20, 1781 (ibid., 221). O'Kelley identifies the substitute commander as Major Charles Harden. O'Kelley, *Unwaried Patience,* 543.

181   **Heading out at night on August 22 . . . too sick to fight:** FM to NG, September 3, 1781 (*NGP*9:288–289); Swager, *The Valiant Died,* 72.

181   **Neither Peter Horry . . . Hugh, was present:** Sherman, *Calendar*, 63,
        598; FM to NG, September 3, 1781 (*NGP9:289–290*); PH to NG,
        August 26, September 4, 1781 (*NGP9:259, 294*). Although Rankin,
        at page 236, states that Hugh Horry was detached to ride far to the
        north to "Cheraw," the letter actually reads "Chehaw"—that is, the
        Chehaw River, which was near where Marion was camped.

181   **just over four hundred . . . Ferdinand Ludwig von Benning:** FM to
        NG, September 3, 1781 (*NGP9:288–289*). Marion's report of the bat-
        tle at Parker's Ferry lists a "Lieut. Col. De Benin" as the enemy com-
        mander. FM to NG, September 3, 1781 (ibid., 289). A loyalist
        newspaper identified this person as "Lieut. Col. de Borck," which most
        historians have assumed to be Hessian lieutenant colonel Ernst Leop-
        old von Borck. *Royal Georgia Gazette* (Savannah), September 13,
        1781. But von Borck was only a major, not a lieutenant colonel, at the
        time. Max von Eelking, *The German Allied Troops in the American War
        of Independence, 1776–1783*, trans. J. G. Rosengarten (Albany: 1893),
        305. It is also unlikely that Marion would have referred to von Borck
        as "de Benin." Some sources identify the Hessian commander as Fried-
        rich Wilhelm von Benning, whose last name closely matches "Benin."
        Conrad, *NGP9:289*; Sherman, *Calendar*, 86, 102, 602–603. But an of-
        ficer by that name was killed at Trenton in December 1776. David
        Hackett Fischer, *Washington's Crossing* (2004; repr., Oxford: Oxford
        University Press, 2005), 405; Phillip Thomas Tucker, *George Washing-
        ton's Surprise Attack: A New Look at the Battle That Decided the Fate of
        America* (New York: Skyhorse, 2014), 518. Most likely the actual
        commander was Lieutenant Colonel Ferdinand Ludwig von Benning,
        who arrived in America in August 1781 and thereafter commanded a
        Hessian regiment at Charleston. Rodney Atwood, *The Hessians: Mer-
        cenaries from Hessen–Kassel in the American Revolution* (1980; repr.,
        Cambridge: Cambridge University Press, 2002), 197n71, 264; A. Les-
        lie to Col. von Benning, May 19, 1782, Letterbook of Alexander
        Leslie, Thomas Addis Emmet Collection, New York Public Library.

181   **The British were not . . . two field pieces:** FM to NG, September 3,
        1781 (*NGP9:290*); Stephen Jarvis, "An American's Experience in the
        British Army," *Journal of American History* 1, no. 4 (1907): 728; Ste-
        phen Jarvis, *The King's Loyal Horseman: His Narrative, 1775–1783*, ed.
        John T. Hayes (Ft. Lauderdale, FL: Saddlebag, 1996), 74–75; Sher-
        man, *Calendar*, 603; Baxley, "Marion at Parker's Ferry."

182   **night of August 27 . . . Marion aborted:** FM to NG, September 3,
        1781 (*NGP9:289*).

182   **August 30 . . . waiting for von Benning:** Ibid.; Jarvis, *King's Loyal
        Horseman*, 74–75; Jarvis, "An American's Experience," 728.

182   **Brigadier General Robert Cunningham:** "Memorial of Patrick Lisitt
        of North Carolina," April 1, 1786, reprinted in *Online Institute for*

Advanced Loyalist Studies, Todd Braisted, manager, February 23, 2015, www.royalprovincial.com/military/mems/nc/clmlis.htm; Lambert, *South Carolina Loyalists*, 153; Clark, *Loyalists in the Southern Campaign*, 1:222, 268.

182   **spot for an ambush . . . The second group:** FM to NG, September 3, 1781 (*NGP9:289*); Solomon Freer Pension, W8826; William Smith Pension, R9875; *Royal Georgia Gazette* (Savannah), September 13, 1781.

182   **A third group . . . "to follow them . . . at all hazards":** FM to NG, September 3, 1781 (*NGP9:289*).

182   **It was near sunset . . . shot them as they passed by:** Ibid., 289–290; Jarvis, "An American's Experience," 728; Jarvis, *King's Loyal Horseman*, 75; Solomon Freer Pension, W8826; William Smith Pension, R9875; James, 70; Rankin, 237; Aiken, 138.

184   **"running the gauntlet":** FM to NG, September 3, 1781 (*NGP9:290*); Jarvis, *King's Loyal Horseman*, 75. Marion's 2nd South Carolina Regiment soldiers often had to run the gauntlet, a form of punishment in which the condemned runs between two parallel lines of soldiers facing each other, who slap and thrash him as he passes between them. O'Kelley, *Unwaried Patience*, 211, 230, 392, 627n329, 634n399, 648n563, 656n669, 666n822.

A two-sided ambush would have been a complicated deployment requiring placement of the riflemen so as to avoid shooting into each other. In addition, archaeological work to date has located buckshot, rifle, and musket balls on only one side of the road (the east). Smith, *The Search for Francis Marion*, 79, 81. Marion and Jarvis therefore may have used "running the gauntlet" not as a technical military term but in the more generic sense of being made to endure some sort of painful ordeal. Still, it seems too coincidental for both Marion and Jarvis, independently, to have chosen the same classic military phrase to describe the ambush if they did not intend it in the classic sense. The likelihood is that Marion's men formed some type of double line "gauntlet" at Parker's Ferry, although the actual configuration remains unknown.

I particularly thank Charles Baxley and Jack Parker for their helpful insights on Parker's Ferry and Jack for his "one-way street" analogy.

184   **"the most galling fire ever troops experienced":** Jarvis, "An American's Experience," 728.

184   **cavalry was annihilated . . . "all of them capital horses" . . . rode over him:** FM to NG, September 3, 1781 (*NGP9:290*).

184   **"shot through . . . in the head":** Evidence on the Claim of Edward Williams, Transcripts of the Manuscript Books and Papers of the Commission of Enquiry into the Losses and Services of the American

Loyalists, vol. 26, p. 310 (microfilm reel RW 3167, South Carolina Dept. of Archives and History).

184 **Marion's success . . . "villains" . . . to refresh them:** FM to NG, September 3, 1781 (*NGP*9:290).

184 **The next morning . . . Marion sent a small party:** Ibid.; James, 70; Jarvis, *King's Loyal Horseman*, 75.

185 **All told . . . one killed:** FM to NG, September 3, 1781 (*NGP*9:290); O'Kelley, *Unwaried Patience*, 544; Jarvis, "An American's Experience," 728; Jarvis, *King's Loyal Horseman*, 75. Jarvis states that 125 British were killed in addition to many wounded, but given Marion's estimate of 20 enemy killed and 80 wounded, it seems more likely that Jarvis's figure represents total British casualties. Jarvis also mistakenly believed the Americans suffered no casualties.

185 **"Sons of Liberty":** FM to NG, September 3, 1781 (*NGP*9:290).

185 **"the highest honor upon your command":** NG to FM, September 5, 1781 (*NGP*9:298).

185 **"good conduct . . . bravery":** NG to Thomas McKean, September 5, 1781 (*NGP*9:299).

185 **"fresh spirits":** Rutledge to South Carolina Delegates, September 18, 1781, in Barnwell, "Letters of John Rutledge," *SCHGM* 18, no. 4 (October 1917): 157.

185 **rested his men . . . back to Peyre's:** FM to NG, September 3, 1781 (*NGP*9:288, 290); Bass, *Swamp Fox*, 215.

CHAPTER 21: "AT EUTAW SPRINGS THE VALIANT DIED"

186 **Midway Plantation . . . resolved to attack Stewart:** Greene's Orders, July 16, 1781 (*NGP*9:18 and n1); Lee to NG, August 8, 20, 1781 (*NGP*9:150–151, 214 and n4); Swager, *The Valiant Died*, 64, 73–74; Stewart to Cornwallis, August 15, 1781 (CP6:75); Carbone, *Nathanael Greene*, 202. It is possible that Greene's camp was not at Midway but at Singleton's Mills. Sherman, *Calendar*, 570n3392, 621.

186 **Logically . . . about two thousand:** Swager, *The Valiant Died*, 73–76, 80–86; Tonsetic, *1781: The Decisive Year*, 148; Lumpkin, 213–216; William Johnson, *Life of Greene*, 2:216–220; Lee, *Memoirs*, 2:276–278; Bass, *Swamp Fox*, 215; "Journal of Kirkwood," 21–22; McCrady, 442–443; NG to Lee, August 14, 1781 (*NGP*9:181); Edmund Hyrne to Edmund Gamble, August 24, 1781 (ibid., 234); NG to Thomas McKean, September 11, 1781 (ibid., 328); Lee to NG, September 1, 1781 (ibid., 278); NG to Henderson, August 24, 27, 1781 (ibid., 234, 260); NG to Lafayette, August 26, 1781 (ibid., 254); Stewart to Cornwallis, September 9, 1781 (Gibbes, 136–137).

187 **Greene had excused him . . . decided to wait . . . 240:** Greene's Orders, September 2, 3, 1781 (*NGP*9:278, 281); Lee, *Memoirs*, 2:277;

NG to Thomas McKean, September 11, 1781 (*NGP9*:328); William Johnson, *Life of Greene*, 2:216, 219; McCrady, 441–442.

187   **letter on September 4 . . . join him promptly:** Edmund Hyrne to FM, September 4, 1781 (*NGP9*:293); William Pierce Jr. to FM, September 6, 1781 (ibid., 303).

188   **come up as soon as possible:** NG to FM, September 5, 1781 (*NGP9*:298–299).

188   **a night march . . . Laurens's plantations:** FM to NG, September 6, 1781 (*NGP9*:303–304); Greene's Orders, September 15, 1781 (ibid., 346n1); Wallace, *Life of Henry Laurens*, 130.

188   **men and horses were exhausted:** FM to NG, September 6, 1781 (*NGP9*:303–304).

188   **September 7 . . . over two thousand . . . Marion's brigade on the front line:** Greene's Orders, September 7, 1781 (*NGP9*:305); NG to Thomas McKean, September 11, 1781 (*NGP9*:328); Conrad, *NGP9*:333n2; Sherman, *Calendar*, 612–613; William Johnson, *Life of Greene*, 2:219; McCrady, 442–443; "Journal of Kirkwood," 22; Henderson to NG, August 25, 1781 (*NGP9*:245).

189   **Alexander Stewart:** Saberton, *CP5*:295n30; Rawdon to Cornwallis, June 7, 1781 (*CP5*:292); Carbone, *Nathanael Greene*, 202.

189   **nearly caught napping . . . ready to do battle:** Lee, *Memoirs*, 2:282; "Journal of Kirkwood," 22–23; Stewart to Cornwallis, September 9, 1781 (Gibbes, 137); Stedman, *History of the Origin*, 2:377–378; Account of Otho Williams (Gibbes, 145); Stewart to Cornwallis, September 26, 1781 (*CP6*:168–169). Sources differ on the size of the rooting party. Kirkwood and Williams put it at 60 and 100, respectively, while a British return after the battle lists 310, of whom 149 were captured. Sherman, *Calendar*, 612; McCrady, 447n1; Conrad, *NGP9*:334n7. In his September 26 letter to Cornwallis, Stewart claimed that the rooting party, consisting of parts of the flank battalion and Buffs, had four rounds of ammunition per man and that they were captured because they stayed to fight rather than return to camp.

189   **Greene deployed . . . held down by Major John Marjoribanks:** Swager, *The Valiant Died*, 93–100, 103–108, 146, 153; NG to McKean, September 11, 1781 (*NGP9*:328–329); McCrady, 444–445; Lee, *Memoirs*, 2:281–284; Ames, *Cantey Family*, 45; Stewart to Cornwallis, September 9, 1781 (Gibbes, 138–139); FM to NG, September 9, 11, 1781 (*NGP9*:309, 341); Sherman, *Calendar*, 613n3650. Modern archaeological research locates Stewart's main battle line about three hundred yards west of the western edge of the British camp, whereas most histories place it farther east—two or three hundred yards west of the brick house and adjacent springs. Scott Butler, *Battlefield Survey and Archaeological Investigations at the Eutaw Springs, South Carolina*

Revolutionary War Battleground, 8 September 1781 (Atlanta: Brockington & Associates, November 2008), 44, 50–51, 59, 61–62.

192 **no two opposing armies . . . as evenly matched:** No definitive count
of the forces engaged at Eutaw Springs exists. Surveying the various
sources in 1997, the editors of the Greene Papers concluded that the
two armies were "roughly equal in size" at about 2,000 each. Conrad,
NGP9:333n2. Some sources have put Greene's total as low as 1,900
and Stewart's as high as 2,300. Others place Greene's total force much
higher, at nearly 2,800. Piecuch and Beakes, *Lee*, 200; Jim Piecuch,
"The Evolving Tactician: Nathanael Greene at the Battle of Eutaw
Springs," in *General Nathanael Greene and the American Revolution in
the South*, ed. Gregory D. Massey and Jim Piecuch (Columbia: University of South Carolina Press, 2012), 226–227. The 2,800 figure as-
sumes a Continental force of 1,775 based on returns from six weeks
before the battle, when Greene was still resting in the High Hills
(ibid., 226–227, 236n40). William Johnson, by contrast, cites a September 4 field return, prepared specifically for battle, showing only
1,256 Continentals. William Johnson, *Life of Greene*, 2:219; Greene's
Orders, September 4, 1781 (*NGP9:291*).

Stewart claimed to Cornwallis that he had only 1,200 fighting
men. Stewart to Cornwallis, September 26, 1781 (*CP6:169*). However, less than three weeks before the battle Lee estimated Stewart's
force at 1,800 fit for duty, and a week before that, Marion put the number at 2,000. Lee to NG, August 20, 1781 (*NGP9:214* and n4); FM to
NG, August 13, 1781 (ibid., 180). A return on the morning of September 8, adjusted for those sick or on detached duty, gives Stewart a
total of 1,945 men of all ranks fit for duty. A separate return from the
same day lists only 1,396. Piecuch, "The Evolving Tactician," 226.

If one were to credit the low-end estimates of Stewart's force, it
would imply an unprecedented casualty rate of more than 50 percent.
Stewart's wild exaggeration to Cornwallis that Greene had between
4,000 and 5,000 men further undermines the credibility of his lower
figures for himself. Stewart likely had a minimum of 1,600 effectives in
the Battle, even if one believes that he had more than 300 high-
quality soldiers (a quarter of his claimed force) out digging for potatoes at five in the morning and that none of them made it back to the
battle.

193 **Marion's seven hundred . . . celebrating with food and spirits:** NG
to McKean, September 11, 1781 (*NGP9:328–333, 335nn8–10, 336–
337n14*); Stewart to Cornwallis, September 9, 1781 (Gibbes, 137–
138); Lumpkin, 216–219; Swager, *The Valiant Died*, 109–112, 152,
159; Stedman, *History of the Origin*, 2:378–379; William Washington
to NG, September 8, 1781 (*NGP9:306*); John Langley Pension

(transcribed by Max Miller), S4502; Lee, *Memoirs*, 2:283–291; Account of Otho Williams (Gibbes, 146–156); FM to PH, September 14, 1781 (Gibbes, 160–161); Rutledge to South Carolina Delegates, September 9, 1781, *SCHGM* 18, no. 3 (July 1917): 139; H. G. Purdon, "An Historical Sketch of the 64th Regiment," lib.jrshelby.com/64th _sketch.htm; William Johnson, *Life of Greene*, 2:221, 225–230. According to one soldier who was present, Greene ordered Marion's men to fire twelve rounds, which they did before shifting right to launch additional volleys against the British right flank. William Vaughan Pension, W11691.

195   **"utterly unmanageable":** Account of Otho Williams (Gibbes, 154). One source disputes that there could have been any significant source of food or rum available in the British camp for the Americans to get into and posits that what actually stopped the American advance was the complex of camp tents, ropes, and stakes. Piecuch, "The Evolving Tactician," 231. But Otho Williams's firsthand report, supported by several other officers, states that the Americans became unruly after they "fastened upon the liquors and refreshments" in the camp. Account of Otho Williams (Gibbes, 154). That does not seem like the kind of story Williams would invent, especially as he was severely censuring his own men for lack of discipline, which would reflect poorly upon him and his fellow officers. Williams's account is supported by a pension applicant who stated that "the British were driven beyond their baggage, when our men commenced rummaging their tents, drinking rum &c &c which the enemy discovering, came back upon us, & drove us back into the woods." James Magee Pension, S1555.

195   **busy re-forming his line in a diagonal:** Lumpkin, 219.

195   **Marion was sent forward:** James, 74; Jim Piecuch, "Francis Marion at the Battle of Eutaw Springs," *Journal of the American Revolution*, June 4, 2013, allthingsliberty.com/2013/06/francis-marion-at-the -battle-of-eutaw-springs.

195   **Marjoribanks assaulted . . . a filthy pond:** Account of Otho Williams (Gibbes, 154–156); Lumpkin, 219–220; Stedman, *History of the Origin*, 2:379–380; Stewart to Cornwallis, September 9, 1781 (Gibbes, 138–139); Stewart to Cornwallis, September 26, 1781 (CP6:169); FM to PH, September 14, 1781 (Gibbes, 161); Royster, *Light-Horse Harry Lee*, 43–44; Piecuch and Beakes, *Lee*, 205–208; Conrad, NGP9:335–336n11; Sherman, *Calendar*, 81n324; *Charleston City Gazette Commercial*, January 30, 1826; James, 75.

196   **"with an avidity which seemed insatiable":** James, 75.

196   **"by far . . . I ever saw":** NG to Thomas Burke, September 17, 1781 (NGP9:355).

196   **The casualties . . . Pickens . . . Campbell . . . Howard:** Aiken, 239; O'Kelley, *Unwaried Patience*, 549; Stewart to Cornwallis, September

9, 1781 (Gibbes, 139); Stewart to Cornwallis, November 29, 1781 (CP6:172); Account of Otho Williams (Gibbes, 157–158); Conrad, NGP9:338nn22, 24; Carbone, *Nathanael Greene*, 206; Tonsetic, *1781: The Decisive Year*, 155; Sherman, *Calendar*, 614–615; Swager, *The Valiant Died*, 115–119, 155; Lee, *Memoirs*, 2:292; William Johnson, *Life of Greene*, 2:233–234; "John Eager Howard: Revolutionary War Patriot," *The Federalist*, February 2, 2014, thefederalist-gary.blogspot.com /2014/02/john-eager-howard-revolutionary-war.html.

197   **On the British side . . . Stewart was wounded:** Stewart to Cornwallis, September 9, 1781 (Gibbes, 139); Stewart to Cornwallis, November 29, 1781 (CP6:171); Swager, *The Valiant Died*, 119; FM to PH, September 14, 1781 (Gibbes, 160–161); NG to McKean, September 11, 1781 (NGP9:332).

197   **Marjoribanks died . . . reinterred:** Lumpkin, 220; William Johnson, *Life of Greene*, 2:236; "Glimpses at the Country of the Olden Time," *Russell's Magazine* 2, no. 1 (October 1857): 65; Dubose, "Reminiscences of St. Stephens Parish," 64–65.

197   **Marion listed . . . Hugh Horry:** O'Kelley, *Unwaried Patience*, 551; FM to PH, September 14, 1781 (Gibbes, 161).

197   **Private Jehu Kolb:** Jehu Kolb Pension, W8011; Marika Ann Manuel-Kolb, "Descendants of Dielman Kolb" (nos. 27, 109), Genealogy.com, August 25, 2005, www.genealogy.com/ftm/k/o/l/Marika-A-Kolb /GENE3-0005.html; www.genealogy.com/ftm/k/o/l/Marika-A-Kolb /GENE3-0011.html.

197   **Jim Capers:** Jim Capers Pension (transcribed by C. Leon Harris), R1669.

198   **James Delaney:** Thomas McDow Pension, S9427; Piecuch, "Francis Marion at Eutaw Springs."

198   **Jenkins clan . . . James Jenkins:** Jenkins, *Experience*, 43–44.

198   **"a degree . . . class of soldiers":** NG to McKean, September 11, 1781 (NGP9:329).

198   **"my Brigade behaved well":** FM to PH, September 14, 1781 (Gibbes, 161).

198   **"distinguished part . . . intrepid attack":** *Independent Ledger* (Boston), December 24, 1781.

198   **Both commanding generals claimed . . . victory:** NG to George Washington, September 17, 1781 (NGP9:362); NG to Thomas Burke, September 17, 1781 (NGP9:355); Stewart to Cornwallis, September 9, 1781 (Gibbes, 136); Stewart to Cornwallis, September 26, November 29, 1781 (CP6:168, 171); Swager, *The Valiant Died*, 137–142; John Marshall, *The Life of George Washington* (Philadelphia, 1805), 4:551–552.

198   **But in reality . . . Greene buried:** Account of Otho Williams (Gibbes, 156–157); Swager, *The Valiant Died*, 118–119, 136–137; Marshall,

Life of Washington, 4:552; SCAR 2, no. 12 (December 2005): 13 (ed. note); NG to McKean, September 11, 1781 (*NGP*9:332); Stewart to Cornwallis, November 29, 1781 (*CP*6:172).

199   **"The more he is beaten . . . in the end":** Diary of Roderick Mackenzie, quoted in *NGP*9:338n25.

199   **"The honor . . . last to us":** Lee, *Memoirs,* 2:293.

CHAPTER 22: "WATCHFUL ANXIETY"

200   **told Marion to be prepared:** NG to FM, September 17, 19, 1781 (Gibbes, 166–167, 170); William Johnson, *Life of Greene,* 2:243–245.

200   **Greene had dispatched . . . Gould . . . leave matters . . . to Stewart:** FM to NG, September 9, 11, 21, 1781 (*NGP*9:309, 341, 382–383 and nn1–2); McCrady, 464; Sherman, *Calendar,* 76, 527; Stewart to Cornwallis, September 26, November 29, 1781 (*CP*6:169, 172); Saberton, *CP*5:294n29; Conrad, *NGP*9:337–338nn20–21.

201   **Passing Greenland Swamp . . . attributed Harry's murder:** Certification of John Doyle and John McKinnon, November 27, 1782, reprinted in "Black Loyalists—Beheading of Harry," *Online Institute for Advanced Loyalist Studies,* Todd Braisted, manager, February 27, 2015, www.royalprovincial.com/military/black/blkharry.htm; Alan Gilbert, *Black Patriots and Loyalists: Fighting for Emancipation in the War for Independence* (Chicago: University of Chicago Press, 2012), 157; Parker, 68. Because the certification of Harry's death is from November 1782, most sources assign that as the date nearest Harry's beheading. However, the only documented time Gould was ever near Greenland Swamp (about ten miles from Eutaw Springs) was in September 1781; by November 1782 the British army was no longer in the field, and Gould had long since retired to Charleston. The likelihood is that Harry was taken prisoner and executed in September 1781 after the battle of Eutaw Springs when Marion was still in that area. The certification memorializing that earlier episode was signed by Major John Doyle, who also was near Eutaw Springs shortly after the battle. FM to NG, September 21, 1781 (*NGP*9:382); William Johnson, *Life of Greene,* 2:245–246; Gould to Clinton, September 30, 1781, in Willcox, *Clinton's Narrative,* 578–579.

   Marion's September 21 letter to Greene from Murray's Ferry near Greenland Swamp notes that he captured "a negro" from the British force in that same area who then provided him information about enemy movements. Could this have been Harry? Rutledge's order to hang African American spies is in his September 2, 1781 letter to Marion (Gibbes, 131). For a more detailed discussion of the incident see Steven D. Smith, "Beheading of Harry," *Military Collector & Historian* 68, no. 4 (Winter 2016), in press.

201 **Gould turned back . . . Greene retired:** Sherman, *Calendar*, 611, 619, 624; Nathaniel Pendleton to Wade Hampton, September 17, 1781 (*NGP9*:357 and n1); FM to NG, October 9, November 2, 10, 14, 18, 25, 1781 (*NGP9*:439, 521, 557 and n1, 573, 589–590, 628nn2–3); Conrad, *NGP9*:583n3; Willcox, *Clinton's Narrative*, 354, 356; Gould to Clinton, September 30, 1781, in *Clinton's Narrative*, 578–579; Stewart to NG, October 27, 1781 (*NGP9*:493 and n2); Balfour to Germain, October 12, 1781 (*CP6*:222–223); Gould to NG, November 16, 1781 (*NGP9*:578–579 and n1); Stewart to Cornwallis, November 29, 1781 (*CP6*:172); William Johnson, *Life of Greene*, 2:258–261; Piecuch, *Three Peoples*, 309.

201 **Marion remained . . . slowed by the fever:** FM to NG, September 21, 23, 25, 27, October 9, 1781 (*NGP9*:382–383, 386, 396–397, 403, 439); Rutledge to FM, October 10, 1781 (Gibbes, 185–186); Boddie, *Traditions*, 226.

202 **Rutledge . . . "severe examples" . . . wanted the names:** Conrad, *NGP9*:646n1; Rutledge to FM, September 2, 3, 6, 1781 (Gibbes, 131–132, 134–135) (quotation at 131); O'Kelley, *Unwaried Patience*, 552.

202 **sought Marion's recommendations:** Rutledge to FM, August 13, September 14, 1781 (Gibbes, 126–127, 159–160).

202 **Rutledge decided to offer . . . detailed lists:** Rutledge to FM, September 15, 26, October 10, 1781 (Gibbes, 162–163, 175, 184–185); Simms, 187; Rutledge Proclamation (Gibbes, 175–178).

203 **Rutledge also kept him busy:** Rutledge to FM, September 17, 26, October 11, 13, 16, 24, 1781 (Gibbes, 164–165, 174, 188, 190, 197); Haw, *John and Edward Rutledge*, 159.

203 **"I wish . . . winter cloths":** FM to William Richardson, October 28, 1781, American Antiquarian Society, *Books and Autographs*, Carnegie Book Shop, New York: 1948, Catalog 134 (citation courtesy of David Neilan).

203 **a serious dressing down . . . sent Horry a list:** FM to PH, September 23, October 11, 1781 (Gibbes, 171–172, 188); Boddie, *Traditions*, 233–234.

204 **"The time is lost . . . agreeably to his orders":** FM to PH, October 11, 1781 (Gibbes, 188).

204 **"behaved very much amiss":** Rutledge to PH, October 10, 1781 (Gibbes, 184).

204 **"every step . . . exasperate the militia":** Rutledge to PH, October 27, 1781 (Gibbes, 198–199).

204 **point-by-point rebuttal . . . "Gen. Marion's charges . . . in particular":** PH to Rutledge, October 30, 1781 (Gibbes, 200–203).

204 **"I used to submit . . . his late usage":** PH to NG, October 31, 1781 (Gibbes, 205).

204 **"obvious . . . no other person but yourself":** Ibid.

204 **He concluded . . . Rutledge had ordered a stop:** Ibid.; Rutledge to FM, September 26, 1781 (Gibbes, 173–174); Rutledge to PH, October 22, 1781 (ibid., 194–195).

205 **"It is high time . . . commanding you or not":** FM to Maham, October 18, 1781 (Gibbes, 194) (quotation); Boddie, *Traditions*, 234–235.

205 **"You will please . . . command of General Marion":** NG to Maham, October 23, 1781 (*NGP*9:468).

205 **"no man . . . better than yourself":** NG to FM, October 23, 1781 (*NGP*9:468).

205 **Maham returned the horse:** Joseph Johnson, *Traditions and Reminiscences*, 287. Johnson identifies the horse as belonging to the son of Mr. Oliver.

205 **"General Marion cannot wish . . . avoiding them":** NG to PH, November 6, 1781 (Gibbes, 207).

205 **meant nothing personal . . . "the very action itself":** FM to PH, November 9, 1781 (Gibbes, 210).

206 **he and Horry met . . . satisfied:** FM to PH, October 29, 1781 (Gibbes, 199); PH to NG, November 8, 1781 (*NGP*9:546–547); NG to PH, November 11, 1781 (Gibbes, 210).

206 **they learned . . . Cornwallis had surrendered:** FM to PH, October 29, 1781 (Gibbes, 199); NG to FM, October 30, 1781 (*NGP*9:496–497).

206 **Marion hosted a ball:** Bass, *Swamp Fox*, 224; Ames, *Cantey Family*, 31.

206 **"The general's heart . . . his breast":** James, 80.

206 **John Postell . . . would remain in jail:** FM to NG, August 18, November 8, 30, 1781 (*NGP*9:204 and n2, 549, 642); Conrad, *NGP*9:643n7; FM to NG, January 26, 1782 (*NGP*10:265); NG to FM, January 28, 1782 (*NGP*10:275); Rankin, 252; McCrady, 155.

206 **Peter Sinkler . . . denied a farewell visit:** Dubose, "Address at the 17th Anniversary," 7–8; Dubose, "Reminiscences of St. Stephens Parish," 45–48; Ames, *Cantey Family*, 35; Nason McCormick, "South Carolina: The Revolutionary Generation," *Comments on Life and Culture in These United States*, June 6, 2010, nasonmac.wordpress.com/tag /hezekiah-maham.

207 **"between ourselves" . . . had or could "get":** Rutledge to FM, October 24, 1781 (Gibbes, 196).

207 **Greene wrote Marion . . . inappropriate:** NG to FM, October 30, 1781 (*NGP*9:497 and n3). Greene repeated the admonition a few days later. NG to FM, November 5, 1781 (ibid., 531).

207 **written to Gould . . . to complain:** NG to Gould, October 29, 1781 (*NGP*9:495).

207 **Sinkler . . . died soon thereafter:** Dubose, "Address at the 17th Anniversary," 8.

207   Initially Greene hoped . . . "Mad Anthony" Wayne: Swager, *The Valiant Died*, 126; William Johnson, *Life of Greene*, 2:256–257, 276–277; Royster, *Light-Horse Harry Lee*, 47–48; Pancake, *This Destructive War*, 236; NG to FM, October 16, 1781 (*NGP9:448*); Alexander Martin to NG, November 28, 1781 (ibid., 634–635); Wayne to NG, November 30, 1781 (ibid., 644 and n2); NG to Wayne, January 9, 1782 (*NGP10:175–176*); O'Kelley, *Unwaried Patience*, 559.

208   three or four hundred "over mountain" men . . . left to go home: Otho Williams to Elie Williams, November 10, 1781, Calendar of Otho Holland Williams Papers, 1744–1839, MS 908, Maryland Historical Society; NG to John Farr, October 24, 1781 (*NGP9:470*); FM to NG, November 2, 18, 25, 27, 1781 (ibid., 522, 590, 628, 632); Sevier to NG, November 9, 1781 (ibid., 552); NG to FM, November 24, 1781 (ibid., 618); Simms, 189–190; Christine Swager, "Marion After Eutaw Springs," address at 5th Francis Marion/Swamp Fox Symposium, Manning, SC, October 20, 2007, DVD.

208   Pickens had recovered . . . Sumter was back . . . defending backcountry raids: William Johnson, *Life of Greene*, 2:258; Charles B. Baxley, "Gen. Nathanael Greene's Moves to Force the British into the Charlestown Area, to Capture Dorchester, Johns Island and to Protect the Jacksonborough Assembly, November 1781–February 1782," *SCAR* 12, no. 1.1 (January 23, 2015), 3–5; Swager, *The Valiant Died*, 129–131; NG to Sumter, November 2, 1781 (*NGP9:517–518*); Sumter to NG, December 9, 22, 1781 (*NGP10:24–25* and n2, 89–90 and n4).

209   "the worst men": Sumter to NG, November 14, 1781 (*NGP9:576*).

209   a secret plan . . . war's end: Sumter to FM, November 23, 1781 (Gibbes, 213–214).

209   no longer viewed Sumter . . . free to coordinate: NG to McKean, August 25, 1781 (*NGP9:242*); NG to FM, November 5, 1781 (ibid., 531).

209   "As you are at liberty . . . avoid a surprise": NG to FM, November 15, 1781 (*NGP9:577*).

209   Marion sent Maham . . . watched without intervening: FM to NG, November 18, 1781 (*NGP9:589–590*); Maham to NG, November 27, 1781 (ibid., 630–631 and nn2, 4); Henry A. M. Smith, "The Colleton Family in South Carolina," *SCHGM* 1, no. 4 (October 1900): 333–335; Parker, 62; Stedman, *History of the Origin*, 2:183n. Tarleton apparently sympathized with the women and also supported hanging one of the offenders. Borick, *A Gallant Defense*, 152–153.

209   "dragging away . . . civilized nations": John Doyle to FM, November 20, 1781 (Gibbes, 213).

209   Marion's initial report: FM to NG, November 18, 1781 (*NGP9:590*).

210   **Shelby later claimed:** Conrad, *NGP*9:613n4.
210n   **attack in a far different light:** NG to FM, November 24, 1781 (*NGP*9:618); Maham to NG, November 27, 1781 (ibid., 630–631).
210   **Within a matter of days . . . below Goose Creek:** FM to NG, November 21, 25, 27, 30, 1781 (*NGP*9:606, 628, 631, 642); Baxley, "Gen. Nathanael Greene's Moves," 6–7.
210   **leave the High Hills . . . now were in possession:** Baxley, "Gen. Nathanael Greene's Moves," 7–15; Henry A. M. Smith, "The Town of Dorchester, in South Carolina: A Sketch of Its History," *SCHGM* 6, no. 2 (April 1905): 84–85; NG to Otho Williams, December 2, 1781 (*NGP*9:649–650 and n2); Conrad, *NGP*9:xiv–xv.
210   **"melancholy state . . . almost intolerable":** Willcox, *Clinton's Narrative,* 356–357.
211   **Yet the Americans . . . The British still . . . could forage:** Simms, 191; William Johnson, *Life of Greene,* 2:266; NG to PH, December 14, 1781 (Gibbes, 222–223); NG to FM, December 14, 1781 (ibid., 223); Baxley, "Gen. Nathanael Greene's Moves," 17, 22.
211   **Greene lived in constant fear . . . countermand his orders:** NG to FM, December 16, 17, 22, 31, 1781 (Gibbes, 224–228); FM to NG, December 18, 21, 23, 30, 1781 (*NGP*10:74, 86, 94, 137); Boddie, *Traditions,* 232.
211   **Neither King George nor Lord Germain:** Carbone, *Nathanael Greene,* 209; Swager, *The Valiant Died,* 128.
211   **"will not . . . so soon":** FM to NG, November 18, 1781 (*NGP*9:590).
211   **"If we are not supported . . . better days":** NG to FM, December 14, 1781 (Gibbes, 223).

CHAPTER 23: "AS SOON AS THEY CAN SPARE ME"

212   **Governor John Rutledge . . . called for elections:** FM to NG, December 1, 1781 (*NGP*9:646 and n1).
212   **"I am sorry . . . cannot be full":** Ibid., 646.
212   **General Assembly at Jacksonboro:** Haw, *John and Edward Rutledge,* 160; McCrady, 555, 560; NG to Rutledge, December 14, 1781 (*NGP*10:51 and n1); NG to FM, December 31, 1781 (Gibbes, 227).
212   **up to Marion to cover:** NG to FM, January 3, 1782 (Gibbes, 228).
213   **most of those elected . . . turnout was low . . . changed the composition:** McCrady, 557–563, 739–742; FM to NG, December 1, 1781, January 1, 1782 (*NGP*9:646, 10:147); Rogers, *History of Georgetown County,* 145; Haw, *John and Edward Rutledge,* 162; Brannon, "Reconciling the Revolution," 113–114; Postell, "Notes on the Postell Family," 51; Bailey and Cooper, *South Carolina House,* vol. 3, *1775–1790,* 346–347, 376–377, 453–454, 574–577; N. Louise Bailey, ed., *Biographical Dictionary of the South Carolina Senate,* vol. 2, *1776–1785*

(Columbia: University of South Carolina Press, 1986), 753–754, 1035–1036, 1050–1052.

213 **On January 11 . . . Mepkin Plantation:** FM to PH, January 10, 1782 (Gibbes, 228–229); O'Kelley, *Unwaried Patience*, 559.

213 **reaching a quorum . . . January 18 . . . DuBose's tavern:** McCrady, 560–561, 563; Conrad, *NGP10*:147–148n4; FM to PH, January 18, 1782 (Gibbes, 232); A. S. Salley, ed., *Journal of the Senate of South Carolina: January 8, 1782–February 26, 1782* (Columbia, SC: The State Company, 1941), 3–5 and n1, 44, 142nn1–2; A. S. Salley, ed., *Journal of the House of Representatives of South Carolina: January 8, 1782–February 26, 1782* (Columbia, SC: The State Company, 1916), 3–9; Steve Coker, "Tavern of Peter DuBose," Rootsweb.com, January 1, 2007, archiver.rootsweb.ancestry.com/th/read/DuBose/2007–01/1167692640.

214 **a dramatic scene . . . keynote speech:** McCrady, 561–568; Salley, *Journal of the Senate*, 5–10.

214 **"emaciated victims . . . That is Marion":** George Washington Greene, *The Life of Nathanael Greene, Major-General in the Army of the Revolution*, vol. 3, *The War in the South, 1780–1783* (New York, 1871), 432–433.

214 **passed laws . . . legislators bought him:** McCrady 570–574; Conrad, *NGP10*:412n2.

214 **Confiscation Act . . . "inveterate enemies of the state":** McCrady, 576–580; Brannon, "Reconciling the Revolution," 79–84, 87–99, 103, 107; Phil Norfleet, "The South Carolina Estate Confiscation Act of 26 February 1782," Tripod.com, n.d., sc_tories.tripod.com/estate _confiscation_lists_of_february_1782.htm.

215 **"Well, gentlemen . . . Confiscation Act":** Weems, 236.

215 **help raise needed revenue:** FM to PH, February 10, 1782 (Gibbes, 249).

215 **list of persons subject to confiscation:** David J. McCord, ed., *The Statutes at Large of South Carolina*, vol. 6, *Containing the Acts from 1814 . . . to 1838* (Columbia, SC, 1839), 629–635.

216 **The original bill . . . were either moved from . . . or were dropped:** McCrady, 584–588; McCord, *Statutes, 1814–1838*, 6:629–635; Salley, *Journal of the Senate*, 74–79, 97–98, 114–115, 117, 124, 129–131; Rachel N. Klein, *Unification of a Slave State: The Rise of the Planter Class in the South Carolina Backcountry, 1760–1808* (Chapel Hill: University of North Carolina Press, 1990), 120–123; Lambert, *South Carolina Loyalists*, 286–293.

216 **on the Senate committee:** *Journal of the Senate, Jan. 6 to Mar. 17, 1783*, South Carolina Dept. of Archives and History, 11–59, 68, 237–239, 248–250.

216 **"at least mitigated where there is room":** Gadsden to FM, November 17, 1782, in Walsh, *Writings of Christopher Gadsden*, 196.

216   "he that forgets . . . best citizen": Ibid., 197.

216   Marion was willing to forgive . . . readily welcomed: Brannon, "Reconciling the Revolution," 147, 252, 255, 268.

216   undertook . . . John Brockinton . . . confiscation remained: John Faucheraud Grimke Pension, W11088; *Journal of the Senate, Jan. 6 to Mar. 17, 1783*, South Carolina Dept. of Archives and History, 239, 250.

216   "in conjunction . . . arms against us": Brannon, "Reconciling the Revolution," 266; Lambert, *South Carolina Loyalists*, 287.

216   Gordon was . . . switched: McCord, *Statutes, 1814–1838*, 6:635.

216   also served on a committee: Salley, *Journal of the Senate*, 28, 30, 39 41, 45–49.

216   "one sound negro": Thomas Cooper, ed., *The Statutes at Large of South Carolina*, vol. 4, *Containing the Acts from 1752 . . . to 1786* (Columbia, SC, 1838), 513–515.

217   He and Charles Cotesworth Pinckney: NG to PH, March 29, 1782 (Gibbes, 281); David Neilan, "Marion and the Jacksonboro Assembly," address at 9th Francis Marion/Swamp Fox Symposium, October 15, 2011, DVD.

217   never received their promised slaves: John Carter Pension, W8587; James Chitwood Pension, S1751.

217   "the natural strength . . . not the least doubt": NG to Rutledge, December 9, 1781 (NGP10:22).

217   "opposed by common prejudices . . . two years past": NG to Rutledge, January 21, 1782 (NGP10:228).

217   "people returned to their senses": Edward Rutledge to Arthur Middleton, February 8, 1782, in "Correspondence of Hon. Arthur Middleton, Signer of the Declaration of Independence," annotated by Joseph W. Barnwell, SCHGM 27, no. 1 (January 1926): 4.

217   "The Northern people . . . general Emancipation": Aedanus Burke to Middleton, January 25–February 5, 1782, in Middleton, "Correspondence," SCHGM 26, no. 4 (October 1925): 194.

217   despite rumors . . . only seven hundred: Carbone, *Nathanael Greene*, 210; NG to FM, April 15, 1782 (NGP11:64).

217   urgent messages . . . deserting him: NG to FM, January 16, 1782 (Gibbes, 230); PH to FM, January 31, 1782 (ibid., 246–247); James, 90.

218   face-to-face meeting . . . despite Marion's orders: O'Kelley, *Unwaried Patience*, 558; FM to PH, February 3, 1782 (Gibbes, 248).

218   could call on Maham . . . militia work: FM to PH, January 18, 1782 (Gibbes, 231–232); Maham to PH, January 20, 1782 (Gibbes, 239).

218   referred to as a Legion: Hezekiah Maham Orderly Book, September 26, December 27, 1781, January 12, 13, 25, 1782, Manuscripts and Archives Division, New York Public Library. Marion also referred to

Maham's unit as a "Legion" (ibid., December 28, 1781, January 11, 1782).

218   "I . . . shall not obey . . . pleased to send": Maham to PH, January 20, 1782 (Gibbes, 238).

218   Maham was issuing . . . "interferes with my command . . . can scarcely act": PH to FM, January 31, 1782 (Gibbes, 246).

218   Marion prevailed upon Greene . . . "obstinate": FM to NG, January 26, 1782 (*NGP*10:265–266).

218   Greene had just recently: Maham to NG, January 4, 1782 (*NGP*10:157–158); NG to Maham, January 17, 1782 (ibid., 212–213).

218   "a just . . . it is actions": NG to Maham, February 1, 1782 (*NGP*10:297).

218   advise him not to gloat: NG to PH, February 1, 1782 (Gibbes, 247).

218   "I esteem you both . . . his folly": NG to PH, February 14, 1782 (Gibbes, 252).

218   stuck in Jacksonboro . . . barely had a quorum: FM to PH, January 18, 20, February 3, 10, 14, 1782 (Gibbes, 232, 240, 248–249, 253).

218   "As soon as . . . will return": FM to PH, January 18, 1782 (Gibbes, 232).

218   "I assure you . . . with you": FM to PH, February 10, 1782 (Ibid., 249).

218   "would stop all business here": FM to NG, February 19, 1782 (*NGP*10:391).

219   Senate had to adjourn: Salley, *Journal of the Senate*, 30, 41.

219   on February 20: Ibid., 106, 112, 138, 145.

CHAPTER 24: "TO PREVENT THE EFFUSION OF BLOOD"

220   Benjamin Thompson . . . immediate assignment: Sanford C. Brown, *Benjamin Thompson, Count Rumford* (1979; repr., Cambridge, MA: MIT Press, 1981), 17, 24–39, 58, 78–82; Jim Piecuch, "Francis Marion Meets His Match: Benjamin Thompson Defeats the 'Swamp Fox,'" *Journal of the American Revolution*, April 29, 2014, allthingsliberty .com/2014/04/francis-marion-meets-his-match-benjamin-thompson -defeats-the-swamp-fox; FM to NG, March 1, 1782 (*NGP*10:431); Conrad, *NGP*10:419n3, 420n5.

220   Peter Horry, incapacitated . . . Maham rode to Jacksonboro: PH to NG, February 28, 1782 (*NGP*10:419–421 and nn4, 6); O'Kelley, *Unwaried Patience*, 560; Salley, *Journal of the House*, 84; Linder and Thacker, *Rice Plantations*, 561–562.

221   Lee . . . asked for Greene's permission: Lee to NG, January 26, 1782 (*NGP*10:264–265); Bass, *Swamp Fox*, 226; Royster, *Light-Horse Harry Lee*, 48, 52.

221   **"I have the highest opinion . . . a friend":** NG to Lee, January 27, 1782 (Gibbes, 243).

221   **Thompson struck . . . withdrew:** PH to NG, February 28, 1782 (*NGP*10:419–420 and nn4, 5); James, 90–91; McCrady, 602–604; Piecuch, "Francis Marion Meets His Match"; Thompson to Leslie, February 24, 1782, in *Report on Manuscripts in the Royal Institution of Great Britain* (Dublin: John Falconer, 1906), 2:403–405.

221   **Benison's "neglect of duty":** PH to NG, February 28, 1782 (*NGP*10:419).

221   **"reformed" Tories:** James, 90–91; Rankin, 272–273.

221   **Marion, accompanied by Maham . . . rallied his troops:** Rankin, 273–275; James, 91; FM to PH, March 2, 1782 (Gibbes, 260–261); Maham to NG, March 1, 1782 (*NGP*10:429–430); O'Kelley, *Unwaried Patience*, 564; *New-York Gazette*, April 15, 1782; Piecuch, "Francis Marion Meets His Match"; Thompson to Leslie, February 25, 1782, in *Report on Manuscripts*, 2:405–407.

222   **"chosen corps . . . in person:** Thompson to Leslie, February 25, 1782, in *Report on Manuscripts*, 2:405.

222   **elated . . . three days celebrating:** Gray, "Observations," 156–157.

223   **Marion had drowned:** *New-York Gazette*, April 15, 1782.

223   **"which was the only thing . . . saved our men":** Maham to NG, March 1, 1782 (*NGP*10:430).

223   **"a glorious opportunity . . . British cavalry":** FM to NG, March 1, 1782 (*NGP*10:431).

223   **Smith resigned:** Rankin, 275.

223   **"I repeatedly . . . in triumph":** PH to NG, February 28, 1782 (*NGP*10:419).

223   **"drooping spirits . . . so superior a force":** NG to FM, March 1, 1782 (*NGP*10:427).

223   **did clear the area . . . sailed for New York:** Conrad, *NGP*10:421n6, 535n4; Brown, *Benjamin Thompson*, 83–84; Piecuch, "Francis Marion Meets His Match."

223   **"uneventful":** *Dictionary of National Biography* (London, 1898), s.v. "Thompson, Benjamin (1754–1814)."

223   **Marion suggested . . . Marion to decide:** Mathews to NG, March 10, 1782 (*NGP*10:474); NG to Mathews, March 10, 1782 (ibid., 477); NG to FM, March 19, 1782 (ibid., 526); Mathews to FM, April 1, 1782 (Gibbes2, 149); Rankin, 275–276.

224   **Marion made clear . . . tried, without success:** FM to NG, March 13, 23, 1782 (*NGP*10:498–499, 534–535); NG to FM, March 27, 1782 (ibid., 546–547); NG to Mathews, March 27, 1782 (ibid., 547); Mathews to FM, March 12, 1782 (Gibbes, 270–271); Mathews to FM, April 10, 1782 (Gibbes2, 157); NG to FM, April 10, 1782 (Gibbes2, 159).

224 **"The preference . . . extorted from Marion":** James, 92.

224 **"to whom . . . Maham continued":** PH to FM, April 1, 1782 (Gibbes, 285–286).

224 **"which of . . . preferred" . . . Horry remaining in command there:** FM to PH, March 31, 1782 (Gibbes, 284–285).

224 **Georgetown assignment . . . Trade was again flowing:** Rogers, *History of Georgetown County*, 149–154.

224 **"salt must not . . . per bushel":** FM to PH, March 7, 1782 (Gibbes, 264). When Mathews learned about the price regulations he told Horry to end them and to "give every encouragement to a free uninterrupted trade." Mathews to PH, May 1, 1782 (Gibbes2, 172–173).

224 **Confessing to hurt feelings:** PH to FM, April 1, 1782 (Gibbes, 285–286).

224 **In July . . . rode off:** PH to FM, June 29, 1782 (Gibbes2, 196); PH to NG, July 20, 1782 (*NGP*11:450); Bass, *Swamp Fox*, 232–233.

225 **"in the hour . . . her deliverance":** NG to PH, August 10, 1782 (*NGP*11:515).

225 **As for Maham . . . "in the most horrid manner":** Maham to NG, May 20, 1782 (*NGP*11:225–226).

225 **loophole . . . Greene told him:** Ibid.; FM to NG, May 18, 1782 (*NGP*11:206); NG to Maham, May 23, 1782 (ibid., 234).

225n **Maham's cantankerous behavior:** Michael E. Stevens, "'Wealth, Influence or Powerful Connections': Aedanus Burke and the Case of Hezekiah Maham," *SCHM* 81, no. 2 (April 1980): 163–168.

225 **"with great good faith":** Gray, "Observations," 156.

225 **so-called neutral zone . . . haven for bloody raids:** PH to FM, January 31, 1782 (Gibbes, 245–246); Thomas Burke to Rutledge, March 6, 1782 (Gibbes, 265–266); Mathews to FM, March 18, 1782 (Gibbes, 275); Mathews to FM, April 1, 1782 (Gibbes2, 149); Joseph Graham Pension, S6937; Hershel Parker, "Fanning Outfoxes Marion," *Journal of the American Revolution*, October 8, 2014, allthingsliberty.com/2014/10/fanning-outfoxes-marion.

225 **Ganey . . . would personally try:** FM to NG, March 23, 1782 (*NGP*10:534); FM to Thomas Burke, April 13, 1782 (*CSR*16:283).

226 **ever-fretful Greene:** NG to John Laurens, April 2, 1782 (Gibbes2, 150); NG to PH, April [10], 1782 (ibid., 159–160); NG to FM, April 12, 15, 28, May 1, 1782 (ibid., 161, 164, 171–173); James, 93.

226 **maniacal David Fanning:** Hershel Parker, "Fanning Outfoxes Marion."

226 **"dead or alive":** NG to FM, July 9, 1782 (Gibbes2, 198).

226 **"for a handsome reward":** Thomas Farr to NG, September 9, 1782 (*NGP*11:639).

226 **By late May 1782:** Hershel Parker, "Fanning Outfoxes Marion"; Mathews to FM, May 21, 1782 (Gibbes2, 176–177); FM to NG, May 21, 1782 (*NGP*11:232 and nn2–3).

226   **"act as ... most conducive to the service":** Alexander Martin to FM, June 9, 1782 (CSR16:691).

226   **Taking Maham's dragoons ... without violence:** Bass, *Swamp Fox*, 236; O'Kelley, *Unwaried Patience*, 570; Pierce to FM, May 24, 1782 (*NGP*11:238).

226   **"we shall very soon ... on the carpet":** FM to PH, May 21, 1782 (Gibbes2, 177).

226   **"prevent the effusion ... your people's destruction":** FM to Ganey, June 2, 1782 (Gibbes2, 188).

227   **A conference ... "leader of banditti":** Garden, *Anecdotes* (1822), 26–27.

227   **At Burch's Mill ... one horse apiece:** Mathews to FM, May 21, 1782 (Gibbes2, 176–177); FM to PH, June 9, 1782 (ibid., 187–188); FM to NG, June 9, 1782 (*NGP*11:313–314); Moultrie, *Memoirs*, 2:419–421; Parker, 226, 326. The full treaty, reprinted in Moultrie's *Memoirs*, is erroneously dated in 1781.

227   **Marion even allowed Ganey:** Rankin, 282–283.

227   **not to be molested ... "private satisfaction":** O'Kelley, *Unwaried Patience*, 570.

227   **"It is recommended ... by our enemies":** Ibid.

227   **"so many enormities" ... sent off a group:** FM to NG, June 9, 1782 (*NGP*11:313–314 and n2).

228   **One of them ... killed Abel Kolb:** James, 93; Piecuch, *Three Peoples*, 287; Gregg, *Old Cheraws*, 360–361; O'Kelley, *Unwaried Patience*, 529. James and Piecuch identify the man as an African American loyalist leader named Gibson. Gregg and O'Kelley say his name was Mike Goings, a mulatto and only a private. Rankin states that the man excepted from the treaty was Joseph Jones, the captain who led the raiding party to Kolb's home. Rankin, 282.

228   **Another was David Fanning:** James, 93.

228   **"not let her have ... wait on her":** *The Narrative of Colonel David Fanning (a Tory in the Revolutionary War with Great Britain), Giving an Account of His Adventures in North Carolina, 1775–1783, as Written by Himself*, ed. Thomas H. Wynne (Richmond, VA, 1861), 63–64.

228   **He shortly left ... charge of rape:** Linley S. Butler, "David Fanning," in *Dictionary of North Carolina Biography*, ed. William S. Powell (Chapel Hill: University of North Carolina Press, 1986), 179–181.

228   **As 1782 turned ... that was the only way:** Pancake, *This Destructive War*, 238–239; Carbone, *Nathanael Greene*, 213–214; McCrady, 635–637; James, 97; Simms, 218; O'Kelley, *Unwaried Patience*, 571, 576; Conrad, *NGP*11:xi–xiv.

229   **"much fatigued":** FM to NG, April 16, 1782 (*NGP*11:71).

229   **Greene kept ordering:** NG to FM, April 28, May 1, July 24, 27, 30, August 9, 1782 (*NGP*11:134, 148, 453–454, 459–460, 472, 509–510);

Burnet to FM, July 26, 1782 (ibid., 457); Pierce to FM, August 4, 23, 1782 (ibid., 486, 570).

229 **"keep . . . and the enemy":** FM to PH, May 3, 1782 (Gibbes2, 173).

CHAPTER 25: "AN AFFECTIONATE FAREWELL"

230 **John Laurens:** Wallace, *Life of Henry Laurens*, 464, 472–473, 478–482, 487, 490; Greene's Orders, NGP11:323–324; Massey, *John Laurens*, 148, 211–213; Baxley, "Gen. Nathanael Greene's Moves," 19 and n86, 21–30.

230 **"unless intrepidity . . . purest motives":** Wallace, *Life of Henry Laurens*, 489.

230 **leapt from his sickbed . . . charge his men through:** Simms, 218–219; Massey, *John Laurens*, 226–227; Parker, 186; Gordon, *Battlefield History*, 174–175.

231 **"Poor Laurens . . . hardly survive it":** NG to Otho Williams, September 17, 1782 (NGP11:670).

231 **George Sinclair Capers . . . Black Dragoons . . . "cut them to pieces":** James, 94 (quotation); Parker, 131; Jim Piecuch, "The 'Black Dragoons': Former Slaves as British Cavalry in Revolutionary South Carolina," in Piecuch, *Cavalry*, 215–222.

231n **shot two German Hessian deserters:** Atwood, *The Hessians*, 197.

231 **Marion lay camped . . . Wadboo Barony:** James, 94–95; Parker, 57.

231n **Wadboo . . . not to be confused:** Henry A. M. Smith, "Notes and Queries," *SCHGM* 2, no. 1 (January 1901): 246–248; Cross, *Historic Ramblin's*, 34; Parker, 57, 62.

231 **Marion had his headquarters . . . shifted their positions:** FM to PH, February 3, 10, 1782 (Gibbes, 248–249); FM to PH, April 12, 1782 (Gibbes2, 162); James, 93–95; Simms, 214–216; Parker, 57; O'Kelley, *Unwaried Patience*, 577–579, 651–652n606, 706n1571; FM to NG, August 30, September 2, 1782 (NGP11:606–608 and nn2–3, 620–621).

233 **"The militia . . . great spirit":** FM to NG, August 30, 1782 (NGP11:607).

233 **"They fought . . . cord and tree":** Simms, 216.

233 **"the very honorable check . . . the enemy":** NG to FM, August 31, 1782 (NGP11:611–612).

233 **"Fraser attempted . . . was repulsed":** NG to George Washington, October 4, 1782 (NGP12:26).

234 **"hint . . . superior judgment":** FM to NG, September 24, 1782 (NGP12:694–695).

234 **"in the most perfect . . . any operations":** Burnet to FM, November 3, 1782 (NGP12:178).

234   **sporadic reports . . . nothing ever came:** NG to FM, September 4, 15, 1782 (*NGP*12:624 and n1, 662 and nn2–3); FM to NG, September 8, 10, 1782 (ibid., 637, 642 and n2).

234   **"It does not suit me . . . few negroes I have":** Robert Blair to FM, September 7, 1782 (Gibbes2, 224–225).

234   **moved . . . to the amercement list:** McCord, *Statutes, 1814–1838,* 6:631, 634.

234   **Marion's informants:** FM to NG, November 8, 1782 (*NGP*12:161).

234   **Greene and Leslie agreed . . . Wemyss:** Conrad, *NGP*12:xii, 291n3.

234   **On December 14 the great day:** Joseph W. Barnwell, "The Evacuation of Charleston by the British in 1782," *SCHGM* 11, no. 1 (January 1910): 1–26; Fraser, *Patriots,* 150–152; McCrady, 671–674.

235   **Mathews ordered . . . enter Charleston:** Mathews to NG, November 17, 1782 (*NGP*12:198).

235   **Greene took pains:** NG to FM, November 22, 1782 (*NGP*12:210).

235   **"I wish you not . . . too near":** NG to FM, November 15, 1782 (*NGP*12:187).

235   **"three or four of your particular friends":** NG to FM, November 22, 1782 (*NGP*12:211).

235   **Mathews gave Marion permission . . . no desire to go:** FM to NG, November 24, 1782 (*NGP*12:217).

235   **He gathered his men:** James, 98–99.

236   **"was conducted . . . affectionate farewell":** Ibid., 99.

236   **"His appearance . . . his country":** Ibid.

Chapter 26: "The Purest Patriotism"

237   **Pond Bluff . . . went back with him:** Boddie, *Traditions,* 260–261; James, 99; Dubose, "Address at the 17th Anniversary," 19; Dubose, "Reminiscences of St. Stephens Parish," 66–67. An "Ab Marrion, 26," identified as "formerly property of General Marrion," was listed among the slaves who escaped to the British lines. He settled in Shelburne, Nova Scotia, in a large black loyalist settlement known as Birchtown (named for British General Samuel Birch). Gilbert, *Black Patriots and Loyalists,* 198–199, 307n113. Boddie identifies the cousin who managed Belle Isle as "Henry Gignilliat," who had married the oldest sister of Marion's father. Simons, "Marion Family." But Henry Gignilliat was deceased, so it was probably his son Benjamin Gignilliat, who later served as an appraiser for Marion's estate, who tended to Belle Isle during Marion's absence.

238   **new legislative session:** *Journal of the Senate, Jan. 6 to Mar. 17, 1783,* South Carolina Dept. of Archives and History, 1–4.

238   **"I am much obliged . . . goes by favor":** FM to PH, January 18, 1783, Bancroft Collection, NYPL.

238 **"I have no prospect . . . my principles":** Ibid.

239 **"eminent and conspicuous service . . . her inhabitants":** *South Carolina Weekly-Gazette* (Charleston), March 8, 1783.

239 **302-acre land grant:** Francis Marion, Plat for 302 acres in St. John's Parish, August 25, 1785, South Carolina Dept. of Archives and History, series S213190, vol. 14:298.

239 **never applied . . . heirs would claim it:** Declarations of Louisa C. Marion, Catharine Palmer, Mary V. Yeadon, and Gabriella M. Kirk, January 31, 1835, Fold3.com, Revolutionary War Collection; A. D. Hiller to J. Stuart Pittman, January 24, 1935 (ibid.)

239 **"promoted" . . . twenty-six other:** Rankin, 292; O'Kelley, *Unwaried Patience*, 344.

239 **"villains . . . heat of the day":** Lamb (Lemuel) Benton to Mathews, August 20, 1782 (Gibbes2, 208).

239 **received a sinecure . . . resigned the position:** James, 99–100; Cooper, *Statutes, 1752–1786*, 4:588; Thomas Cooper, ed., *The Statutes at Large of South Carolina*, vol. 5, *Containing the Acts from 1786 . . . to 1814* (Columbia, SC, 1839), 73–74; FM to Charles Pinckney, November 10, 1789, "Governors' Messages," South Carolina Dept. of Archives and History, series S165009, message 512, p. 15. Five shillings equaled one-quarter of a pound.

240 **"For if . . . suffer for it":** Garden, *Anecdotes* (1822), 20.

240 **A bill did pass:** Cooper, *Statutes, 1752–1786*, 4:598–600.

240 **Mary Esther Videau . . . rebuilt at Pond Bluff:** Richard Yeadon, "The Marion Family, No. 10: The Widow of Gen. Marion," *Charleston Courier*, August 7, 1858; Boddie, *Traditions*, 18, 28, 35–36, 57, 76, 99, 140, 261, 266–267; James, 100; Bass, *Swamp Fox*, 242; J. H. Robinson, "Marion's Brigade," *Cook County Herald* (Arlington Heights, IL), April 20, 1906; *Columbian Herald* (Charleston, SC), April 24, 1786; Kirk, "Pond Bluff Plantation, Marion Family"; MacNutt, "Gen. and Mrs. Marion"; Inventory of Estate of Francis Marion, September 21, 1795, South Carolina Dept. of Archives and History, transcript and notes provided by David Neilan to the author. One source states that the house at Pond Bluff had two stories with a porch, sitting room, and nine other rooms. Cross, *Historic Ramblin's*, 279.

241 **Charlotte Videau Ashby . . . Anthony Ashby:** Yeadon, "The Widow of Gen. Marion"; Boddie, *Traditions*, 272; Bass, *Swamp Fox*, 242; Simons, "Marion Family."

241 **For Marion's part . . . "Dwight":** Boddie, *Traditions*, 272; Last Will and Testament of Francis Marion, October 16, 1787, July 16, 1792, Ancestry.com; Simons, "Marion Family."

242 **did legally change his name . . . surname disappeared:** *Acts of the General Assembly of the State of South-Carolina, from December, 1795,*

to December, 1804, Both Inclusive (Columbia, SC, 1808), 2:251; Simons, "Marion Family."

242 **hired out some of his slaves . . . at Fort Johnson:** Voucher from Commissioners at Fort Johnson for work done by negroes in 1785, Francis Marion Miscellaneous File, 1783–1785, Manuscripts and Archives Division, New York Public Library.

242 **six thousand acres . . . extended loans:** Inventory of Estate of Francis Marion, September 21, 1795, South Carolina Dept. of Archives and History, transcript and notes provided by David Neilan to the author.

242 **"moderate Federalist":** James, 100.

242 **convention that ratified . . . William Clay Snipes:** Francis Newton Thorpe, *Constitutional History of the United States*, vol. 2, *1788–1861* (Chicago: Callaghan & Co., 1901), 69; Jonathan Elliot, ed., *Debates in the Several State Conventions on the Adoption of the Federal Constitution, as Recommended by the General Convention at Philadelphia in 1787, Together with the Journal of the Federal Convention*, vol. 4 (Washington, DC, 1836), 339.

243 **convention that drafted:** James, 100.

243 **Marion urged . . . free public schools:** Weems, 239–247.

243 **kept up command . . . resigned:** Bass, *Swamp Fox*, 243–244.

243 **Pinckney . . . compromise candidate:** Michael E. Stevens, ed., *Journals of the House of Representatives, 1792–1794* (Columbia: University of South Carolina Press, 1988), x–xi and n5.

244 **"constant pain . . . ardent fever":** FM to Francis Marion Dwight, November 8, 1794, Francis Marion Miscellaneous File, 1783–1785, Manuscripts and Archives Division, New York Public Library. The letter was sent to Stratford, Connecticut, which is fifteen miles from New Haven, the site of Yale.

244 **6,453 . . . half a million dollars . . . seventy-four slaves:** Inventory of Estate of Francis Marion, September 21, 1795, South Carolina Dept. of Archives and History, transcript and notes provided by David Neilan to the author.

244 **He willed . . . mahogany furniture:** Ibid.; Cross, *Historic Ramblin's*, 280; Last Will and Testament of Francis Marion, October 16, 1787, July 16, 1792, Ancestry.com.

244 **will was invalid . . . She died in 1815:** Yeadon, "The Widow of Gen. Marion"; Cooper, *Statutes, 1786–1814*, 5:162–164. Marion made out his last will in 1787 and re-signed and dated it in 1792; in neither case was it witnessed.

244 **Francis (Dwight) Marion . . . 150 slaves:** Appraisal and Division of Negroes Belonging to the Estate of Francis (Dwight) Marion, December 27–28, 1833, South Carolina Dept. of Archives and History, Ancestry.com; John J. Simons III, "Francis Marion Dwight," *The Early Families of the South Carolina Low Count[r]y*, Rootsweb.com, Septem-

ber 3, 2011, wc.rootsweb.ancestry.com/cgi-bin/igm.cgi?op=GET&db =syf&id=I21087.

245 **"Scipio":** Last Will and Testament of Mary Esther (Videau) Marion, December 6, 1814, Ancestry.com; Boddie, *Traditions*, 280. See also McCord, *Statutes . . . Relating to Slaves*, 7:396, 442–443, 459–460.

245 **Had he been so:** Daniel Littlefield, commentary in *Chasing the Swamp Fox*, executive producer Thomas Fowler, producers James H. Palmer Jr. and Sanford Adams (Columbia: South Carolina ETV Commission, 2004), YouTube video, 12:27, posted by Butch Hills, December 8, 2013, www.youtube.com/watch?v=9Lc9-C8dGGM.

245 **and some did:** Bobby G. Moss and Michael C. Scoggins, *African-American Patriots in the Southern Campaign of the American Revolution* (Blacksburg, SC: Scotia-Hibernia Press, 2004), 36–37, 43–44, 183–184.

245 **a slave named Antigua:** Ibid., 10–11.

245 **"forever delivered . . . yoke of slavery":** Cooper, *Statutes*, 4:545.

246 **"History affords no . . . peculiar to yourself":** NG to FM, April 24, 1781 (*NGP*8:144).

246 **In November 1794 . . . first signer . . . Peter Horry:** James, 100; Smith, "Archaeological Perspectives," 345–346.

246 **"Your achievements . . . purest patriotism":** James, 100–101.

247 **"Washington of the South":** Weems, v. See also Busick, introduction to Simms, xi–xii.

Selected Bibliography

The works in this list are those cited in shortened form periodically in the notes as well as those consulted more generally in the preparation of this book.

Primary Sources

Balfour, Nisbet. Letterbook of Lt. Col. Nisbet Balfour, January 1–December 1, 1781. Society of the Cincinnati, Digitized Collections, 2012. societyofthe cincinnati.org/collections/library/digitized_collections.

Brown, Tarleton. *Memoirs of Tarleton Brown, a Captain in the Revolutionary Army.* New York, 1862.

Clinton, Henry. *The American Rebellion: Sir Henry Clinton's Narrative of His Campaigns, 1775–1782, with an Appendix of Original Documents.* Edited by William B. Willcox. New Haven, CT: Yale University Press, 1954.

Colonial and State Records of North Carolina. Vols. 14–17. In *Documenting the American South.* Chapel Hill: University Library, University of North Carolina, 2010. docsouth.unc.edu/csr/index.html/document/csr14–0518.

Cornwallis, Charles. *The Cornwallis Papers: The Campaigns of 1780 and 1781 in the Southern Theatre of the American Revolutionary War.* 6 vols. Edited by Ian Saberton. Uckfield, East Sussex, UK: Naval & Military Press, 2010.

———. *Correspondence of Charles, First Marquis Cornwallis.* Vol 1. Edited by Charles Ross. London, 1859.

Fanning, David. *The Narrative of Colonel David Fanning (a Tory in the Revolutionary War with Great Britain), Giving an Account of His Adventures in North Carolina, 1775–1783, as Written by Himself.* Edited by Thomas H. Wynne. Richmond, VA, 1861.

French, Christopher. "Journal of an Expedition to South Carolina." *Journal of Cherokee Studies* 2, no. 3 (Summer 1977): 275–301.

Gadsden, Christopher. *The Writings of Christopher Gadsden, 1746–1805.* Edited by Richard Walsh. Columbia: University of South Carolina Press, 1966.

Gates, Horatio. "Orders Issued by Major Genl. Gates While Commanding the Southern Army, July 26th to August 31st 1780." Edited by Thomas

Addis Emmet. *Magazine of American History* 5, no. 4 (October 1880): 310–320.

———. Papers. Manuscripts and Archives Division, New York Public Library.

———. Papers. Thomas Cooper Library, University of South Carolina.

———. "The Southern Campaign 1780: Letters of Major General Gates from 21st June to 31st August." Edited by Thomas Addis Emmet. *Magazine of American History* 5, no. 4 (October 1880): 281–310.

Gibbes, Robert W., ed. *Documentary History of the American Revolution . . . 1764–1776.* New York, 1855.

———. *Documentary History of the American Revolution, Consisting of Letters and Papers Relating to the Contest for Liberty, Chiefly in South Carolina . . . 1776–1782.* New York, 1857.

———. *Documentary History of the American Revolution, Consisting of Letters and Papers Relating to the Contest for Liberty, Chiefly in South Carolina, in 1781 and 1782.* Columbia, SC, 1853.

Grant, James. "Journal of Lieutenant-Colonel James Grant, Commanding an Expedition Against the Cherokee Indians, June–July, 1761." *Florida Historical Quarterly* 12 (1933): 24–36.

Gray, Robert. "Colonel Robert Gray's Observations on the War in Carolina." *SCHGM* 11, no. 3 (July 1910): 139–159.

Greene, Nathanael. *The Papers of General Nathanael Greene.* Vol. 6. Edited by Richard K. Showman. Vol. 7. Edited by Richard K. Showman and Dennis M. Conrad. Vols. 8–12. Edited by Dennis M. Conrad. Chapel Hill: University of North Carolina, 1991, 1994, 1995–2002.

Horry, Peter. "Horry's Notes to Weems's 'Life of Marion.'" Edited by Alexander S. Salley. *SCHM* 60, no. 3 (July 1959): 119–122.

———. "Journal." Edited by A. S. Salley. *SCHGM* 38, nos. 2 and 3 (April and July 1937): 49–53, 81–86; *SCHGM* 39, no. 3 (July 1938): 125–128.

Jarvis, Stephen. "An American's Experience in the British Army." *Journal of American History* 1, no. 3 (1907): 441–464; 1, no. 4 (1907): 727–740.

———. *The King's Loyal Horseman: His Narrative, 1775–1783.* Edited by John T. Hayes. Ft. Lauderdale, FL: Saddlebag, 1996.

Jenkins, James. *Experience, Labours, and Sufferings of Rev. James Jenkins, of the South Carolina Conference.* Columbia, SC, 1842.

Kirkwood, Robert. "The Journal and Order Book of Captain Robert Kirkwood of the Delaware Regiment of the Continental Line, Part I: A Journal of the Southern Campaign, 1780–1782." Edited by Joseph Brown Turner. *Papers of the Historical Society of Delaware* 56 (1910): 7–45.

Laurens, Henry. *The Papers of Henry Laurens.* Vol. 3, *Jan. 1, 1759–Aug. 31, 1763.* Edited by Philip M. Hamer and George C. Rogers Jr. Columbia: University of South Carolina Press, 1972.

———. *The Papers of Henry Laurens.* Vol. 16, *September 1, 1782–December 17, 1792.* Edited by David R. Chesnutt and C. James Taylor. Columbia: University of South Carolina Press, 2003.

Lee, Henry. *Memoirs of the War in the Southern Department.* 2 vols. Philadelphia, 1812.

Maham, Hezekiah. Orderly Book. Manuscripts and Archives Division, New York Public Library.

Marion, Francis. "Francis Marion's Regimental Muster Roll, 1778." Thomas Cooper Library, University of South Carolina, Rare Books and Special Collections.

———. Miscellaneous File, 1783–1785. Manuscripts and Archives Division, New York Public Library.

———. Papers. Edited and annotated by Charles B. Baxley and David Neilan. 2015, in progress.

McKay, James, Robert Robinson, and Thomas B. Campbell. "Journal of the Blockade at Scott's Lake, [SC] Fort Watson, 15–23 April 1781." *SCAR* 4, no. 2.1 (April–June 2007): 52.

Middleton, Arthur. "Correspondence of Hon. Arthur Middleton, Signer of the Declaration of Independence." Annotated by Joseph W. Barnwell. *SCHGM* 26, no. 4 (October 1925): 183–213; 27, no. 1 (January 1926): 1–29.

Monypenny, Alexander. "Diary of Alexander Monypenny: March 20–May 31, 1761." *Journal of Cherokee Studies* 2, no. 3 (Summer 1977): 320–331.

Moultrie, William. *Memoirs of the American Revolution, So Far as It Related to the States of North and South Carolina, and Georgia.* 2 vols. New York, 1802.

Nase, Henry. *Diary of Henry Nase, King's American Regiment.* Transcribed by Todd Braisted. New Brunswick Museum, Archives Division, Nase Family Papers.

O'Kelley, Patrick. *Unwaried Patience and Fortitude: Francis Marion's Orderly Book.* West Conshohocken, PA: Infinity, 2007.

Rutledge, John. "Letters of John Rutledge." Annotated by Joseph W. Barnwell. *SCHGM* 17, no. 4 (October 1916): 131–146; 18, no. 2 (April 1917): 59–69; 18, no. 3 (July 1917): 131–142; 18, no. 4 (October 1917): 155–167.

Saunders, John. Papers. Loyalist Collection, Harriet Irving Library, University of New Brunswick, Fredericton, NB, Canada.

Simcoe, John Graves. *Simcoe's Military Journal: A History of the Operations of a Partisan Corps, Called the Queen's Rangers.* 1787. Reprint, New York, 1844.

Sparks, Jared. Jared Sparks Collection of American Manuscripts, 1560–1843 (MS Sparks 22), Houghton Library, Harvard University.

Stedman, Charles. *The History of the Origin, Progress, and Termination of the American War.* Vol. 2. London, 1794.

Tarleton, Banastre. *A History of the Campaigns of 1780 and 1781, in the Southern Provinces of North America.* London, 1787.

Thompson, Benjamin. Letters. In *Report on Manuscripts in the Royal Institution of Great Britain.* Vol. 2. Dublin: John Falconer, 1906.

Watson, John. "Narrative." Transcribed by Donald J. Gara. *SCAR* 4, no. 2.1 (April–June 2007): 55–61.

Williams, Otho Holland. Calendar of Papers, 1744–1839 (MS 908). Maryland Historical Society.

———. "A Narrative of the Campaign of 1780." In Johnson, *Nathanael Greene*, vol. 1, Appendix B, 485–510.

Secondary Sources

Books

Aiken, Scott D. *The Swamp Fox: Lessons in Leadership from the Partisan Campaigns of Francis Marion.* Annapolis, MD: Naval Institute Press, 2012.

Ames, Joseph S. *Six Generations of the Cantey Family of South Carolina.* Charleston, SC: Walker, Evans, and Cogswell, 1910.

Atwood, Rodney. *The Hessians: Mercenaries from Hessen–Kassel in the American Revolution.* 1980. Reprint, Cambridge: Cambridge University Press, 2002.

Bailey, N. Louise, ed. *Biographical Dictionary of the South Carolina House of Representatives.* Vol. 4, *1791–1815.* Columbia: University of South Carolina Press, 1984.

———, ed. *Biographical Dictionary of the South Carolina Senate.* Vol. 2, *1776–1785.* Columbia: University of South Carolina Press, 1986.

Bailey, N. Louise, and Elizabeth Ivey Coopers, eds. *Biographical Dictionary of the South Carolina House of Representatives.* Vol. 3, *1775–1790.* Columbia: University of South Carolina Press, 1981.

Barbour, R. L. *South Carolina's Revolutionary War Battlefields: A Tour Guide.* Gretna, LA: Pelican, 2002.

Bass, Robert D. *Gamecock: The Life and Campaigns of General Thomas Sumter.* New York: Holt, Rinehart and Winston, 1961.

———. *The Green Dragoon: The Lives of Banastre Tarleton and Mary Robinson.* 1957. Reprint, Columbia, SC: Sandlapper, 1973.

———. *Swamp Fox: The Life and Campaigns of General Francis Marion.* 1959. Reprint, Orangeburg, SC: Sandlapper, 1974.

Beckett, Ian F. W. *Modern Insurgencies and Counter-Insurgencies: Guerillas and Their Opponents Since 1750.* London: Routledge, 2001.

Boddie, William Willis. *History of Williamsburg: Something About the People of Williamsburg County, South Carolina, from the First Settlement by Europeans About 1705 Until 1923.* Columbia, SC: The State Company, 1923.

———. *Traditions of the Swamp Fox: William W. Boddie's Francis Marion. With an Introduction by Steven D. Smith.* Spartanburg, SC: The Reprint Company, 2000.

Boot, Max. *Invisible Armies: An Epic History of Guerrilla Warfare from Ancient Times to the Present.* New York: Liveright, 2013.

Borick, Carl P. *A Gallant Defense: The Siege of Charleston, 1780.* Columbia: University of South Carolina Press, 2003.

Bowden, David K. *The Execution of Isaac Hayne.* Orangeburg, SC: Sandlapper, 1977.

Brown, Sanford C. *Benjamin Thompson, Count Rumford.* 1979. Reprint, Cambridge, MA: MIT Press, 1981.

Buchanan, John. *The Road to Guilford Courthouse: The American Revolution in the Carolinas.* New York: John Wiley & Sons, 1997.

Carbone, Gerald M. *Nathanael Greene: A Biography of the American Revolution.* New York: Palgrave Macmillan, 2008.

Clark, Murtie June. *Loyalists in the Southern Campaign of the Revolutionary War.* Vol. 1, *Official Rolls of Loyalists Recruited from North and South Carolina, Georgia, Florida, Mississippi, and Louisiana.* Baltimore: Genealogical Pub. Co., 1981.

Cross, J. Russell. *Historic Ramblin's Through Berkeley.* Columbia, SC: R. L. Bryan, 1985.

Davis, Henry Edwards. *A Southern Sportsman: The Hunting Memoirs of Henry Edwards Davis.* Edited by Ben McC. Moïse. 2010. E-book edition, Columbia: University of South Carolina Press, 2014. Chap. 1.

Deas, Anne Simons. *Recollections of the Ball Family of South Carolina and the Comingtee Plantation.* Summerville, SC, c. 1909.

Dubose, Samuel, and Frederick A. Porcher. *A Contribution to the History of the Huguenots of South Carolina, Consisting of Pamphlets.* Edited by Theodore Gaillard Thomas. New York, 1887.

Edgar, Walter. *Partisans and Redcoats: The Southern Conflict That Turned the Tide of the American Revolution.* 2001. Reprint, New York: Perennial, 2003.

Fraser, Walter J., Jr. *Patriots, Pistols, and Petticoats: "Poor Sinful Charles Town" During the American Revolution.* 1976. Reprint, Columbia: University of South Carolina Press, 1993.

Gaillard, Frye. *Lessons from the Big House: One Family's Passage Through the History of the South, A Memoir.* Asheboro, NC: Down Home Press, 1994.

Garden, Alexander. *Anecdotes of the American Revolution, Illustrative of the Talents and Virtues of the Heroes and Patriots, Who Acted the Most Conspicuous Parts Therein.* Charleston, SC, 1828.

———. *Anecdotes of the Revolutionary War in America, with Sketches of Character of Persons the Most Distinguished, in the Southern States, for Civil and Military Service.* Charleston, SC, 1822.

Gilbert, Alan. *Black Patriots and Loyalists: Fighting for Emancipation in the War for Independence.* Chicago: University of Chicago Press, 2012.

Golway, Terry. *Washington's General: Nathanael Greene and the Triumph of the American Revolution.* 2005. Reprint, New York: Owl Books, 2006.

Gordon, John W. *South Carolina and the American Revolution: A Battlefield History.* Columbia: University of South Carolina Press, 2003.

Gregg, Alexander. *History of the Old Cheraws . . . and Sketches of Individuals*. New York, 1867.

Groves, Joseph A. *The Alstons and Allstons of North Carolina and South Carolina*. Atlanta: Franklin Printing, 1901.

Hatley, Tom. *The Dividing Paths: Cherokees and South Carolinians Through the Revolutionary Era*. New York: Oxford University Press, 1995.

Haw, James. *John and Edward Rutledge of South Carolina*. Athens: University of Georgia Press, 1997.

Heitzler, Michael J. *Historic Goose Creek, South Carolina, 1670–1980*. Edited by Richard N. Côté. Easley, SC: Southern Historical Press, 1983.

Higgins, W. Robert, ed. *The Revolutionary War in the South: Power, Conflict and Leadership*. Durham, NC: Duke University Press, 1979.

Holbrook, Stewart H. *The Swamp Fox of the Revolution*. 1959. Reprint, New York: Sterling, 2008.

Holt, Mack P. *The French Wars of Religion: 1562–1629*. 1995. Reprint, Cambridge: Cambridge University Press, 2005.

Horry, Peter and M. L. Weems. *The Life of Gen. Francis Marion, a Celebrated Partisan Officer in the Revolutionary War, Against the British and Tories in South Carolina and Georgia*. 1809. Reprint, Philadelphia, 1845.

Howe, George. *History of the Presbyterian Church in South Carolina*. Vol. 1. Columbia, SC, 1870.

James, William Dobein. *A Sketch of the Life of Brig. Gen. Francis Marion and a History of His Brigade from Its Rise in June 1780 Until Disbanded in December, 1782*. 1821. Reprint, Feather Trail Press, 2010.

Joes, Anthony James. *America and Guerrilla Warfare*. Lexington: University Press of Kentucky, 2000.

Johnson, Daniel McDonald. *Blood on the Marsh: The Adventures of Brigadier William Mackintosh . . . Sergeant Allen McDonald and Alexander McDonald*. Rev. ed. Allendale, SC: CreateSpace, 2014.

Johnson, Joseph. *Traditions and Reminiscences, Chiefly of the American Revolution in the South*. Charleston, SC, 1851.

Johnson, William. *Sketches of the Life and Correspondence of Nathanael Greene*. 2 vols. Charleston, SC, 1822.

Jouanna, Arlette. *The Saint Bartholomew's Day Massacre: The Mysteries of a Crime of State*. Translated by Joseph Bergin. Manchester: Manchester University Press, 2013.

Kaufman, Scott. *Francis Marion: Swamp Fox of South Carolina*. Stockton, NJ: OTTN, 2007.

Lambert, Robert Stansbury. *South Carolina Loyalists in the American Revolution*. Columbia: University of South Carolina Press, 1987.

Linder, Suzanne Cameron, and Marta Leslie Thacker. *Historical Atlas of the Rice Plantations of Georgetown County and the Santee River*. Columbia: South Carolina Dept. of Archives and History, 2001.

Lumpkin, Henry. *From Savannah to Yorktown: The American Revolution in the South*. 1981. Reprint, New York: Paragon House, 1981.

Marshall, John. *The Life of George Washington*. Vol. 4. Philadelphia, 1805.

Massey, Gregory D. *John Laurens and the American Revolution*. Columbia: University of South Carolina Press, 2000.

McCrady, Edward. *The History of South Carolina in the Revolution, 1775–1780*. New York: Macmillan, 1901.

———. *The History of South Carolina in the Revolution, 1780–1783*. New York: Macmillan, 1902.

Moss, Bobby G., and Michael C. Scoggins. *African-American Patriots in the Southern Campaign of the American Revolution*. Blacksburg, SC: Scotia-Hibernia Press, 2004.

Nelson, Paul David. *Francis Rawdon-Hastings, Marquess of Hastings: Soldier, Peer of the Realm, Governor-General of India*. Madison, NJ: Fairleigh Dickinson University Press, 2005.

———. *General James Grant: Scottish Soldier and Royal Governor of East Florida*. Gainesville: University Press of Florida, 1993.

O'Kelley, Patrick. *"Nothing but Blood and Slaughter": The Revolutionary War in the Carolinas*. Vol. 3, *1781*. Bradenton, FL: Booklocker.com, 2005.

Oliphant, John. *Peace and War on the Anglo–Cherokee Frontier, 1756–1763*. Baton Rouge: Louisiana State University Press, 2001.

Pancake, John S. *This Destructive War: The British Campaign in the Carolinas, 1780–1782*. 1985. Reprint, Tuscaloosa: University of Alabama Press, 2003.

Parker, John C., Jr. *Parker's Guide to the Revolutionary War in South Carolina*. 2nd ed. West Conshohocken, PA: Infinity, 2013.

Piecuch, Jim, ed. *Cavalry of the American Revolution*. Yardley, PA: Westholme, 2012.

———. *Three Peoples, One King: Loyalists, Indians, and Slaves in the Revolutionary South, 1775–1782*. Columbia: University of South Carolina Press, 2008.

Piecuch, Jim, and John Beakes. *"Light Horse Harry" Lee in the War for Independence: A Military Biography of Robert E. Lee's Father*. Charleston, SC: Nautical and Aviation Pub. Co. of America, 2013.

[Poyas, Elizabeth Anne]. *Our Forefathers: Their Homes and Their Churches*. Charleston, SC, 1860.

Ramsay, David. *The History of the Revolution of South-Carolina, from a British Province to an Independent State*. Vol. 2. Trenton, NJ, 1785.

Rankin, Hugh F. *Francis Marion: The Swamp Fox*. New York: Thomas Y. Crowell, 1973.

Raphael, Ray. *Founding Myths: Stories That Hide Our Patriotic Past*. New York: The New Press, 2004.

Rogers, George C., Jr. *The History of Georgetown County, South Carolina*. Columbia: University of South Carolina Press, 1970.

Royster, Charles. *Light-Horse Harry Lee and the Legacy of the American Revolution.* 1981. Reprint, Baton Rouge: Louisiana State University Press, 1994.

Ryan, William R. *The World of Thomas Jeremiah: Charleston on the Eve of the American Revolution.* New York: Oxford University Press, 2010.

Sabine, Lorenzo. *Biographical Sketches of Loyalists of the American Revolution: With an Historical Essay.* Vol. 1. Boston, 1864.

Savage, Henry. *River of the Carolinas: The Santee.* Chapel Hill: University of North Carolina Press, 1968.

Scheer, George F., and Hugh F. Rankin. *Rebels and Redcoats: The American Revolution Through the Eyes of Those Who Fought and Lived It.* 1957. Reprint, New York: Da Capo Press, 1987.

Schlotterbeck, John T. *Daily Life in the Colonial South.* Santa Barbara, CA: Greenwood Press, 2013.

Simms, William Gilmore. *The Life of Francis Marion: The True Story of South Carolina's Swamp Fox. With a New Introduction by Sean Busick.* 1844. Reprint, Charleston, SC: History Press, 2007.

Swager, Christine R. *The Valiant Died: The Battle of Eutaw Springs, September 8, 1781.* Westminster, MD: Heritage Books, 2007.

Swisher, James K. *The Revolutionary War in the Southern Back Country.* 2008. Reprint, Gretna, LA: Pelican, 2012.

Taylor, Ann. *Colonial America: A Very Short Introduction.* Oxford: Oxford University Press, 2013.

Tonsetic, Robert L. *1781: The Decisive Year of the Revolutionary War.* Havertown, PA: Casemate, 2011.

Tortora, Daniel J. *Carolina in Crisis: Cherokees, Colonists, and Slaves in the American Southeast, 1756–1763.* Chapel Hill: University of North Carolina Press, 2015.

Wallace, David Duncan. *The Life of Henry Laurens, with a Sketch of the Life of Lieutenant-Colonel John Laurens.* New York: G. P. Putnam's, 1915.

Wickwire, Franklin B., and Mary Wickwire. *Cornwallis: The American Adventure.* Boston: Houghton Mifflin, 1970.

Wood, Gordon S. *The American Revolution: A History.* New York: The Modern Library, 2003.

Articles/Book Chapters

Baskin, Marg. "Friends, Comrades, and Enemies: James Wemyss (1748–1833)." *Oatmeal for the Foxhounds: Banastre Tarleton and the British Legion,* January 2, 2011. home.golden.net/~marg/bansite/friends/wemyss.html.

———. "John Watson Tadwell Watson (1748–1826)." *SCAR* 4, no. 2.1 (April–June 2007): 61–64.

Bass, Robert D. "John Tadwell-Watson, Builder of Fort Watson." *Independent Republic Quarterly* 12, no. 2 (Spring 1978): 9–16.

————. "The South Carolina Rangers: A Forgotten Loyalist Regiment." *Proceedings of the South Carolina Historical Society* (1977): 64–71.

Baxley, Charles B. "Gen. Nathanael Greene's Moves to Force the British into the Charlestown Area, to Capture Dorchester, Johns Island and to Protect the Jacksonborough Assembly, November 1781–February 1782." *SCAR* 12, no. 1.1 (January 23, 2015): 1–33.

Calmes, Holley. "Banastre Tarleton, A Biography." *Oatmeal for the Foxhounds: Banastre Tarleton and the British Legion*, January 2, 2011. home.golden .net/~marg/bansite/btbiog.html.

Cavanaugh, John C. "American Military Leadership in the Southern Campaign: Benjamin Lincoln." In Higgins, *Revolutionary War in the South*, 101–131.

Davies, Nell Weaver. "New Facts About an Old Story." *Carologue: Bulletin of the South Carolina Historical Society* 15, no. 4 (Winter 1999): 16–21.

Dennis, Jeff W. "Southern Campaign Against the Cherokees: A Brief Compilation." *SCAR* 2, no. 10.1 (October 2005): 17.

Dornfest, Walter T. "John Watson Tadwell Watson and the Provincial Light Infantry, 1780–1781." *SCAR* 4, no. 2.1 (April–June 2007): 47–55.

Dubose, Samuel. "Address at the 17th Anniversary of the Black Oak Agricultural Society, April 27, 1858." In Dubose and Porcher, *Contribution*, 1–33.

————. "Reminiscences of St. Stephens Parish, Craven County, and Notices of Her Old Homesteads." In Dubose and Porcher, *Contribution*, 35–85.

Du Pont, H. A. "Address of Col. H. A. Du Pont . . . April 13, 1917." *Huguenot Society* 23 (1917): 24–36.

Ervin, Sam J., Jr. "Entries in Colonel John Ervin's Bible." *SCHM* 79, no. 3 (July 1978): 219–227.

Farley, M. Foster. "The South Carolina Negro in the American Revolution, 1775–1783." *SCHM* 79, no. 2 (April 1978): 75–86.

Ferguson, Clyde R. "Functions of the Partisan–Militia in the South During the American Revolution: An Interpretation." In Higgins, *Revolutionary War in the South*, 239–258.

Frierson, John L. "Col. Abel Kolb–SC Patriot Militia." *SCAR* 3, no. 5 (May 2006): 27–29.

————. "Discipline by the Lash: The Order Books of Gen. Francis Marion." *Carologue* 15, no. 4 (Winter 1999): 8–13.

Gaillard, Thomas. "Copious Extracts by the Committee on Publication from the History of Huguenots of South Carolina, and Their Descendants." *Huguenot Society* 5 (1897): 6–42.

Graves, William T. "The South Carolina Backcountry Whig Militia: 1775–1781, an Overview." *SCAR* 2, no. 5 (May 2005): 7–11.

Gruber, Ira D. "Britain's Southern Strategy." In Higgins, *Revolutionary War in the South*, 206–238.

Kiel, John Loran, Jr. "War Crimes in the American Revolution: Examining the Conduct of Lt. Col. Banastre Tarleton and the British Legion During the Southern Campaigns of 1780–1781." *Military Law Review* 213 (Fall 2012): 29–64.

Kyte, George W. "Francis Marion as an Intelligence Officer." *SCHM* 77, no. 4 (October 1976): 215–226.

Lossing, Benson J. "Francis Marion." *Harpers New Monthly Magazine* 17, no. 98 (July 1858): 145–170.

Miskimon, Scott A. "Anthony Walton White, a Revolutionary Dragoon." In Piecuch, *Cavalry*, 104–144.

Parker, Hershel. "Fanning Outfoxes Marion." *Journal of the American Revolution*, October 8, 2014.

Piecuch, Jim. "The 'Black Dragoons': Former Slaves as British Cavalry in Revolutionary South Carolina." In Piecuch, *Cavalry*, 213–223.

———. "The Evolving Tactician: Nathanael Greene at the Battle of Eutaw Springs." In *General Nathanael Greene and the American Revolution in the South*, edited by Gregory D. Massey and Jim Piecuch, 214–237. Columbia: University of South Carolina Press, 2012.

———. "Francis Marion at the Battle of Eutaw Springs." *Journal of the American Revolution*, June 4, 2013.

———. "Francis Marion Meets His Match: Benjamin Thompson Defeats the 'Swamp Fox.'" *Journal of the American Revolution*, April 29, 2014.

———. "Massacre or Myth? Banastre Tarleton at the Waxhaws, May 29, 1780." *SCAR* 1, no. 2 (October 2004): 4–10.

Powers, Thomas L. "In Defense of General Thomas Sumter." *SCAR* 5, no. 2 (2nd ed. 2008): 31–34.

Ravenel, Daniel. "Historical Sketch of the Huguenot Congregations of South Carolina." *Huguenot Society* 7 (1900): 7–74.

Rubin, Ben. "The Rhetoric of Revenge: Atrocity and Identity in the Revolutionary Carolinas." *Journal of Backcountry Studies* 5, no. 2 (Fall 2010): 1–46. www.partnershipsjournal.org/index.php/jbc/article/viewFile/102/84.

Scheer, George H. "The Elusive Swamp Fox." *American Heritage* 9, no. 3 (April 1958): 40–47.

Scoggins, Michael C. "South Carolina's Back Country Rangers in the American Revolution: 'A Splendid Body of Men.'" In Piecuch, *Cavalry*, 145–181.

Smith, Steven D. "Beheading of Harry," *Military Collector & Historian* 68, no. 4 (Winter 2016), in press.

———. "Imagining the Swamp Fox: William Gilmore Simms and the National Memory of Francis Marion." In *William Gilmore Simms's Unfinished Civil War: Consequences for a Southern Man of Letters*, edited by David Moltke-Hansen. Columbia: University of South Carolina Press, 2013, 32–47.

———. Introduction. In Boddie, *Traditions*, xi–xliv.

Tortora, Daniel J. "The Alarm of War: Religion and the American Revolution in South Carolina, 1774–1783." *SCAR* 5, no. 2 (2nd ed. 2008): 43–55.

Wates, Wylma Anne. "Meanderings of a Manuscript: General Peter Horry's Collection of Francis Marion Letters." *SCHM* 81, no. 4 (October 1980): 352–361.

Yeadon, Richard. "The Marion Family." *Southern and Western Monthly Magazine and Review*, edited by W. Gilmore Simms. Vol. 1, no. 1 (March 1845): 209–219; no. 2 (April 1845): 270–284; no. 3 (May 1845): 347–356; no. 4 (June 1845): 412–426; no. 5 (July 1845): 50–58; Vol. 2, no. 6 (August 1845): 121–127; no. 7 (September 1845): 200–204; no. 8 (October 1845): 265–276; no. 9 (November 1845): 333–341.

———. "The Marion Family, No. 10: The Widow of Gen. Marion." *Charleston Courier*, August 7, 1858.

Dissertations/Theses

Brannon, Rebecca Nathan. "Reconciling the Revolution: Resolving Conflict and Rebuilding Community in the Wake of Civil War in South Carolina, 1775–1860." PhD diss., University of Michigan, 2007. deepblue.lib.umich.edu/bitstream/handle/2027.42/57715/brannonr_1.pdf.

Jacobsen, Kristen E. "Conduct of the Partisan War in the Revolutionary War South." Master's thesis, University of Rhode Island, 1999. www.dtic.mil/dtic/tr/fulltext/u2/a416929.pdf.

Smith, Steven D. "Archaeological Perspectives on Partisan Communities: Francis Marion at Snow's Island in History, Landscape, and Memory." PhD diss., University of South Carolina, 2010. ProQuest, search.proquest.com/docview/823439460.

Archaeological Reports and Surveys

Butler, Scott. *Battlefield Survey and Archaeological Investigations at the Eutaw Springs, South Carolina Revolutionary War Battleground, 8 September 1781.* Atlanta: Brockington & Associates, November 2008.

Ferguson, Leland G. "Exploratory Archeology at the Scott's Lake Site (38CR1) Santee Indian Mound–Ft. Watson Summer 1972." In *Research Manuscript Series*, Book 30. Columbia: University of South Carolina, South Carolina Institute of Archeology and Anthropology, 1973. scholarcommons.sc.edu/archanth_books.

Smith, Steven D. *The Search for Francis Marion: Archaeological Survey of 15 Camps and Battlefields Associated with Francis Marion.* With contributions by Tamara S. Wilson and James B. Legg. Columbia: University of South Carolina, South Carolina Institute of Archaeology and Anthropology, July 2008.

Smith, Steven D., James B. Legg, Tamara S. Wilson, and Jonathan Leader. *"Obstinate and Strong": The History and Archaeology of the Siege of Fort Motte.* Columbia: University of South Carolina, South Carolina Institute of Archaeology and Anthropology, 2007. scholarcommons.sc.edu/cgi /viewcontent.cgi?article=1052&context=anth_facpub.

Whitacre, Stacey R. "An Analysis of Lead Shot from Fort Motte, 2004–2012: Assessing Combat Behavior in Terms of Agency." Master's thesis, University of South Carolina, 2013. scholarcommons.sc.edu/etd/2479.

Legislative Materials

Cooper, Thomas, ed. *The Statutes at Large of South Carolina.* Vol. 4, *Containing the Acts from 1752 . . . to 1786.* Columbia, SC, 1838.

———, ed. *The Statutes at Large of South Carolina.* Vol. 5, *Containing the Acts from 1786 . . . to 1814.* Columbia, SC, 1839.

Journals of the Senate, 1783–1785, South Carolina Dept. of Archives and History.

McCord, David J., ed. *The Statutes at Large of South Carolina.* Vol. 6, *Containing the Acts from 1814 . . . to 1838.* Columbia, SC, 1839.

———, ed. *The Statutes at Large of South Carolina.* Vol. 7. *Containing the Acts Relating to Charleston, Courts, Slaves, and Rivers.* Columbia, SC, 1840.

Salley, A. S., ed. *Journal of the House of Representatives of South Carolina: January 8, 1782–February 26, 1782.* Columbia, SC: The State Company, 1916.

———, ed. *Journal of the Senate of South Carolina: January 8, 1782–February 26, 1782.* Columbia, SC: The State Company, 1941.

Thompson, Theodora J., Rosa S. Lumpkin, Lark Emerson Adams, and Michael E. Stevens, eds. *Journals of the House of Representatives [1783–1794].* 6 vols. Columbia: University of South Carolina Press, 1977–1988.

Miscellaneous Online Sources

EleHistory Research. *American Revolution Sites, Events, and Troop Movements.* 2011. elehistory.com/amrev/SitesEventsTroopMovements.htm.

Graves, William T., and C. Leon Harris. *Southern Campaigns Revolutionary War Pension Statements and Rosters.* 2015. revwarapps.org.

Kirk, F. M. "Pond Bluff Plantation, Marion Family." c. 1930s. www.rootsweb .ancestry.com/~scbchs/pondbluff.htm.

Lewis, J. D. *The American Revolution in South Carolina.* Little River, SC, 2014. www.carolana.com/SC/Revolution/home.html.

———. *The Evolution of Marion's Brigade After the Fall of Charleston, 1780–1782.* Little River, SC, 2014. www.francismarionsymposium.com/Evolution_of _Marion's_Brigade_1780_to_1782_JDL.pdf.

Online Institute for Advanced Loyalist Studies. Managed by Todd Braisted. February 23, 2015. www.royalprovincial.com/index.htm.

Robertson, John A. *Global Gazetteer of the American Revolution*. 2011. www.gaz
.jrshelby.com.

Sciway.net. *South Carolina Plantations*. 2014. south-carolina-plantations.com
/georgetown/greenwich.html.

Sherman, William Thomas. *Calendar and Record of the Revolutionary War in the
South, 1780–1781*. 9th ed. Seattle: Gun Jones, 2014. battleofcamden.org
/sherman9.pdf.

Simons, John. "Marion Family." Rootsweb.com, May 13, 2004. www.hay
genealogy.com/hay/patriots/marion-descendants.html.

Swamp Fox Murals Trail. Managed by George and Carole Summers. August 29,
2015. www.clarendonmurals.com.

Documentaries and Instructional Media

*And Then There Were Thirteen: The Early Campaigns of Francis Marion, 1780;
The Later Campaigns of Francis Marion, 1781–1782*. Narrated with commentary by Henry Lumpkin. Columbia: University of South Carolina
and South Carolina Educational Television, 1976. Two videocassettes
(VHS). On file at Francis Marion University, Cauthen Educational Media Center, Florence, SC.

Chasing the Swamp Fox. Produced by Thomas Fowler, executive producer, and
James H. Palmer Jr. and Sanford Adams, producers. With commentary by
Walter B. Edgar, Daniel Littlefield, Steven D. Smith, Christine Swager,
and Roy Talbert. Columbia: South Carolina ETV Commission, 2004.
YouTube video, 56:45, posted by Butch Hills, December 8, 2013. www
.youtube.com/watch?v=9Lc9-C8dGGM.

Addresses (all at annual Francis Marion/Swamp Fox Symposium, Manning, SC)

Baxley, Charles B. "Marion at Parker's Ferry." 9th Symposium, October 15,
2011.

MacNutt, Karen. "After the Fox in Georgetown." 11th Symposium, October 19, 2013.

———. "Francis Marion and Georgetown." 9th Symposium, October 15, 2011.

———. "Gen. and Mrs. Marion, Families of the Revolution." 7th Symposium,
October 17, 2009.

———. "Images of Francis Marion." 8th Symposium, October 16, 2010.

Neilan, David. "The Life of General Francis Marion: The Weems–Horry Controversy, Where Fiction Trumped History." 12th Symposium, October 25, 2014.

———. "Marion Letters and Research." 8th Symposium, October 16, 2010.

———. "Marion and the Jacksonboro Assembly." 9th Symposium, October 15, 2011.

————. "Marion and the Trials and Tribulations of Peter Horry." 11th Symposium, October 19, 2013.

Owens, Dusty. "The Role of Marion's Subordinate Commanders in Marion's Early Success with Hugh Giles." 11th Symposium, October 19, 2013.

Parker, John C., Jr. "Blue Savannah and Marion vs. Ganey." 8th Symposium, October 15, 2010.

Powers, Thomas L. "Marion and his Commanders." 7th Symposium, October 17, 2009.

Swager, Christine. "Marion After Eutaw Springs." 5th Symposium, October 20, 2007.

Index